Computer Graphics
with Java

Computer Graphics with Java

Glenn W. Rowe

palgrave

First published 2001 by
PALGRAVE
Houndmills, Basingstoke, Hampshire RG21 6XS and
175 Fifth Avenue, New York, N.Y. 10010
Companies and representatives throughout the world

PALGRAVE is the new global academic imprint of
St. Martin's Press LLC Scholarly and Reference Division and
Palgrave Publishers Ltd (formerly Macmillan Press Ltd).

ISBN 0–333–92097–X paperback

This book is printed on paper suitable for recycling and
made from fully managed and sustained forest sources.

A catalogue record for this book is available
from the British Library.

10   9   8   7   6   5   4   3   2   1
10   09   08   07   06   05   04   03   02   01

Printed and bound in Great Britain by
Antony Rowe Ltd, Chippenham, Wiltshire

By the same author

- *Theoretical Models in Biology* (1994); Oxford University Press.

- *Introduction to Data Structures and Algorithms with C++* (1997); Prentice-Hall.

- *Introduction to Data Structures and Algorithms with Java* (1998); Prentice-Hall.

- *The Essence of Java Programming* (1999); Prentice-Hall.

Contents

Preface

Computer graphics is a subject that, perhaps more than many other computer-related disciplines, has come of age in recent years. The main reason for this is the exponential increase in the power of computer hardware. The power and capacity of processors, graphics cards and memory have continued to increase at rates that could not have been forecast some years ago, and prices continue to fall, thus making high-powered graphics systems available to virtually all computer users, from multinational industries to the average home computer buff.

The evidence of this explosion is all around us. Films and television are filled with 'special effects', most of which are generated using the techniques of computer graphics. Computer games have advanced from the simple graphics of a decade ago to fully immersive experiences with realistic three-dimensional images and surround sound. Computer-aided design systems are used to produce blueprints for everything from jumbo jets to the electronic circuits from which computers themselves are made. Computer simulations, with high-resolution, three- dimensional animations, are used to study areas of research as diverse as climate change, models of the economy, and theories of the evolution of the universe. In short, there is hardly any area of human endeavour that has been left untouched by the revolution in computer graphics and the increase in computing power that made it possible.

Another, somewhat quieter, revolution has also been taking place in the world of computing languages. Although new computing languages are frequently developed, few of them become quite as popular in such a short time as the Java language. Originally developed by Sun Microsystems, Java first gained widespread popularity as a language that could be used to embed sophisticated graphical components called *applets* in web pages. In a few short years, however, Java has become a serious rival to established languages such as C and C++ in many industrial applications. A glance through lists of jobs on offer in the computing area shows that Java is now in high demand.

Part of the reason for Java's success is that it allows graphics to be produced fairly easily. Graphical capabilities are built into Java, rather than provided as add-ons that only work within one programming environment or on one type of operating system, as is the case with many other graphical systems. Java's platform independence means that graphics code can be written on a PC, a UNIX machine or a Macintosh and run on any of the other machines with no changes.

Although the early versions of Java had fairly limited graphical capabilities, the evolution of the language over the past few years has seen many more features being added. The latest versions of Java and its associated packages now support many of the two- and three-dimensional features that would be expected in a professional graphics development package. Since Java is still an actively developing language, the number of these features will no doubt continue to grow over the coming years.

There are already many excellent textbooks available which give an in-depth treatment of graphics theory. Some of these books provide sample code in one language or another, while others restrict themselves to a clear exposition of the underlying principles without tying themselves to a specific programming language.

This book does not attempt to compete with these established texts. Rather, it seeks to provide the reader with a comprehensive survey of the graphical features, both two- and three-dimensional, that are available in the core Java package (which now contains Java 2D), and in its sister package, Java 3D.

Such a book could have been written purely as a 'recipe book', in that the reader could simply be told how to use the various Java graphics classes and provided with a few code examples. However, it is the author's belief that, had the book been written in that way, the reader would come away with a sense of being cheated, for although some coding skills would no doubt have been learned, no deeper understanding of how the methods work would be gained.

For this reason, the basic theory required to understand how the methods in Java's graphics packages work has been provided. The theory in the book should be seen as an underpinning for the explanations of how to use Java's graphics classes. As such, the theory is restricted mainly to those areas of graphics that are implemented in the latest versions of Java 2D and 3D at the time of writing.

Having said that, the theory that is actually contained in the book covers most of the material that would be found in a first university course in computer graphics, so the book could certainly be used as a textbook for such a course. However, the main purpose of the book is as an exposition of the graphical features of Java for those who wish to gain an understanding not only of how to write graphics programs in Java, but also to understand *how* these programs work.

The main approach of the book for each of its topics is to begin by describing the theory that underpins a particular graphical method, and then to introduce the classes and programming techniques by which the method is implemented in Java. To this end, numerous coding examples are given, with detailed explanations of how the code works. The code in the book does not contain any comments, since it is fully documented in the accompanying text and inserting additional comments into the code would only cause a distracting clutter. The code that may be downloaded from the web site (see below) is, however, fully commented.

No matter how complete an explanation is, however, the reader can only learn to write graphical Java programs by actually *doing* it. Readers are therefore urged to download the source code in the book and *play* with it—change things, try new methods and so on. It is only by this means that real understanding can be gained. The code may be downloaded from www.palgrave.com/resources. To further urge the readers to pursue their own explorations, exercises are provided at the end of each chapter.

There are two main requirements for readers of this book. First, they should be familiar with the basics of Java, to a level that would be gained by an introductory programming course using Java as the language. Such a course should cover the basics of Java syntax and object oriented programming, and should include some experience in simple graphical user interface (GUI) programming. Thus a typical reader of this book should know how to construct programs using Java classes, how to add components such as buttons and text areas to a graphical interface, and how to handle events generated by these components. Since many universities today use Java as their first teaching language, this level of understanding should be gained after the first year.

Second, readers should feel comfortable with basic mathematics, particularly with vectors, matrices and linear algebra. Much of the underlying theory in the book relies heavily on these areas of mathematics, since this is the most natural and precise way of describing the basic ideas. The level of mathematics expected of the reader is usually achieved by the end of high school, and certainly by the end of a first year course at a university.

Readers are not expected to have any prior exposure to the theory of graphics or to graphics programming, although a first course in Java will probably have introduced its students to some simple drawing.

Although the book was written with the idea that the reader would read the chapters in sequence, there is not a strong dependence on what has gone before in many of the chapters. A deep understanding of the theory in Chapters 1 and 2 is not required for most of Chapter 3 (on Java 2D) to be followed. For the 3D material, Chapters 4 and 5 are essential to the understanding of the remaining chapters, but chapters after Chapter 5 are more or less independent of each other, although some examples do make use of concepts from earlier chapters.

All of the code in this book was developed using the standard Java Development Kit (JDK), version 1.3, and the Java 3D pack, version 1.2.1 (beta 2), both of which are available free of charge from Sun's web site. The main web page for Java products in general is `http://www.javasoft.com/`. Follow the 'Products and APIs' link to download specific Java packages. The main Java 3D page is

```
http://www.javasoft.com/products/java-media/3D/index.html
```

It is certainly possible to write your Java code using nothing more than a text editor and console window in which to run the compiler and the resulting programs. Without wishing to become embroiled in 'editor wars', one popular environment is emacs (which is now available on all common platforms) with its JRE extension, which contains many features specifically designed for writing Java programs. Again, all emacs software is free and download sites may easily be found by doing a web search.

For those wishing to use a more sophisticated programming environment, there are many commercial offerings available. A free package worth trying is Borland's JBuilder 4, *Foundation Edition*, which may be downloaded from Borland's web site at

```
http://www.borland.com/jbuilder
```

Further reading

Without a doubt, the most important 'further reading' for anyone involved with Java development is the on-line documentation that comes with the JDK and with

Java 3D. This is a set of HTML pages giving complete documentation of all classes in all packages that come with these libraries. Although this book does give a comprehensive survey of the graphical capabilities of Java 2D and 3D, it is expected that readers will explore the topics further by looking up the classes in the documentation and exploring their abilities and properties. Get into the habit of having the documentation running in a web browser alongside any text editor or coding environment, since you should refer to it early and often while writing any code. Several exercises throughout the book encourage you to look things up in the documentation and find things out for yourself.

For readers wishing to review the basics of Java, there is an enormous number of books now available. At the risk of egotism, readers might wish to try the present author's *The Essence of Java Programming* (Prentice Hall, 1999, ISBN 0-13-011377-8) for a compact, easily readable introduction. A weighty, comprehensive coverage of basic Java may be found in Deitel and Deitel's *Java How to Program* (Prentice Hall, 1997, ISBN 0-13-899394-7). For those interested in a clear, detailed discussion of the guts of the language, you cannot beat Bruce Eckel's *Thinking in Java, 2nd edition* (Prentice Hall, 2000, ISBN 0-13-027363-5; also available on-line at `www.bruceeckel.com`). A popular reference (not for beginners, although readers familiar with C++ will find this book especially useful) is David Flanagan's *Java in a Nutshell, 3rd edition*, (O'Reilly, 1999, ISBN 1-56592-487-8). Finally, Wrox Press has produced a good series of books on Java, including Ivor Horton's *Beginning Java 2 – JDK 1.3 Version* (Wrox, 2000, ISBN 1861003668).

Books on graphics with Java are much more difficult to come by (one of the reasons this book was written). A reasonable survey of Java 2D may be found in Vincent J Hardy's *Java 2D API Graphics* (Sun Microsystems Press, 2000, ISBN 0-13-014266-2) and Jonathan Knudsen's *Java 2D Graphics* (O'Reilly, 1999, ISBN 1-56592-484-3). The author has yet to find another suitable book on Java 3D.

For readers interested in Java 3D who cannot find what they are looking for either in this book or in the on-line documentation, a good source of information and help is the `java3d-interest` mailing list run by Sun. A link to the email archives from the list may be found on Sun's Java 3D web page given above. You may also register on the list yourself, which allows you to post articles to the list and receive email delivery of all articles posted. The list is read by many of Sun's engineers who work on Java 3D, so you can sometimes expect authoritative responses to queries.

For a more comprehensive treatment of graphics theory, there are several well-respected texts. Probably the most famous is *Computer Graphics* by Foley, van Dam, Feiner and Hughes (Addison Wesley Longman, 1995, ISBN 0-201-84840-6), although it is not a recreational read. Another popular text is Hearn and Baker's *Computer Graphics, C Version* (Prentice Hall, 1996, ISBN 0-13-530924-7, or international edition with ISBN 0-13-578634-7). An honourable mention goes to Alan Watt's *3D Computer Graphics, 2nd edition* (Addison-Wesley, 1993, ISBN 0-201-63186-5).

Acknowledgements

First and foremost, I would like to thank the staff at Palgrave (in particular Jackie Harbor for starting the book off and Tracey Alcock for seeing it through) for helping me along the way in this project. Contributors to the `java3d-interest` newsgroup provided invaluable assistance in coping with some of the intricacies of Java 3D. Several anonymous referees managed to read through two drafts of the manuscript and provided very helpful advice and suggestions. Graham Douglas did a masterful job of the typesetting. Finally, I would like to thank several students, particularly Iain Milne and Marc Nebbett, for reading through part or all of the manuscript and providing some useful feedback from a student's point of view.

Two-dimensional graphics

1.1 Computer graphics

Most textbooks on computer graphics begin with a chapter or two giving examples of areas where graphics have been used in research, industry, or entertainment. Today, this scarcely seems necessary. Examples of computer graphics in action surround us during almost all our waking hours. Television (both the programmes themselves and the advertisements that interrupt them) is laden with graphical enhancement. Feature films rely more on 'special effects' than on plot or acting (but still make millions). The computer games industry is rivalling the film industry, both in terms of use of graphics and size of profits.

In industry, computer aided design (CAD) packages are used in the design of everything from food packaging to aircraft. In research, computer simulations are used routinely to model systems as diverse as global climate change and the national economy.

In short, anyone who lives in the industrialized world cannot avoid being exposed to computer graphics in some form.

The aim of this book is to allow you to learn the main techniques that are used to produce a wide variety of graphical effects, and to see how these techniques can be implemented using the Java language and some of the graphics packages that are now part of the Java world. Since graphics is such a large field, we will not be examining all topics in exhaustive detail. Indeed, most of the topics in this book have books of their own devoted to them. It is hoped, though, that by the time you have finished the book, you will know enough about each of the topics to hold your own in the graphics field, and perhaps be inspired to continue your studies in one or more specialized areas.

1.2 Digital and analog displays

Despite the diversity of graphical methods available to the computer artist, all graphical algorithms must have one thing in common—a method of displaying their results. Since this is primarily a software book, we will not dwell on the various types of hardware that can be used to display images. There are a few bits of terminology derived from hardware, however, that we must consider.

Graphical output is displayed on two main types of device: monitors (display screens) and printers. These devices, in turn, come in two main forms: digital and analog. To understand the difference between digital and analog devices, suppose you wished to draw a circle (either onto a monitor screen or on paper).

A mathematical circle is, of course, a smooth curve with no sharp corners. A *digital* graphical display device uses a grid of discrete points called *pixels* (the word being a contraction of 'picture elements'). The vast majority of monitors on personal computers (of any size from palmtop to desktop) use a digital display. In its simplest form, each pixel is either 'on' or 'off', so that any image displayed on a digital device must be composed of a number of small dots, rather than a collection of smooth curves. In particular, a circle is approximated by a jagged curve formed from individual pixels. The higher the *resolution* of the display device (that is, the more pixels per centimetre), the smoother the circle will look, but at the pixel level, the circle is still being approximated by a collection of dots. See Figure 1.1.

Figure 1.1:
A digital
circular arc.

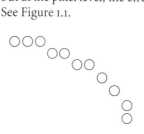

An *analog* device uses an electron beam (in a monitor) or a pen plotter (for hardcopy) which is not constrained to individual pixel locations, so that it can produce a smooth curve without jagged edges. Such displays can produce very crisp, clear output of graphics requiring precise curves, and are often used in industrial design work. Analog devices, however, are relatively rare in the personal computer arena. Since it is most likely that readers of this book will be using digital displays, we will concentrate exclusively on them in this book.

A digital display may be thought of as a rectangular array of points (Figure 1.2). On a monitor, each point is a single pixel on the screen; on a printer, each point is a dot of ink on the page.

Figure 1.2:
A digital display,
with lit pixels shown.

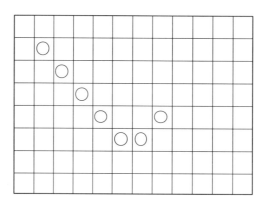

All images produced on a digital display are composed of these points.

1.3   Points and lines

Even the most complex graphics operations ultimately reduce to specifying which pixels to turn on (and with which colour or intensity), and which to turn off.

Before we consider more complex situations, we can get a feel for the problems that we will encounter by considering the simplest 'curve'—the straight line. The standard equation for a straight line is:

$$y = mx + b \qquad (1.1)$$

Here, m is the *slope* of the line and b is the *y-intercept*, or point where the line intersects the y axis.

Before we go any further, we should notice that the two-dimensional coordinate systems used by most display devices differ from what you may be used to in high school mathematics. In mathematics, the x axis is the horizontal axis which increases from left to right, and the y axis is the vertical axis which increases from bottom to top. The usual coordinate system used for monitors and printers uses the same x axis, but inverts the y axis, so that it increases from top to bottom. On a monitor screen, the origin (0, 0) is located in the upper-left corner, x increases to the right, and y increases downwards, so that all pixels on screen have both a positive x and a positive y coordinate.

The reason for this seemingly perverse way of doing things is related to the way a monitor image is drawn by the electron gun. The image starts in the upper-left corner and is scanned left-to-right and top-to-bottom, so that the pixel coordinates actually mirror the way in which the image is drawn.

At this point, we therefore need to decide how we are going to treat pixel coordinates in this book. Since a special transformation is required if we wish to draw things using 'mathematical' coordinates (that is, with y increasing upwards), we will use the coordinate system that is built into the monitor, with y increasing downwards. Initially this may cause some confusion if you are used to dealing with graphs in mathematics, but since you need to learn to think in terms of monitor coordinates, it seems the most sensible thing to do.

We can therefore draw the graph of the straight line given in equation 1.1 as shown in Figure 1.3.

Figure 1.3: A straight line with positive slope, using the monitor's coordinate system.

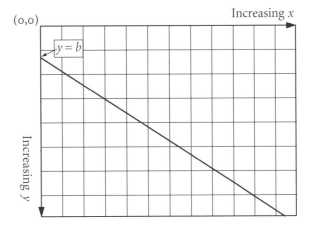

Straight lines are easy enough to draw on graph paper with a pencil and a ruler, but the problem facing the graphics programmer is how to draw such a line on a digital display. To see why this may cause a problem, consider the line with the equation

$$y = 7x + 2 \qquad (1.2)$$

Suppose we want to draw this line over the range $x = 0$ to $x = 10$, and that we want the image on the screen to be drawn in a window that is 5 cm square. The number of pixels in a 5 cm distance on the screen depends on the size and display resolution of the monitor, but for a 17-inch monitor running at a resolution of 1280 by 1024 pixels, the display area for the graph of the line would be approximately 200 pixels on each side.

We therefore need to plot the graph at 200 equally spaced points along the x axis, for values of x between 0 and 10. Let us use equation 1.2 to calculate the first few values:

x	y
0.0	2.0
0.05	2.35
0.10	2.70
0.15	3.05

Let us assume that the area on the screen onto which the graph is to be drawn occupies pixels numbered 0 through 200 in both horizontal and vertical directions, and that the upper-left corner of the square therefore corresponds to the origin. If both the horizontal and vertical axes have the same scale of 1 unit per 20 pixels, we can map the values given in the table above to pixel coordinates by multiplying them all by 20. We get:

x pixel	y pixel
0	40
1	47
2	54
3	61

Illuminating only the pixels shown in the table results in Figure 1.4.

Figure 1.4: First attempt at drawing a line leaves gaps in the y direction. The pixel in the upper-left corner has coordinates (0, 40).

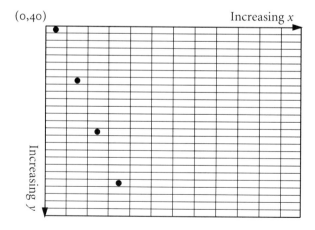

(0,40) Increasing x

Increasing y

We can see that the result of our first attempt at drawing a line on a digital display contains a serious problem—we have ended up with a few isolated points with large gaps in between them. We need a better algorithm that fills in the gaps.

Aha, you may be thinking: the problem is obviously that the slope of the line is greater than 1, meaning that a unit change in the x direction will result in greater than a unit change in the y direction. Therefore, rather than calculating y for unit changes in x, we can calculate x for unit changes in y.

Doing this does, in fact, result in a better line (you can try it yourself), but there are still problems.

First, consider the line generated by equation 1.2. When we used it to calculate the coordinates of the points that were to be plotted, we obtained floating point values. We were lucky when we converted these values to pixel coordinates, since they all came out to be integers at that point, but that won't be true in general. Floating point arithmetic is considerably more time-consuming than integer arithmetic, so if we have a large number of lines to draw, using a floating point algorithm will increase the display time noticeably. If possible, we would like to use only integer calculations to determine the pixels to be plotted.

The other problem wasn't apparent in the example above, but will occur in most cases. Suppose that, when we converted the raw data generated by equation 1.2 to pixel values, these values had fractional parts as well. For example, suppose we discovered that we were supposed to plot a pixel with coordinates (3, 47.5). Do we turn on the pixel at (3, 47), the one at (3, 48) or possibly both?

1.4 Bresenham's algorithm

Fortunately, there is a line-drawing algorithm that neatly solves both these problems. Known as *Bresenham's algorithm* (a variant of Bresenham's algorithm called the *mid-point algorithm* is sometimes used), it provides a way of determining all the pixels in a line segment using exclusively integer arithmetic.

The algorithm assumes that the pixel coordinates of the endpoints of the lines are known, and are integers. Slight variations in the algorithm are needed for the four cases of (i) positive slope < 1; (ii) negative slope > -1; (iii) positive slope ≥ 1; negative slope ≤ -1. We will present the algorithm for the first case; the alterations to obtain the other three cases should be fairly obvious.

Since the slope of the line is less than 1, the y coordinate varies more slowly than the x coordinate, so we can obtain all the required pixels in the line by stepping through x one pixel at a time and calculating the y coordinate at each x value. We can adapt equation 1.1 to a digital display by adding a subscript to x indicating the pixel number:

$$y = mx_k + b \tag{1.3}$$

The y value generated by equation 1.3 will not, in general, be an integer, so we cannot rely on it being used as a pixel coordinate.

Bresenham's algorithm assumes that we are given the coordinates of the first pixel to be plotted; let us call this pixel (x_0, y_0). We now wish to discover what pixel should be plotted at position x_1. Since the slope is positive and less than 1, we know this will be either y_0 or $y_0 + 1$. How can we decide which, and at the same time use only integer arithmetic?

Let's generalize the problem slightly by assuming that we have determined the pixel to be plotted at location (x_k, y_k) and wish to find the y value corresponding to position $x_k + 1$. We know this value will be either y_k or $y_k + 1$. Using equation 1.3, we have:

$$y = m(x_k + 1) + b$$

Choosing the smaller y value, y_k, we calculate the distance between the exact value, y, and this value, calling it d_1:

$$d_1 = y - y_k = m(x_k + 1) + b - y_k$$

In a similar way, we find d_2, the distance between the larger pixel value, $y_k + 1$, and y:

$$d_2 = y_k + 1 - y = y_k + 1 - m(x_k + 1) - b$$

Clearly, we would like to choose the pixel corresponding to the smaller of d_1 and d_2. If we find the difference between d_1 and d_2, we get:

$$d_1 - d_2 = 2m(x_k + 1) + 2b - 2y_k - 1 \qquad (1.4)$$

The sign of this difference will tell us which pixel to choose: if the difference is negative, then y_k is closer to the actual y value, while if it is positive, $y_k + 1$ is closer. If the difference is exactly zero, the line passes exactly halfway between the two pixels, so either may be chosen.

So far, however, we have not managed to eliminate non-integer calculations. To do this, we begin by recalling that one of the conditions of Bresenham's algorithm is that the endpoints of the line segment are known, and are already in integer pixel coordinates. This means we can express the slope m of the line as the ratio of two integer values:

$$m = \Delta y / \Delta x$$

where Δy is the difference between the y values at the endpoints, and similarly for Δx. Using this substitution for m in equation 1.4, and multiplying through by Δx, we obtain:

$$\Delta x(d_1 - d_2) = 2\Delta y x_k - 2\Delta x y_k + [2\Delta y + \Delta x(2b - 1)] \qquad (1.5)$$

The quantity in square brackets does not depend on the pixel index k, and the quantity $\Delta x(d_1 - d_2)$ on the left-hand side of the equation has the same sign as $(d_1 - d_2)$, since Δx is always positive (we always scan the line from left to right).

Every factor on the right-hand side of this equation is an integer with the possible exception of the intercept b. To simplify the notation, we define C to be the constant quantity in square brackets:

$$C = 2\Delta y + \Delta x(2b - 1)$$

Further, we define the *pixel choice* parameter p_k as:

$$p_k = \Delta x(d_1 - d_2) = 2\Delta y x_k - 2\Delta x y_k + C \qquad (1.6)$$

If p_k is positive, we choose $y_k + 1$; if negative, y_k. But how can we get rid of C, which is the only parameter that may require non-integer calculations? The answer is to use a recursive method for calculating the series of p_k values. The pixel choice at the next location is determined by p_{k+1}:

$$p_{k+1} = 2\Delta y x_{k+1} - 2\Delta x y_{k+1} + C$$

Now we can eliminate C by subtracting equation 1.6 from this equation, to get:

$$p_{k+1} - p_k = 2\Delta y(x_{k+1} - x_k) - 2\Delta x(y_{k+1} - y_k)$$

But we know that $x_{k+1} = x_k + 1$, since we are stepping along the x axis one pixel at a time. We also know that y_{k+1} is either y_k or $y_k + 1$, depending on the sign of p_k. (In any case, y_{k+1} will be known by the time this equation is used.) We therefore have our recursive relationship for choosing pixels:

$$p_{k+1} = p_k + 2\Delta y - 2\Delta x(y_{k+1} - y_k) \qquad (1.7)$$

Note that all quantities in this equation are integers. The only thing still required is a starting value p_0. We can get this from equation 1.5 by using the starting point of the line (x_0, y_0), and substituting the following for b:

$$b = y_0 - mx_0 = y_0 - (\Delta y/\Delta x)x_0$$

Multiplying out and cancelling off terms, we obtain:

$$p_0 = 2\Delta y - \Delta x \qquad (1.8)$$

We can now summarize Bresenham's algorithm for the case where the slope is $0 < m < 1$.

1. Provide the two endpoints of the lines in pixel coordinates. The left endpoint is at position (x_0, y_0), and the right endpoint is at (x_n, y_n), where n is the number of pixels to draw after the starting point.

2. Calculate the constants $2\Delta y$ and $2\Delta y - 2\Delta x$, where $\Delta y = y_n - y_0$ and $\Delta x = x_n - x_0$.

3. Plot (x_0, y_0) as the first point.

4. Calculate the pixel choice parameter p_k, (starting at $k = 0$ using equation 1.8), and use it to find the next y value, as follows:

   If $p_k < 0$, the next point to plot is $(x_k + 1, y_k)$, and, from equation 1.7:

   $$p_{k+1} = p_k + 2\Delta y$$

   Otherwise, the next point to plot is $(x_k + 1, y_k + 1)$, and, from equation 1.7:

   $$p_{k+1} = p_k + 2\Delta y - 2\Delta x$$

5. Repeat step 4 until x_n is reached.

The alterations in this algorithm to cope with the other 3 types of slope should be fairly obvious, and are left as exercises for the reader.

1.5 Java implementation of Bresenham's algorithm

Translating Bresenham's algorithm as given above into Java is relatively straightforward, since we are dealing with a series of simple arithmetic calculations. To make the algorithm completely general, however, we should allow for lines of any slope and orientation (for example, we should allow the start point to be to the right of the endpoint).

The following code assumes that the endpoints of the line have been determined externally (for example, from mouse clicks). These points are stored in a couple of Point variables in the LineCanvas class, which is derived from the Canvas class in the Java AWT. Once the two Point variables have been determined, the line itself is drawn in the paint() method.

The LineCanvas class begins as follows:

```
1    public class LineCanvas extends java.awt.Canvas
2    {
3        static int START_POINT = 0;
4        static int END_POINT = 1;
5
6        int x0, y0, x1, y1;
```

```
7        int slopeSign;
8        boolean slopeLT1;
9        int param;
10       int twoDeltaY, twoDYDX, twoDeltaX, twoDXDY;
11
12       Point startPoint = null, endPoint = null;
13
14       public void setPoint(int type, Point point)
15       {
16          if (type == LineCanvas.START_POINT) {
17             startPoint = point;
18          } else if (type == LineCanvas.END_POINT) {
19             endPoint = point;
20          }
21       }
22
23       public void clearPoints()
24       {
25          startPoint = endPoint = null;
26       }
27
28       public void paint(Graphics g)
29       {
30          if (startPoint == null || endPoint == null)
31             return;
32          drawBresenhamLine(g, startPoint, endPoint);
33       }
34
35       // ... other code follows
36    }
```

Lines 6 through 10 declare the various parameters that are used in the algorithm, and will be described as we encounter them in the code. Line 12 declares the two Point variables marking the endpoints of the line. Lines 14 through 26 define a couple of methods used to set and clear these points. For example, setPoint() would be called by the method that handles the mouse button events to set the respective endpoints chosen by the user.

Lines 28 through 33 check that both points are defined and, if so, call a method to draw the line using Bresenham's algorithm.

This method implements the algorithm given above, and is as follows.

```
1     void drawBresenhamLine(Graphics g, Point start,
2        Point end)
3     {
4        slopeLT1 = selectEndPoints(start, end);
5
6        int x, y;
7        if (slopeLT1) {
8           x = x0+1; y = y0;
9           while (x < x1) {
10             if (param < 0) {
```

```
11              param += twoDeltaY;
12            } else {
13              param += twoDYDX;
14              y += slopeSign;
15            }
16            g.drawLine(x, y, x, y);
17            x++;
18          }
19      } else {
20          x = x0; y = y0+1;
21          while (y < y1) {
22            if (param < 0) {
23              param += twoDeltaX;
24            } else {
25              param += twoDXDY;
26              x += slopeSign;
27            }
28            g.drawLine(x, y, x, y);
29            y++;
30          }
31      }
32    }
```

On line 4 we call a separate method to determine if the slope is less than 1, and also set up a few parameters that are used in the algorithm. All parameters that are not declared as local variables are class variables.

The variable slopeLT1 is true if the line's slope is between −1 and +1 (it can be shown that the version of the algorithm given above also works if the slope is between −1 and 0), and is calculated by the method selectEndPoints(). We will consider this method below.

The line is to be drawn between (x0, y0) and (x1, y1). The variable param is the p_k parameter. The variables twoDeltaY and twoDYDX are $2\Delta y$ and $2\Delta y - \Delta x$, respectively. The slopeSign variable is +1 if the slope is positive and −1 if it is negative. The code in the while loop (lines 9 to 15) applies the recursive formula for calculating successive values of p_k and determining the various y values that should be plotted.

Line 16 plots the point using Java's drawLine() method from the Graphics class. Java does not have a method for plotting a single point (except in Java 3D), so we simply specify the starting and ending points to be the same. (Obviously this is a horribly inefficient way of drawing a line, but we are merely trying to illustrate that Bresenham's algorithm does, in fact, produce a proper line by plotting each point separately.)

The remaining code (lines 20 through 31) handle lines with slopes of 1 or greater in magnitude. As you can see by looking at the variables, it is essentially obtained by taking the first block of code and interchanging x and y. Points are plotted using y as the index rather than x, and it is therefore the x coordinate that must be determined using Bresenham's algorithm.

Finally, we examine the method selectEndPoints():

```
1     boolean selectEndPoints(Point point0, Pointpoint1)
2     {
3        x0 = point0.x;
4        y0 = point0.y;
5        x1 = point1.x;
6        y1 = point1.y;
7
8        int deltaY = y1 - y0, deltaX = x1 - x0;
9        slopeSign = 1;
10       slopeLT1 = true;
11       if (Math.abs(deltaY) > Math.abs(deltaX)) {
12           slopeLT1 = false;
13       }
14       if (slopeLT1) {
15           if (x1 < x0) {
16               int temp = x0;  x0 = x1;  x1 = temp;
17               temp = y0;  y0 = y1;  y1 = temp;
18               deltaX = -deltaX;
19               deltaY = -deltaY;
20           }
21           if (deltaY < 0) {
22                   slopeSign = -1;
23                   deltaY = -deltaY;
24           }
25           twoDeltaY = 2 * deltaY;
26           twoDYDX = 2 * (deltaY - deltaX);
27           param = twoDeltaY - deltaX;
28       } else {
29           if (y1 < y0) {
30               int temp = x0;  x0 = x1;  x1 = temp;
31               temp = y0;  y0 = y1;  y1 = temp;
32               deltaX = -deltaX;
33               deltaY = -deltaY;
34           }
35           if (deltaX < 0) {
36               slopeSign = -1;
37               deltaX = -deltaX;
38           }
39           twoDeltaX = 2 * deltaX;
40           twoDXDY = 2 * (deltaX - deltaY);
41           param = twoDeltaX - deltaY;
42       }
43       return slopeLT1;
44   }
```

The main purposes of this method are to initialize the various parameters and to ensure that the endpoints are specified in the correct order (for example, in the case with the slope less than 1, that the start point is to the left of the endpoint).

The method receives as input the two Point variables chosen by the user. These two points could be in any relative position on the canvas. On lines 3 through 6, we extract the coordinates. Lines 8 through 13 determine if the magnitude of the slope is less than 1.

If the slope is less than 1 in magnitude, lines 15 through 20 ensure t leftmost point is the one with coordinates (x0, y0), and lines 21 to 24 the sign of the slope. Lines 25 to 27 set up the constants and the initia param (equivalent to p_o).

The remainder of the method does the same things for the case where the slope has a magnitude greater than or equal to 1.

The selectEndPoints() method is called only once per line, after which the algorithm generates successive points. In a real graphics system, of course, the actual plotting of the points is done at a more primitive level (it is often built into the hardware), so the algorithm would be much more efficient than the software version given here.

1.6 Generating circles

Next to line segments (and figures such as polygons that are composed from them), the circle is probably the most commonly used figure in simple graphics.

The equation of a circle with centre (x_c, y_c) and radius r may be specified in rectangular coordinates:

$$(x - x_c)^2 + (y - y_c)^2 = r^2 \qquad (1.9)$$

Using polar coordinates, the same circle may be specified using the parametric equations:

$$x = r\cos\theta + x_c$$
$$y = r\sin\theta + y_c \qquad (1.10)$$

where $0 \le \theta < 2\pi$.

We could attempt to generate a circle by, say, solving equation 1.9 for y in terms of x, and then obtaining a set of y coordinates for each x coordinate. There are two problems with this approach. First, the equation giving y in terms of x involves a square root, which is costly to calculate. Second, because of the curvature of the circle, the points generated by this approach will not be equally spaced, so that gaps will appear in the circle when it is drawn.

We can generate a more uniform circle by using equation 1.10, since here we can vary the angle θ by constant increments. However, trigonometric functions are also costly to calculate, so the algorithm would not be very efficient.

Figure 1.5:
The eight-fold symmetry of a circle.

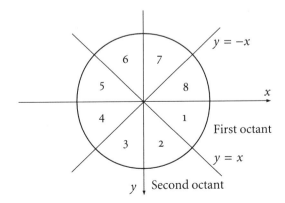

It turns out that there is another algorithm, also discovered by Bresenham, that allows circles to be drawn using only integer arithmetic. The algorithm is similar in spirit to that for drawing line segments.

Before we present the details of the algorithm, it is worth noting that the symmetry of the circle can also be used to reduce the work required to draw it. We can divide a circle into eight octants (see Figure 1.5). Because we are using the monitor's coordinate system with the y axis increasing downwards, the octants are numbered in a clockwise direction starting at the positive x axis. Thus the first octant is that portion of the circle between the positive x axis and the line $y = x$, the second octant lies between the line $y = x$ and the positive y axis, and so on.

Suppose we have an algorithm that generates the pixels in the second octant of a circle centred at the origin. (If the circle's centre is elsewhere, we can just add the coordinates of the centre to each pixel value after calculating it.) For a point (x, y) generated by this algorithm, we can draw seven other pixels in the other seven octants by using the following table.

Octant	x coord	y coord
1	y	x
2	x	y
3	$-x$	y
4	$-y$	x
5	$-y$	$-x$
6	$-x$	$-y$
7	x	$-y$
8	y	$-x$

Now let us consider how to generate the pixels in the second octant of a circle centred at the origin. In this octant, the circle begins at a location given by $(0, r)$, where r is the radius of the circle and is assumed to be given in pixel coordinates so that it is an integer. As we increase x in the second octant, the value of y decreases until we reach the line $y = x$, where the second octant finishes. Thus, if we have decided that a pixel with coordinates (x_k, y_k) is part of the circle, the next pixel at location (x_{k+1}, y_{k+1}) must satisfy the conditions that $x_{k+1} = x_k + 1$ and $y_{k+1} =$ either y_k or $y_k - 1$, depending on whether the curve of the circle takes it to the next level of pixels in the y direction.

Since we have a choice of two possible pixels at each stage, we can set up a system similar to the algorithm for drawing a line: find which of these two pixels is closer to the true circle for that value of x_k.

From equation 1.9 with $x_c = y_c = 0$, we can find the actual y value corresponding to x_{k+1}:

$$y^2 = r^2 - x_{k+1}^2$$
$$= r^2 - (x_k + 1)^2$$

We will use y^2 rather than y so that we can use integer arithmetic throughout. Now we wish to compare the distance from the actual y value at position x_{k+1} with the two possible pixel values at y_k and y_{k+1}. Of the two choices for the next pixel, the one with the larger value will be that with y coordinate y_k. We can find the difference between this point and the true circle, and call this difference d_i:

$$d_1 = y_k^2 - y^2$$

$$= y_k^2 - r^2 + (x_k + 1)^2 \tag{1.11}$$

Similarly, the other pixel will have y coordinate $y_k - 1$, so we can find the difference d_2 between this pixel and the true circle:

$$d_2 = y^2 - (y_k - 1)^2$$

$$= r^2 - (x_k + 1)^2 - (y_k - 1)^2 \tag{1.12}$$

$$= r^2 - (x_k + 1)^2 - y_k^2 + 2y_k - 1$$

As in the line algorithm, we now define a *decision parameter* p_k as the difference between d_1 and d_2:

$$p_k = d_1 - d_2$$

$$= 2y_k^2 + 2(x_k + 1)^2 - 2y_k - 2r^2 + 1 \tag{1.13}$$

Since both d_1 and d_2 are positive, if p_k is negative, the pixel y_k lies closer to the true circle, while if p_k is positive, we should use the pixel at $y_k - 1$.

Since all quantities in equation 1.13 are integers (recall that r was required to be an integer at the start of the algorithm), we could just use this formula to calculate p_k at each step. However, it is more efficient to derive a recursive relationship as we did in the case of the line algorithm. To do this, we write out equation 1.13 for p_{k+1}:

$$p_{k+1} = 2y_{k+1}^2 + 2(x_{k+1} + 1)^2 - 2y_{k+1} - 2r^2 + 1$$

We can now subtract equation 1.13 from this equation to get:

$$p_{k+1} - p_k = 2y_{k+1}^2 + 2(x_{k+1} + 1)^2 - 2y_{k+1} - 2y_k^2 - 2(x_k + 1)^2 + 2y_k$$

We now have two cases. If p_k is negative, then $y_{k+1} = y_k$. Substituting this, together with $x_{k+1} = x_k + 1$, we obtain, after cancelling off terms:

$$p_{k+1} - p_k = 4x_k + 6 \qquad (p_k < 0) \tag{1.14}$$

If $p_k \geq 0$, then $y_{k+1} = y_k - 1$, and we obtain:

$$p_{k+1} - p_k = 4(x_k - y_k) + 10 \qquad (p_k \geq 0) \tag{1.15}$$

All that remains is to derive the starting value p_0, which we can obtain directly from equation 1.13, by substituting $x_0 = 0$ and $y_0 = r$:

$$p_0 = 3 - 2r \tag{1.16}$$

We therefore have our algorithm for choosing the pixels in the second octant of a circle:

1. Specify (in integer pixel coordinates) the radius r and centre (x_c, y_c) of the circle.
2. Set $x_0 = 0$ and $y_0 = r$, and plot the first point at position $(x_0 + x_c, y_0 + y_c)$.
3. Calculate p_0 from equation 1.16.
4. While $x_k < y_k$:

   Set $x_{k+1} = x_k + 1$.

   If $p_k < 0$, set $y_{k+1} = y_k$, plot the next pixel at location $(x_{k+1} + x_c, y_{k+1} + y_c)$ and calculate p_{k+1} from equation 1.14.

   Else, set $y_{k+1} = y_k - 1$, plot the next pixel at location $(x_{k+1} + x_c, y_{k+1} + y_c)$ and calculate p_{k+1} from equation 1.15.

To obtain pixels in other octants, use the table above.

1.7 Java code for circle generation

The Java code for generation of a full circle is quite straightforward using the algorithm above. We draw the pixels for the second octant and use symmetry to produce the other seven octants.

```java
void drawBresenhamCircle(Graphics g, Point centre,
    int radius)
{
    int centreX = centre.x;
    int centreY = centre.y;

    int param = 3 - 2 * radius;
    int x = 0, y = radius;
    drawCircleOctant(g, x, y, centreX, centreY, 1);
    drawCircleOctant(g, x, y, centreX, centreY, 2);
    drawCircleOctant(g, x, y, centreX, centreY, 4);
    drawCircleOctant(g, x, y, centreX, centreY, 7);
    while (x <= y) {
        if (param < 0) {
            param += 4 * x + 6;
        x++;
        } else {
            param += 4 * (x - y) + 10;
            x++;
            y--;
        }
        for (int i = 1; i < 9; i++)
            drawCircleOctant(g, x, y, centreX,
            centreY, i);
    }
}

void drawCircleOctant(Graphics g, int x, int y,
    int centreX, int centreY, int octant)
{
    switch (octant) {
    case 1:
        g.drawLine(y + centreX, x + centreY,
            y + centreX, x + centreY);
        break;
    case 2:
        g.drawLine(x + centreX, y + centreY,
            x + centreX, y + centreY);
        break;
    case 3:
        g.drawLine(-x + centreX, y + centreY,
            -x + centreX, y + centreY);
    break;
```

```
44          case 4:
45             g.drawLine(-y + centreX, x + centreY,
46                -y + centreX, x + centreY);
47             break;
48          case 5:
49             g.drawLine(-y + centreX, -x + centreY,
50                -y + centreX, -x + centreY);
51             break;
52          case 6:
53             g.drawLine(-x + centreX, -y + centreY,
54                -x + centreX, -y + centreY);
55             break;
56          case 7:
57             g.drawLine(x + centreX, -y + centreY,
58                x + centreX, -y + centreY);
59             break;
60          case 8:
61             g.drawLine(y + centreX, -x + centreY,
62                y + centreX, -x + centreY);
63             break;
64       }
65    }
```

The method `drawBresenhamCircle()` takes the centre and radius of the circle as arguments (along with the `Graphics` object). On line 7 we calculate p_0, and on line 8 we initialize x_0 and y_0.

Lines 9 through 12 draw the four pixels that lie on the coordinate axes using the utility method `drawCircleOctant()`. This method, on lines 28 to 65, implements the table above to draw points in the selected octant.

The while loop starting on line 13 implements the algorithm given above by updating x_k, y_k and p_k. The for loop on line 22 maps the pixel generated by the algorithm to all eight octants in the circle.

Note that, since the usual coordinate system for graphics on a monitor screen inverts the y axis, the first octant is that sector of the circle immediately *below* the positive x axis, rather than above, as is the case with the usual mathematical graph of a circle. In addition, the octants are then numbered clockwise around the circle rather than counterclockwise.

1.8 Plotting general curves—the ellipse

Many of the techniques we have used in the line and circle algorithms in the previous sections can be applied to create algorithms for plotting more general curves. In this section, we will identify the general principles that can be used to plot a wide variety of curves, and illustrate the procedure by deriving an algorithm for plotting ellipses.

Let us consider the essentials of the algorithms presented above. The first problem we needed to solve was how to avoid gaps in the curve. We can do this by identifying those regions of the curve where the slope (strictly speaking, the slope of the tangent line) is less than or greater than 1, and changing the strategy we use for determining pixels to plot. In general, for those portions of a curve with a slope less than 1 (in magnitude), we can step along the x axis one unit at a time and calculate the corresponding y coordinate for the pixel to be plotted. Since the slope is less than 1, the y value can change at most one unit up or down from its previous position.

Conversely, for regions of the curve where the slope is greater than or equal to 1 (again, we are considering the magnitude of the slope), we step along the y axis one unit at a time and calculate the corresponding x value for each pixel. In this way, we can guarantee a digital display of the curve without any gaps.

For a general curve, therefore, we must first determine those points where the slope of the curve is ± 1, and then determine the relative magnitude of the slope of the curve between these points.

For simple curves, such as lines and circles, we can determine these points either by direct inspection of the equation (as in the case of the line, where the slope is given as the parameter m in equation 1.1), or by considering the symmetry of the curve (in a circle centred at the origin, for example, the slope has magnitude 1 where the circle intersects the lines $y = \pm x$).

For more complex curves, we can determine the slope of the tangent line to the curve by calculating the derivative dy/dx. For example, to determine the slope of the tangent line to an ellipse, we begin with the general equation of an ellipse centred at the origin.

$$\frac{x^2}{a^2} + \frac{y^2}{b^2} = 1 \tag{1.17}$$

Here, a and b are constants called the *semi-major* and *semi-minor* axes of the ellipse. (Which of the constants is which depends on which one is larger: the semi-major axis is the larger of the two.) If $a = b$, the ellipse becomes a circle.

By using implicit differentiation, we can find the derivative dy/dx from equation 1.17:

$$\frac{2x}{a^2} + \frac{2y}{b^2}\frac{dy}{dx} = 0 \tag{1.18}$$

Since ellipses have four-fold symmetry, we can determine the algorithm for plotting the pixels in the first quadrant and then use this symmetry to determine the points in the other three quadrants. In the first quadrant (see Figure 1.6, and recall that we are using monitor coordinates with the y axis increasing downwards) the ellipse will have one point where the slope of the tangent is -1. To find this point, we set $dy/dx = -1$ in equation 1.18, and obtain the condition:

$$a^2 y = b^2 x \tag{1.19}$$

Figure 1.6:
An ellipse.

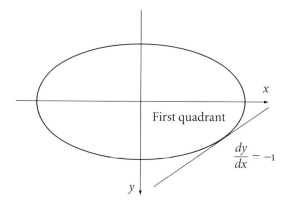

First quadrant

$$\frac{dy}{dx} = -1$$

From the graph of an ellipse, it is obvious that the magnitude of the slope is less than 1 in the region from $x = 0$ to the point defined by equation 1.19, and greater than 1 from that point up to the point where the ellipse crosses the x axis, at $y = 0$. We can therefore design our algorithm so that we begin with $x = 0$ and step through x one unit at a time until the point specified by equation 1.19 is reached. Then, we can complete the first quadrant of the ellipse by starting at $y = 0$ and stepping through y one unit at a time until the same point is reached. In this way, we are building up the ellipse by starting at the points where it crosses the two coordinate axes and working from both directions towards the point defined by equation 1.19.

The second stage of a general curve plotting algorithm is, having just plotted a pixel, to decide which pixel should be plotted next. In the cases of the line and circle, we identified the two possible candidates for the next pixel and calculated the distance from these two pixels to the actual curve. The difference between these two distances defined our decision parameter p_k, the sign of which told us which pixel to choose.

The calculation of p_k is straightforward once we have the equation of the curve, but it is also a good idea to attempt to simplify the algorithm for finding p_k in order to speed up the algorithm. In the cases of the line and circle, we were able to find an algorithm which used exclusively integer arithmetic. We will see we can also do this for the ellipse, but for more general curves this will not always be possible. However, even for such curves, we can still use the principle of comparing the distances from two candidate pixels to the actual curve in order to choose which pixel to plot next.

Let us see how we can obtain p_k for the ellipse. We will begin by considering that part of the ellipse in the first quadrant where the magnitude of the slope is less than 1. In this region, we step through successive values of x and calculate the corresponding y coordinate. We therefore need the equation of the ellipse in a form which allows us to calculate y (or at least y^2) in terms of x. We can rearrange equation 1.17 to get:

$$a^2 y^2 = b^2 \left(a^2 - x^2 \right)$$

Let us assume that the pixel at position (x_k, y_k) has just been plotted, and try to determine which pixel should be plotted next. Since the slope in this region is negative, we know that y_{k+1} must be either y_k or $y_k - 1$. We therefore need to find the distances from each of the pixels to the true curve, and choose whichever pixel minimizes this distance. In order to simplify the calculations, we will consider the quantity $a^2 y^2$ rather than y itself for comparing the distance between the pixel and the curve. We then have, for $y_{k+1} = y_k$:

$$d_1 = a^2 \left(y_k^2 - y^2 \right)$$
$$= a^2 y_k^2 - b^2 \left(a^2 - x_{k+1}^2 \right)$$

For $y_{k+1} = y_k - 1$:

$$d_2 = a^2 \left(y^2 - \left(y_k - 1 \right)^2 \right)$$
$$= b^2 \left(a^2 - x_{k+1}^2 \right) - a^2 \left(y_k - 1 \right)^2$$

We now define the decision parameter p_k as the difference between these two quantities:

$$p_k = d_1 - d_2$$
$$= 2a^2\left(y_k^2 - y_k\right) - 2b^2\left(a^2 - x_{k+1}^2\right) + a^2 \qquad (1.20)$$

If $p_k < 0$, we choose $y_{k+1} = y_k$, otherwise we choose $y_{k+1} = y_k - 1$. We could stop here, but as with the circle, it is possible to derive a recursive formula for calculating p_k which improves the efficiency. The derivation of this formula is similar to that for the circle: we use the preceding equation to calculate p_{k+1} and subtract the first equation from the second to get a formula for $p_{k+1} - p_k$. Working out the algebra, and substituting $x_{k+1} = x_k + 1$, we obtain two formulas. If $p_k < 0$, we have:

$$p_{k+1} = p_k + 2b^2\left(2x_k + 3\right) \qquad (1.21)$$

Otherwise, we have:

$$p_{k+1} = p_k + 4a^2\left(1 - y_k\right) + 2b^2\left(2x_k + 3\right) \qquad (1.22)$$

The initial condition can be obtained from equation 1.20 with $x_0 = 0$ and $y_0 = b$:

$$p_0 = a^2\left(1 - 2b\right) + 2b^2 \qquad (1.23)$$

We have now completed the algorithm for determining that portion of the ellipse in the first quadrant where the slope has magnitude less than 1. To determine the remainder of the first quadrant portion of the ellipse, we start with $x = a$ and $y = 0$. Since the procedure is entirely symmetric in x and y, we can obtain the recursion formulas for p_k by simply interchanging x with y, and a with b, in equations 1.21 through 1.23, to obtain the following. If $p_k < 0$, we have:

$$p_{k+1} = p_k + 2a^2\left(2y_k + 3\right) \qquad (1.24)$$

Otherwise, we have:

$$p_{k+1} = p_k + 4b^2\left(1 - x_k\right) + 2a^2\left(2y_k + 3\right) \qquad (1.25)$$

The initial condition is now:

$$p_0 = b^2\left(1 - 2a\right) + 2a^2 \qquad (1.26)$$

The Java code to implement this algorithm is very similar to that for the circle, and is left as an exercise for the reader.

1.9 Line thickness

In addition to providing a set of primitive shapes such as lines, circles, and ellipses, most graphics libraries also allow the programmer to specify several properties of the lines or curves used to draw the figures. Two of the most common attributes of lines that may be specified are the *thickness* of the line and the *style* (solid, dashed, dotted, etc.) of the line.

Despite their apparent simplicity, both of these features prove surprisingly difficult to implement consistently for all types of lines and curves. In this section, we will consider line thickness, leaving line style till later.

1.9.1 Pixel duplication

Consider first a straight line segment. How might we draw this line with a specified thickness of, say, 3 pixels? If the line is horizontal, we begin by plotting the line with a thickness of 1 pixel, and then just add another row of pixels on either side.

Now suppose we wish to plot a 3-pixel-wide line that has a non-zero slope. One way of doing this would be to generate the basic 1-pixel-wide line using Bresenham's algorithm above, and for each pixel produced by the algorithm, add another pixel on either side to produce the thicker line. If the slope of the line satisfies $|m| < 1$, we add the extra pixels above and below the original pixel; otherwise we add the extra pixels to the left and right. This is called the *pixel duplication algorithm*.

Does this really provide a line with a thickness of 3 pixels? It depends on how we measure the thickness. The most intuitive way of measuring thickness of a line is to measure the thickness perpendicular to the line itself. Because the 3 pixels are always drawn either horizontally or vertically, the thickness of the line measured in this way will be less than 3 for any line at an angle to the coordinate axes.

Figure 1.7 shows a line with slope less than 1 drawn with a width of 10 pixels using the pixel duplication algorithm. Note that the ends of the line are clipped vertically, and not perpendicular to the line itself as might be more natural. It is this vertical distance that is 10 pixels in size, so a cross section of the line perpendicular to its length will be less than 10 pixels wide.

Figure 1.7:
A line with slope less than 1 produced using the pixel duplication algorithm.

There is another problem with the pixel duplication method: if we want a thickness of an even number of pixels, we will need to put more extra pixels on one side of the original line than on the other. To see this, it is easiest to consider a line with a thickness of 2 pixels. We draw the original line using Bresenham's algorithm and then wish to thicken the line by adding an extra pixel at each point. On which side do we put it? Either way, the centre line of the new thicker line will not be the same as it was when the original line was generated.

Despite these problems, the pixel duplication method works well if precise accuracy is not that important. It is also fairly easy to generalize the method to more complex curves. If we are drawing a curve with varying slope, we can thicken the curve by adding extra pixels on either side (above and below) in those areas of the curve where the slope of its tangent line has magnitude less than 1, and to the left and right otherwise.

Figure 1.8 shows a circle with a thickness of 10 pixels, drawn using the pixel duplication algorithm. The circle appears thicker at top, bottom, left and right than in between these points, and this is not an optical illusion. There are also four noticeable notches at the thinner points in the circle. These notches occur where the algorithm switches over from drawing horizontal rows of pixels (where the slope is greater than 1) to vertical rows (where the slope is less than 1). Although these flaws are quite noticeable in Figure 1.8, if the line thickness is only 2 or 3 pixels rather than 10 or more, the representation is quite good.

Although this algorithm works passably well for projects where precision is not vital, in detailed graphic design work, the inaccuracies in thickness and line placement may be unacceptable. We therefore need to consider some alternative algorithms.

Figure 1.8:
A circle with a 10-pixel thickness, drawn using the pixel duplication algorithm.

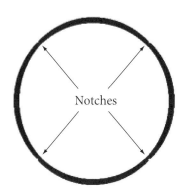

1.9.2 The moving pen

The moving pen algorithm is actually a variant of the pixel replication algorithm above, but allows different effects to be generated depending on the type of pen used. The idea is that rather than just thickening each pixel by duplicating it on either side, we define a pen nib with a specified cross section and trace out the curve. For example, if we wished to draw a curve with a thickness of 3 pixels, we could define a pen with a cross section (sometimes called a *footprint*) which is a square with 3 pixels on each side. For each pixel generated by Bresenham's algorithm, we stamp out this imprint centred on that pixel.

A 3-pixel-thick curve drawn using the moving pen tends to appear thicker on screen than the same curve drawn using the pixel duplication algorithm. However, the thickness is still not uniform for lines of different slopes, or over the extent of curves such as circles and ellipses.

Figure 1.9 shows a line with a slope less than 1 and a thickness of 10 pixels drawn using the moving pen algorithm with a square footprint, 10 pixels on each side. Measured perpendicular to its length, this line is noticeably thicker than the one in Figure 1.7, which was drawn using pixel duplication. As well, the ends of the line reflect the square that was used to draw it.

Figure 1.9:
A line with slope less than 1, drawn using the moving pen algorithm with a square footprint.

Figure 1.10 shows a circle with a thickness of 10 pixels drawn using the moving pen algorithm with a square footprint. Compared with Figure 1.8, we see that the moving pen circle is thinner where the pixel duplication circle was thicker, and vice versa. However, one improvement noticeable with the moving pen algorithm is that there are no notches in the circle's outline. This is because the same shape is used to thicken every pixel in the circle—a square is drawn around every point. There is no discontinuity at points where the slope is 1.

Figure 1.10:
A circle with thickness 10 pixels, drawn using the moving pen algorithm with a square footprint.

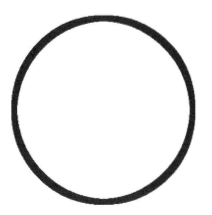

Another advantage is that we can compensate for some of the variations in thickness by changing the shape of the pen. For example, rather than using a square pen, we could use a circular one. Circles, of course, have the same 'thickness' from any viewing angle, but they are also somewhat more difficult to compute than squares or rectangles.

1.10 Line style

The *style* of a line is usually taken to refer to the dash or dot pattern that is used to draw it. All lines we have drawn so far are *solid* lines, in that every pixel along the line's path is drawn. By leaving periodic gaps in the line, we can create a dashed or dotted pattern.

An algorithm for drawing a dashed line therefore only needs to figure out which pixels should be drawn and which should not. The pixels of which the line is composed are still calculated using Bresenham's algorithm, with one of the line thickness algorithms in the previous section being applied if necessary.

There are various ways that dashed or dotted lines can be specified. Some graphics packages contain a fixed set of options, such as 'solid', 'dashed', 'dotted' and 'dash-dotted'. Java 2D is much more flexible in that it allows any pattern to be created by the programmer (as we will see in Chapter 3).

There is only one difficulty with producing dashed lines. Suppose, for example, that we wish to draw a line with a dash pattern consisting of 5 pixels drawn followed by 3 pixels blank. If the line is horizontal or vertical, we can simply draw 5 pixels, leave the next 3 blank, then draw 5 more and so on.

However, if the line is at an angle of 45 degrees (with a slope of 1), drawing 5 successive pixels will produce a dash that is longer by a factor of the square root of 2 than a dash on a horizontal line. Thus, to ensure that dashes are all roughly the same size when a line is drawn, we need to take account of the slope of the line. In the case of the line with a slope of 1, for example, we could draw only $5/\sqrt{2}$ (which is roughly 3.53, so we could round it up to 4) pixels. In general, for a line that subtends an angle of between 0 and 45 degrees (that is, it has a slope between 0 and 1), we can scale the length of the dash by multiplying it by the cosine of the subtended angle. Lines subtending an angle between 45 and 90 degrees are scaled by multiplying the length by the sine of the angle.

When drawing dashed lines with a thickness of greater than a single pixel, we must also ensure that the end style of each dash is appropriate. The most commonly used end style is one where the end of the dash is perpendicular to the direction of the line, but obviously this can be varied if desired.

1.11 Polygons

A polygon is any plane figure bounded by straight line segments. Once we have decided on algorithms for drawing lines (and for implementing thick lines, if desired), drawing polygons is fairly easy. Usually, the vertices ('corners') of the polygon are stored in a data structure such as an array or list, and the polygon is drawn by traversing the list and joining each pair of adjacent vertices with a line segment. The polygon is closed by joining the last vertex in the list with the first.

Drawing a polygon with lines that are a single pixel in thickness is thus quite easy, once we have a routine for drawing lines. However, there are a few problems when we wish the lines to be thicker than a single pixel. One problem is the same as that with circles or ellipses: if we make the border of a polygon thicker, do we add the extra thickness on the inside or outside of the original border, or do we add a bit on each side? It all depends on the specific application. If the polygon is part of a larger image, and must fit snugly next to other geometric shapes (for example, a square on a chessboard), then we probably want to specify the vertices of the polygon as its outside dimensions, so any extra line thickness should be added to the interior. In other applications, the polygon may be serving as a border or frame for other graphics of a fixed size (such as border around some text), and increasing the line thickness on the inside of the polygon might overwrite some of the graphics. In this case, it makes more sense to add the thickness on the outside. A versatile graphics package will allow us to make the choice for ourselves.

Figure 1.11:
A polygon drawn using the pixel duplication line thickness algorithm.

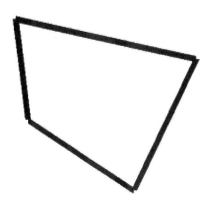

Another problem specific to polygons arises where two line segments meet at a vertex. In most cases, we would like a smooth join where two lines meet, but different line thickness algorithms provide different results.

For example, in Figure 1.11, a polygon with a 10-pixel-thick border is drawn using the pixel duplication algorithm to produce the thick lines. We can see that there are notches or gaps at the points where the lines meet.

Using the moving pen algorithm produces the result shown in Figure 1.12. The square footprint produces much cleaner junctions at the corners.

Figure 1.12:
A polygon drawn using the moving pen line thickness algorithm.

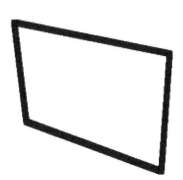

Other more complex algorithms exist for producing different types of joins at vertices. These algorithms take into account such things as the orientation of the line so that they can produce ends that are properly aligned with the lines they adorn. We will see in Chapter 3 that Java provides some of these more sophisticated methods for joining lines.

1.12   Filling

Up to now, all the figures we have drawn consisted solely of outlines. Frequently, we need to *fill* a figure. There are two main effects that can be realized by filling a figure: a *solid* fill (where all interior pixels are set to the same colour) and a *pattern* fill (where some repeating pattern, such as hatched lines, is drawn over the interior of the figure).

Since filling often involves drawing many more pixels that the outline, it is important to have an efficient algorithm for doing it. As with the drawing algorithms we have considered so far, the most desirable filling algorithm uses only integer arithmetic.

Some of the problems associated with filling may not be immediately obvious, so let us take a moment to consider just what needs to be done.

First, *filling* a figure implies that we should colour all the *interior* pixels, but what exactly do we mean by 'interior'? For simple polygons such as those shown in Figures 1.11 and 1.12, the interior of the polygon may seem obvious, but some polygons can be self-intersecting. Consider the polygon shown in Figure 1.13. Which portions are interior and which are exterior?

Figure 1.13:
Can you identify the
interior regions of this
polygon?

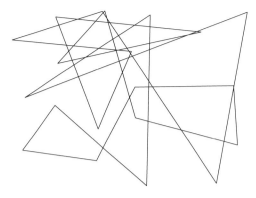

Once the interior regions have been identified, we still need an algorithm for colouring in these regions efficiently.

1.12.1 The scan-line algorithm

The most common method for filling polygons is called the *scan-line algorithm*. It is based on the fact that, when an image is drawn on a monitor, the electron beam starts at the top and *scans* across the screen one line at a time until it reaches the bottom of the screen. The idea is to identify those regions on each scan line that are to be coloured in, and draw in these regions one scan line at a time. That is, we take a series of horizontal cross-sections of the figure and identify the interior regions of the polygon in each cross-section.

Before we get to the actual filling, we can use the scan lines to determine the interior points of the polygon on any given row. To see how, consider Figure 1.14, which contains an example of a *concave* polygon. A polygon is concave if a straight line can be found that intersects the boundary at more than 2 points. (If a straight line can intersect a polygon at no more than 2 points, the polygon is called *convex*. Common polygons such as triangles and rectangles are all convex.)

A sample scan line is shown in Figure 1.14. We can determine the interior points of the polygon along this scan line by defining a quantity called *parity*. We begin by placing ourselves on the scan line at its left-hand end (so we are definitely outside the polygon). The idea is to count the number of times this scan line intersects the polygon's border as it crosses it. The parity of a point along this line is either *even* or *odd*, depending on whether we have encountered an even or odd number of intersections up to that point. Since the first intersection passes from the outside to the inside, the *inside* of a polygon is defined as the set of all points with odd parity.

The first intersection occurs when the scan line crosses edge AB, so the parity becomes odd at that point. The second intersection occurs with edge AF, so the parity becomes even. We can therefore say that points along the scan line between edges AB and AF are interior, points between edges AF and EF are exterior, and points between EF and DE are interior.

The method is quite general, and could even be used to identify interior points in a polygon as complex as the one shown in Figure 1.13.

Figure 1.14:
Using a scan line to
determine the interior
points of a polygon.

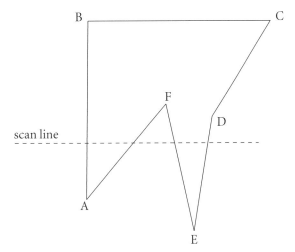

Figure 1.14: Using a scan line to determine the interior points of a polygon.

There are a couple of special cases that we need to consider, however. First, what happens if the scan line coincides with a horizontal edge in the polygon, such as edge BC in Figure 1.14? The convention is to ignore horizontal edges in the determination of parity. This means that edge BC would be considered as exterior using this algorithm.

The second case is a bit more subtle. What happens when a scan line passes through a vertex that is not part of a horizontal edge, such as vertex A or F above? Intuitively, we feel that such a vertex should not change the parity, since the portion of a scan line passing through vertex F that is between edges AB and CD, for example, should be entirely interior. Similarly, a scan line passing through vertex A should not enter an interior zone until it crosses line EF.

Another convention solves this problem as well. The convention relies on looking at the boundary of a polygon as being composed of a number of separate line segments, each with a distinct start- and end-point. If a scan line passes through a vertex where two edges meet, we treat the vertex as the property of both line segments that meet at that point. In the case of vertex A above, the lines AB and AF share the vertex.

The convention then is that the parity changes at a vertex for each line that has its *minimum* point (that is, lowest y value) at that point. If a line has its *maximum* value (highest y value) at a vertex, the parity does *not* change in response to that point.

For vertex A, both AB and AF have minimum points, so the parity will change *twice* at that vertex (that is, from even to odd and back to even again), meaning that there is no effective change at all. At vertex F, both AF and EF have their maximum points, so the parity does not change at all.

At a vertex such as D where one line has a maximum and another a minimum, the parity *does* change.

You should try this algorithm for yourself on a few simple figures with various configurations of vertices and convince yourself that it does work in all possible cases.

Given these conventions, we can state the first version of the scan-line algorithm for polygon filling.

1. Define a data structure for representing an edge. This data structure should contain the minimum and maximum y values (y_{min} and y_{max}, respectively) for the edge, and the x value corresponding to y_{min}, which we will call x_{min} (although it must be remembered that it is not necessarily the minimum x value on the edge—it is the x value that corresponds to the point with minimum y value).

2. Create an *edge table* in which the edges (represented by the data structures defined in step 1) are listed, sorted in ascending order by their y_{min} value. Omit any horizontal edges from the table. (In practice, an array or linked list is used for the edge table.)

3. Set the scan line value y_{scan} to the minimum y_{min} value for all edges (that is, to the lowest y value reached by the polygon). This is easily done by taking the y_{min} value from the first entry in the edge table, since the table was sorted on y_{min}. We will begin scanning the polygon at this point.

4. Create a second table called the *active edge table*. This table contains all edges currently intersected by the scan line. Like the original edge table, the active edge table is usually implemented as an array or linked list.

5. Add to the active edge table (and delete from the master edge table) any edges whose y_{min} value is equal to the current y_{scan}.

6. Sort the active edge table in ascending order on x. In this way, the edges will be listed in the order they are intersected by the scan line as it travels left to right.

7. Traverse the active edge table, taking pairs of edges at each step. Draw all pixels between the x value for the first edge in a pair and the x value in the second edge in the same pair. For example, with the scan line positioned as shown in Figure 1.14, pixels along this line between edges AB and AF would be drawn from the first pair of edges in the active edge table, then pixels between EF and ED. (It is a good exercise at this point to convince yourself that, using the conventions for determining parity described above, the active edge table will *always* contain an even number of edges.)

8. Increment y_{scan} by 1 to move to the next scan line.

9. Delete any edges from the active edge table if their y_{max} value is equal to y_{scan}. Note that we do not draw the pixel corresponding to the y_{max} value before deleting the edge—this is consistent with the rule above that y_{max} values are not to be used in determining the parity of a pixel.

10. Having moved the scan line, we must now determine the location on each edge where the scan line intersects the edge, so we know where to draw the next pixel. This means we must change the x coordinate for each edge to reflect the new intersection point. Doing this efficiently requires an additional algorithm, which we consider below.

11. While either the master edge table or the active edge table have edges remaining in them, repeat the algorithm from step 5.

1.12.2   **Edge coherence**

We now consider the algorithm for finding the intersection point between a scan line and a polygon edge. In principle, of course, this is easy—we just use the equation of the line, substitute $y = y_{scan}$ and solve for x. If x is not an integer, we round it to the nearest integer.

However, this 'brute force' technique suffers from the same problem that motivated us to consider the Bresenham-style algorithm for drawing the line in the first place—it involves floating point arithmetic. It turns out that there is a more efficient algorithm which allows us to calculate the x value on a scan line directly from the x value on the previous scan line, and also which allows us to use exclusively integer arithmetic. The technique relies on the so-called *edge coherence* property of a polygon edge.

The idea behind coherence of any sort is that most geometric figures have regions where their properties are relatively constant. For example, the interior points of a polygon are all equivalent in that they are all to be treated the same way by a filling algorithm. The specific case of edge coherence means that any non-horizontal edge in a polygon will be intersected by more than one scan line, so we can develop an efficient algorithm to generate the intersection points iteratively, rather than having to use the equation of the line from scratch for each scan line.

To develop the intersection algorithm, we need to consider two main cases: those where the magnitude of the line's slope is less than 1, and where it is greater than or equal to 1. We will consider the latter case first.

To begin, let us rewrite equation 1.1 of a line to give x as a function of y:

$$x = \frac{1}{m}(y - b) \qquad\qquad (1.27)$$

In going from one scan line to the next, y changes by an increment of 1 unit, so we can use equation 1.27 to calculate how much x changes over a single scan line. We find that this change is $1/m$ (the reciprocal of the slope).

Now if the slope is greater than 1, its reciprocal will, of course, be less than 1, which means that x changes by less than a single pixel over a scan line. Thus, it will sometimes take several scan lines before the cumulative change in x is enough to merit incrementing it by a single pixel. The number of scan lines required to allow x to change by a single pixel is the minimum integer which, when multiplied by $1/m$, gives a result that is greater than or equal to 1.

How do we determine when this should be done, and at the same time restrict ourselves to integer arithmetic?

The trick is to split the slope into its numerator $\Delta y = y_{max} - y_{min}$ and denominator $\Delta x = x_{max} - x_{min}$, both of which are integers, since the endpoints of the edge are given in pixel coordinates. The slope m is then given as $\Delta y / \Delta x$, and its reciprocal is $\Delta x / \Delta y$.

Now suppose we define a quantity called the *increment* for an edge. We initialize the increment to zero when that line is first scanned (that is, when it is added to the active edge table). For each increase in the scan line, we add Δx to the increment and test to see if the increment has equalled or exceeded Δy. If it has, we increase x by 1 pixel, and subtract Δy from the increment for that edge. We continue in the same way until the scan line reaches y_{max}.

For example, suppose we have an edge with a slope of $7/4$ with a starting x value of 10. Then $\Delta x = 4$ and $\Delta y = 7$. At the time this edge is added to the active edge table, we plot a pixel at $x = 10$ on that scan line. When we move to the next scan line, we add $\Delta x = 4$ to the increment, giving the increment a value of 4. This is not greater than $\Delta y = 7$, so we leave x alone and plot another pixel at $x = 10$ on the next scan line.

Moving to the third scan line for that edge, we add $\Delta x = 4$ to the increment again, giving it a cumulative value of 8. This is now greater than Δy, so we increase x by 1 and plot the pixel at $x = 11$ on this scan line. We adjust the increment by subtracting Δy from it, giving it a value of 1.

For the next few scan lines, the increment will have values of 5, 9 (x increased to 12), 6, 10 (x increased to 13), 7 (x increased to 14), 4, and so on.

If the slope of the line is negative and less than –1, the algorithm works in much the same way, except that Δx is negative (we have defined the edge data structure so that lines are sorted by their minimum y values so that Δy is always non-negative). This means that the increment will be negative as well, so we must compare its magnitude with Δy to determine when x should be changed, and x is decreased by 1, rather than increased, when it is changed.

The other main case is that where the slope is less than 1. In this case, Δy is less than Δx, so x will change at every scan line. The catch here is that sometimes x will change by more than 1 pixel, so we need some way of determining how many pixels x should be moved.

The technique works in the same way, however. For each scan line, we add to the increment the value Δx. To find the number of pixels by which x should be moved, we divide the magnitude (in case Δx is negative) of the increment by Δy, ignoring the remainder (that is, we use integer division). The quotient is the number of pixels to move. The increment itself is then adjusted by subtracting Δy multiplied by the number of pixels moved.

For example, if a line has a slope of $3/13$, and a starting x value of 10, then the value $x = 10$ is plotted on the first scan line. Moving up one scan line, we add $\Delta x = 13$ to the increment. To discover how many pixels to move, we divide 13 by 3 (ignoring the remainder) to get 4, so on the next line, we have $x = 14$. The increment is adjusted by subtracting $4 \times \Delta y = 12$, to give a value of 1. Over the next few scan lines, the increment has the values 14 (x increased by 4), 15 (x increased by 5), 13 (x increased by 4), and so on.

We can summarize the edge coherence algorithm for determining scan line intersection points as follows:

1. When a scan line is added to the active edge table, initialize x to x_{min} and the increment to 0. Calculate and store Δx and Δy.

2. When a scan line is increased by 1, add Δx to the increment.

3. If the magnitude of the slope is greater than or equal to 1, compare the magnitude of the increment with Δy. If it is less than Δy, leave x as it is. Otherwise, increase x by 1, and subtract (add) Δy to the increment if the increment is positive (negative).

4. If the magnitude of the slope is less than 1, determine the number of pixels to increase x by dividing the magnitude of the increment by Δy (ignoring the remainder). The remainder (positive if the increment is positive, and negative if it is negative) becomes the new value of the increment.

You may notice that steps 3 and 4 are actually identical, since in step 3 we are effectively dividing the increment by Δy to get the number of pixels by which x

should be moved. If the quotient is zero, we do not move *x*. It may be argued that it is worth making step 3 separate from step 4 as division (even integer division) is more costly than other arithmetic operations, but if you would rather have a simpler algorithm, you can apply step 4 to all line slopes, and omit step 3.

With the addition of the edge coherence algorithm for finding intersection points, the scan-line algorithm for filling polygons is now complete.

1.12.3 Java code for the scan-line polygon filling algorithm

We now present the Java code necessary for drawing and filling a polygon using the scan-line algorithm presented above. We shall assume that the vertices of the polygon have been stored as Point objects in a Vector. The Vector class is part of the java.util package, and is fully described in the Java documentation. Basically, a Vector acts as a variable-length array, which will grow or shrink as elements are added or deleted from it. It is also possible to add or remove elements from the interior of the array, with the remainder of the array expanding or contracting to allow for the change.

Associated with the Vector class (and a number of other so-called *collection classes*, or classes that allow data to be stored in an array or list) is the Enumeration class. We can connect an Enumeration object with an existing Vector, and use it to step through the elements of the vector in sequential order. Again, the Enumeration class is fully documented in the Java Development Kit, and in any Java development environment that you may be using. We shall explain any references to the Vector or Enumeration classes as we meet them in the code.

Before we get to the actual algorithm, however, we need a class to represent an edge in a polygon. We define the Edge class for this purpose:

```
1    public class Edge
2    {
3        int m_yMin, m_yMax;
4        int m_xMin, m_xMax;
5        int m_deltaX, m_deltaY;
6        int m_increment;
7
8        Edge(int xMin, int yMin, int xMax, int yMax)
9        {
10           m_xMin = xMin;
11           m_xMax = xMax;
12           m_yMin = yMin;
13           m_yMax = yMax;
14           m_deltaX = xMax - xMin;
15           m_deltaY = yMax - yMin;
16           m_increment = 0;
17       }
18
19       boolean lessThan(Edge other)
20       {
21           if (m_yMin < other.m_yMin) {
22               return true;
23           }
```

```
24        if (m_yMin == other.m_yMin &&
25            m_xMin < other.m_xMin) {
26            return true;
27        }
28        return false;
29    }
30
31    boolean lessThanX(Edge other)
32    {
33        if (m_xMin < other.m_xMin) {
34            return true;
35        }
36        return false;
37    }
38 }
```

The data fields in this class have the same meanings as their counterparts in the scan-line algorithm. m_yMin and m_yMax are the *y* coordinates of the endpoints of the edge, and m_xMin and m_xMax are the corresponding *x* coordinates. The constructor on lines 8 through 17 initializes all the data values.

In constructing the edge table below, we will need to sort the edges by their y_{min} values, so we provide a comparison method called lessThan() on lines 19 through 29. This method compares the y_{min} values of two edges, and if these are equal, it then compares the edges by their x_{min} values.

In sorting the active edge table, we need to sort the edges based on their x_{min} values alone, so we provide another comparison method, lessThanX(), on lines 31 to 37.

If we follow the scan-line algorithm above, the first thing we must do is create the master edge table. The method calculateEdgeTable() achieves this:

```
1     void calculateEdgeTable()
2     {
3         Enumeration vertex = m_polygonPoints.elements();
4         if (!vertex.hasMoreElements()) {
5             return;
6         }
7         m_startPoint = (Point)vertex.nextElement();
8         m_endPoint = m_startPoint;
9         m_edgeTable = new Vector();
10        while (vertex.hasMoreElements()) {
11            m_endPoint = (Point)vertex.nextElement();
12            addEdge(m_startPoint, m_endPoint);
13            m_startPoint = m_endPoint;
14        }
15        addEdge(m_startPoint,
16            (Point)m_polygonPoints.elementAt(0));
17    }
```

The Vector storing the polygon's vertices is m_polygonPoints. On line 3, we create an Enumeration object and attach it to m_polygonPoints by calling the elements() method. An Enumeration of a Vector begins by creating a marker which points to the first element in the Vector (if any). The marker is hidden from the direct view of the programmer, although it can be read and changed through various methods in the Enumeration class.

There are two main methods in the Enumeration class that we need to step through the elements in a Vector. The first is hasMoreElements() which returns true or false, depending on whether we have reached the last element in the Vector yet. We use this method on line 4 to test if the polygon contains any vertices at all, and if it doesn't, we return immediately.

The second Enumeration method is nextElement(), which does two things: it *returns* the element currently pointed to by the marker, and then it *advances* the marker to the next element in the Enumeration. Note that a Vector stores any object derived from Java's Object class, which is at the root of the entire class hierarchy. When we retrieve one of the elements in a Vector, therefore, we must explicitly cast it to its actual data type. On line 7, we retrieve the first Point stored in the Vector, and we apply a cast to tell the compiler that the object being retrieved is of class Point.

Since we are interested in storing *edges*, not individual vertices, in our edge table, we need to calculate each edge from a pair of vertices. We therefore need a second Point object to store the other end of the edge. This is the m_endPoint object, initialized on line 8. (Both m_startPoint and m_endPoint are Points, and are variables declared in the class in which the calculateEdgeTable() method is defined.)

We will use another Vector to store the edge table, which is initialized on line 9. We therefore need to step through the m_polygonPoints vector, calculate each edge, and add it to m_edgeTable. This is done in the loop on lines 10 through 14, in which the addEdge() method is called. Its code follows.

```
void addEdge(Point start, Point end)
{
    if (start.y == end.y) {
        return;
    }

    Edge newEdge;
    if (start.y < end.y) {
        newEdge = new Edge(start.x, start.y,
            end.x, end.y);
    } else {
        newEdge = new Edge(end.x, end.y,
            start.x, start.y);
    }
    insertEdge(newEdge);
}
```

The addEdge() method omits horizontal lines, which can be detected by comparing the *y* values of the two Points passed into the method. Then, a new Edge object is created, and the edge is stored with its minimum *y* value as the starting point.

After the edge is created, it is inserted into the edge table with the method insertEdge():

```
        void insertEdge(Edge edge)
        {
            Enumeration edgeList = m_edgeTable.elements();
            int counter = 0;
            while (edgeList.hasMoreElements()) {
                Edge currentEdge = (Edge)edgeList.nextElement();
                if (currentEdge != null &&
                    edge.lessThan(currentEdge))
                {
                    m_edgeTable.insertElementAt(edge, counter);
                    return;
                }
                counter ++;
            }
            m_edgeTable.insertElementAt(edge, counter);
        }
```

This method uses a version of the standard insertion sort routine for adding a new element to a sorted list. We attach an Enumeration object to the current edge table (which, on the first call to insertEdge(), will be empty). We use a counter to count the number of elements we step over in the edge table before we find the correct place to insert the new edge. The loop uses the lessThan() method defined earlier in the Edge class to compare the edge to be inserted with an edge already in the table and, when the correct location is found, the insertElementAt() method in the Vector class is used to insert the new element at the required point.

If the new edge belongs at the end of the table, it will be larger than all existing elements in the table, and the last line in the insertEdge() method takes care of that case.

To complete the creation of the edge table, we return to lines 15 and 16 in the calculateEdgeTable() method above. This inserts the edge from the last vertex in the list back to the first vertex, thus closing the polygon.

The master edge table is now complete. At this point, we know that the first element in the edge table will contain the minimum y value for the entire polygon, so that will be the location of the first scan line.

We can now start the actual filling of the polygon by calling fillPolygon():

```
1      void fillPolygon(Graphics g)
2      {
3          calculateEdgeTable();
4          Edge currentEdge = (Edge)m_edgeTable.elementAt(0);
5          int y = currentEdge.m_yMin;
6
7          Vector activeEdgeTable = new Vector();
8          while (m_edgeTable.size() > 0 ||
9              activeEdgeTable.size() > 0)
10         {
11             while (currentEdge != null &&
12                 currentEdge.m_yMin == y)
13             {
14                 activeEdgeTable.addElement(currentEdge);
15                 m_edgeTable.removeElementAt(0);
16                 if (m_edgeTable.size() > 0) {
```

```
17              currentEdge =
18                  (Edge)m_edgeTable.elementAt(0);
19          } else {
20              currentEdge = null;
21          }
22        }
23
24        sortTable(activeEdgeTable);
25        fillScanLine(g, y, activeEdgeTable);
26        y++;
27        removeDoneEdges(y, activeEdgeTable);
28        incrementX(activeEdgeTable);
29      }
30    }
```

The edge table is created on line 3, the first edge is extracted on line 4, and the scan line number is set on line 5.

On line 7 we create the active edge table, and lines 8 and 9 start the loop that actually draws in the filling pixels for each scan line. As stated by the algorithm above, the loop should continue until both the master edge table and the active edge table are empty.

The first thing to do in an iteration is to add to the active edge table any edges that begin at the current scan line, and this is done in lines 11 through 22. The addElement() method called on line 14 is part of the Vector class, and adds the element at the end of the list. Similarly, the removeElementAt(0) call on line 15 removes the first element from the master edge table.

The code on lines 16 through 21 reads the next edge from the master edge table (if there is one) and makes it ready for the next time an edge is to be transferred to the active edge table. Note that we always refer to the first element in the master edge table since, once an edge has been added to the active edge table, it is removed from the master edge table. The remaining edges in the master edge table are moved up automatically (by the Vector removeElementAt(0) method call) to fill in the gap, so the next edge is always at the start of the Vector.

After adding edges to the active edge table, we need to sort it by x coordinate. Although the edges added initially will be in the right order, the fact that we have to adjust the x coordinate on each scan line means that the lines could get out of order after a few scans. The call to sortTable() on line 24 uses insertion sort to do this, and is left as an exercise for the reader (the insertion sort algorithm is also used in insertEdge()).

The pixels to be filled in on the current scan line are drawn by the call to fillScanLine() on line 25:

```
void fillScanLine(Graphics g, int y,
    Vector activeEdgeTable)
{
    Edge startEdge, endEdge;
    Enumeration xPoints = activeEdgeTable.elements();
    while (xPoints.hasMoreElements()) {
        startEdge = (Edge)xPoints.nextElement();
        endEdge = (Edge)xPoints.nextElement();
        for (int x = startEdge.m_xMin;
                x <= endEdge.m_xMin; x++)
```

```
                {
                    g.drawLine(x,y,x,y);
                }
            }
    }
```

We see that edges are extracted in pairs from the active edge table, and pixels are drawn between the respective m_xMin values in each pair of edges.

Returning to the fillPolygon() method, line 26 increments the scan line, and line 27 removes any edges whose y_{max} value coincides with this scan line (thus we do not draw pixels at the y_{max} end of an edge, as explained in the algorithm above). The method for removing edges is:

```
void removeDoneEdges(int y, Vector activeEdgeTable)
{
    Edge startEdge;
    Enumeration edgeList = activeEdgeTable.elements();
    while (edgeList.hasMoreElements()) {
        startEdge = (Edge)edgeList.nextElement();
        if (startEdge.m_yMax == y) {
            activeEdgeTable.removeElement(startEdge);
            edgeList = activeEdgeTable.elements();
        }
    }
}
```

We step through the active edge table searching for edges where m_yMax is equal to the scan line value y, and remove such edges using removeElement(), a method in the Vector class. Note that after each removal, we must reinitialize edgeList to a new Enumeration, since removing an element disrupts the marker used for an enumeration, meaning that some edges could be missed if we don't start again.

Finally, the method incrementX() implements the edge coherence algorithm for changing x values from one scan line to the next. The code that follows implements the shorter of the two algorithms for edge coherence: that is, the one that does not check the slope of the line, but uses integer division to calculate the increment in all cases.

```
void incrementX(Vector activeEdgeTable)
{
    Edge currentEdge;
    int increment;
    Enumeration xPoints = activeEdgeTable.elements();
    while (xPoints.hasMoreElements()) {
        currentEdge = (Edge)xPoints.nextElement();
        currentEdge.m_increment += currentEdge.m_deltaX;
        increment = currentEdge.m_increment /
            currentEdge.m_deltaY;
        currentEdge.m_xMin += increment;
        currentEdge.m_increment -= increment *
                currentEdge.m_deltaY;
    }
}
```

We step through all edges in the active edge table and apply the algorithm to each one. The code should be easy enough to follow by referring back to the edge coherence algorithm above.

1.13 Text and characters

Probably the most commonly generated graphical objects are the various character symbols that make up lines of text. The generation of text is done using two main methods: as fixed bitmap images or as mathematically defined outlines.

Using a bitmap to display a character such as 'A' is computationally quite cheap, as once the image of the character has been created (usually by scanning in a high resolution version of the character and touching it up in an art package), the pixels are simply copied from the bitmap to wherever they are to appear on the display device.

The main problem with bitmapped characters is that it is difficult to scale them (or transform them in other ways that we will consider in the next chapter), so a separate set of bitmaps is often required for each size and variant (such as bold or italic) of the original font. Although the actual memory required to store several sizes and typefaces of a single font is not excessive, since the individual images are small, the flexibility offered by bitmapped text is limited to the sets of fonts that have been supplied—it is not possible to generate a transformed version of the font 'on the fly'.

The second method of character generation requires a polygonal or curved outline of the character to be specified. As can be imagined, the mathematical representation of a character is not always simple, but once such a representation is obtained, the character can be scaled, rotated, and transformed in many other ways without the need to generate any further representations. Defining a character as an outline also allows such effects as filling with a solid colour or a pattern, providing different colours for the outline and the interior, and other effects.

In Java, characters are produced using mathematical descriptions of their outlines, and utilities are provided which allow the programmer to produce new fonts by transforming existing ones. We will see some examples of the use of fonts in Java in Chapter 3, but for now, we will define some terminology.

As of the introduction of the Java 2D package (included with the Java JDK version 1.2), characters are produced using *glyphs*. A glyph is a single mathematically defined shape which can be transformed just like any other standard shape, such as a rectangle or ellipse. A character such as 'A' is composed of a single glyph, but some characters, such as the lower-case 'i', which contains two separated parts (the lower bit and the dot) or letters with accents, such as á, are composed of two glyphs.

A Java programmer rarely needs to be concerned with glyphs on their own (in fact, there is no Glyph class as such), although there are some classes that allow their handling. The Font class usually provides the necessary methods for dealing with text; besides providing the basic fonts such as Times Roman and Helvetica, it also contains methods for generating new fonts by applying various transformations.

EXERCISES

1. Extend Bresenham's algorithm for drawing lines to the cases where the slope m is greater than 1.

2. Extend Bresenham's line algorithm so that it can handle lines with negative slope.

3. Bresenham's circle algorithm divides a circle into eight symmetric parts so that the pixels need be calculated for only one of these parts. Carry this logic one step further by dividing the circle into 16 parts, calculating the pixels for one of these sections and attempting to apply symmetry arguments to calculate the pixel values for the other 15 sections. Does this actually increase the efficiency of the algorithm?

4. Implement in Java your algorithm from question 3.

5. Modify Bresenham's circle algorithm to obtain an algorithm for drawing circular arcs. A circular arc should be specified by giving its centre, radius, and starting and ending angles (in degrees or radians).

6. Implement in Java the circular arc algorithm you developed in question 5.

7. Implement in Java the ellipse drawing algorithm given in the text.

8. Repeat questions 5 and 6 for the case of elliptic arcs.

9. Adapt the techniques used in the text for drawing ellipses to produce an algorithm for drawing parabolas. The general equation for a parabola with a vertical axis of symmetry is $y = k(x - a)^2 + b$, where k, a and b are constants. The point (a, b) defines the vertex of the parabola.

10. Implement in Java your parabola algorithm from question 9.

11. Implement in Java the pixel duplication and moving pen (with a square footprint) algorithms for drawing thick lines. For fairly thick lines (20 pixels or more) compare the drawing times of these two algorithms. (The difference should be easily visible on screen unless you have a *very* powerful graphics card and processor).

12. One reason the moving pen algorithm is slow is that it consists of many overlapping squares, with the result that many pixels are overwritten several times. Try to improve the efficiency of the algorithm by drawing only those pixels that have not been drawn by an earlier square. Can you detect the difference on screen?

13. Write and implement a moving pen algorithm using a circular footprint. Try to use an efficient way of calculating and drawing the circles.

14. Write a Java program which draws a polygon given an array of vertex points, using Bresenham's line algorithm to draw each side of the polygon. The array of points may be specified in the program, but to make the program easier to use, allow the user to specify the first $n - 1$ vertices by clicking the left mouse button. Clicking the right mouse button specifies the nth vertex and draws the full polygon.

15. Write the `sortTable()` method called on line 24 of the `fillPolygon()` method given in the text (page 33).

16. [Research project] An alternative algorithm sometimes used to fill polygons is based on the *nonzero winding rule*. Suppose we wish to determine if a point P is inside or outside the polygon. We choose a point Q on the perimeter of the polygon and trace the outline of the polygon all the way round the perimeter until we come back to Q. In the process, we count the number of times we have wound around the point P (counterclockwise rotation counts as positive and clockwise as negative). If this number is non-zero, P is defined to be inside the polygon.

   By doing a Web search or consulting other graphics textbooks, find an easier way of computing the winding number, and thus of using this method to build a polygon-filling algorithm. Implement your algorithm in Java. Note that the nonzero winding rule will not always produce the same results as the scan-line filling algorithm given in the text.

Two-dimensional transformations

2.1 Simple transformations

In the previous chapter, we studied the main methods used in producing two-dimensional graphics. Once we have constructed an image, we can *transform* it in various ways without adding any new components to the image. There are many ways an image can be transformed, but the most common ones are:

- *translation*—an object (such as a line segment or polygon) is moved rigidly to a new location, without altering its shape, size, or orientation.

- *rotation*—an object is rotated about a fixed point, again without changing its size or shape.

- *scaling*—an object is made larger or smaller. The object can be scaled by the same factor in both the horizontal and vertical dimensions, so that it maintains its proportions; or the scaling factor can be different in the two dimensions, causing the object to get taller and thinner, or shorter and fatter.

- *shearing*—an object can be distorted by translating different portions of it by different amounts. Shearing can occur in both dimensions, with varying amounts in each dimension.

A number of other effects can be obtained by applying various mathematical transformations to simple objects. These effects are often used in films and television programs, so you have probably seen many examples in everyday life.

In this chapter we will examine the theory behind the simpler transformations listed above, and show how they can be implemented in Java.

2.1.1 Translations

The *translation* is the simplest transformation that can be applied to an image, as it consists of merely moving the image from one place to another, without altering its appearance or orientation in any way. To produce a translation of an image, we add a constant x_t to the x coordinate, and another constant y_t to the y coordinate of every point in the image. That is, to translate a point with coordinates (x, y) to a new position (x', y') we apply the following transformation:

$$x' = x + x_t$$
$$y' = y + y_t$$

(2.1)

In practice, of course, we need only translate those points that are required to define the geometric figure that we wish to draw. For example, to translate a line segment, we need only translate its endpoints.

We can express equation 2.1 using matrix notation as follows:

$$\begin{bmatrix} x' \\ y' \end{bmatrix} = \begin{bmatrix} x \\ y \end{bmatrix} + \begin{bmatrix} x_t \\ y_t \end{bmatrix}$$

(2.2)

The Java code for translation of an image is obviously very straightforward—we need only add the constant x_t to all x coordinates of the points defining the image, and the constant y_t to all y coordinates.

One note of caution may be worth sounding at this point, however. A common mistake made by those who are relatively new to Java is to forget that all objects are referred to *by reference*. For example, suppose we have used the Point class to represent the points that define an image, such as the two endpoints of a line segment. We may wish to translate this line segment to a new location, and later return it to its original position. The following code, although incorrect, is a common first attempt at solving this problem.

```
Point startPoint = new Point(100, 200);
Point endPoint = new Point(300, 350);
Point tempStart = startPoint;
Point tempEnd = endPoint;
tempStart.x += 50;
tempStart.y += 75;
tempEnd.x += 50;
tempEnd.y += 75;
```

We have created two Points to serve as the endpoints of a line segment extending from (100, 200) to (300, 350). It is then assumed that the third and fourth lines in this code copy these two Points into two other temporary Point objects, which are subsequently translated by adding constants to the x and y components of each Point. (The Point class also contains a translate() method that translates both coordinates as a shortcut.) If this assumption were correct, the original endpoints would still be stored in startPoint and endPoint.

In fact, because Java treats all objects as references (that is, pointers), a line of code such as

```
Point tempStart = startPoint;
```

simply makes tempStart point to the same memory location as startPoint, so that both variables in fact refer to the same Point object. As a result, the lines

```
tempStart.x += 50;
tempStart.y += 75;
```

will translate the coordinates of the *original* startPoint object, so that its original position is lost.

The correct way to solve the problem to use the Point constructor that creates a new Point object from an existing one, so we should replace the third and fourth lines in the code above with:

```
Point tempStart = new Point(startPoint);
Point tempEnd = new Point(endPoint);
```

With this definition, `tempStart` is a separate `Point` object, so that the translation will not affect the original `startPoint` object.

2.1.2 Rotations

A *rotation* of an image requires that the image be rotated rigidly about some fixed point in the xy plane. The shape and size of the image do not change.

The simplest rotation is one where the fixed point about which the image is rotated is taken as the origin of the coordinate system, that is, $x = 0$ and $y = 0$. We shall see that all other rotations can be reduced to a rotation about the origin, so we shall study that special case in detail here.

In Figure 2.1, the point (x, y) is to be rotated by an angle θ about the origin. We can see that the line segment extending from the origin to the point (x, y) makes an angle ϕ with the x axis. After rotation, the point will be at location (x', y') and make an angle of $(\theta + \phi)$ with the x axis. We can use this fact to derive a pair of equations giving x' and y' in terms of x and y. Letting the distance of the point (x, y) from the origin be d, we have, using basic trigonometry:

$$x = d\cos\phi$$
$$y = d\sin\phi \tag{2.3}$$

The rotated point (x', y') can be expressed in terms of the angle $(\theta + \phi)$ as follows:

$$x' = d\cos(\theta + \phi) = d\cos\theta\cos\phi - d\sin\theta\sin\phi$$
$$y' = d\sin(\theta + \phi) = d\sin\theta\cos\phi + d\cos\theta\sin\phi$$

Figure 2.1:
Rotation of a point about the origin.

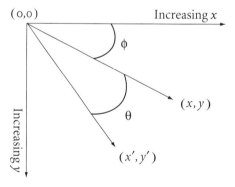

Using equation 2.3, we can simplify these equations to:

$$x' = x\cos\theta - y\sin\theta$$
$$y' = x\sin\theta + y\cos\theta \tag{2.4}$$

In matrix form, this equation becomes:

$$\begin{bmatrix} x' \\ y' \end{bmatrix} = \begin{bmatrix} \cos\theta & -\sin\theta \\ \sin\theta & \cos\theta \end{bmatrix} \begin{bmatrix} x \\ y \end{bmatrix} \tag{2.5}$$

We can give each of the three matrices in this equation single-letter symbols, so that the equation can be written as $P' = RP$, where R is the rotation matrix, P is the coordinate matrix before rotation and P' is the coordinate matrix after rotation.

If we wished to apply another rotation through an angle α, say, to P', we can left-multiply P' by a new rotation matrix R' in which the angle θ is replaced by α. It is left as an exercise for the reader to show that the matrix product $R'R$ gives a single rotation matrix in which the rotation angle is $(\theta + \alpha)$, which is what we should expect. We can see, therefore, that we can apply as many rotations as we like by multiplying together the corresponding rotation matrices and applying the result to the original coordinate matrix P.

How can we handle rotations about points other than the origin? For example, suppose we wish to rotate a line segment about its midpoint, which has coordinates (x_m, y_m). The key is to notice that if we first *translate* the line so that its midpoint is at the origin, then rotate the line about the origin, then *translate* the line so its midpoint returns to its original position, we have achieved our goal. That is, we first apply equation 2.2 with $x_t = -x_m$ and $y_t = -y_m$, then equation 2.5 to rotate the line through the desired angle, and then equation 2.2 with $x_t = x_m$ and $y_t = y_m$ to restore the line to its original position.

The rotation algorithm we have given above applies to single points. How can we extend the algorithm to rotate more general figures such as polygons and curves?

Rotating a polygon is quite simple, as all we need to do is rotate the endpoints of its edges. More general curves (those with boundaries that are not line segments) can pose problems, however.

In the previous chapter, we examined an algorithm for drawing an ellipse whose axes were aligned with the coordinate axes. Using the equation for an ellipse, we were able to produce the algorithm given only the semi-major and semi-minor axis parameters a and b, and the coordinates of the centre of the ellipse.

If we wish to rotate an ellipse, our first thought might be that all we need to do is work out the coordinates of the endpoints of the two axes, rotate these endpoints, and then draw in the ellipse using the same algorithm. The problem with this approach is that the algorithm for drawing pixels in an ellipse depends on whether we are in a region of the ellipse where the slope of its tangent line is greater than or less than 1. When the axes of the ellipse are aligned with the coordinate axes, we can work out the point on the ellipse where the slope is ± 1, so we know where to switch from one drawing mode to the other. When we rotate the ellipse, the points on the ellipse where the slope is ± 1 will change, so if we used the same algorithm to attempt to draw the rotated ellipse, gaps would appear in the outline.

It turns out that there is a general algorithm for drawing ellipses (and other *conic sections*, such as hyperbolas and parabolas) at any angle, but the algorithm is quite complex and beyond the scope of this book. In addition, the algorithm will not help us if we wish to draw more general curves (that are not conic sections) at various rotation angles.

For applications where we have a small number of curves that we wish to rotate, the simplest solution is a brute force one: use the original algorithm for producing the curve, and rotate each point produced by the algorithm to obtain the rotated curve. This works reasonably well, although there may still be some slight gaps in the rotated curve caused by round-off error. When two pixels are adjacent in the original (unrotated) curve, the application of the rotation formulae and subsequent rounding and casting to ints may result in the points being mapped onto the same location, leaving a gap of a single pixel.

This brute-force method of rotating curves may also cause some problems if thick lines are being used, since some line thickness algorithms (such as the pixel duplication algorithm considered in the previous chapter) rely on the slope of the curve. Rotating an ellipse drawn with the pixel duplication algorithm does not work well if the line thickness is greater than 2 or 3 pixels (although the result with thicker lines is quite artistic). Algorithms such as the moving pen algorithm, which do not rely on the slope of the line to produce the thickness, do not suffer from these problems.

2.1.3 Java code for rotations

As with translations, the Java code for rotating a point is straightforward, but, also as in the translation case, there is a hidden pitfall. As a first attempt at rotating a point about the origin, we might write the following Java code:

```
Point startPoint = new Point(200, 300);
double angle = 0.5;
int xRotated = Math.cos(angle) * startPoint.x -
    Math.sin(angle) * startPoint.y;
int yRotated = Math.sin(angle) * startPoint.x +
    Math.cos(angle) * startPoint.y;
startPoint.x = xRotated;
startPoint.y = yRotated;
```

We create a new Point object, and declare an angle variable (note that trigonometric functions in the Math class require their arguments in radians, not degrees). Then we declare a couple of temporary integer variables xRotated and yRotated and use them to store the rotated values of the x and y coordinates. (Why is it incorrect to just use startPoint.x and startPoint.y in place of xRotated and yRotated, respectively?) Finally, we assign the rotated values to the x and y fields of the original startPoint object. (Note that if we wished to 'undo' the rotation later, that is, we wished to return to the original location of the point, we would need to perform the rotation on a copy of startPoint, just as in our translation example above.)

The code looks reasonable, but contains a hidden problem: the coordinates of points to be drawn on screen must be ints, but the trigonometric methods return doubles, so a cast is required to convert the results of the rotation formulae to ints. The code above will produce a compiler error because of this problem.

A second try at the third and fourth lines in the above code would then look like this:

```
int xRotated = (int)(Math.cos(angle) * startPoint.x -
    Math.sin(angle) * startPoint.y);
int yRotated = (int)(Math.sin(angle) * startPoint.x +
    Math.cos(angle) * startPoint.y);
```

This will compile without errors, but if you use the code repeatedly to rotate the point through a succession of angles, you will find that rather than rotating around the origin at a fixed distance, it will tend to spiral in towards the origin and eventually lodge itself at the origin permanently. Why?

The problem is that casting a `double` value to an `int` performs the conversion by simply truncating the fractional part of the `double` to produce an `int` value. This rather severe case of round-off error means that with every application of the rotation code, the point moves a bit closer to the origin. We can solve the problem by using the `round()` method in Java's `Math` class, so our final version of the rotation code is:

```
int xRotated = (int)Math.round(Math.cos(angle) *
    startPoint.x - Math.sin(angle) * startPoint.y);
int yRotated = (int)Math.round(Math.sin(angle) *
    startPoint.x + Math.cos(angle) * startPoint.y);
```

The `round()` method rounds a `double` to the nearest `int` rather than just throwing away the fractional part, so on average, the distance from the origin of the rotated point should remain roughly constant. We say 'roughly', since there will always be some loss of accuracy in converting a `double` value to an `int`, and in some cases, the error could compound itself over successive rotations, but on average, the rounding operations should cancel each other out.

2.1.4 Homogeneous coordinates

In practice, we often need to combine a series of translations, rotations, and some other transformations. It would be convenient if we could represent each transformation in the series as a matrix, and the overall set of transformations as a matrix product, as we have done with the series of rotations above.

We can see, however, that the matrix equation 2.2 representing a translation requires a sum rather than a product, so our plans do not seem to work. However, we can convert the translation transformation from a sum to a product if we introduce a third, dummy, coordinate to each point, so that a point is now represented as (x, y, w). The w coordinate does not represent any actual property of the point as it appears in an image—it is simply there to allow a *homogeneous* representation of all the basic geometric transformations.

How does this help us? Let us return to equation 2.2, giving a translation as a matrix sum. If we add the extra coordinate w to each point, and set $w = 1$, we can now write the translation equation as a matrix product:

$$\begin{bmatrix} x' \\ y' \\ 1 \end{bmatrix} = \begin{bmatrix} 1 & 0 & x_t \\ 0 & 1 & y_t \\ 0 & 0 & 1 \end{bmatrix} \begin{bmatrix} x \\ y \\ 1 \end{bmatrix} \tag{2.6}$$

It is straightforward to verify that x' and y' are related to x and y in the same way as in equation 2.2, and that the w coordinate does indeed remain equal to 1 in this equation. Thus the introduction of w allows the translation to be written as a matrix product rather than a sum.

As a first example of the power of the homogeneous coordinate notation, we can revisit the procedure for rotating a point (x, y) about an arbitrary fixed point (rather than the origin), to obtain a new point (x_r, y_r). As we stated above, we first translate the centre of rotation to the origin, then perform the rotation, and then translate the centre of rotation back to its original position. We can do this using a product of three matrices, and arrange them in right-to-left order.

Let us set the centre of rotation at coordinates (c_x, c_y). The first translation shifts the image so that the centre of rotation is moved to the origin. This can be done using the transformation:

$$\begin{bmatrix} x' \\ y' \\ 1 \end{bmatrix} = \begin{bmatrix} 1 & 0 & -c_x \\ 0 & 1 & -c_y \\ 0 & 0 & 1 \end{bmatrix} \begin{bmatrix} x \\ y \\ 1 \end{bmatrix}$$

Next, we wish to rotate the point by an angle θ, which can be done using the transformation:

$$\begin{bmatrix} x'' \\ y'' \\ 1 \end{bmatrix} = \begin{bmatrix} cos\theta & -sin\theta & 0 \\ sin\theta & cos\theta & 0 \\ 0 & 0 & 1 \end{bmatrix} \begin{bmatrix} x' \\ y' \\ 1 \end{bmatrix}$$

Finally, we translate the centre of rotation back to its original location, using the transformation:

$$\begin{bmatrix} x_r \\ y_r \\ 1 \end{bmatrix} = \begin{bmatrix} 1 & 0 & c_x \\ 0 & 1 & c_y \\ 0 & 0 & 1 \end{bmatrix} \begin{bmatrix} x'' \\ y'' \\ 1 \end{bmatrix}$$

In full, the transformation is:

$$\begin{bmatrix} x_r \\ y_r \\ 1 \end{bmatrix} = \begin{bmatrix} 1 & 0 & c_x \\ 0 & 1 & c_y \\ 0 & 0 & 1 \end{bmatrix} \begin{bmatrix} cos\theta & -sin\theta & 0 \\ sin\theta & cos\theta & 0 \\ 0 & 0 & 1 \end{bmatrix} \begin{bmatrix} 1 & 0 & -c_x \\ 0 & 1 & -c_y \\ 0 & 0 & 1 \end{bmatrix} \begin{bmatrix} x \\ y \\ 1 \end{bmatrix}$$

It should be clear that any number of rotations and translations can be combined simply by multiplying their matrices together.

While homogeneous coordinates do simplify the process of combining transformatons, we need to be a bit careful about blindly converting these equations into Java code. The reason is efficiency. If we consider, for example, the first translation process considered above, we note that if we use homogeneous coordinates, we need to multiply a 3×3 matrix into a 3-component vector, which requires 9 multiplications and 6 additions. If we use the original equation 2.2, we have only 2 additions and no multiplications at all. Similarly, with a rotation about the origin, the homogenous coordinate system requires another 9 multiplications and 6 additions, while using the straightforward equations for a rotation requires 4 multipications and 2 additions (although the trigonometric functions are the most time-consuming operation in performing a rotation, they must be calculated in any case, so we can disregard them in comparing the two methods).

The bottom line is that homogeneous coordinates are very useful for working out your transformations on paper, but from the point of view of implementing translations and rotations in code, it is often better to use the original non-homogeneous equations.

2.1.5   Scaling

Now that we have seen how a couple of the basic transformations (translation and rotation) work, and how they can be expressed in a consistent matrix notation using homogeneous coordinates, we can expand our repertoire by adding a few other transformations.

An image may be *scaled* in the horizontal and vertical directions by multiplying the corresponding coordinates of each point in the image by a constant factor. If the scaling factor is the same in both the horizontal and vertical directions, the effect is to magnify or shrink the image while maintaining its relative proportions (sometimes known as keeping a constant *aspect ratio*). If the scaling factors differ, the appearance, as well as the size, of the image will change as well.

Like rotation, scaling must be done relative to some fixed point in the *xy* plane. If this fixed point is the origin, we can define two scaling factors, x_s and y_s, which are used to scale in the horizontal and vertical directions, respectively. For each point in the figure, we can then scale the coordinates using the equations:

$$x' = x_s x$$
$$y' = y_s y$$

In homogeneous coordinates, we can express a scaling transformation as follows.

$$\begin{bmatrix} x' \\ y' \\ 1 \end{bmatrix} = \begin{bmatrix} x_s & 0 & 0 \\ 0 & y_s & 0 \\ 0 & 0 & 1 \end{bmatrix} \begin{bmatrix} x \\ y \\ 1 \end{bmatrix} \tag{2.7}$$

In addition to magnifying or shrinking an image, the scaling transformation will change the distance of the image from the reference point being used for the scaling. For example, if a square with a side length of 100 pixels and with its upper-left corner at position (50, 50) is scaled by a factor of 2 in both the *x* and *y* directions (using the origin as the reference point), the resulting square will have a side length of 200 pixels, but its upper-left corner will now be at position (100, 100).

If we wish to scale an image relative to a point other than the origin, we can use the same solution as for rotations. We first translate the image so that the reference point is at the origin, then apply a scaling relative to the origin, then translate the image back so that the reference point is at its original location.

Scaling more complex figures may be done in a similar way to rotating them, although, as with rotation, some problems appear. Let us consider the example of the ellipse again, as it illustrates these problems.

If we adopt the brute-force approach of applying the scaling algorithm to each point generated by the ellipse drawing algorithm in the previous chapter, we will find that gaps will appear if we magnify the object, since two points that were adjacent in the original figure will have a distance appear between them after scaling. As with rotation, we can solve this problem for the ellipse by using a more general algorithm to redraw the ellipse taking into account its scaled axes, but for more general curves, no mathematical representation may be available.

One way of filling in the gaps generated by magnifying a curve is to draw a line segment (using Bresenham's algorithm) between each pair of points after scaling. If the magnification factor is not too great, the approximation of the curve by a series of straight line segments should be acceptable.

The Java code for scaling is quite straightforward, as it merely consists of multiplying the x and y coordinates of a `Point` by the corresponding scaling factors.

2.1.6 Shearing

All the transformations we have considered so far have left the relative proportions of the object unchanged. A *shearing* transformation distorts the object in the *x* or *y* direction. To get the feel of a shear, picture the rectangle formed by looking at a pack of cards end-on. If you now push the pack to one side in such a way that the bottom card does not move, the first card is pushed 1 mm over, the second card 2 mm over and so on, then the rectangle will be transformed into a parallelogram (Figure 2.2).

Figure 2.2:
The rectangle on the left is sheared by multiplying each *x* coordinate by a value that is proportional to the corresponding *y* coordinate.

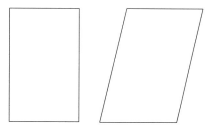

Looking at the shear mathematically, suppose that the rectangle initially had one of its corners at the origin, so that the equation of its left-hand edge was $x = 0$. After shearing, the equation becomes $x' = x + x_h y$, where x_h is a constant giving the degree of shearing. The *y* coordinate of any point on the left edge does not change (each card in the pack retains the same height above the bottom card), so $y' = y$.

We can write this in homogeneous coordinates as

$$\begin{bmatrix} x' \\ y' \\ 1 \end{bmatrix} = \begin{bmatrix} 1 & x_h & 0 \\ 0 & 1 & 0 \\ 0 & 0 & 1 \end{bmatrix} \begin{bmatrix} x \\ y \\ 1 \end{bmatrix} \tag{2.8}$$

In a similar way, we can shear an object vertically using the equation:

$$\begin{bmatrix} x' \\ y' \\ 1 \end{bmatrix} = \begin{bmatrix} 1 & 0 & 0 \\ y_h & 1 & 0 \\ 0 & 0 & 1 \end{bmatrix} \begin{bmatrix} x \\ y \\ 1 \end{bmatrix} \tag{2.9}$$

2.2 Affine transformations

The transformations we have considered in this chapter are all examples of *affine transformations*. A precise definition of an affine transformation requires mathematical notation, but the essential aspects of such a transformation can be stated in two properties:

- The *curvature* of an object remains unaltered (for example, a straight line segment that undergoes any affine transformation will still be a straight line segment).

- Two lines that are parallel before an affine transformation will also be parallel afterwards

Note that the last statement does *not* necessarily imply that, if two lines are not parallel, the angle between them remains the same after an affine transformation—this is not the case in shearing, for example.

Any affine transformation (or combination of transformations) can be expressed in homogeneous coordinates by means of the matrix equation:

$$\begin{bmatrix} x' \\ y' \\ 1 \end{bmatrix} = \begin{bmatrix} m_{00} & m_{01} & m_{02} \\ m_{10} & m_{11} & m_{12} \\ 0 & 0 & 1 \end{bmatrix} \begin{bmatrix} x \\ y \\ 1 \end{bmatrix} \tag{2.10}$$

where the m_{ij} entries in the matrix are constants for any given transformation. It can be shown mathematically that all combinations of rotations, translations, scaling and shearing are affine transformations.

2.2.1 Windows and viewports

Up to now, we have assumed that all graphical components that we draw are expressed in pixel units, so that we can plot them directly to the output device, whether that device is a monitor or a printer. In many cases, however, it is more convenient to calculate the graphical data in some other coordinate system and then transform it to pixel units when we wish to display it. For example, suppose we have written a letter (or a book, as I am doing at the moment) using a word processor. Unless the letter is short enough to fit on a single page, we will need to store more data than can be displayed at one time on the screen (or on a single sheet of paper, if we are sending the data to a printer). Let us suppose that the letter consists of 2 pages, and that we are viewing the letter in a word processor, which is being displayed in a window on our computer screen. The word processor's view of the letter is as a single long document, rather as if the letter were written on a long roll of paper. When the person writing the letter wishes to view page 1 on the computer screen, the word processor must find that portion of the letter that represents the first page, and convert the graphical data it has stored internally into pixel coordinates so that the required page can be displayed. If the user now wishes to view page 2, the word processor must move down inside the document to find the data for page 2, and convert the data so that it can now be displayed on screen.

The important point is that two *different* areas from within the document representing the letter are being displayed in the *same* area on the computer screen, so that the formula giving the transformation from document to screen depends on what part of the document the user wishes to see.

As a second example, suppose that you have created a large drawing of, say, a landscape, in a drawing package. The drawing may be too large for all of it to be visible on the screen (or within the window being used by the drawing package) at once. We therefore need to find a section of the drawing and map that section to the display area on the screen. As before, the transformation between the data representing the drawing and the viewing area on the screen depends on which area of the drawing is to be displayed.

In both of these cases, we might be using different measurement units to set out the display in its original form. In the landscape drawing, we might represent the distances between objects in the landscape using large units such as kilometres, while in the word processing example, we might use much smaller units such as millimetres (or possibly *points*, which are used in the printing industry to measure the size of the type used in printing a book). As suggested above, we may wish to view only a portion of the original data on screen. We might also like to be able to zoom in or out, so that we get a larger or smaller representation of the area we wish to view. Finally, we might want to rotate, shear, or transform in some more exotic fashion the data in the original document. In other words, we need a general transformation formula to relate the data in the original representation of the view to the actual pixel coordinates that will be used to display it.

In computer graphics, the coordinate system used to represent the original graphical data is called the *world* coordinate system, and the coordinate system used to display data on a monitor or printer is called the *device* system. In the landscape example above, for instance, the units of the world coordinate system could be kilometres, and in the word processing example, they could be millimetres. The units of the device system, however, are always pixels, since any digital display device always uses pixels to display its data.

That section of the original world view that is to be displayed on screen at one time is called a *window*, and the area on the display device into which the view is to be drawn is called the *viewport*. The use of the term 'window' for the portion of the world view that is to be displayed may cause some confusion, because the term 'window' is, these days, much more often used to refer to a rectangular area on the monitor in which a program is running. It is important to understand that these two types of 'window' are not the same—a window in computer graphics is an abstract concept that identifies that portion of an overall world view that is to be transformed so that it can be displayed in a viewport. (If it's any consolation, the term 'window' was used in its computer graphics sense before the introduction of window-based displays on computer screens.) To summarize: windows are measured in world coordinates, and viewports are measured in device coordinates (pixels).

The transformation between the window and the viewport depends, naturally, on what effect the user desires, but the most common transformation is a simple scaling so that the window's contents are displayed in the viewport with the same orientation (that is, no rotation) and in the same proportions (that is, the scale factors in the x and y directions are equal).

Figure 2.3:
Relation between a window and a viewport.

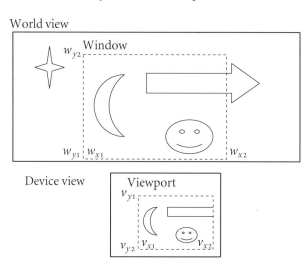

In Figure 2.3 we see some basic shapes forming the overall image in the world view. The dashed rectangle identifies the window within the world view that we wish to map onto a viewport on a device such as a monitor. This window is defined by the coordinates (in world units) defining its edges. The left and right edges are given by w_{x1} and w_{x2} respectively, and the bottom and top edges by w_{y1} and w_{y2} respectively. (We are assuming that in the world view, the y axis is oriented so that y increases upwards, as is normal in mathematics.)

The device view shows how this window will be drawn onto a monitor or other display device. The dashed rectangle within the device shows the viewport, which will, in general, be a rectangular region within one of the monitor's windows (here, we are using 'window' in the sense of a rectangular display area on a computer screen, not in the sense of an area in the world view). The left and right edges of the viewport are given by v_{x1} and v_{x2} respectively, and the top and bottom edges by v_{y1} and v_{y2}, respectively. Note the order of the top and bottom edges— they are reversed relative to the world view since display devices measure y from the top down, rather than from the bottom up.

To work out the equations giving the transformation from the window to the viewport, we will assume that the window and viewport have the same proportions (that is, the same ratio of height to width). That is, we are assuming that:

$$\frac{w_{y2} - w_{y1}}{w_{x2} - w_{x1}} = \frac{v_{y2} - v_{y1}}{v_{x2} - v_{x1}}$$

We now need a formula for transforming a point (w_x, w_y) in the world view's window to its corresponding point (v_x, v_y) in the device's viewport. To maintain the relative position of the point with respect to the enclosing rectangle, we must have, for the x coordinate:

$$\frac{w_x - w_{x1}}{w_{x2} - w_{x1}} = \frac{v_x - v_{x1}}{v_{x2} - v_{x1}}$$

and, for the y coordinate (remembering that the direction of y is inverted in the viewport):

$$\frac{w_y - w_{y1}}{w_{y2} - w_{y1}} = \frac{v_{y2} - v_y}{v_{y2} - v_{y1}}$$

We can solve these two equations for v_x and v_y respectively, to obtain:

$$v_x = v_{x1} + \frac{v_{x2} - v_{x1}}{w_{x2} - w_{x1}}(w_x - w_{x1}) \qquad (2.11)$$

and:

$$v_y = v_{y2} - \frac{v_{y2} - v_{y1}}{w_{y2} - w_{y1}}(w_y - w_{y1}) \qquad (2.12)$$

2.3 Clipping

As a glance at Figure 2.3 will show, when mapping from a window in the world view to viewport on a display device, we usually must *clip* the image so that we can draw a part of the original scene. Clipping is also important in managing the layout of windows on a monitor screen. When one window overlaps another, the window 'underneath' the other one must have part of its display clipped so that the upper window can be displayed.

The algorithm used for clipping depends, as you might expect, on the type of image that is being clipped. If the image consists of a bitmapped picture, for example, then the viewport must simply be told which areas to draw and which not to draw—the display device will then just display those pixels in the picture that fall into the visible area.

However, when the image is composed of geometric figures produced using the algorithms in the previous chapter, we do not have a bitmapped image—we have a set of objects that are drawn from mathematical specifications each time the window must be refreshed. It is true that we *could* draw the image once, create a bitmap from the resulting drawing, and store the bitmap in memory so that we could then just redraw the portions of the image using the simple bitmap algorithm, but this turns out to be very wasteful of memory, and is in many cases slower than redrawing the components of the image.

Since most viewports are rectangles, most clipping algorithms are designed to clip objects to a rectangular area. In addition, since many geometric shapes are built from line segments, the most common clipping algorithms deal with clipping line segments that extend beyond the boundaries of a rectangle.

2.3.1   The Cohen–Sutherland clipping algorithm

We will examine the most popular line-clipping algorithm, known as the *Cohen–Sutherland algorithm*. It is not the most efficient algorithm for clipping images that contain a large number of line segments, since it tends to do more calculation than is necessary in some cases, but for images with relatively few lines (or if your computer is particularly fast), it is certainly adequate.

Before we examine the algorithm itself, we need to consider the various cases that can occur when a line segment crosses a rectangular clipping area (see Figure 2.4). A line segment might be entirely within the clipping area (such as EF), in which case it need not be clipped at all. The line segment might be entirely outside the clipping area (as with AB and IJ), in which case the line can be discarded altogether. The line might cross a single edge of the rectangle (as with GH), in which case one end of the line must be clipped. Finally, the line may pass right through the rectangle (as with CD), in which case it must be clipped at both ends.

Figure 2.4:
Possibilities
in line clipping.

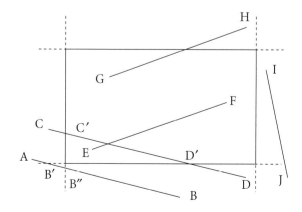

We need a method of classifying a line segment based on the locations of its endpoints. To this end, we divide the xy plane into five (overlapping) regions, by means of the dashed lines in Figure 2.4. The regions are (1) inside the clipping rectangle; (2) to the left of the left edge; (3) to the right of the right edge; (4) below the bottom edge; (5) above the top edge.

A line that lies entirely within region 1 can be drawn without clipping, while any line with both its endpoints lying *entirely* within any one of the other four regions can be rejected immediately, since it must lie entirely outside the rectangle. In Figure 2.4, for example, line IJ has both endpoints to the right of the right edge (region 3) and can therefore be rejected immediately.

Lines with endpoints in different regions must be analyzed further. For example, line AB lies entirely outside the rectangle, but point A lies in region 2 while point B lies in region 4. However, line CD *does* intersect the rectangle, even though its endpoints lie in the same two regions.

The Cohen–Sutherland algorithm solves this problem by clipping lines against the edges of the rectangle until the remaining segments can be either accepted or rejected according to the criteria given above. For example, consider line CD. If we first clip it against the bottom edge of the rectangle, we are left with line CD′. The point D now lies in the interior of the rectangle (the 'interior' is assumed to include the boundary) but point C still lies outside the rectangle, in region 2. So we clip the line against the left edge, giving us line segment C′D′, which can now be accepted, since both points lie in the interior of the rectangle.

Line AB can be subjected to the same procedure. We first clip the line against the bottom edge of the rectangle (or rather against the line that runs through the bottom edge), giving us line AB′. This line now lies entirely to the left of the rectangle, so can be rejected.

Note that the number of iterations required for a line to be accepted or rejected can depend on the order in which the clipping is done. For example, with line AB, if we had clipped it first against the left edge of the rectangle (rather than the bottom edge), we would be left with line AB″, which cannot yet be rejected since the points A and B″ do not lie entirely on one side of the rectangle. Here A lies to the left of the left edge, but B″ does not—but it does lie *below* the bottom edge. Hence we must also clip the line AB″ against the bottom edge to reduce it to line AB′ as before, which can now be rejected since both endpoints lie to the left of the left edge.

The Cohen–Sutherland algorithm associates a 4-bit code with each endpoint of a line segment. Each bit in the code corresponds to one of the four exterior regions surrounding the clipping rectangle, as follows:

- bit 0 (least significant bit): left of the left edge;
- bit 1: right of the right edge;
- bit 2: below the bottom edge;
- bit 3: above the top edge.

A bit is switched on (set to 1) if the point lies in the corresponding region. For example, point H in Figure 2.4 has the bit code 1000, since it lies above the top edge and in no other region. Point J has the bit code 0110 since it lies both below and to the right of the rectangle. Points that lie within the rectangle have a bit code of 0000.

The advantage of using the bit code to identify a point's position is that simple Boolean logic operations can be used to accept or reject line segments. For example, the endpoints of line segment IJ have bit codes 0010 and 0110. We know that a line may be rejected if both endpoints lie in the same external region (in this case, both lie to the right of the right edge). This can easily be checked by taking the bitwise AND (in Java, this operation is provided by the operator &) of the two codes: 0010 AND 0110 = 0010. If this operation is non-zero, the two endpoints must both lie in at least one external region, and the line can therefore be rejected, since it must lie entirely outside the clipping rectangle.

A line can be accepted if the bitwise OR (the Java operator being |) of the two codes is zero, since this means that both endpoints must have a bit code of 0000, indicating that they both lie inside the clipping rectangle.

Lines that do not satisfy one of these two conditions (the bitwise AND is non-zero, or the bitwise OR is zero) will be clipped by the Cohen–Sutherland algorithm, the bit codes recalculated for the new endpoints of the line, and the acceptance and rejection tests repeated. The process continues until the line segment is either accepted or rejected. The algorithm requires a minimum of zero clips (for lines that satisfy the acceptance or rejection criteria immediately) and a maximum of two clips. (Lines that intersect a corner of the rectangle will be clipped against one of the edges that meet at that corner, so that clipping against the other edge is not required.)

The only remaining step in the algorithm is the calculation of the intersection point when a line is clipped. We can do this using the point–slope equation for a line:

$$y = y_1 + m(x - x_1) \tag{2.13}$$

where the point (x_1, y_1) is a point on the line and m is the slope.

Equation 2.13 can be used to calculate the new y value when a line is clipped against the left or right edge of the rectangle, where the x value will be known (it is just the x value of the edge of the rectangle). For intersections with the top or bottom of the rectangle, the y value will be known so we need to invert equation 2.13 to provide x in terms of y:

$$x = x_1 + (y - y_1)/m \tag{2.14}$$

We can calculate the slope from the two endpoints (x_1, y_1) and (x_2, y_2):

$$m = (y_2 - y_1)/(x_2 - x_1) \tag{2.15}$$

provided that $x_2 \neq x_1$. In the latter case, the line is vertical and must be treated as a special case.

2.3.2   Java code for clipping lines

Coding the Cohen–Sutherland algorithm in Java presents no major obstacles. Since the smallest integer data type available in Java is the byte, we use this to represent the 4-bit code required. Within the class containing the clipping code, we define four constant byte values representing the four areas outside the clipping rectangle.

```
static final byte LEFT_EDGE = 1;
static final byte RIGHT_EDGE = 2;
static final byte BOTTOM_EDGE = 4;
static final byte TOP_EDGE = 8;
```

In what follows, we will assume that coordinates of the upper-left and lower-right corners of the clipping rectangle have been specified, and are stored in the int variables clipXStart and clipYStart for the upper-left corner, and clipXEnd and clipYEnd for the lower-right corner. We may then write a method that generates the code value for a given endpoint stored in a Point variable named point.

```
private byte getCode(Point point)
{
    byte code = 0;
    if (point.x < clipXStart) code |= LEFT_EDGE;
    if (point.x > clipXEnd) code |= RIGHT_EDGE;
    if (point.y < clipYStart) code |= TOP_EDGE;
    if (point.y > clipYEnd) code |= BOTTOM_EDGE;
    return code;
}
```

Notice that we are using the viewport's coordinate system here, with a *y* value that increases downwards, so that the top edge of the clipping rectangle has the minimum *y* value, and the bottom edge the maximum value.

We begin by declaring a byte variable named code and setting it to 0. We compare the *x* and *y* coordinates of point with the boundaries of the rectangle and use the bitwise | operator to set bits for each region in which the point lies. The |= operator works in a similar way to the += operator: the bitwise | operation is performed between its left and right operands and the result stored in the left operand. Before we get into the main portion of the algorithm, we can define a few utility methods for dealing with lines:

```
private boolean acceptLine(byte codeStart, byte codeEnd)
{
    return((codeStart | codeEnd) == 0);
}

private boolean rejectLine(byte codeStart, byte codeEnd)
{
    return((codeStart & codeEnd) != 0);
}

private void zeroLine(Point start, Point end)
{
    start.x = start.y = end.x = end.y = 0;
}

private void swapPoints(Point point1, Point point2)
{
    int temp;
    temp = point1.x;
    point1.x = point2.x;
    point2.x = temp;
    temp = point1.y;
    point1.y = point2.y;
    point2.y = temp;
}
```

The acceptLine() method compares the codes of the endpoints of a line, and if the bitwise OR is zero, accepts the line as lying entirely within the clipping rectangle. Similarly, the rejectLine() method calculates the bitwise AND to see if line lies entirely within a single exterior region and can therefore be rejected.

The zeroLine() method sets the coordinates of both endpoints to zero, and the swapPoints() method swaps the coordinates of two Point objects. Both of these are used in the main algorithm below.

We can now present the central method of the algorithm.

```
1    public void clipLine(Point start, Point end)
2    {
3        byte codeStart = 0, codeEnd = 0;
4        boolean clipped = false;
5        while (!clipped) {
6            codeStart = getCode(start);
7            codeEnd = getCode(end);
8
9            if (acceptLine(codeStart, codeEnd))
10               clipped = true;
11           else if (rejectLine(codeStart, codeEnd)) {
12               zeroLine(start, end);
13               clipped = true;
14           } else {
15               if (codeStart == 0) {
16                   swapPoints(start, end);
17                   byte tempCode = codeStart;
18                   codeStart = codeEnd;
19                   codeEnd = tempCode;
20               }
21               double slope = 0.0;
22               if (start.x != end.x) {
23                   slope = (end.y - start.y) /
24                       (double)(end.x - start.x);
25               }
26               if ((codeStart & LEFT_EDGE) != 0) {
27                   start.y += (int)((clipXStart -
28                       start.x) * slope);
29                   start.x = clipXStart;
30               } else if ((codeStart & RIGHT_EDGE) != 0) {
31                   start.y += (int)((clipXEnd -
32                       start.x) * slope);
33                   start.x = clipXEnd;
34               } else if ((codeStart & TOP_EDGE) != 0) {
35                   if (start.x != end.x) {
36                       start.x += (int)((clipYStart -
37                           start.y) / slope);
38                   }
39                   start.y = clipYStart;
40               } else if ((codeStart & BOTTOM_EDGE) != 0) {
41                   if (start.x != end.x) {
42                       start.x += (int)((clipYEnd -
43                           start.y) / slope);
```

```
44                        }
45                        start.y = clipYEnd;
46                    }
47                }
48            }
49        }
```

The `clipLine()` method requires as its arguments the two endpoints of the line to be clipped. As stated above, it is assumed that the coordinates defining the clipping rectangle are provided as class variables—alternatively, they may be provided as arguments to the `clipLine()` method if desired. It is important to note at the outset that this method will *permanently change* the coordinates of the line it clips. In some applications, of course, this is undesirable, so you may wish to alter the method by having it make a local copy of the line's endpoints before clipping it.

We declare the two bit codes on line 3, and a `boolean` variable `clipped` on line 4, which is used to specify when the line has either been accepted or rejected by the algorithm.

The main loop beginning on line 5 continues until the line is fully processed. Lines 6 and 7 calculate the endpoint bit codes using the `getCode()` method given above. Lines 9 and 10 test if the line lies within the clipping area, and if so, accepts it, ending the algorithm. Lines 11 through 13 test for rejection. If the line is rejected, a method `zeroLine()` is called which sets all coordinates in both endpoints to zero. What is to be done with rejected lines may vary with the application, so this method can be replaced by a different method if desired.

If the algorithm reaches line 15, the line has not been accepted or rejected and must be clipped. This means that at least one endpoint of the line must lie outside the clipping rectangle. In order to streamline the algorithm, it is more convenient to assume that the `start` point is outside the clipping area. Lines 15 to 19 ensure that this is so by testing the bit code of `start` and, if it is zero (meaning that `start` is inside the clipping rectangle), swapping it with `end`, using the `swapPoints()` method given above. Having swapped the endpoints, we must also swap their bit codes.

The actual clipping begins on lines 21 to 24 with the calculation of the slope, provided that the line is not vertical. The remainder of the method clips the line against one of the edges of the clipping rectangle. The edges are tested in order, and only one clip per iteration is allowed, since after each clip, we must recalculate the bit codes to see if the line can now be accepted or rejected.

To clip a line against the left edge (lines 26 to 29) we first test to see if the line's `start` point lies in the left region by comparing its bit code with the `LEFT_EDGE` constant defined earlier. If it does, we use equation 2.13 to calculate the new *y* value and then set the x and y values of `start` to the point where it intersects the left edge of the clipping rectangle.

Intersections with the top and bottom edges work in a similar way, except that we must deal with vertical lines as special cases. The x coordinate of a vertical line need not be changed, so we test to see if the line is vertical (line 35) and, if not, we apply equation 2.15 to calculate the new *x* value.

2.3.3   Clipping polygons

It might be thought that clipping polygons against a rectangular area should be easy once we have an algorithm for clipping line segments. However, the problem with clipping polygons by simply clipping their individual edges using an algorithm such as the Cohen–Sutherland algorithm is that we are sometimes left with a few disconnected line fragments, as in Figure 2.5(b).

Figure 2.5:
The polygon in (a) is to be clipped by the dashed rectangle. Using a line clipping algorithm produces the result in (b), whereas we would like a properly clipped polygon as shown in (c).

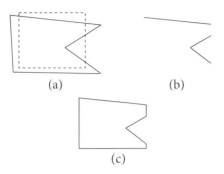

Since polygons are typically specified in a program as a list or array of vertices, the output of a polygon clipping algorithm should be a new polygon in the same format. In Figure 2.5(c), we see the proper outcome of a polygon clipping algorithm applied to the polygon and clipping rectangle shown in Figure 2.5(a). This is particularly important if the polygon is filled, since merely applying a line clipping algorithm will not result in a closed polygon to which we can apply the scan-line filling algorithm described in Chapter 1.

The standard polygon clipping algorithm was devised by Sutherland and Hodgman in 1974, and is therefore known as the Sutherland–Hodgman algorithm. In its most general form, the algorithm allows the clipping of a polygon against any polygonal clipping outline, not just the rectangle that is the most common case. To keep things simple, we will illustrate the algorithm only for the case where the clipping region is rectangular, but the generalization should be fairly obvious once this case is understood.

Figure 2.6:
The Sutherland–Hodgman algorithm for polygon clipping.

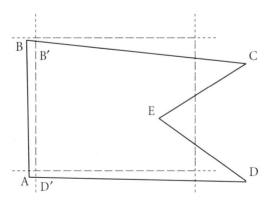

The algorithm works in four stages, each of which (except the last) involves clipping the polygon against one of the four edges of the rectangle, and then feeding the resulting clipped polygon into the next stage of the algorithm, where it is clipped against another edge of the rectangle. At the end of the fourth stage, the resulting polygon is a properly clipped version of the original.

We illustrate the algorithm in Figure 2.6, in which the polgyon's vertices are labelled A, B, C, E, D, which is the order in which they are stored in the linked list or array. The algorithm requires that we identify an 'inside' and an 'outside' for each edge in the clipping rectangle (or for the clipping polygon, in the more general case). It is conventional to define the 'inside' of an edge to be that area on your left as you walk around the clipping rectangle in a counterclockwise direction. For a rectangle, this is fairly obvious, but if we apply the algorithm to a general polygonal clipping region, the rule is a useful guide to which area is which.

The relation of a given polygon edge to a clipping rectangle can be one of four possible cases:

1. Both the starting vertex and the ending vertex of the edge are inside the edge of the clipping rectangle being considered.

2. The starting vertex is inside and the ending vertex is outside.

3. Both vertices are outside.

4. The starting vertex is outside and the ending vertex is inside.

For example, considering the left edge of the rectangle in Figure 2.6, the line DA is of case 2, since vertex D is inside relative to the left edge (even though it is outside the clipping area, it is still on the 'inside' the left edge) and vertex A is on the outside. The idea behind the algorithm is to create the clipped polygon as a list of vertices.

The rules for adding vertices to the list for the clipped polygon are, for each case above:

1. Add the ending vertex only to the list.

2. Find the intersection of the polygon edge with the edge of the clipping rectangle. Add only this intersection point to the list.

3. Add nothing to the list.

4. Find the intersection of the polygon edge with the edge of the clipping rectangle. Add the intersection point *and* the ending vertex (in that order) to the list.

Applying these rules to edge DA in the polygon in Figure 2.6, we find the intersection point D′ and add it to the list (making it the first vertex in the new list). Next, we consider the edge AB, and find that both vertices are 'outside' the left edge (case 3). We therefore add nothing to the list.

Edge BC is of case 4 (B is outside the left edge and C is inside). We therefore find intersection point B′ and add both it and vertex C to the list. Edge CE is of case 1 (both vertices inside the edge, so we add vertex E only. Note that adding only the end vertex when voth vertices lie inside an edge avoids adding vertices twice.

Finally, edge ED is also entirely inside the left edge, so we add vertex D.

After clipping the polygon relative to the left edge of the rectangle, the resulting clipped polygon has vertices D′B′CED. We now clip this new polygon relative to the right, bottom and top edges in turn, applying the same rules, and generating a new polygon after each clipping. The end result is the polygon shown in Figure 2.5(c).

The algorithm as stated here is not as efficient as it could be, since it requires three temporary lists or arrays to store the results of clipping the polygon against the first three edges. Sutherland and Hodgman, in their original paper, produced a recursive version of the algorithm in which vertices and intersection points are clipped against all four edges in turn, and only added to the list if they survive all clipping processes, thus avoiding the intermediate lists. The algorithm is fairly complex and somewhat beyond the scope of this book.

However, we can produce some improvement in efficiency without resorting to recursion by slightly modifying the four rules above. The idea is that instead of generating four separate lists of vertices, three of which are discarded, we modify the original list by adding and deleting vertices as appropriate. So, starting with the list representing the original unclipped polygon, we apply the following rules for each of the four cases above.

1. Do nothing to the list (since the ending vertex is one of those vertices already in the list, we just leave it there).

2. Find the intersection of the polygon edge with the edge of the clipping rectangle. Add this intersection point to the list immediately before the ending vertex, then delete the ending vertex from the list.

3. Delete the ending vertex from the list.

4. Find the intersection of the polygon edge with the edge of the clipping rectangle. Add this intersection point to the list immediately before the ending vertex, but leave the ending vertex in the list.

If we use a `Vector` to store the vertices of a polygon (as we did in Chapter 1) the insertion and deletion operations are all provided in the `Vector` class, so the implementaton of the algorithm in this form is particularly easy. All we really need to provide is the code for finding the intersection points, and we have already worked this out for the line clipping algorithm earlier. This version of the algorithm does store some vertices temporarily (and delete them later), but it uses the same `Vector` throughout the calculation.

2.3.4 Java code for polygon clipping

The Java code for implementing the Sutherland–Hodgman algorithm requires three methods. The first is a method for determining whether a point is 'inside' relative to an edge of the clipping rectangle.

```
static final int LEFT = 0;
static final int RIGHT = 1;
static final int BOTTOM = 2;
static final int TOP = 3;

private boolean isInside(Point point, int edge)
{
    switch (edge) {
    case LEFT:
        return (point.x >= clipXStart);
```

```
        case RIGHT:
            return (point.x <= clipXEnd);
        case BOTTOM:
            return (point.y <= clipYEnd);
        case TOP:
        return (point.y >= clipYStart);
        }
        return false;
    }
```

Four constants representing the four sides of the rectangle are defined within the class containing the clipping code. The point coordinates are then compared with the coordinates of the clipping rectangle, assumed to be provided within the class as in the line clipping algorithm.

Next, we need a method to calculate the intersection of a polygon edge with an edge of the clipping rectangle. This code is very similar to that for the line clipping algorithm, except it produces a new Point object.

```
    private Point intersect(Point start, Point end, int edge)
    {
        Point intersection = new Point();
        double slope = 0.0;
        if (start.x != end.x) {
            slope = (end.y - start.y) /
                (double)(end.x - start.x);
        }
        switch (edge) {
        case LEFT:
            intersection.y = start.y + (int)((m_clipXStart -
                start.x) * slope);
            intersection.x = m_clipXStart;
            break;
        case RIGHT:
            intersection.y = start.y + (int)((m_clipXEnd -
                start.x) * slope);
            intersection.x = m_clipXEnd;
            break;
        case TOP:
            if (start.x != end.x) {
                intersection.x = start.x + (int)((m_clipYStart -
                start.y) / slope);
            } else {
                intersection.x = start.x;
            }
            intersection.y = m_clipYStart;
            break;
        case BOTTOM:
            if (start.x != end.x) {
                intersection.x = start.x + (int)((m_clipYEnd -
                    start.y) / slope);
            } else {
                intersection.x = start.x;
            }
            intersection.y = m_clipYEnd;
```

```
        break;
      }
      return intersection;
    }
```

Refer back to the description of the line clipping algorithm for details on how the intersections are calculated.

Finally, we have the method which implements the algorithm itself.

```
 1    private void clipPolygon()
 2    {
 3      Point lineStart = null, lineEnd = null;
 4      Point intersection = null;
 5      for (int edge = 0; edge < 4; edge++) {
 6        int numVertices = m_polygonPoints.size();
 7        if (numVertices > 0) {
 8          lineStart = (Point)m_polygonPoints.lastElement();
 9        } else {
10          return;
11        }
12        for (int vertex = 0; vertex < numVertices; vertex++) {
13          lineEnd = (Point)m_polygonPoints.elementAt(vertex);
14          if (isInside(lineEnd, edge)) {
15            if (!isInside(lineStart, edge)) {
16              intersection = intersect(lineStart,
17                lineEnd, edge);
18              m_polygonPoints.insertElementAt(intersection,
19                m_polygonPoints.indexOf(lineEnd));
20              numVertices++;
21              vertex++;
22            }
23          } else {
24            if (isInside(lineStart, edge)) {
25              intersection = intersect(lineEnd,
26                lineStart, edge);
27              m_polygonPoints.insertElementAt(intersection,
28                m_polygonPoints.indexOf(lineEnd));
29              numVertices++;
30              vertex++;
31            }
32            m_polygonPoints.remove(lineEnd);
33            numVertices--;
34            vertex--;
35          }
36          lineStart = lineEnd;
37        }
38      }
39    }
```

The for loop beginning on line 5 loops over the four edges of the clipping rectangle. The vertices of the polygon to be clipped are stored in the Vector m_polygonPoints, as in Chapter 1 when we were considering the polygon filling algorithm. The `Point` objects `lineStart` and `lineEnd` are used to store the endpoints of the polygon edge being considered at any one time. We initialize `lineStart` to the last vertex in the polygon on line 8.

Line 12 begins the loop over all edges in the polygon, clipping them against the current edge of the rectangle. We extract the endpoint of the current polygon edge and store it in `lineEnd` on line 13. Line 14 tests if `lineEnd` is inside the current edge, using the `isInside()` method mentioned earlier. If it is inside, we are dealing with either case 1 or case 4 described above. The second test, on line 15, determines if the starting point is not inside the edge, which narrows things down to case 4 (recall that in case 1, we do nothing to the existing list). Lines 16 through 19 determine the intersection of the polygon edge with the rectangle edge, and insert this intersection point before `lineEnd` in the `m_polygonPoints` vector. The `insertElementAt()` method of the `Vector` class inserts the object passed as its first argument at the index specified by its second, and moves all elements from that point onwards up one index. Lines 18 and 19 therefore insert `intersection` at the point currently occupied by `lineEnd` and then shift `lineEnd` and all following vertices up by one index.

Since the size of the vertex list has been increased by 1, lines 20 and 21 adjust the loop counters to account for this.

The `else` on line 23 refers to `lineEnd` beginning on the outside of the rectangle edge, thus dealing with cases 2 and 3 above. If `lineStart` is on the inside (line 24) we are dealing with case 2, and we must find and insert the intersection point, then delete `lineEnd`. If `lineStart` is also on the outside, we just delete `lineEnd`. The code on lines 25 through 34 performs these operations and adjusts the loop counters accordingly.

On line 36 we end the loop by setting `lineStart` to `lineEnd`, getting ready to look at the next polygon edge.

2.4   Antialiasing

One undesirable side-effect of using a digital display device for drawing lines and curves is that these objects tend to acquire jagged edges (sometimes called the 'jaggies'). In the case of a straight line, for example, the stair-step effect is a natural consequence of Bresenham's algorithm, which we discussed in Chapter 1. When we draw a line with a slope of, say, 0.5, the algorithm must decide at each step in the *x* direction whether the next pixel should be drawn with the same *y* value, or whether *y* should be increased by one and the next pixel drawn one row down from the previous one. If the latter decision is made, an abrupt step appears in the display, which of course is not present in the mathematical description of the line. Similar problems occur with most other curves, since the finite mesh of pixels cannot represent a curve precisely.

The jagged-edge effect is known as *aliasing*. The term arises in *sampling theory* which was originally concerned with the sampling of electronic signals, such as radio waves, that consist of a signal that oscillates in some fashion. Consider, for example, a simple sine wave signal that oscillates (with a constant amplitude) with a frequency of 1000 HZ (cycles per second). If we *sample* this signal (measure its strength) 2000 times per second, we will get two measurements of the signal strength per oscillation. If we time the sampling correctly, we could get one measurement when the signal is at its maximum and the other when it is at its minimum. From this we could conclude that the signal has a frequency of 1000 Hz, and we would be correct.

However, if we sampled the signal only twice every three oscillations, we would get the first reading at the peak of the first oscillation and the next reading at the minimum of the *second* oscillation, with the next reading at the peak of the fourth oscillation, and so on. From this we might conclude that 1.5 cycles of the true signal actually represents only half a cycle of the frequency we measure, so we are fooled into thinking that the frequency is only a third of its true value, or 333.3 HZ. The error has occurred because our sampling procedure is too coarse-grained to be able to see the finer details of the signal. The result is that the true signal appears as an *alias* signal—a signal with a 'secret identity' which in this case is manifested by the apparently lower frequency.

The jaggies appear in digital graphics displays due to the same effect—because we are sampling the 'true' mathematical shape with a relatively coarse-grained pixel grid, the actual shape that is displayed is only an approximation to the original. Methods that attempt to reduce or eliminate aliasing are called *antialiasing algorithms.*

We might think that any attempt at antialiasing is doomed to failure, since unless we physically alter the hardware used to display the graphics, we cannot change the resolution of the pixel grid, so we cannot display a finer-grained image. It is true that we cannot increase the resolution of the pixel grid, so antialiasing algorithms aim instead to smooth out the jagged edges rather than provide a higher resolution in the display.

To see how the smoothing process works, let us consider plotting a straight line with unit thickness using Bresenham's algorithm, as described in Chapter 1. As can be seen from Figure 2.7, a line with unit thickness is actually a rectangle that is superimposed on the pixel grid. Bresenham's algorithm finds the pixel in each column of the grid that is closest to the line's midpoint and displays this pixel at full intensity. All other pixels in the same column are turned off. The result is the jagged stair-step approximation to the true line segment.

Figure 2.7: A line with a non-zero thickness is actually a rectangle superimposed on the pixel grid.

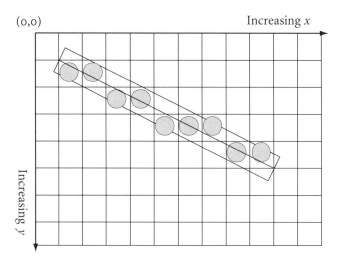

(0,0)

Increasing *x*

Increasing *y*

Antialiasing algorithms smooth out the rough edges by observing that the rectangle which represents the line segment actually overlaps some pixels that are not selected by Bresenham's algorithm. The idea is to compute what fraction of a pixel's area is overlapped by the rectangle, and illuminate that pixel by an amount proportional to this overlap. Thus a pixel area that lies entirely within the rectangle would be fully illuminated, just as given by Bresenham's algorithm. One with half its area overlapping with the rectangle would be illuminated with half its full intensity, and so on.

Clearly, antialiasing algorithms will only work on display devices that allow intermediate illumination values. Virtually all modern monitors have this ability, but many printers do not. For example, an inkjet printer may only be able to place a dot of ink at full strength at one location, or else skip that location entirely. Antialiasing algorithms that produce good results on a monitor will fail completely when the graphics are printed on such a printer.

Most monitors have colour displays, of course, so we need to modify the definition of 'intensity' to cope with the more general situation of a line of one colour drawn on a background of a different colour. To see how to apply the edge-smoothing algorithms to the two-colour case, let us define the colour of the foreground as C_f and that of the background as C_b. A colour can be defined in terms of its red, green and blue components, so we can write the foreground colour, for example, as $C_f = (r_f, g_f, b_f)$. Each of the three components can be represented as an integer with values between 0 and the maximum (usually 255) for the particular display device. Alternatively, the Java `Color` class allows red, green and blue components to be represented as `floats`, with values between 0.0 and 1.0.

With colours represented this way, we can now implement the antialiasing algorithm as a linear combination of the two colours. Suppose that application of an antialiasing algorithm states that the intensity of illumination of a pixel should be 0.6. We can apply this to a two-colour display to generate the actual colour of that pixel as $C = 0.6C_f + 0.4C_b = 0.6(r_f, g_f, b_f) + 0.4(r_b, g_b, b_b)$. That is, the foreground colour is represented at the intensity level given by the antialiasing algorithm, and the background colour is assigned whatever intensity is left over. This formula works equally well with colour and greyscale monitors.

2.4.1   Supersampling and filtering

Two main versions of antialiasing are in common use, each of which uses its own form of smoothing of the jagged edges as described above. The *supersampling* algorithm simulates a finer grid of pixels than that available on the hardware. It does this by dividing each pixel area into a number of *subpixels*, as shown in Figure 2.8, where we have divided each pixel into a sub-grid of 3 by 3 subpixels. The number of subpixels that overlap with the rectangle representing the line to be drawn is counted, and the overall pixel is lit to a level that is proportional to the number of subpixels that overlap with the line.

Since the line's rectangle may overlap only part of a subpixel, some rule must be adopted to decide whether or not to count a partially overlapped subpixel. The rule we shall use is that if the subpixel's upper-left corner is within the line's rectangle, we will count that subpixel. In Figure 2.8, the subpixels that overlap with the rectangle are shaded.

Using this technique, we can calculate the intensities assigned to some of the pixels in Figure 2.8. In the upper-left pixel, 3 subpixels overlap with the line, so that pixel would be assigned a colour composed of the foreground and background colours in the ratio 3:6 (or, equivalently, 1:2). The pixel with coordinates (1, 1) (one row down and one column in from the left) has 8 subpixels shaded, so its colour is composed of the foreground and background colours in the ratio 8:1. Other pixels are evaluated similarly.

A variant of the supersampling technique applies different *weights* to each subpixel, giving more weight to the centre subpixel, and less weight to those pixels near the edge of the enclosing pixel. The logic here is that if a line overlaps with the centre subpixel, it is likely that the pixel containing that subpixel is closer to the centre of the line's rectangle than if only a corner subpixel overlaps with the line.

Figure 2.8:
The subpixels used in the supersampling algorithm.

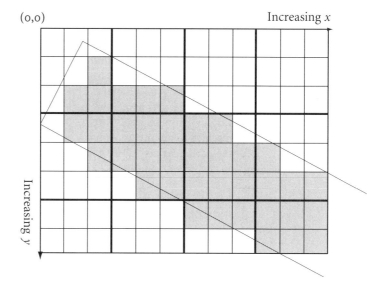

We will consider the supersampling method in more detail below.

The other main antialiasing technique is known as *filtering*. Here, each pixel is assumed to have an area of influence (which may overlap with the areas of influence of other pixels). If the line's rectangle overlaps the pixel's area of influence, the pixel should be illuminated by an amount determined by the area of overlap.

The amount of illumination is determined by defining a *filter function* for each pixel. The filter function is essentially a weighting function that determines how much each portion of the area of influence contributes to the overall illumination.

A common filtering technique defines a circular area of influence centred at the centre of the pixel, and with a radius of 1 pixel. Thus the area of influence of a pixel extends as far as the centres of its four nearest neighbours. The filter function is defined to be cone with its base being the circle and its apex lying directly above the centre of the pixel. The volume of the cone is normalized (by adjusting the height of the apex) so that its volume is 1.

To determine the amount by which a pixel should be illuminated, the area defined by the intersection of the area of influence (the circle) and the line's rectangle is determined. The volume enclosed by that portion of the cone directly above this intersection is then calculated, which will give a value between 0 and 1 (since the cone's total volume is normalized to 1), which in turn provides the fraction of total illumination assigned to that pixel.

As we might expect, the main problem with the filtering technique is the calculation of the area of intersection between the area of influence of a pixel and the line's rectangle, and the subsequent determination of the volume of the portion of the cone that lies above this area. In practice, this must be done by numerical integration, which is a time-consuming process on a computer.

The problem is usually solved by pre-calculating a table of these numerical integrals, which is accurate for a particular filter function. Unfortunately, the table is only valid for one choice of filter function, one choice of area of influence, one line thickness and one set of colour resolutions. For example, if we have decided that we wish to use the conical filter function, an area of influence that is a circle of radius 1, a line of thickness 1, and a colour resolution that allows 16 different colours per pixel, we can generate a table of the numerical integrals for lines that pass varying distances from the centre of a pixel. If we subsequently want to draw lines of thickness 2, we need a new table, even if all the other factors remain the same. Thus the filtering technique for antialiasing is quite restrictive.

Antialiasing algorithms partially illuminate pixels other than those selected by Bresenham's algorithm. The effect of this is to smooth the edges of the line, but at the same time, the line is also broadened slightly. This effect is most noticeable for thinner lines.

2.4.2 The supersampling algorithm

Due to the restrictive nature of the filtering algorithm, we will consider only the supersampling algorithm in detail here.

The first step in implementing this algorithm is to determine the rectangle that encloses the line we wish to draw. We will assume that the line's endpoints are specified in the same way as in Chapter 1, that is, that the line begins and ends on integer coordinates which correspond exactly to pixel coordinates. Since the line has a finite width, we will also assume that these endpoints define the ends of the *middle* of the rectangle.

This may not always be the desired case. For example, if we define a horizontal line of thickness 5 pixels, we might want the pixel coordinates to define the upper or lower edge of the rectangle, rather than its midline. If such is the case, the algorithm below will need to be modified, but the principle is the same.

We begin by writing the equation of the line using the point–slope form, where the two endpoints have coordinates (x_0, y_0) and (x_1, y_1) respectively.

$$y - y_0 = m(x - x_0) \tag{2.16}$$

Here, the line's slope is given by $m = (y_1 - y_0)/(x_1 - x_0)$, assuming that $x_1 \neq x_0$. To find the coordinates of the corners of the rectangle, we need to travel a perpendicular distance equal to half the line's thickness each way from each endpoint (see Figure 2.7). The line perpendicular to the line that is to be drawn has slope $-1/m$, so the equation of the perpendicular line containing the point (x_0, y_0) is:

$$y - y_0 = -\frac{1}{m}(x - x_0) \tag{2.17}$$

Now if the line's thickness is t, we wish to find the two points that lie on the line given by equation 2.17 and are a distance $t/2$ from (x_0, y_0). Let the point (x_p, y_p) be one of these two points. Since this point must be a distance $t/2$ from (x_0, y_0), it must satisfy the equation:

$$\left(y_p - y_o\right)^2 + \left(x_p - x_o\right)^2 = \frac{t^2}{4} \tag{2.18}$$

Since (x_p, y_p) lies on the line defined by equation 2.17, we can substitute for $(y_p - y_o)$ and solve for x_p to obtain:

$$x_p = \pm\frac{t}{2}\frac{m}{\sqrt{1+m^2}} + x_o$$

From equation 2.17 we can solve for y_p to obtain:

$$y_p = \mp\frac{t}{2}\frac{1}{\sqrt{1+m^2}} + y_o$$

Defining the constant k as

$$k \equiv \frac{t}{2}\frac{1}{\sqrt{1+m^2}}$$

we have the two points that define the corners of the rectangle nearest the line endpoint (x_o, y_o):

$$\left(x_p, y_p\right) = \begin{cases} \left(km + x_o, \ -k + y_o\right) \\ \left(-km + x_o, \ k + y_o\right) \end{cases} \tag{2.19}$$

The two points that define the corners at the other endpoint may be obtained from this equation by replacing the subscript 0 by 1.

All that remains is to determine which subpixels lie within this rectangle. This can be done using a variant of the scan-line algorithm we used for filling polygons in Chapter 1. For a subpixel whose upper-left corner has coordinates (x_s, y_s) we determine if the scan line at $y = y_s$ intersects the rectangle and, if so, what the corresponding x coordinates are for the two points of intersection. If x_s lies between these two points, the subpixel (or at least the upper-left corner, which is what we are using as our test to see if the subpixel is to be counted) must lie within the rectangle.

In the Java implementation of this algorithm below, we will cheat a bit and use Java 2D's GeneralPath class to construct the rectangle. This class has a method called contains() which tests a point to see if it lies within the shape defined by the GeneralPath object. Although we could have implemented the algorithm the long way (by calculating the intersections of the rectangle with the scan line), we have used the shortcut in order not to detract from the clarity of the algorithm for antialiasing. We will now consider the Java code to implement the supersampling algorithm.

The antialiasing code is implemented as an add-on to the code for Bresenham's algorithm that we presented in Chapter 1. We reproduce the central method from that algorithm here, for convenience:

```
1    void drawBresenhamLine(Graphics g, Point start,
2        Point end)
3    {
4        slopeLT1 = selectEndPoints(start, end);
5        int x, y;
6        if (slopeLT1) {
7            x = x0 + 1; y = y0;
8            while (x < x1) {
```

```
9            if (param < 0) {
10               param += twoDeltaY;
11           } else {
12               param += twoDYDX;
13               y += slopeSign;
14           }
15           g.drawLine(x, y, x, y);
16           x++;
17       }
18   } else {
19       x = x0; y = y0 + 1;
20       while (y < y1) {
21           if (param < 0) {
22               param += twoDeltaX;
23           } else {
24               param += twoDXDY;
25               x += slopeSign;
26           }
27           g.drawLine(x, y, x, y);
28           y++;
29       }
30   }
31 }
```

If antialiasing is enabled, we must first calculate the rectangle that bounds the line that is to be drawn. We will use a GeneralPath for this rectangle, so we must import the java.awt.geom package to obtain this class:

```
import java.awt.geom.*;
```

At the start of the drawBresenhamLine() method, we create the GeneralPath object, so we can insert the following line after line 3.

```
GeneralPath antialiasPolygon = new GeneralPath();
```

Now we can concentrate on the code for the supersampling algorithm. We insert the code for this after line 4:

```
1    if (m_antialias) {
2        if(x1 != x0) {
3            double slope = (double)(y1 - y0)/(double)(x1 - x0);
4            double value = m_thickness / 2.0 /
5                Math.sqrt(1.0 + slope * slope);
6            Line2D.Double edge = new Line2D.Double(
7                x0 + value * slope, y0 - value,
8                x0 - value * slope, y0 + value);
9            antialiasPolygon.append(edge, false);
10           edge = new Line2D.Double(x0 - value * slope,
11               y0 + value, x1 - value * slope, y1 + value);
12           antialiasPolygon.append(edge, true);
13           edge = new Line2D.Double(x1 - value * slope,
14               y1 + value, x1 + value * slope, y1 - value);
15           antialiasPolygon.append(edge, true);
```

```
16        edge = new Line2D.Double(x1 + value * slope,
17            y1 - value, x0 + value * slope, y0 - value);
18        antialiasPolygon.append(edge, true);
19    } else {
20        Line2D.Double edge =
21            new Line2D.Double(x0 - m_thickness/2.0, y0,
22                x0 + m_thickness/2.0, y0);
23        antialiasPolygon.append(edge, false);
24        edge = new Line2D.Double(x0 + m_thickness/2.0, y0,
25            x1 + m_thickness/2.0, y1);
26        antialiasPolygon.append(edge, true);
27        edge = new Line2D.Double(x1 + m_thickness/2.0, y1,
28            x1 - m_thickness/2.0, y1);
29        antialiasPolygon.append(edge, true);
30        edge = new Line2D.Double(x1 - m_thickness/2.0, y1,
31            x0 - m_thickness/2.0, y0);
32        antialiasPolygon.append(edge, true);
33    }
34 }
```

Line 1 assumes that the class has a boolean flag m_antialias which is true if antialiasing is required for this line. Line 2 checks if the line is vertical, since we cannot calculate a slope for such a line. If the line is not vertical, lines 3 through 18 build the rectangle that bounds the line. The code uses equation 2.19 to calculate the coordinates, with the constant k represented by the variable value in the code.

This code makes use of a few classes that we have not studied yet, but their application should be fairly obvious. We will study these classes in more depth in Chapter 3. On line 6, we use the Line2D.Double class to create a line segment with its endpoints specified as double coordinates (rather than integer pixel coordinates, as we have used up to now). We need to use doubles since the rectangle's corners will not be at the exact centres of pixels. Line 9 uses the append() method from the GeneralPath class to add this line to the rectangle. The first argument of append() is the edge to be added to the shape, and the second argument is a boolean value that indicates whether this edge should be attached to the preceding edge, or whether it is a separate shape. Since the edge added on line 9 is the first edge to be added, we do not connect it to anything, but the other 3 edges of the rectangle, added on lines 12, 15 and 18, are connected to their predecessors. The code on lines 20 to 32 handles the special case of a vertical line.

Note that we cannot use the Rectangle class to create the bounding rectangle for the line, since Rectangle objects always have their edges aligned with the coordinate axes, which will not in general be true here.

Having constructed the line's bounding rectangle, we must now count the number of subpixels that lie within this rectangle for every pixel it intersects. We will define a separate method to do this. To call this method for lines with a slope less than 1, we replace line 15 (the call to drawLine()) in the listing for drawBresenhamLine() above with the following call:

```
drawXPixel(g, x, y, antialiasPolygon);
```

The code for this method is as follows.

```
1     void drawXPixel(Graphics g, int x, int y,
2         Shape antialiasPolygon)
3     {
4         float intensity;
5         int yStart = y;
6         do {
7             intensity = getIntensity(antialiasPolygon, x, y);
8             if (intensity > 0.0f) {
9                 g.setColor(colorMix(intensity));
10                g.drawLine(x,y,x,y);
11            }
12            y++;
13        } while (intensity > 0.0f);
14        y = yStart - 1;
15        do {
16            intensity = getIntensity(antialiasPolygon, x, y);
17            if (intensity > 0.0f) {
18                g.setColor(colorMix(intensity));
19                g.drawLine(x,y,x,y);
20            }
21            y--;
22        } while (intensity > 0.0f);
23    }
```

The ints x and y in the argument list on line 1 are the coordinates of the pixel in which we wish to count subpixels. We pass the bounding rectangle as a Shape rather than a GeneralPath since the Shape interface lies at the base of a hierarchy of graphical shapes that includes GeneralPath among other classes. This allows the drawXPixel() method to be used for any class that implements the Shape interface.

The idea behind this method is that, starting with the central pixel (x, y), we calculate the intensity of the foreground colour by calling the getIntensity() method (described below). If this intensity is greater than zero, the line's rectangle overlaps with this pixel and we need to illuminate the pixel to some extent. The colour to which this pixel should be set is calculated by the colorMix() method (also described below), and then the pixel is drawn.

The drawXPixel() method uses a fixed value for x, and, starting with y, explores y values above and below the starting y value until a zero intensity value is returned by getIntensity(), at which point we have found a pixel that lies outside the bounding rectangle. The first do...while loop explores values of y greater than the starting value (so it explores pixels below the starting pixel, as seen on the display device), and the second loop explores the other side of the starting pixel.

For lines with a slope greater than 1, we can write a method drawYPixel() which is almost identical to drawXPixel() except that it keeps y fixed and explores x values either side of the starting pixel. We would then call drawYPixel() from line 27 in the original drawBresenhamLine() method, instead of the call to drawLine() that is in the listing above.

The getIntensity() method counts the number of subpixels whose lower-left corner lies inside the bounding rectangle:

```
1    float getIntensity(Shape antialiasPolygon, int x, int y)
2    {
3        float increment = 1.0f / ANTIALIAS_SIZE;
4        float xSubPixel = x;
5        float ySubPixel = y;
6        int subPixelCount = 0;
7        for (int xStep = 0; xStep < ANTIALIAS_SIZE; xStep++) {
8            for (int yStep = 0; yStep < ANTIALIAS_SIZE; yStep++) {
9                if (antialiasPolygon.contains(xSubPixel, ySubPixel))
10                   subPixelCount ++;
11               ySubPixel += increment;
12           }
13           xSubPixel += increment;
14       }
15       float intensity = 0.0f;
16       if (subPixelCount > 0)
17           intensity = (float)subPixelCount/
18               ANTIALIAS_SIZE / ANTIALIAS_SIZE;
19       return intensity;
20   }
```

The getIntensity() method assumes that the class has an int constant named ANTIALIAS_SIZE declared. This specifies the number of segments into which each side of the overall pixel is divided. A typical value is 3, so that the pixel itself is subdivided into 9 subpixels in a 3 by 3 grid.

The increment variable on line 3 calculates the length of each side of a subpixel, and the variables xSubPixel and ySubPixel will contain the precise coordinates of a corner of a subpixel. Since we are dealing with fractions of a pixel, we must use floating point variables rather than integers.

The nested loop on lines 7 to 14 uses the contains() method (specified by the Shape interface and therefore implemented by all classes that implement Shape) to check if a subpixel is contained by the bounding rectangle. If so, subPixelCount is incremented.

Once the number of subpixels that intersect the bounding rectangle is known, we convert this number into an intensity value on lines 15 to 18. This is done by dividing subPixelCount by the total number of subpixels within the pixel.

Finally, we examine the colorMix() method:

```
Color colorMix(float intensity)
{
    Color foreground = getForeground();
    Color background = getBackground();
    float[] foregroundCompArray =
        foreground.getRGBColorComponents(null);
    float[] backgroundCompArray =
        background.getRGBColorComponents(null);
    float[] mixCompArray = new float[3];
    for (int comp = 0; comp < 3; comp++) {
        mixCompArray[comp] = foregroundCompArray[comp] *
            intensity + backgroundCompArray[comp] *
            (1.0f - intensity);
    }
```

```
        Color mix = new Color(mixCompArray[0], mixCompArray[1],
        mixCompArray[2]);
    return mix;
}
```

This method is quite straightforward, as it extracts the red, green and blue components of the foreground and background colours and stores them in float arrays using the getRGBColorComponents() method from the Color class. We then create a new colour using the weighted average of the foreground and background colours.

EXERCISES

1. By drawing a simple geometric figure, such as a triangle, on a piece of paper, convince yourself that translations and rotations are, in general, not commutative. For example, if the triangle is translated 1 unit in the $+y$ direction and then rotated by 90 degrees about the origin, the effect is not the same as doing the rotation first, followed by the translation.

2. Verify the case in question 1 by working out the transformation matrices for the translation and rotation, multiplying them both ways to produce the two composite transformations, and observing that the products are different.

3. Implement in Java the translation transformation for a single line segment. The graphical interface for this program should consist of a drawing area where the line is drawn, and a single button control. Pushing the button control should cause the line to move a fixed number of pixels horizontally.

4. Implement in Java the rotation transformation for a single line segment, with the rotation occurring relative to the origin (the upper-left corner of the drawing canvas). Use a similar interface to that in question 3: the button causes the line to rotate by 0.1 radians (approximately 5.7 degrees) each time it is pushed.

5. Extend question 4 so that the line is rotated about one of its endpoints, rather than the origin.

6. Modify question 5 so that the Math.round method is *not* called to convert the pixel values from doubles to ints. Observe the effect of round-off error by pushing the button many times and watching the length of the line change over time.

7. [Programming project] Write a more comprehensive Java package which allows the user to experiment with all four affine transformations covered in this chapter (translation, rotation, scaling and shearing). The package should allow the user to draw a polygon by specifying its vertices with the mouse, and then apply a combination of the four transformations to this polygon, in any order. The user should be able to select the required transformation from a combo box or set of radio buttons, and then drag the mouse over the drawing area to produce the transformation. For example, if the user selects 'rotation' and drags the mouse over the drawing area, the polygon should rotate as the mouse is dragged.

You may wish to investigate the `AffineTransform` class in the `java.awt.geom` package (this class is discussed in the next chapter).

8. Devise a line clipping algorithm that uses a triangular clipping region. You may use the ideas from the Cohen–Sutherland algorithm, but you will need a way of determining whether an endpoint of the line to be clipped lies on one side or the other of an edge of the triangle. Use some simple vector algebra to work out an equation that will tell you this, and then use this condition to create the clipping algorithm.

9. Generalize the algorithm from question 8 so that you can clip a line using a clipping region that is a convex polygon of any number of sides. (A convex polygon is, roughly speaking, one where all corners point outwards. Why is this restriction necessary?)

10. Implement in Java the algorithms from questions 8 and 9.

11. Devise an algorithm for clipping a line using a circular clipping region. To do this, you will first need a test that determines if a point lies within the circle. You can then use this test to determine if both endpoints of the line lie within the circle (in which case the line is left untouched), both endpoints lie outside the circle (in which case the line is erased completely), or whether the line crosses the circle boundary. In the latter case, you will then need to find the intersection of the line with the circle by solving simultaneous equations.

12. [Research project] The Cohen–Sutherland algorithm can be inefficient since it sometimes requires more than one clip operation to clip a line relative to the clipping region. A more efficient algorithm was developed in 1978 by Cyrus and Beck that avoids this problem. The Cyrus–Beck algorithm (sometimes called just the *parametric clipping algorithm*) may be applied to any convex polygonal clipping region. By consulting other graphics textbooks or searching the internet, find out how the Cyrus–Beck algorithm works and implement it in Java.

13. [Research project] An even more efficient version of the Cyrus–Beck algorithm was developed in 1984 by Liang and Barsky, which works for the special case of upright rectangular clipping regions, such as those we have been using in this chapter. Find out more about the Liang–Barsky algorithm and implement it in Java.

14. Generalize the Sutherland–Hodgman polygon clipping algorithm so that it can be used to clip a polygon using a clipping region that is itself a convex polygon, with any number of sides. You may find it helpful to work out the general algorithm for the special case of a triangular clipping region first.

15. Modify the `getIntensity()` method used in antialiasing so that each sub-pixel within a particular pixel has a weight attached to it. A common technique is to give the central subpixels a greater weight than those further from the centre. The weights should be normalized so that the maximum possible intensity for a given pixel is still 1.0. Compare lines drawn with this weighted antialiasing system with those drawn using the algorithm given in the text. Do you think the results justify the extra computational load?

The Java 2D packages

3.1 The Java 2D model

Readers who have used earlier versions of Java to draw simple graphics will no doubt be familiar with the Graphics class. Although the features provided by the Graphics class were enough for basic graphical operations such as display of simple figures (rectangles, ellipses, lines and so on), they fell far short of what is expected in a professional graphics system.

The Java 2D set of packages extends the 2D drawing capabilities of Java immensely. Despite this increase in functionality, the Java 2D system is still quite simple to use, once we understand the models used to produce two-dimensional images (as covered in this book, for example).

Using Java 2D effectively, however, does require an understanding of its overall structure, above and beyond the theory required to produce the actual images. To this end, we will state at the outset the two main principles that lie at the centre of all Java 2D functionality. We will consider each of these topics in more depth later in this chapter, but for now it is important that you fix these concepts in your mind.

- Java 2D provides *device independent* rendering to three main types of output: monitors, printers, and off-screen buffers (where graphical data is stored in memory but not displayed). Device independence means that an object should appear the same physical size no matter what device is used to display it.

- Java 2D renders three main classes of graphical objects: *shapes* (graphical objects given by mathematically-defined outlines such as rectangles and ellipses), *images* (objects specified as pixel patterns, such as scanned photographs), and *text*.

We will examine Java 2D's capabilities by looking first at how it addresses different display devices, and then at how it can be used to produce various graphical objects.

3.2 Rendering graphics to various display devices

3.2.1 Monitors

The most common destination for graphical output is a monitor screen. In Java, the graphics are drawn within the paint() method, which is available in any class that is derived from the Component class. The paint() method requires a Graphics argument, which provides the interface between the program and the monitor on which the graphics are to be displayed. The Graphics object is generated for you by the Java virtual machine, and the paint() method is called whenever the display needs updating.

All this was true from the earliest versions of Java. In Java 2D, which was first included as part of the JDK with version 1.2, extra features are available if a Graphics2D object is used instead of the original Graphics object. However, no new versions of the paint() method have been provided—the paint() method still expects an old-fashioned Graphics argument. A Graphics2D object is obtained from the Graphics argument by an explicit cast within the paint() method. Thus, in a Java 2D program, the paint() method usually has the following form:

```
public void paint(Graphics g)
{
    Graphics2D gg = (Graphics2D)g;

    // other statements generating the graphics using gg
}
```

A simple example of such a paint() method is given in the next section, when we display a rectangle on a monitor and also allow it to be printed.

3.2.2 Printers

Printing was only possible in Java with the release of JDK 1.1, where it was introduced as an add-on available in the Toolkit class. As of JDK 1.2, printing has been elevated to the point where it now has its own package of classes in java.awt.print. This package allows printing of all graphical elements that can be displayed on screen. It also provides the traditional dialog boxes that allow the user access to the properties of the printer and of the page to be printed. Multi-page printing has also been introduced.

Printing is accomplished by providing two main components. First, we must create a PrinterJob object which provides the interface between the Java program and the printer. It does this by allowing the user to specify the properties of the printer and the pages to be printed, either through dialog boxes or directly in the code.

Once we have a PrinterJob set up, we must give it something to print. This is done by creating a class that implements the Printable interface. The interface contains only a single method, print(), which acts much like the paint() method in a class that draws graphics to the screen. A Printable object may produce only a single page, or it may create a Book object which contains several pages to be printed.

It is easiest to see how all these parts fit together by considering a simple example. The following program displays a window on screen in which a rectangle is drawn. The window's frame has a menu which allows the user to print the rectangle. For completeness, we will show the entire program, including the code to attach the menu to the frame and handle the events generated by the menu items.

```
1    import java.awt.*;
2    import java.awt.event.*;
3    import java.awt.print.*;
4
```

```
5    class SimplePrint extends Frame implements
6        Printable, ActionListener
7    {
8        MenuItem printItem = new MenuItem("Print");
9        MenuItem exitItem = new MenuItem("Exit");
10       Menu fileMenu = new Menu("File");
11       MenuBar menuBar = new MenuBar();
12
13       public static void main(String[] argv)
14       {
15           SimplePrint testPrint = new SimplePrint();
16           testPrint.setSize(600, 700);
17           testPrint.setVisible(true);
18       }
19
20       public SimplePrint()
21       {
22           WindowHandler windowHandler = new WindowHandler();
23           this.addWindowListener(windowHandler);
24           setTitle("Java 2D printing test");
25           fileMenu.add(printItem);
26           fileMenu.add(exitItem);
27           printItem.addActionListener(this);
28           exitItem.addActionListener(this);
29           menuBar.add(fileMenu);
30           setMenuBar(menuBar);
31       }
32
33       public void paint(Graphics g)
34       {
35           Graphics2D gg = (Graphics2D)g;
36           Shape testShape = getTestShape();
37           gg.draw(testShape);
38       }
39
40       public int print(Graphics g, PageFormat pageFormat,
41           int pageIndex)
42       {
43           if (pageIndex > 0)
44               return NO_SUCH_PAGE;
45           Graphics2D gg = (Graphics2D)g;
46           Shape testShape = getTestShape();
47           gg.draw(testShape);
48           return PAGE_EXISTS;
49       }
50
51       public void actionPerformed(ActionEvent event)
52       {
53           String command = event.getActionCommand();
54           if (command.equals("Exit")) {
55               exitApplication();
56           } else if (command.equals("Print")) {
```

```
57            PrinterJob printerJob = PrinterJob.getPrinterJob();
58            PageFormat pageFormat = printerJob.defaultPage();
59            if(!printerJob.printDialog()) return;
60            pageFormat = printerJob.pageDialog(pageFormat);
61            printerJob.setPrintable(this, pageFormat);
62            try {
63                printerJob.print();
64            } catch (PrinterException e) {
65                System.out.println(e.toString());
66            }
67        }
68    }
69
70    private Shape getTestShape()
71    {
72        Shape testShape = new Rectangle(50, 50, 100, 200);
73        return testShape;
74    }
75
76    class WindowHandler extends WindowAdapter
77    {
78        public void windowClosing(WindowEvent event)
79        {
80            Object object = event.getSource();
81            if (object == SimplePrint.this)
82                SimplePrint_windowClosing(event);
83        }
84    }
85
86    void SimplePrint_windowClosing(WindowEvent event)
87    {
88        exitApplication();
89    }
90
91    void exitApplication()
92    {
93        this.setVisible(false);
94        this.dispose();
95        System.exit(0);
96    }
97 }
```

Lines 1 to 3 include the required packages for generating the graphics, handling events, and printing. The class declaration on lines 5 and 6 shows that the Printable interface is implemented to allow the SimplePrint class to generate a printable image, and the ActionListener interface is implemented to allow the class to handle ActionEvents, which are generated by selecting menu items.

As menus are not central to the discussion here, we will not dwell on the code that implements them, apart from pointing out that the parts of the menu are created on lines 8 through 11, and the menu itself is built in the constructor starting on line 20. The constructor also attaches a handler allowing the window itself to be closed by clicking on the 'close window' button in the title bar. (In

Windows, this is the small 'x' button at the upper-right of the window. In other systems, the location of the button may vary.)

The on-screen image is drawn by the paint() method on line 33 by calling the getTestShape() method to create the shape to be drawn. (We will consider the Shape interface in more detail later in this chapter.) The getTestShape() method on line 70 creates a rectangle and returns it. The Rectangle class is one of several classes that implements the Shape interface, so it is legal to assign a Rectangle object to a Shape variable, as we do on line 72.

Running the program will produce a window in which the rectangle appears on screen. To print the rectangle, the 'Print' menu item must be selected. Let us see what happens when this is done.

The action begins in the actionPerformed() method on line 56, where we find the code for handling the 'Print' menu item. First, we must set up the *printer job*, which we do by creating a PrinterJob object on line 57. The getPrinterJob() method is a *static* method of the PrinterJob class. (Recall that static methods refer to the class as a whole and not to any particular instance of that class, so we must prefix a call to a static method with the *class* name, not an object name.) This method queries the operating system to discover what printer or printers are connected to the computer on which the program is being run.

Next, on line 58, we create a PageFormat object, which describes the characteristics of the page on which the printing is to occur. The PageFormat class contains information on such things as the dimensions of the paper, the sizes of the margins, and so on. A PrinterJob object can supply a *default* PageFormat object through its defaultPage() method. In theory, this method should query the default printer on your computer and discover its default page properties. In practice, this sometimes does not work. In particular, in Britain, the default paper size on most printers *should* be A4 (210 mm by 297 mm). However, the defaultPage() method may return a paper size of 8.5 inches by 11 inches, which is the default letter paper size in North America (which is wider and shorter than A4). We will see below how we can specify the paper size in a PageFormat object.

On line 59 we call printDialog() to display the dialog box allowing the user to set the properties of the printer. Again, the results of altering parameters in this dialog are unpredictable—in many cases, the selections seem to be ignored. In some cases this may be due to the fact that modern printers tend to have more complex printer dialogs, often containing several tabbed panes allowing a multitude of parameters to be set. For example, the printer in the author's university department allows the user to staple the printed pages, and even allows a choice as to what angle the staple should be inserted into the paper! Java's printing facilities do not extend to this level of detail.

One use of the printDialog() method is its return value, which is a boolean parameter that is false if the user pressed the 'Cancel' button and true if the user pressed 'OK'. That is, the print dialog does allow the user to prevent a print job from proceeding. On line 59 we test the return value and, if it is false, we return from the method without printing anything.

On line 60 we display the second dialog box controlled by the PrinterJob class: the *page dialog*. This dialog allows the user to set the page size and the margin widths. The argument of the pageDialog() method is a PageFormat which is cloned (a new copy is made). The values specified by the user in the dialog are passed along to the clone, which is then returned when the user clicks 'OK' in the dialog. This dialog *does* have an effect—values specified by the user do get recorded in the PageFormat object that is returned. This is therefore one way of allowing the user to override the default PageFormat if required.

At this stage, we have created the PrinterJob and set its properties. We must now provide something for it to print. This is done in two stages: first, we attach a Printable object to the PrinterJob (on line 61). The first argument of the setPrintable() method must be a Printable object—since the SimplePrint class was declared as implementing Printable, we can pass this as the required object. The second argument is the PageFormat object which tells the PrinterJob what page properties should be used to print the Printable object. Note that we can change the page format for each printing if we wish.

Finally, we proceed with the actual printing process by calling the print() method on line 63. This method takes no arguments, since we have already told the PrinterJob what is to be printed by calling setPrintable() on line 61. The print() method can throw a PrinterException, which is a non-runtime exception and therefore must be caught, so the try and catch blocks are required whenever print() is called.

We pointed out earlier that the default PageFormat object generated by the defaultPage() method in the PrinterJob class does not always produce the correct page layout. It is possible to redefine the page layout in code, without requiring the user to input the details in the page dialog. To do this, we must define a Paper object.

The Paper class allows the overall dimensions and the *imageable area* of a sheet of paper to be defined. To do this, the paper dimensions must be set in *points*, where 1 point is equivalent to 1/72 of an inch (which is a standard unit in typesetting). For example, to define an A4 sheet we must convert the dimensions of the page from millimetres to points. The width of an A4 sheet is 210 mm = 8.268 inches = 595.28 points. Similarly, the height of an A4 sheet is 297 mm = 11.693 inches = 841.89 points. We can define a Paper object to represent A4 as follows:

```
Paper a4Paper = new Paper();
a4Paper.setSize(595.28, 841.89);
```

We can also define the *imageable area* of the sheet of paper, which defines the area on which drawing will occur. Basically, it is a way of specifying the margins on each page. The imageable area is defined by four numbers: the x and y coordinates of the upper-left corner of the drawing area, and the width and height of the area.

For example, to define an A4 sheet with half-inch margins on all sides, we need to set the upper-left corner of the imageable area at (36, 36) (since half an inch is equal to 36 points), and set the width and height of the imageable area to 523.28 (= 595.28 − 72) and 769.89 (= 841.89 − 72) points respectively. We would do this to the a4Paper object defined above with the statement:

```
a4Paper.setImageableArea(36, 36, 523.28, 769.89);
```

Finally, we can assign this Paper object to a PageFormat object with the statement:

```
pageFormat.setPaper(a4Paper);
```

To avoid using a page dialog as in the program example above, we could replace line 60 in that program with the four lines just given—this would hard-code an A4 paper format into the program.

Note that the coordinate system used for drawing the image (in the `print()` method, for example) is the same as that used for specifying the page size and imageable area. This means that any parts of the image that overlap the margins (that is, that extend outside the imageable area) will be clipped and will not appear on the printout. For example, if we attempted to print a rectangle with upper-left corner at (20, 20), width 100 and height 200 on the A4 sheet defined above, we would not see the top or left edges of the rectangle since these lie outside the imageable area. We would only see part of the bottom and right edges of the rectangle. In other words, if we want all of an image to appear on the page, we must ensure that all the drawing is done inside the imageable area.

One further note of caution is needed at this point, however. The setting of a `Paper` object or a `PageFormat` object does not guarantee that the drawing area will be set up correctly on all printers. For example, on some printers, extra margin widths appear in addition to those specified by the imageable area in the Java code, effectively reducing the drawing area even more than that specified by the imageable area parameters. Sometimes this 'unprintable area' can be changed by accessing the driver settings for the printer—methods for doing this are system dependent, but if you are on a Windows system, for example, you can access the 'Properties' dialog for your printer from the Windows control panel. It is best to experiment with your own printer setup to see what results you get.

3.2.3 Off-screen buffers

Java allows graphics to be drawn into an *off-screen buffer*, which is just an area of memory that stores image data without displaying the data on a monitor or printer. The main advantage of drawing into an off-screen buffer is speed: it is much faster to construct an image by writing into memory without displaying each component on screen as it is produced.

Off-screen buffers have two main applications. They are most commonly used in producing animations, where successive images are displayed on screen with a delay of only a few milliseconds between each pair of images. Each frame in the animation is drawn to an off-screen buffer, and the completed frame is then drawn to the screen in a single operation. This technique, often called *double buffering*, can help reduce the flickering that is often observed with animations. It cannot eliminate flickering entirely on a machine using a graphics card with too little memory, however, but the image quality is almost always improved when double buffering is used.

Another application of off-screen buffering is the ability to write an image into a disk file. We will illustrate the use of off-screen buffering by describing a program that creates a JPEG image file containing a simple shape.

Although the required classes for creating JPEG images are not technically part of the standard JDK package, they are included with the JDK download from Sun, and are to be found in the `com.sun.image.codec.jpeg` package.

The procedure for drawing into an off-screen buffer is very similar to that for producing an image on the monitor. The main difference is that a `BufferedImage` object is created and a `Graphics2D` object is attached to it. The graphics are then produced in the `BufferedImage` by using this `Graphics2D` object.

The following complete program creates an off-screen buffer that is a square 200 pixels on each side, draws a square 100 pixels on each side within it, and saves the image as a JPEG file.

```
1    import java.awt.*;
2    import java.awt.image.*;
3    import java.io.*;
4    import com.sun.image.codec.jpeg.*;
5
6    class JPGFile
7    {
8        public static void main(String[] argv)
9        {
10           JPGFile jpgFile = new JPGFile();
11       }
12
13       JPGFile()
14       {
15           BufferedImage image = new BufferedImage(200, 200,
16               BufferedImage.TYPE_INT_RGB);
17           Graphics2D gg = image.createGraphics();
18           gg.setPaint(Color.red);
19           Shape rect = new Rectangle(50, 50, 100, 100);
20           gg.draw(rect);
21           saveJPGImage(image);
22           System.exit(0);
23       }
24
25       private void saveJPGImage(BufferedImage image)
26       {
27           try {
28                   FileOutputStream outFile =
29                       new FileOutputStream("rect.jpg");
30                   JPEGImageEncoder encoder =
31                       JPEGCodec.createJPEGEncoder(outFile);
32                   encoder.encode(image);
33                   outFile.close();
34               } catch (Exception e) {
35               System.out.println(e.toString());
36           }
37       }
38   }
```

The import statement on line 1 is required to draw the square, and that on line 2 is required to create the BufferedImage. Line 3 is required to write output to the disk, and line 4 is needed to create the JPEG image.

The off-screen buffer is created on line 15 by specifying its dimensions in pixels and stating the graphics type that is to be stored. In this case, we specify TYPE_INT_RGB, indicating that an int is to be used to store each pixel's colour information, and that we are using RGB data, which allows a colour image. We will see another example later in this chapter that produces a greyscale image.

Line 17 creates a Graphics2D object connected to the BufferedImage. This object may be used to add graphics to the off-screen buffer, as we do on lines 18 to 20 where we create a red square and draw it into the buffer.

Line 21 calls the saveJPGImage() method which creates the JPEG image and saves it to disk. Several of the methods used here can throw exceptions, so we have included all the code in `saveJPGImage()` within a `try-catch` block, covering lines 27 to 36. Lines 28 and 29 create and open the output file stream. Lines 30 and 31 create the JPEG encoder object and associate it with the file stream. Line 32 converts the `BufferedImage` to a JPEG image and stores it in the disk file. The file stream is closed on line 33.

The program itself produces no visible output on screen, but it does create the file named `rect.jpg`. Displaying this file (in a Web browser, for example) will show a red square centred within an image that is 200 pixels on each side.

3.3   Graphics with Java 2D

As mentioned in the introduction to this chapter, Java 2D provides many more features than the `Graphics` class that was provided with the earlier versions of the JDK. Java 2D treats graphics objects in three broad areas: *shapes*, *images*, and *text*.

A *shape* is a graphical object constructed from a set of mathematically defined curves and areas. Simple shapes include rectangles, lines, and ellipses, but shapes of arbitrary complexity may be represented. Graphics drawn by using mathematical formulae to specify the shapes is known as *vector graphics*.

A mathematical shape is represented in Java 2D by an object from a class that implements the Shape interface. A `Shape` object may be constructed from a series of components, each of which is a straight line segment, a *quadratic spline* curve, or a *cubic spline* curve. (We will consider splines in Chapter 6). Close approximations to most geometric figures (such as circles and ellipses) may be drawn using splines, so the implementations of the `Shape` interface are capable of drawing complex figures with a good degree of precision.

An *image* is a graphical object defined as an array of pixels, and includes such objects as scanned photographs and other bitmapped images. Java 2D provides classes for loading, displaying and filtering (changing the appearance of) images.

Graphics created using arrays of pixels, rather than mathematically determined curves, are known as *raster graphics*.

Java 2D also contains several classes that allow text to be displayed and transformed. The facilities go considerably further than the simple `drawText()` method familiar from the `Graphics` class.

3.3.1   Drawing shapes

Mathematically defined shapes may be specified by creating a class that implements the Shape interface. A `Shape` consists of a list of separate components, where each component consists of two parts: from zero to three geometric points, and a label specifying the type of component. There are five types of component that can be added to the list in a `Shape` object:

- *move to*: appends a single point to the component list, and specifies that the drawing routine should move to that point, but not actually draw anything.
- *line to*: appends a single point, and specifies that a straight line should be drawn to this point from the last specified point.
- *quad to*: appends two points to the list, and specifies that a *quadratic spline* curve be drawn using these two points together with the last specified point. (We will examine splines in more detail in Chapter 6)

- *cubic to*: appends three points to the list, and specifies that a *cubic spline* curve be drawn using these three points together with the last specified point.
- *close*: adds no points to the list, but specifies that a straight line segment should be drawn from the last specified point back to the last 'move to' point, thus closing a curve to make an enclosed space.

Any geometric shape must be composed of a list of these components. Although it is not possible to represent *all* geometric figures *exactly* using these components (for example, a circle cannot be drawn exactly using only quadratic and cubic splines), the approximation to any curve is very good, and in practice will differ from the most precise algorithm by only a pixel or two at some places along the curve.

A shape is thus represented by a linked list of geometric components. Java 2D provides the PathIterator class to allow an iteration through this list to be done. The various components of a Shape are, in fact, represented by constants in the PathIterator class, being respectively SEG_MOVETO, SEG_LINETO, SEG_QUADTO, SEG_CUBICTO, and SEG_CLOSE.

Since Shape is an interface, we must have a class to implement it. Java 2D provides several classes that allow common shapes to be produced using the Shape interface, and two more general purpose classes called Area and GeneralPath that allow completely general geometric shapes to be produced. We will examine some examples below.

Before we get to some code, though, it is worth giving an overview of some of the other capabilities of the Shape interface.

The interface allows the specification of an 'interior' for any given shape. The Shape interface specifies several contains() methods, which allow the programmer to test if a specified point (or an entire rectangle) is contained within the Shape. There are also some intersects() methods that test if the Shape intersects a specified rectangle.

A Shape object can be transformed using any combination of the affine transformations (translation, rotation, scaling and shearing) described in Chapter 2. The AffineTransform class is used for this.

Finally, Java 2D treats fonts as collections of Shapes as well, which means that the same affine transformations can be applied to them, thus allowing great flexibility in the generation of new font types on the fly. Scaling allows different sizes of font to be created, rotation allows the text to appear at any angle, and other transformations allow the text to be distorted in various ways. Text can also be filled with solid colours or patterns.

3.3.2 Drawing basic shapes with Graphics2D

As we have seen, Java 2D has its own graphics context class called Graphics2D, which inherits the Graphics class. The inheritance, of course, allows Graphics2D to do everything that Graphics can, but Graphics knows nothing about the Shape interface. In order to deal with Shape objects, a Graphics2D object must be used.

Let us consider the code to create a simple Shape (a line segment) and draw it on the screen. The complete program is as follows.

```
import java.awt.*;
import java.awt.geom.*;
```

```
class LineShape extends Frame
{
    public static void main(String[] argv)
    {
        LineShape lineshape = new LineShape();
        lineshape.setSize(100, 100);
        lineshape.setVisible(true);
    }

    public void paint(Graphics g)
    {
        Graphics2D gg = (Graphics2D)g;
        Shape shape = new Line2D.Double(20, 30, 50, 70);
        gg.draw(shape);
    }
}
```

Note that we must import the java.awt.geom package to use Java 2D.

The main() method creates an instance of the main window, sets its size and makes it visible. The paint() method will be called automatically when the window is first displayed, so there is no need to call repaint() explicitly.

The first line in the paint() method is essential if we wish to make use of the Graphics2D package—we must cast the Graphics argument passed to paint() into a Graphics2D object.

The creation of the Shape variable shape may require a bit of explanation. First, recall that Shape is an interface, not a class, so we cannot actually create *objects* of type Shape. However, we can use the principle of polymorphism (one of the foundations of object oriented programming) to declare a Shape pointer, which can then be set to any object from a class that implements Shape. This is what we have done here—we have declared a pointer called shape and then initialized it by creating a new object of the class Line2D.Double, which (among other things) implements the Shape interface. But what is this class with the strange double-barrelled name?

In Java 2D, Line2D is defined as an *abstract* class, which for our purposes here means much the same thing as if it were an interface, since objects cannot be created directly from abstract classes either. The abstract Line2D class contains two *inner classes* (classes whose code is nested inside that of Line2D), both of which inherit Line2D and provide concrete implementations of all the methods in Line2D. These inner classes are named Double and Float, and allow straight line segments to be specified using either double or float values, respectively, as the coordinates of the endpoints of the line.

After all that, we can now state what the middle line in the paint() method is doing. It creates a line segment with endpoints of (20, 30) and (50, 70) (where all coordinates are stored as doubles), and stores that line segment in the Shape variable called shape. In terms of the five component types specified above for a Shape object, the line segment is stored as a 'move to (20, 30)' followed by a 'line to (50, 70)'.

Merely creating a Shape object doesn't display it on screen, however, so we need to complete the job by calling the draw() method in the Graphics2D class.

Other simple shapes may be created in much the same way. There is an abstract Rectangle2D class, also with Double and Float inner classes, that can be used to create a rectangular Shape. The Ellipse2D class can be used to create ellipses and circles, the Arc2D class creates elliptical arcs, and the RoundRectangle2D class creates rectangles with rounded corners. All these classes are abstract, so we need to use either the Double or Float inner class that each contains. In each case, the corresponding geometric figure is represented as a Shape by calculating the appropriate set of commands from the set of five basic components given above, and constructing the corresponding component list. In some cases (such as Rectangle2D), the figures can be represented exactly as Shape components, but in other cases (such as Ellipse2D), the Shape representation using splines is only an approximation (although a reasonably good one) to the desired figure. For example, if we draw a circle using the Ellipse2D class and compare it with a circle of the same size drawn using Bresenham's circle algorithm from Chapter 1, the circle drawn with Ellipse2D has a slightly more ragged outline. For most purposes, however, the Shape versions of geometric figures are satisfactory.

As a second example, we will illustrate the use of the GeneralPath and PathIterator classes. We replace the paint() method in the previous program with the following:

```
1    public void paint(Graphics g)
2    {
3        Graphics2D g2d = (Graphics2D)g;
4        GeneralPath testShape = new GeneralPath();
5        testShape.moveTo(130, 130);
6        testShape.lineTo(200, 200);
7        testShape.quadTo(20, 150, 40, 30);
8        testShape.curveTo(300, 150, 250, 250, 75, 50);
9        g2d.draw(testShape);
10
11       PathIterator pathIter =
12           testShape.getPathIterator(null);
13       double[] coords = new double[6];
14       while (!pathIter.isDone()) {
15           int segType = pathIter.currentSegment(coords);
16           System.out.print("Seg: " + segType);
17           for (int i = 0; i < 6; i++) {
18               System.out.print(" " + coords[i]);
19           }
20           System.out.println("");
21           pathIter.next();
22       }
23   }
```

The GeneralPath class is another class that implements the Shape interface, but it allows us to construct any curve we like by constructing a linked list composed of the five component types described above. In the method shown here, we create a new GeneralPath object on line 4. We then move to (130, 130) and then draw a line from there to (200, 200) (lines 5 and 6). We then add a quadratic spline curve segment on line 7. As we will see in Chapter 7, a quadratic spline requires three control points, so the curve here uses the last point plotted in the previous segment (200, 200) as the first control point, and requires the programmer to specify the remaining two control points as arguments to the quadTo() method. Here these points are (20, 150) and (40, 30).

Finally, on line 8, we use the curveTo() method to add a cubic spline segment, which requires four control points. The first control point is (40, 30) and the remaining three points are given as arguments to the method. After drawing the curve, we obtain the result shown in Figure 3.1.

Figure 3.1:
A curve drawn using a GeneralPath.

The remainder of the code in the paint() method illustrates the use of the PathIterator class. This class retrieves the individual components in the linked list of segments making up a GeneralPath and stores their coordinates in an array. On line 11 we create the PathIterator using the getPathIterator() method from the GeneralPath class. This method takes an AffineTransform (see next section) as an argument, which allows the components within the list to be transformed. If we pass a null argument to the method (as we do here), no transformation is performed.

On line 13 we prepare the array that is to receive the data from the PathIterator. Line 14 begins a loop that traverses the linked list. The isDone() method checks if we have processed the last segment in the list.

On line 15 the currentSegment() method loads the coordinates of the current segment into the coords array that is passed to it as an argument, and returns an int flag that indicates the type of segment (SEG_MOVE_TO, SEG_LINE_TO, etc.). The remainder of the loop prints out the data in a text window. For the GeneralPath object we have just defined, the output is:

```
Seg: 0 130.0 130.0 0.0 0.0 0.0 0.0
Seg: 1 200.0 200.0 0.0 0.0 0.0 0.0
Seg: 2 20.0 150.0 40.0 30.0 0.0 0.0
Seg: 3 300.0 150.0 250.0 250.0 75.0 50.0
```

By comparing this with the code on lines 5 to 8, we see that segment type 0 is SEG_MOVE_TO, with similar assignments to the other curve segments. We can also see the coordinates that were specified in the original code returned to us by the PathIterator.

It is instructive to examine the PathIterator for some of the built-in shape classes such as Rectangle2D and Ellipse2D, where you can see what fundamental segment types are used to build these objects.

Those readers familiar with the old Graphics class and the methods within it for generating shapes such as rectangles and ellipses may be relieved to hear that these methods still work in Java 2D. However, as we shall see later in this chapter, it is better to use the new classes for drawing these basic shapes.

3.4   Filling and the Paint interface

Objects may be filled with solid colours or patterns by using the Paint interface in Java 2D. A Paint object is associated with the current Graphics2D and is then used in all filling operations until it is replaced by a different Paint.

There are three classes that implement the Paint interface: Color, GradientPaint, and TexturePaint. The Color class is probably familiar to you as it has been part of the JDK since the earliest days, and is used in simple drawing to specify the drawing colour for text, lines, and areas. In Java 2D, Color is extended by having it implement the Paint interface, so that it can be used to specify solid colours for filling Shape objects.

We will consider colour theory in more depth in Chapter 7, but for now it is easiest if we confine ourselves to the simple RGB (red–green–blue) model. All colours that are produced by *projected* light (as on a monitor screen) can be composed of the three *primary* colours red, green and blue. (Colours that are formed from *reflected* light, as in a painting, are formed from the colours red, yellow and blue. Many colour printers use the CMYK (cyan, magenta, yellow and black) system.)

In Java's RGB colour model, a colour is specified by providing a value between 0 and 255 for each of the three colour components. We often write a colour in RGB notation as a triplet of integers, as in (255, 255, 0). This means that red and green are both on maximum, and blue is turned off completely (the resulting colour is bright yellow).

The Color class provides 13 fixed colours as static parameters. Thus, to use an orange colour, we may say Color.orange, rather than having to work out the RGB coordinates for orange. Refer to the JDK documentation for a complete list of colours available.

A simple example of the use of the Color class is shown below.

```
public void paint(Graphics g)
{
    Shape shape;
    Graphics2D gg = (Graphics2D)g;
    shape = new Polygon();
    ((Polygon)shape).addPoint(20, 70);
    ((Polygon)shape).addPoint(350, 110);
    ((Polygon)shape).addPoint(80, 270);
    gg.setPaint(Color.orange);
    gg.fill(shape);
    gg.setPaint(Color.black);
    gg.draw(shape);
}
```

This code draws a triangle with a solid outline, filled with a solid orange colour. Notice the use of the setPaint() method to select the drawing colour. Notice also that we *fill* the shape (using the fill() method of the Graphics2D class) *before* we draw its outline using draw(). The reason for this is that the filling algorithm used by Java 2D overwrites some of the outline of the figure, so if we want a clean outline to be drawn, we must always draw it on top of the filled figure.

3.4.1 Gradient filling

A *gradient fill* results in a solid fill pattern that gradually merges from one colour to another between two points. A gradient fill can be produced using the GradientPaint class. An example is given in the following code.

```
public void paint(Graphics g)
{
    Shape shape;
    Graphics2D gg = (Graphics2D)g;
    shape = new Polygon();
    ((Polygon)shape).addPoint(20, 70);
    ((Polygon)shape).addPoint(350, 110);
    ((Polygon)shape).addPoint(80, 270);
    Paint pattern =
        new GradientPaint(20, 70, Color.black,
        350, 110, Color.white);
    gg.setPaint(pattern);
    gg.fill(shape);
    gg.setPaint(Color.black);
    gg.draw(shape);
}
```

The code produces the effect shown in Figure 3.2.

Figure 3.2:
A gradient fill.

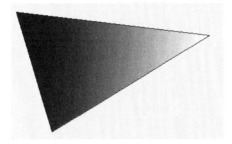

In the GradientPaint constructor, the first two arguments specify the coordinates of the point that is to serve as the anchor point for the first colour (given as the third argument), and the fourth and fifth arguments do likewise for the second colour.

In Figure 3.2, we have chosen the two upper vertices of the triangle as the anchor points, so the gradient covers the entire polygon. It is also possible to choose points within the polygon and generate a *cyclic* fill, which results in the effect shown in Figure 3.3.

Figure 3.3:
A cyclic gradient fill.

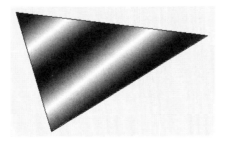

This figure was drawn by replacing the GradientPaint object in the previous example with the call:

```
Paint pattern = new GradientPaint(40, 70, Color.black,
    70, 110, Color.white, true);
```

Notice that there is an extra boolean argument at the end which is true if a cyclic (repeating) pattern is required.

3.4.2 Textured filling

Using *textured fills* it is possible to define your own pattern with which a Shape may be filled. A BufferedImage is required as the image used to define the texture. The single image is tiled to fill the Shape by defining a TexturePaint object to associate the image with the Graphics2D object. An example of a texture fill is given below.

```
public void paint(Graphics g)
{
    Shape shape;
    Graphics2D gg = (Graphics2D)g;
    shape = new Polygon();
    ((Polygon)shape).addPoint(20, 70);
    ((Polygon)shape).addPoint(350, 110);
    ((Polygon)shape).addPoint(80, 270);

    int smileySize = 60;
    Paint pattern = new
        TexturePaint(createSmiley(smileySize),
        new Rectangle2D.
        Double(20, 70, smileySize, smileySize));
    gg.setPaint(pattern);
    gg.fill(shape);
    gg.setPaint(Color.black);
    gg.draw(shape);
}
```

This program fills the triangle with images of a smiley face, the construction of which we will consider in a minute. The TexturePaint constructor takes two arguments—the first is a BufferedImage containing the image of the smiley face (produced by calling the createSmiley() method below), and the second is a reference rectangle which defines the size and location of one of the tiles into which the image is to be drawn. The original BufferedImage will be scaled so that it fits inside this reference rectangle, and then the rectangle will be duplicated horizontally and vertically from its defined location until it fills the Shape.

The BufferedImage object containing the smiley face is created by the following method:

```
// Add this import to top of class definition file
import java.awt.image.*;

private BufferedImage createSmiley(int size)
{
    BufferedImage smiley = new BufferedImage(size, size,
    BufferedImage.TYPE_BYTE_GRAY);
```

```
Graphics2D gg = smiley.createGraphics();
gg.setPaint(Color.yellow);
Shape face = new Ellipse2D.Double(1, 1,
    size-2, size-2);
gg.fill(face);
gg.setPaint(Color.black);
gg.draw(face);
gg.draw(new Ellipse2D.Double(0.3*size, 0.36*size,
    0.1*size, 0.1*size));
gg.draw(new Ellipse2D.Double(0.6*size, 0.36*size,
    0.1*size, 0.1*size));
gg.draw(new Arc2D.Double
    (new Rectangle2D.Double(0.2*size, 0.2*size,
    0.6*size, 0.6*size), 225.0, 90.0, Arc2D.OPEN));
return smiley;
}
```

The BufferedImage class is defined in the java.awt.image package, so we must import that in any code that uses BufferedImages.

We have used the simplest constructor, which takes three arguments. The first two define the size of the image, and the last argument defines its type. We have specified a greyscale image (type TYPE_BYTE_GRAY) so that it will reproduce properly in this book. In practice, you will no doubt want a full-colour image, which can be obtained using TYPE_INT_RGB. Note that although we are drawing the smiley face using greyscale, its colours are specified as yellow and black. To actually see the colours, all we need to do is change the type argument in the constructor. There are numerous other types available, so have a look at the BufferedImage documentation and experiment a bit.

The image of the smiley is defined using a large ellipse for the head, two smaller ellipses for the eyes, and an arc for the mouth. The result of the fill is shown in Figure 3.4.

Figure 3.4:
A texture fill.

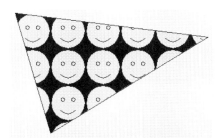

3.5 Clipping

Java 2D allows us to clip objects as they are drawn, with the clipping boundary being defined by another Shape object. This means that we can clip to any shape of boundary we wish.

Clipping requires only that we create the Shape object to define the boundary and then call the setClip() method in the Graphics2D class to set the clipping area. As a simple example, we can clip the texture-filled triangle shown in Figure 3.4 by defining an elliptical clipping boundary. All that is needed is to insert the following lines of code at any point before the call to `gg.fill()` in the preceding example:

```
Shape clip = new Ellipse2D.Double(20, 70, 200, 100);
gg.setClip(clip);
```

Once the clipping boundary is set for the graphics context, all subsequent drawing operations will be clipped relative to this boundary. The clipped output is shown in Figure 3.5.

Figure 3.5

3.5.1 Areas

The classes we have studied so far provide powerful methods for drawing curves of almost any shape, but it can be difficult to specify more complex enclosed areas using these classes. The Area class, which also implements the Shape interface, provides a number of methods which make it much easier to construct regions with complex geometries.

An Area object can be created from an existing Shape object, provided that the Shape specifies an enclosed region. For example, an Area can be created from a Rectangle2D object, but not from a Line2D object. (Well, we *can* create an Area from a Line2D, but it couldn't be used for anything.)

The main use of Area objects is that they can be combined with each other using boolean operations such as OR, AND, NOT and XOR. For example, we could create a slice of Swiss cheese by creating a rectangular Area and then combining several small circular Areas, using the NOT operation, to put some holes in the rectangle.

Having created an Area, we can either display it directly using the draw() method in Graphics2D, or we can use it as a clipping region for other graphics. We will give an example of the latter use here.

Figure 3.6:
A cloverleaf image
drawn using Areas.

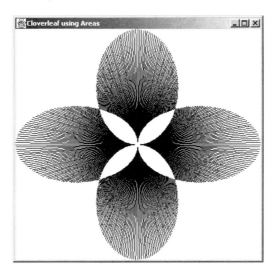

The example program produces the output shown in Figure 3.6—a cloverleaf pattern composed of lines radiating out from the centre of the frame. (This program is a Java version of the demonstration program in Charles Petzold's classic *Programming Windows* book, which uses C as the programming language.)

The idea is to draw a set of radiating lines which fills the entire frame, and then to use Areas to define a mask which is placed over the lines, thus producing the cloverleaf pattern. The pattern should neatly fill the drawing area inside the frame, and should resize itself if the window itself is resized by the user.

The complete program code is as follows:

```java
import java.awt.*;
import java.awt.event.*;
import java.awt.geom.*;

class Clover extends javax.swing.JFrame
{
    int frameWidth, frameHeight;
    Shape contentShape;
    Area cloverArea;

    public static void main(String[] argv)
    {
        Clover testShape = new Clover();
        testShape.setVisible(true);
    }

    public Clover()
    {
        setTitle("Area demo");
        setSize(300,300);
        setBackground(Color.black);
        enableEvents(AWTEvent.WINDOW_EVENT_MASK |
            AWTEvent.COMPONENT_EVENT_MASK);
    }

    protected void processWindowEvent(WindowEvent e) {
        super.processWindowEvent(e);
        if (e.getID() == WindowEvent.WINDOW_CLOSING) {
            System.exit(0);
        }
    }

    protected void processComponentEvent(ComponentEvent e) {
        super.processComponentEvent(e);
        if (e.getID() == ComponentEvent.COMPONENT_RESIZED ||
            e.getID() == ComponentEvent.COMPONENT_SHOWN) {

            frameWidth = getContentPane().getWidth();
            frameHeight = getContentPane().getHeight();
            contentShape = new Rectangle2D.Double(0, 0,
                frameWidth, frameHeight);
```

```
42
43          Area[] ellipse = new Area[4];
44          ellipse[0] =
45              new Area(new Ellipse2D.Double(0, frameHeight/3,
46                  frameWidth/2, frameHeight/3));
47          ellipse[1] =
48              new Area(new Ellipse2D.Double(frameWidth/2,
49                  frameHeight/3, frameWidth/2, frameHeight/3));
50          ellipse[2] =
51              new Area(new Ellipse2D.Double(frameWidth/3, 0,
52                  frameWidth/3, frameHeight/2));
53          ellipse[3] =
54              new Area(new Ellipse2D.Double(frameWidth/3,
55                  frameHeight/2, frameWidth/3, frameHeight/2));
56
57          ellipse[0].add(ellipse[1]);
58          ellipse[2].add(ellipse[3]);
59
60          cloverArea = ellipse[0];
61          cloverArea.exclusiveOr(ellipse[2]);
62          getContentPane().repaint();
63      }
64  }
65
66  public void paint(Graphics g)
67  {
68      Graphics2D g2d =
69          (Graphics2D)getContentPane().getGraphics();
70
71      g2d.setPaint(getBackground());
72      g2d.fill(contentShape);
73      g2d.setPaint(Color.green);
74      g2d.setClip(cloverArea);
75
76      double radius =
77          Math.sqrt(frameWidth*frameWidth +
78              frameHeight*frameHeight)/2.0;
79      GeneralPath clover = new GeneralPath();
80      for (double angle = 0.0; angle <= 2*Math.PI;
81          angle += Math.PI/180.0) {
82          clover.moveTo(frameWidth/2, frameHeight/2);
83          clover.lineTo(
84              (float)(radius * Math.cos(angle)) + frameWidth/2,
85
86              -(float)(radius * Math.sin(angle)) +
87              frameHeight/2);
88      }
89      g2d.draw(clover);
90  }
91 }
```

The variables on lines 7 and 8 are used to keep track of the dimensions of the frame as it is resized. The `Area` on line 9 will contain the mask that defines the cloverleaf pattern.

In the constructor, on lines 22 and 23, we call `enableEvents()` as an alternative method of catching events of certain types. In this case, we catch events that pertain to the window itself, and resizing and displaying components. The latter type of event will allow us to redraw the graphics when the window is resized.

The `processWindowEvent()` method on line 26 overrides a method in the `JFrame` base class, and traps the `WINDOW_CLOSING` event. This is an alternative method to that used in earlier chapters for handling the closing of a window.

The `processComponentEvent()` method on line 33 performs all the calculations required to update the cloverleaf shape each time the window is displayed or resized. We first obtain the dimensions of the drawing area within the frame on lines 38 and 39. Note that call `getContentPane()` first before extracting the width and height, since this ensures that we are considering the actual drawing area within the frame (excluding the title bar). If we omitted the call to `getContentPane()`, the `getHeight()` call would retrieve the height of the outer boundary of the frame, which includes the title bar.

Line 40 creates a `Shape` that covers the entire drawing area, which we use later in the `print()` method to refresh the drawing area.

We begin the definition of the cloverleaf region on line 43 by creating an array of 4 `Area`s. Each of these areas is used to define one of the elliptical lobes of the cloverleaf pattern. On line 44, for example, we create the leftmost lobe as an `Ellipse2D` object, and use this object to create a corresponding `Area`. The other three lobes are created in a similar manner, with array elements 1, 2 and 3 being the right, top and bottom ellipses, respectively.

On line 57 we use the `add()` method from the `Area` class to combine the left and right ellipses using a boolean OR operation. Somewhat confusingly, the methods in the `Area` class that implement the various Boolean operations use names that are drawn from set theory, boolean logic and just plain English. For reference, they are:

- `add()`: Boolean OR, set union. Combines two `Area`s to produce a final area that contains all regions of the original two.

- `subtract()`: Boolean NOT, set difference. Combines two `Area`s A and B such that the final area is A minus the intersection of A and B.

- `intersect()`: Boolean AND, set intersection. Combines two `Area`s to produce the intersection.

- `exclusiveOr()`: Boolean XOR, set union minus set intersection. Combines two `Area`s A and B to produce an area which is (A union B) – (A intersect B).

Line 57 therefore takes the union of the left and right ellipses, and stores the compound area back in `ellipse[0]`. Line 58 similarly combines the top and bottom ellipses.

If we now took the union of `ellipse[0]` and `ellipse[1]`, we would get a cloverleaf pattern without the almond-shaped holes near the centre. To produce these holes, we need to remove the regions where `ellipse[0]` and `ellipse[1]` intersect. We can do this by using an XOR operation, which we do on line 61 to produce the final mask, which is stored in the class variable `cloverArea`.

The paint() method on line 66 clears the existing drawing, draws the radial lines and then uses cloverArea as a clipping mask to produce the cloverleaf pattern.

Notice that we ignore the Graphics object passed into paint(), since this refers to the overall frame (including the title bar), so the coordinates would not be correct. Instead, on line 68, we obtain the graphics context of the content pane and use that for all drawing within paint().

Lines 71 and 72 erase the existing drawing. For drawing areas derived from the Canvas class, a call to repaint() would usually do this for us, since repaint() first calls the default update() method which does erase the background. However, the update() method in the JFrame class merely calls paint() directly without erasing the background, so we need to do this ourselves within paint().

Line 73 sets the drawing colour to green, and line 74 applies the cloverleaf pattern as a clipping region. This means that only those portions of any drawing operations that fall within cloverArea will be displayed—everything else is clipped.

The remainder of the paint() method draws the radial line pattern. We do this by calculating the distance from the centre of the window to one of its corners using Pythagoras' theorem (line 76). We then use a GeneralPath to store all the radial lines. We draw one line per degree (a total of 360 lines).

3.5.2 Transparency and composition

Everything we have drawn so far has used *opaque colour*, in the sense that it obscured whatever was underneath it. The 'paint' that was used as the drawing medium, whether it was a solid colour or a texture composed of smiley faces, completely overwrote any previously-drawn graphics.

In many cases, it is useful to blend the new objects with the existing graphics, rather than simply overwrite it. Using an artistic analogy, we would rather use watercolours than oil paints, so that we can apply semi-transparent washes and objects to a pre-drawn background.

Java 2D offers several facilities for creating objects with varying degrees of transparency. The simplest method involves just adding a fourth component, called *alpha*, to a Color object which is used as a Paint. The alpha parameter specifies the *opacity* of the Color: a value of 0.0 indicates zero opacity, so that the colour is completely transparent (so all background graphics show through unchanged). A value of 1.0 indicates total opacity, so that the Color obscures anything over which it is drawn. An alpha of 1.0 is the default, and is what we have been implicitly using in all the examples so far.

Intermediate values of alpha indicate a partial opacity, giving the effect of viewing the background through stained glass. The alpha value of a Color must be specified in the Color's constructor—there is no 'setAlpha()' method in the Color class.

Thus, if we wished to draw some objects using a red colour with 50% opacity, we must create the red colour as follows:

```
Color transparentRed = new Color(1.0f, 0.0f, 0.0f, 0.5f);
gg.setPaint(transparentRed);
// draw objects using this paint
```

Before we get into the details of the methods by which transparent colours can be produced, the reader should try a few simple programs which produce overlapping rectangles and ellipses, just to get a feel for what effect the alpha parameter has. This can easily be done by adding a few lines to the paint() method of an existing application.

The process of drawing a new object on top of an existing background is known as *composition*. The colour and transparency of each pixel in an overlapping region is worked out according to a composition algorithm. Java 2D provides a choice of eight composition algorithms which can be used to combine new and existing graphical objects.

Newcomers to the art of composition often find the effects of the various algorithms hard to predict, especially as they don't always give the same result in all cases where graphics is drawn onto a display surface. We will study how composition works by examining in detail the default composition algorithm, and then giving an overview of the other seven algorithms.

The default composition algorithm is known as the *source over rule*, because it places the *source* object (the new object that is being added to an existing set of objects) over the *destination* object (the set of objects that has been drawn previously), and allows some of the destination to show through the source, according to the value of the alpha parameter.

The goal of a composition algorithm is to determine the four components (red, green, blue and alpha) of each pixel in the drawing area after a new object has been drawn on top of some existing ones. All the composition algorithms used by Java 2D have the same general form. The three colour components of a Color object (red, green and blue) are all transformed according to the formula:

$$c_d := f_s \alpha_s c_s + f_d \alpha_d c_d \tag{3.1}$$

where α_s and α_d are the alpha values of the source and destination respectively, c_s and c_d represent one of the colour coordinates (red, green or blue) of the source and destination, and f_s and f_d are parameters that are specified by the particular composition algorithm. Note that we have used the assignment operator := indicating the new value of c_d after the composition is determined by evaluating the expression on the right-hand side, and that all values on the right-hand side of the assignment operator refer to values before the composition has taken place.

A similar expression determines how the alpha values are transformed under a composition:

$$\alpha_d := f_s \alpha_s + f_d \alpha_d \tag{3.2}$$

For the source over rule, we have $f_s = 1$ and $f_d = 1 - \alpha_s$. Thus for the source over rule, the composition algorithm becomes:

$$c_d := \alpha_s c_s + (1 - \alpha_s)\alpha_d c_d \tag{3.3}$$

and

$$\alpha_d := \alpha_s + (1 - \alpha_s)\alpha_d \tag{3.4}$$

Before we examine some specific examples of these equations, we need to consider the drawing surfaces that are being used. We have seen earlier in this chapter that we have two main options for drawing graphics: we can draw directly to the screen, or we can draw to an off-screen BufferedImage and then draw the BufferedImage onto the screen later.

The monitor screen is special in that it does not have an *alpha channel*. That is, there is no opacity or alpha value for the screen. If we draw a figure directly to the screen, then, what value do we use for α_d in the equations above? The convention used in compositing is that an alpha value of 1.0 is assumed for any drawing surface that does not have an alpha channel. This value is read-only—it cannot be changed by any composition algorithm.

When equations 3.3 and 3.4 are used to combine a new source with the screen as the destination, the colour components calculated from equation 3.3 are divided by the alpha component calculated from equation 3.4, and the alpha component is then discarded, since the alpha of the screen cannot be changed. If the alpha value is zero, all colour components are set to zero (making the colour black).

A BufferedImage, on the other hand, may or may not have an alpha channel, depending on the image type that is specified when the BufferedImage is created. If it does have an alpha channel, the initial alpha value for the entire image is zero, making it completely transparent. Here, when equations 3.3 and 3.4 are used to combine a source with an existing BufferedImage, the new colour components are divided by the new alpha value, but the alpha value is retained, since the alpha component of each pixel in a BufferedImage is writable. Again, if the alpha is zero, the colour components are set to zero, but since a zero alpha means the colour is transparent, it will not be visible.

To demonstrate that a BufferedImage with an alpha channel is indeed transparent, we can use the following paint() method:

```java
public void paint(Graphics g)
{
    g.drawString("Transparent image", 100, 100);
    BufferedImage buf = new BufferedImage(width, height,
        BufferedImage.TYPE_INT_ARGB);
    g.drawImage(buf, 0, 0, null);
}
```

Here, we draw the string 'Transparent image' directly onto the screen, then create a BufferedImage (where width and height are assumed to match the display area and would be calculated externally). The BufferedImage is then drawn on top of the string. When the program is run, the string will still be visible because the BufferedImage's background colour is transparent.

Now let us consider a simple example where we draw, say, a filled ellipse on top of a filled star using the source over rule.

First, we will draw the figures directly onto the screen, without using an intervening BufferedImage. We will draw a filled, red, opaque star onto the screen first. For the screen, α_d is always 1.0, and if we assume that the background colour is white, we have $c_d = (1.0, 1.0, 1.0)$. The star is opaque, so $\alpha_s = 1.0$, and the colour is red, so $c_s = (1.0, 0.0, 0.0)$. Using equation 3.3, we find that the colour of the destination where the star is drawn is $c_d := c_s$, so the red colour is transferred as we would expect.

Using equation 3.4, the alpha of the destination is 1.0, so there is no change in opacity. The net result is just to draw the solid red star onto the background.

Now let us draw a blue ellipse so that it partially overlaps the star. The ellipse will have an alpha of 0.5 meaning that it is half transparent. The ellipse is now the source, so we have $c_s = (0.0, 0.0, 1.0)$ for the blue colour, and $\alpha_s = 0.5$ for the opacity.

Using equation 3.3 we find that the new colour for the region where the ellipse overlaps the star is $c_d := 0.5c_s + 0.5c_d = (0.5, 0.0, 0.5)$. The new alpha value for the overlap region is $\alpha_d = 0.5 + 0.5 = 1.0$. The final colour is thus an equal mixture of red and blue (giving purple), which is what we expect if we put a semi-transparent blue object over an opaque red object.

For the region where the ellipse overlaps the white background, the background colour is $c_d = (1.0, 1.0, 1.0)$ and the background opacity is $\alpha_d = 1.0$. The resulting colour is thus $c_d := 0.5c_s + 0.5c_d = (0.5, 0.5, 1.0)$, and the new opacity is still 1.0. We thus get a light blue colour, again what we would expect if we placed a semi-transparent blue object over a white background.

Now consider what happens if we do the same drawing but this time onto a `BufferedImage`. Drawing the initial red star onto the image results in the area covered by the star having a solid red colour and an alpha of 1.0. The remainder of the `BufferedImage` still has an alpha of 0.0, however. When we draw the blue ellipse, we will get the same result in the region where the ellipse overlaps the star, but what happens where the ellipse overlaps the transparent background area?

In this area, $\alpha_d = 0$ (so it doesn't matter what c_d is), so using equation 3.3, we find that the new colour is $c_d := 0.5c_s = (0.0, 0.0, 0.5)$. The new alpha value, from equation 3.4, is $\alpha_d = 0.5$. As we mentioned above, the final colour is obtained by dividing c_d by α_d, so we reclaim the original blue colour of the ellipse: $(0.0, 0.0, 1.0)$.

However, we are not finished yet, since we still must draw the `BufferedImage` onto the screen. The image contains three areas: the region where the ellipse overlaps the star, the region where the ellipse overlaps the background, and the remaining background region. The region where the ellipse overlaps the star has an opacity of 1.0, so it gets transferred directly to the screen, overwriting the white background. The region where the ellipse overlaps the background has an opacity of 0.5 and a solid blue colour, so the result of combining this with the screen's white background is to produce a pale blue colour with components $(0.5, 0.5, 1.0)$, just as in the case where we drew both objects to the screen directly. Finally, the region of pure image background is completely transparent, so the screen's white background just shows through in this area.

The final result is the same as drawing both objects directly to the screen, but we can see that the process is a bit more involved.

The results of using the source over rule are shown in Figures 3.7 and 3.8.

Figure 3.7:
An ellipse with $\alpha = 1$ overlapping a star using the source over rule.

Figure 3.8:
An ellipse with
$\alpha = 0.5$ overlapping
a star using the
source over rule.

3.5.3   The AlphaComposite class

The source over rule described in the previous section is the default rule used in Java 2D for compositing images, and is most likely the one we would want to use since it is a 'common sense' rule. When we add an object with a specified opacity over existing graphics, we want the background graphics to 'show through' to a degree corresponding to the opacity of the new object.

However, there are a number of other rules which can be applied. The set usually used in graphics was defined originally by Porter and Duff in 1984 and consisted of twelve rules. Java 2D implements eight of these rules, one of which is the source over rule already described.

All the rules can be described by specifying values for f_s and f_d in equations 3.1 and 3.2. We will briefly describe the rules here and leave it to the exercises to explore their effects in detail.

Rule	AlphaComposite static object	AlphaComposite instance name	f_s	f_d
Source over	SrcOver	SRC_OVER	1	$1 - \alpha_s$
Source	Src	SRC	1	0
Source in	SrcIn	SRC_IN	α_d	0
Source out	SrcOut	SRC_OUT	$1 - \alpha_d$	0
Destination over	DstOver	DST_OVER	$1 - \alpha_d$	1
Destination in	DstIn	DST_IN	0	α_s
Destination out	DstOut	DST_OUT	0	$1 - \alpha_s$
Clear	Clear	CLEAR	0	0

Although the source over rule ultimately gives the same results whether it is applied directly to the screen or to a BufferedImage which is then drawn on the screen, the other rules often give different results in the two cases, so care must be taken to work out exactly what will happen. In general, the behaviour of these rules will be closer to 'what we would expect' if we draw to a BufferedImage rather than directly to the screen.

Before we describe each rule in more detail, it is worth mentioning how to invoke these rules within a Java program.

The AlphaComposite class may be used to set the composition rule for a Graphics2D object. This class contains a number of static predefined AlphaComposite objects which may be used directly to create each of the eight rules given in the above table. The predefined object names are listed in the column labelled 'AlphaComposite static object'. To set the composition rule in a graphics context, use the setComposite() method:

```
public void paint(Graphics g)
{
    Graphics2D gg = (Graphics2D)g;
    gg.setComposite(AlphaComposite.DstOver);
    // draw commands
}
```

All drawing commands in this code will use the destination over rule until another call to setComposite() is made.

There is a second way of using the AlphaComposite class which compensates for the fact that a Color object cannot be changed after it is created. The getInstance() method in the AlphaComposite class allows a rule and an additional alpha parameter to be specified. This new alpha value is multiplied with the existing alpha value in all Colors that are subsequently drawn. Thus, if we have previously defined a Shape object containing a variety of Colors, but all of these Colors have alpha values of 1.0, we can use the getInstance() method to make these Colors semi-transparent without having to redefine the original Shape.

The first argument of the getInstance() method is a static parameter from the AlphaComposite class, and is given in the table above. The second argument is a float specifying the desired alpha value.

We can use getInstance() to invoke the destination over rule and reduce the opacity of all colours by 50% as follows:

```
public void paint(Graphics g)
{
    Graphics2D gg = (Graphics2D)g;
    gg.setComposite(AlphaComposite.getInstance(
        AlphaComposite.DST_OVER, 0.5f));
    // draw commands
}
```

A brief description of each of the available rules follows.

- **Source over**: places the source over the destination and allows the destination to show through the source according to the alpha setting of the source.

- **Source**: The source overwrites the destination. Alpha values are ignored, so the destination will not show through the source.

- **Source in**: Ignores the destination colour. Copies the source to the destination wherever the destination is not totally transparent (essentially uses the destination shapes as clipping boundaries).

- **Source out**: Ignores the destination colour. Copies the source to the destination wherever the destination is not totally opaque.

- **Destination over**: places the source 'under' the destination, and allows the source to show through the destination according to the alpha of the destination. This rule works like an inverse of source over, but may not do what you expect if you draw directly to the screen (see exercises).

- **Destination in**: Similar to source in, except the source's colour is ignored, and the area of overlap with the destination is altered by the source's opacity.

Areas of overlap where the source is completely transparent will remain transparent.

- **Destination out**: Similar to destination in, except areas of overlap where the source is opaque become transparent.
- **Clear**: all areas covered by the source become totally transparent.

Samples of each of these rules are shown in the following figures, but to get a better feel for how the rules work, you should experiment by changing the various alpha values. All figures are drawn using an intervening BufferedImage, with the star as the destination and the ellipse as the source. The alpha values of both the star and ellipse are 0.75.

Figure 3.9: Source rule.

Figure 3.10: Source in rule.

Figure 3.11: Source out rule.

Figure 3.12: Destination over rule.

Figure 3.13: Destination in rule.

Figure 3.14: Destination out rule.

Figure 3.15: Clear rule.

3.5.4 Affine transformations

At this point, you could be forgiven for wondering what the point of the Shape class is. We have seen how to draw simple shapes using Shape together with Graphics2D's draw() method, but all of these shapes can be produced, and with fewer lines of code, using the old Graphics class. What's the big advantage of using Shapes?

The answer to this question is that, unlike the drawings of shapes produced by the Graphics class, a Shape *is* a genuine object with its own methods, so you can interface with it in a variety of ways to produce quite sophisticated effects. One way to see the power of this 'proper' object oriented approach to graphics is to consider how Java 2D allows us to implement the various affine transformations we studied in Chapter 2.

Let's begin with the simplest transformation: the translation. Consider the following paint() method.

```
public void paint(Graphics g)
{
    Graphics2D gg =
        (Graphics2D)getContentPane().getGraphics();
    Shape shape = new Ellipse2D.Double(0,0,40,20);
    for (int x = 0; x < frameWidth; x += 40) {
        for (int y = 0; y < frameHeight; y += 20) {
            AffineTransform transform = AffineTransform.
                getTranslateInstance(x, y);
            gg.setTransform(transform);
            gg.draw(shape);
        }
    }
}
```

Here we have used the Ellipse2D.Double class to create a Shape which is an ellipse bounded by the rectangle with upper-left coordinates at (0,0), width 40 and height 20.

Now look at the nested for loops (the parameters frameWidth and frameHeight have the same meaning as in the cloverleaf example above—they contain the width and height of the drawing area within the frame and are recalculated each time the window is resized). The AffineTransform class contains several static methods which produce the standard transforms we considered in Chapter 2 (translation, rotation, scaling and shearing). To generate a translation, we call the static method getTranslateInstance(). Its two arguments are the horizontal and vertical distance by which the translation is to shift a Shape. (Note that x and y specify the *differences* between the final and initial locations, not the coordinates of the final position.)

Once an AffineTransform has been created and stored in the transform object, we call the setTransform() method of the Graphics2D class to apply the transform to the next Shape that is to be drawn. The result of this program is shown in Figure 3.16.

The main idea behind this program is that a Shape object is built once only, and then translated to each position where it is to be drawn. As we will see below, a Shape can be arbitrarily complex, so the advantage of only having to construct it once can be substantial.

The AffineTransform class provides two methods for rotating a Shape, both of which are named getRotateInstance(). They differ in their arguments. The first method takes one double argument which specifies the angle (in radians) through which the Shape is to be rotated, with the rotation being about the origin. The second method takes three double arguments: the rotation angle and the x and y coordinates of the point about which the rotation occurs.

There are also methods for scaling and shearing a Shape. The getScaleInstance() method takes two double arguments: the scaling factors in the x and y directions, respectively. The getShearInstance() method also takes two double arguments: the first being the multiplier by which coordinates are shifted in the direction of the x axis as a function of their y coordinate, and the second being the same with the roles of x and y reversed. Shearing is always done relative to the origin.

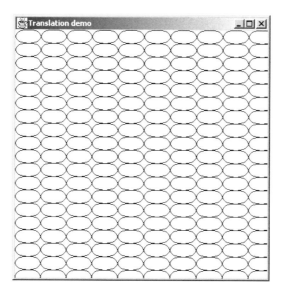

Affine transforms can be combined using the `concatenate()` or `preConcatenate()` methods. These methods work by applying matrix multiplication to combine two affine transforms, as described in Chapter 2. It is easiest to understand how these methods work by seeing an example.

Suppose we wish to generate an ellipse, then rotate it through $\pi/4$ radians (45 degrees) about its centre, and finally scale it by a factor of 2 in the x direction and 1.5 in the y direction. We can do this using the following code.

```java
public void paint(Graphics g)
{
    Graphics2D gg = (Graphics2D)g;
    Shape ellipse = new Ellipse2D.Double(0, 0, 40, 20);
    AffineTransform transform = AffineTransform.
        getRotateInstance(Math.PI / 4.0, 20, 10);
    transform.preConcatenate(AffineTransform.
        getScaleInstance(2.0, 1.5));
    gg.setTransform(transform);
    gg.draw(ellipse);
}
```

We create the ellipse as in the earlier example, and then generate a `transform` for the rotation (note the use of the static `PI` constant value from the `Math` class to provide the value for π). Recall from Chapter 2 that the matrices which contribute to a compound affine transformation are applied from *right* to *left*, so if we wish to do the scaling *after* the rotation, we must multiply the rotation matrix by placing the scaling matrix on its left. We can use the `preConcatenate()` method to do this. The effect of a statement such as:

```java
transform.preConcatenate(otherTransform);
```

is to multiply `otherTransform` by `transform` (with `otherTransform` on the left), and place the matrix product back in `transform`.

If we said instead:

```java
transform.concatenate(otherTransform);
```

we would multiply transform by otherTransform (with transform on the left this time), and store the product in transform. This means that the affine transformation represented by otherTransform would be applied *before* that represented by transform.

If we adapt to thinking of the components of a transformation in reverse order, each of the 'get instance' methods listed above has a corresponding method which generates the same transformation and concatenates it to an existing transformation. For example, we could rewrite the last code example using the rotate() shortcut method as:

```
public void paint(Graphics g)
{
    Graphics2D gg = (Graphics2D)g;
    Shape ellipse = new Ellipse2D.Double(0, 0, 40, 20);
    AffineTransform transform = AffineTransform.
        getScaleInstance(2.0, 1.5);
    transform.rotate(Math.PI / 4.0, 20, 10);
    gg.setTransform(transform);
    gg.draw(ellipse);
}
```

Here we create the transform with the scaling operation (which is to be performed *last*). We then call the rotate() method, which concatenates a rotation matrix by multiplying the existing matrix in the transform object on the right (which means the rotation will be done *before* the scaling).

There are similar translate(), scale(), and shear() shortcut methods, each of which has the same argument list as the corresponding 'get instance' method described above.

We can also define an AffineTransform object directly from the matrix elements m_{ij} as specified in the top two rows of the general transformation matrix we introduced in Chapter 2, and which we reproduce here for reference:

$$\begin{bmatrix} x' \\ y' \\ 1 \end{bmatrix} = \begin{bmatrix} m_{00} & m_{01} & m_{02} \\ m_{10} & m_{11} & m_{12} \\ 0 & 0 & 1 \end{bmatrix} \begin{bmatrix} x \\ y \\ 1 \end{bmatrix}$$

The AffineTransform class has several constructors that allow these matrix elements to be specified directly, either as floats or doubles. For example, we may declare a transformation as:

```
AffineTransform transform = new AffineTransform(1.0, -0.5,
    0.0, -0.341, 2.0, 0.9);
```

which corresponds to the transformation equation:

$$\begin{bmatrix} x' \\ y' \\ 1 \end{bmatrix} = \begin{bmatrix} 1.0 & -0.5 & 0.0 \\ -0.341 & 2.0 & 0.9 \\ 0 & 0 & 1 \end{bmatrix} \begin{bmatrix} x \\ y \\ 1 \end{bmatrix}$$

There are several other useful methods in the AffineTransform class, so the reader is urged to consult the JDK documentation for details.

3.6   Line styles and the Stroke interface

Java 2D offers support for a variety of line styles through the Stroke interface and its implementing class, BasicStroke.

The Stroke interface defines only a single method with the prototype:

```
Shape createStrokedShape(Shape figure);
```

The argument figure is the area (such as a rectangle or ellipse) around which an outline is to be drawn. The implementation of createStrokedShape() must calculate another Shape object that represents this outline. To understand what is meant by this second shape, suppose we wished to draw a very thick dashed line. Each dash in the line is a separate rectangular shape, and the collection of all the individual dashes together make up the overall dashed line. It is this collection of rectangles, each representing one of the dashes in the line, that comprise the Shape object calculated by the createStrokedShape() method.

It is important to realize that the geometric object represented by a Shape can consist of several, unconnected shapes, so that, for example, the collection of all the separate dashes making up a dashed line can be represented by a single Shape object.

The main class provided by Java 2D for producing line styles is BasicStroke, which implements the Stroke interface. The BasicStroke class allows you to specify the following characteristics of a line:

- line width;
- the *cap style*, which determines the appearance of the ends of line segments;
- the *join style*, which determines how two line segments meet at corners;
- the *dash pattern*, which determines the pattern used to create dashed or dotted lines.

3.6.1   Cap styles

Three cap styles are provided as constants in the BasicStroke class: CAP_SQUARE, CAP_BUTT, and CAP_ROUND. The CAP_SQUARE style adds an extra square end that extends the length of the line *at each end* by half its width (thus effectively extending the length of the entire line by an amount equal to its width). The CAP_BUTT style squares off the ends of a line without extending its length, and the CAP_ROUND style adds a semi-circle with radius equal to half the width of the line to each end. Examples of the three cap styles are shown in Figure 3.17.

Figure 3.17:
Cap styles in the
BasicStroke class.
From left to right:
CAP_SQUARE, CAP_BUTT
and CAP_ROUND.

The line segments in Figure 3.17 were drawn using the following code:

```
public void paint(Graphics g)
{
    Graphics2D gg = (Graphics2D)g;
```

```
Shape shape = new Line2D.Double(20, 70, 50, 110);

BasicStroke stroke;
stroke = new BasicStroke(10, BasicStroke.CAP_SQUARE,
    BasicStroke.JOIN_BEVEL);
gg.setStroke(stroke);
gg.draw(shape);

stroke = new BasicStroke(10, BasicStroke.CAP_BUTT,
    BasicStroke.JOIN_BEVEL);
gg.setStroke(stroke);
gg.setTransform(AffineTransform.
    getTranslateInstance(100, 0));
gg.draw(shape);

stroke = new BasicStroke(10, BasicStroke.CAP_ROUND,
    BasicStroke.JOIN_BEVEL);
gg.setStroke(stroke);
gg.setTransform(AffineTransform.
    getTranslateInstance(200, 0));
gg.draw(shape);
}
```

A new BasicStroke object was created for each line segment. There are a variety of constructors provided in the BasicStroke class—the one used here takes three arguments which are, respectively, the line width (here set to 10 pixels), the cap style and the join style. (The join style only has an effect if two line segments meet at a corner, so is not visible in Figure 3.17, but there is no constructor that allows only the cap style to be set.)

3.6.2 Join styles

Three styles are provided for joining line segments at corners in figures such as polygons. The styles are illustrated in Figure 3.18, where a triangle is drawn using each of the styles. Note that the triangle's vertices are the same in all three cases—the differences in appearance are due solely to the join style used.

Figure 3.18:
The join styles (left to right) JOIN_BEVEL, JOIN_MITER, and JOIN_ROUND.

The JOIN_BEVEL style produces blunt corners by joining with a straight line the outside edges of the line segments that meet at the corner. The JOIN_MITER style (note that the American spelling of 'miter' as opposed to the British 'mitre' is used in the style's name) produces pointed corners by extending the outside edges of the two line segments until they meet. The JOIN_ROUND style caps each corner with a circular segment.

In the case of JOIN_MITER, an additional parameter known as the *mitre limit* can be specified, which sets an upper limit on the distance that a corner can be extended to produce a mitre join. If two lines that are almost parallel meet, a very long point could be drawn to produce a mitre joint if no such limit were imposed. The mitre limit is a float parameter, and has a default value of 10.0.

The numerical value of the mitre limit is not used directly to calculate the maximum length of a mitred join. Rather, the maximum allowed length of a join is the mitre limit multiplied by half the width of the line. Thus, with a line thickness of 40 pixels, say, and the default value of 10.0 for the mitre limit, the maximum allowable length of a mitred corner is 200 pixels, not 10. Any corners that would exceed this length are drawn as bevelled joins (that is, using the JOIN_BEVEL algorithm).

3.6.3   Dashed lines

Unlike many graphics packages, Java 2D does not provide default settings for dashed and dotted lines. You must define your own dash pattern by placing values in an array of floats, and then using this array in the construction of a BasicStroke object.

The elements in the array specify the lengths of the alternating dashes and spaces that are to be used in the pattern. This array is then passed as one of the arguments to the BasicStroke constructor. An example follows.

```java
public void paint(Graphics g)
{
    Shape shape;
    Graphics2D gg = (Graphics2D)g;
    float[] dash = {10, 5, 5, 5};
    BasicStroke stroke;
    stroke = new BasicStroke(1, BasicStroke.CAP_BUTT,
        BasicStroke.JOIN_BEVEL, 10.0f,
        dash, 0.0f);
    gg.setStroke(stroke);
    shape = new Polygon();
    ((Polygon)shape).addPoint(20, 70);
    ((Polygon)shape).addPoint(350, 110);
    ((Polygon)shape).addPoint(80, 270);
    gg.draw(shape);
}
```

Here we have defined the float array dash, with 4 elements. This specifies a dashed pattern with a distance of 10 drawn, then a blank space of 5, followed by a dash of 5, followed by another blank space of 5. The final entry in the BasicStroke constructor is a single float value called the *dash phase*, and gives an offset into the array at which the pattern should start. A dash phase of zero means that the dashing pattern should begin with the first element of the array. A dash phase of 7.0, say, means that the first dash would have length 3.0 (10.0 − 7.0), after which the pattern is the same as before.

This code produces the triangle shown in Figure 3.19.

The dash pattern is applied to the Shape by measuring the distance along the outline as it is drawn and comparing it with the array entries. When a distance equal to the total of all entries in the array is reached on the outline, the array is used over again from the start. This may seem obvious, but has an interesting effect if the array contains an odd number of elements. The reader is urged to run the above code sample, except delete the last 5 from the dash array. Try to predict the result before you run the program.

Figure 3.19:
A polygon drawn with dash pattern {10, 5, 5, 5}.

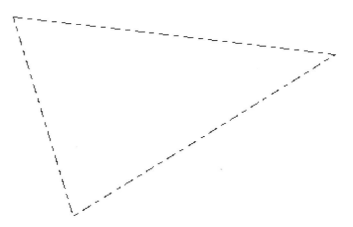

3.6.4 Antialiasing and the RenderingHints class

Recall from Chapter 2 that antialiasing is a technique for reducing the jagged-edge effect seen on lines, curves and text drawn on a digital display. Java 2D allows antialiasing to be implemented on any graphical output. As a simple example, we will apply antialiasing to the dashed polygon drawn in the previous section. To do this, we need to add only a single line to the code given above for drawing the dashed polygon. Adding the following line at any point before the call to draw() will switch antialiasing on, with result shown in Figure 3.20.

```
gg.setRenderingHint(RenderingHints.KEY_ANTIALIASING,
    RenderingHints.VALUE_ANTIALIAS_ON);
```

Figure 3.20:
The dashed polygon with antialiasing switched on.

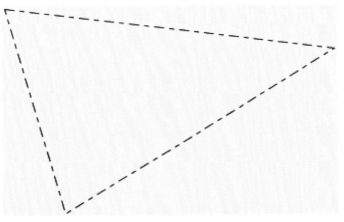

Comparison with Figure 3.19 shows that the jagged effect is much reduced when antialiasing is used.

Note that antialiasing is specified by using the setRenderingHint() method from the Graphics2D class. It may seem odd that the word 'hint' is used in this method's name, but there is a good reason for this. The setRenderingHint() method merely *suggests* options that might be used when the image is drawn—it does not *guarantee* that these features will be implemented. As we mentioned in

Chapter 2, in order for antialiasing to work, the display device must support more than two colours. Attempting to use antialiasing on, say, a printer that only draw black pixels (and not shades of grey) will simply not work, since the antialiasing algorithm depends on the production of colours that are intermediate between that of the line and that of the background on which the line is drawn.

Using a rendering hint to specify that antialiasing should be used therefore tells the graphics renderer that, if the display device supports intermediate colours, use antialiasing, but if it doesn't, then don't bother.

The setRenderingHint() method specifies a hint by means of a *key* and a *value* that corresponds to the key. The key is the first argument to the method, and must be an object of subclass RenderingHints.Key. The key specifies which hint is to be added to the graphics context—in our example above, we specified that antialiasing should be added. The available keys are all declared as static fields in the RenderingHints class. Details are available in the JDK documentation.

The value that corresponds to a given key must be one of the static fields in the RenderingHints class whose name begins with the VALUE prefix. The available values for a given key should be obvious from the list of possible values given in the documentation for RenderingHints. For example, for the KEY_ANTIALIASING key, the possible values are VALUE_ANTIALIAS_ON, VALUE_ANTIALIAS_OFF, and VALUE_ANTIALIAS_DEFAULT. (The 'default' option just uses the default value for the current output device.)

The RenderingHints class may be used specify several features which can be implemented on some, but not all, display devices. For many of the available keys, the choices of value allow the programmer to produce either higher quality, but slower, rendering, or cruder but faster rendering. By switching antialiasing on, for example, the output looks better but takes longer to draw. A more general key is KEY_RENDERING, which has the three corresponding values VALUE_RENDER_SPEED, VALUE_RENDER_QUALITY and VALUE_RENDER_DEFAULT. The value of this hint is used in a number of internal rendering algorithms to choose forms that are either faster but produce poorer quality output, or slower but produce a better image. If our application produces single images with a large amount of detail, the 'quality' value would be more appropriate, but if we are generating animations where each image must be drawn quickly, then the 'speed' option is better.

Many of the rendering hints will only have a noticeable effect in more complex programs or on certain types of display devices. For reference, the complete set of keys available is shown in the following table:

Key	Possible values	Description
KEY_ANTIALIASING	VALUE_ANTIALIAS_ON, _OFF, _DEFAULT	Controls the display of antialiasing in lines and curves (but not text).
KEY_TEXT_ANTIALIASING	VALUE_TEXT_ANTIALIAS_ON, _OFF, _DEFAULT	Controls antialiasing in text.
KEY_COLOR_RENDERING	VALUE_COLOR_RENDER_SPEED, _QUALITY, _DEFAULT	Controls the quality with which colours are rendered (drawn to the display device).

Key	Possible values	Description
KEY_DITHERING	VALUE_ENABLE, _DISABLE, _DEFAULT	On devices with limited colours, intermediate colours can be produced by *dithering*, or mixing available colours on adjacent pixels. Turns this effect on or off.
KEY_ALPHA_INTERPOLATION	VALUE_ALPHA_INTERPOLATION_QUALITY, _SPEED, _DEFAULT	*Alpha compositing* is the process of making a colour or image partially transparent, and thus merging it with background graphics. This key determines the quality with which this is done.
KEY_FRACTIONALMETRICS	VALUE_FRACTIONALMETRICS_ON, _OFF, _DEFAULT	Text displayed with a 'fractional metric' can appear of higher quality.
KEY_INTERPOLATION	VALUE_INTERPOLATION_BICUBIC, _BILINEAR, _NEAREST_NEIGHBOR	If an image is transformed using an affine transformation, the new pixel positions may not correspond with pixels on the display device. The display pixel colours must be determined by an interpolation algorithm, which this hint specifies.
KEY_RENDERING	VALUE_RENDERING_SPEED, _QUALITY, _DEFAULT	Specifies how accurately shapes are drawn to the output device.

3.7 Text

In early versions of Java, text was drawn using the drawString() method of the Graphics class. A Font object could be created and used to set the font of text that was printed, but beyond this, the capabilities for dealing with text were fairly limited.

In Java 2D, a great many powerful text-handling utilities have been added. Many of these features are aimed at applications that include text editing facilities as well as graphics. Since we are concerned mainly with graphics in this book, we will concentrate on those aspects of text handling that deal with the display of text as part of an overall graphical image, rather than its application to word processing.

The manipulation of text in Java 2D has been separated to a large extent from the graphics context. The TextLayout class (which is derived directly from Object) contains most of the functionality that is required. Not only does it contain all the methods needed for creating the string of text, it also contains its own draw() method, distinct from that in Graphics2D.

Let us begin with a simple example of how TextLayout can be used to display some text.

```
import java.awt.font.*;
public void paint(Graphics g)
{
    Shape shape = null;
    Graphics2D gg = (Graphics2D)g;
    FontRenderContext fontRenderContext =
        gg.getFontRenderContext();
    Font font = new Font("SansSerif", Font.BOLD, 48);
    TextLayout text = new TextLayout("Hello world!", font,
        fontRenderContext);
    text.draw(gg, 20, 70);
}
```

Fonts are treated with their own set of classes, and to access them we need to import the java.awt.font package. When creating a TextLayout object, we will always need a FontRenderContext to pass to its constructor. The need for a FontRenderContext arises because of the variations in output devices that may be used to display the text. Devices with different resolutions sometimes display fonts slightly differently, and the FontRenderContext class is designed to cope with these differences. We can always obtain this object directly from the graphics context, as we do here by using the getFontRenderContext() method in the Graphics2D class.

Next, we create a Font in which to display the text. Here we use a SansSerif font (often known as Helvetica or Arial), and make it bold face and quite large (48 points).

To create a TextLayout, we need to pass it only three arguments: the actual text to be displayed (which can be a constant string as here, or a String object), the font, and the FontRenderContext object.

Finally, we call the draw() method for the TextLayout. The arguments of this version of draw() are, firstly, the graphics context, and then the coordinates of the starting point of the text. Running this program will produce the text 'Hello world!'.

So far, we have not seen anything terribly dramatic about the TextLayout class. However, we can begin to realize its power when we understand that the outlines of individual characters in a TextLayout object are represented as Shapes. This means that we can apply all the tools we have studied in this chapter to text as well as to geometric shapes.

First, we need to see how to get hold of the TextLayout object as a Shape. We can do this using the getOutline() method in the TextLayout class. For example, we can insert the line:

```
shape = text.getOutline
    (AffineTransform.getTranslateInstance(20, 100));
```

immediately after the creation of the TextLayout object in the preceding example to obtain the Shape object describing the outline of the text 'Hello world!'. The argument of the getOutline() method is an optional AffineTransform. We have translated the Shape downwards and to the right so that it will lie within the display area of the Frame. If we passed a null argument to getOutline(), the baseline of the Shape's text would be positioned at (0, 0), so that the actual text would lie above the top edge of the Frame and not be visible.

To prove we do in fact have this outline, we can display it in the usual way with the method call:

```
gg.draw(shape);
```

and obtain this result:

Now that we have the text as a Shape, we can apply any affine transformation to it, change the style of the lines that draw the outline, or insert a fill pattern in the interior of the text.

For example, we can apply a shear to the text to slant it to one side, and then fill it with the smiley pattern we used earlier. The code is:

```
public void paint(Graphics g)
{
    Shape shape = null;
    Graphics2D gg = (Graphics2D)g;
    FontRenderContext fontRenderContext =
        gg.getFontRenderContext();
    Font font = new Font("SansSerif", Font.BOLD, 72);
    TextLayout text = new TextLayout("Hello world!", font,
        fontRenderContext);
    shape =
        text.getOutline(AffineTransform.
        getTranslateInstance(20, 100));
    gg.setTransform(AffineTransform.
        getShearInstance(0.5, 0));
    int smileySize = 30;
    Paint pattern = new
        TexturePaint(createSmiley(smileySize),
        new Rectangle2D.Double(20, 70, smileySize,
        smileySize));
    gg.setPaint(pattern);
    gg.fill(shape);
    gg.setPaint(Color.black);
    gg.draw(shape);
}
```

The result is the following:

EXERCISES

1. If you have access to a printer, try running the SimplePrint program given in the text. Experiment with the printer dialog box to see which controls and options have an effect within the program.

2. If the printed output on your printer clips the rectangle so that not all of it can be seen, experiment with setting the imageable area on the page to see if

you can display the entire rectangle without changing its coordinates in the program.

3. Determine how accurate the imageable area parameters are for your printer by attempting to print a rectangle that is exactly the same size as the imageable area. Can you see all four sides of the rectangle?

4. A common feature of Web pages is a *hit counter*, which is a count of the number of times a page has been visited. Many Web counters create a JPEG file containing the number of hits displayed in some exotic font, such as images of building blocks or lottery balls. Using the JPGFile program in this chapter as a model, write a Java program which has a simple graphical front end consisting of a button and a small display area. Initially, the display area shows the number 0. Each time the button is pushed by the user, the number increases by 1. At the same time as you update the on-screen display, write the number to disk as a JPEG file. You way wish to experiment with some of the text drawing methods described at the end of this chapter to produce some fancier output.

5. Experiment with the various '2D' classes that implement the Shape interface, such as Ellipse2D, Rectangle2D, and so on. Initially, you can modify the LineShape program given in the text by just replacing the line that creates the Shape in the paint() method, but you may also wish to write a more sophisticated program with some controls that allow the user to choose which shape to draw, specify its size and position, and so on.

6. Compare a circle drawn using Ellipse2D with one drawn using Bresenham's circle algorithm from Chapter 1. The comparison is easier to make if you draw two circles of the same centre and radius, using a different algorithm for each. Use different colours so you can see whether the two circles coincide. Also, compare these two circle-drawing algorithms with a circle drawn using the drawOval() method from the old Graphics class. Which algorithm do you think drawOval() uses to draw circles?

7. Look up the Polygon class in the Java documentation, and use a Polygon object to draw a regular hexagon (a hexagon with all sides the same length and all internal angles equal).

8. Experiment with GeneralPath and try to draw the outline of a wine bottle (you may choose your favourite type of wine). Use the bilateral symmetry of the bottle.

9. Using a gradient fill, add some shading to the wine bottle, making it appear light green on the right and shading towards a dark green on the left.

10. Create a rectangular label for the wine bottle. The label should be texture-filled with some simple geometric pattern such as cross-hatching, and should have some text in the middle stating the brand and vintage of the wine.

11. Draw a filled circle with a hexagonal hole in the middle by using the Polygon from question 7 and some Area objects.

12. Write a class Star which inherits Polygon. The class should draw a star where the number of points, the centre, the radius (distance from the centre to one of the points), inner radius (distance from the centre to the midpoint of the 'V' between two points) and orientation (angle between the positive x axis and the first point drawn) can all be specified in the constructor. A sample

Star with 8 points is shown in the diagrams used to illustrate the AlphaComposite class in the text.

13. Figure 3.12 shows the result of the destination over rule where the graphics are drawn on a BufferedImage, which is in turn drawn onto the screen. The star is drawn first, using the source over rule, followed by the ellipse, using the destination over rule. When the same sequence of drawing operations is done directly on the screen (without using a BufferedImage), the ellipse is not visible at all. Why?

14. Figure 3.15 shows the effect of using the 'clear' rule to draw an ellipse on top of a star, both of which are drawn onto a BufferedImage. When the same sequence of drawing operations is done directly on the screen, the ellipse appears as solid black, rather than white. Why?

15. An opaque red star is drawn directly onto the screen. Next, a blue ellipse with an alpha of 0.5 is drawn onto a BufferedImage and then the BufferedImage is drawn on top of the red star using the 'destination in' rule. Assuming that part of the ellipse overlaps part of the star (but not all of it), what will appear on screen? Try to predict the result using the composition equations before writing the code to verify your predictions.

16. Rewrite the Clover program in the text using composition rules to create the clover pattern.

17. Use the hexagonal object from question 7 together with an AffineTransform to tile the drawing area with a honeycomb pattern. As a variant on this question, try filling each hexagon with a random Color.

18. Rewrite the Clover program in the text using AffineTransforms to generate the radial line pattern by rotating the first line about the centre of the window.

19. Consider a line of thickness 10 that is to be drawn between points A and B. In the examples in the text, the mathematical line joining A and B splits the thick line down the middle, so that 5 pixels of the drawn line's thickness occur on either side of the mathematical line.

   In many applications, we would like the drawn line to lie entirely on one side of the mathematical line (for example, if the drawn line must fit inside a boundary of some sort). Write an implementation of the Shape interface that draws lines that fit entirely on one side or the other of the mathematical line that joins their endpoints. Note that since the Stroke being used is a property of Graphics2D and not of the Shape, you will need to retrieve the current Stroke and use this to adjust the location of the line.

20. Try to predict the result of using an odd number of elements in the array specifying the dash pattern in a BasicStroke. Test your prediction by running the program.

21. Experiment with some of the rendering hints to see if you can detect any differences between various value settings for a given key. (The results of this exercise will vary, depending on the monitor you are using. On some systems, you can change the capabilities of a display by setting some system parameters. On Windows, for example, you can change the number of colours and screen resolution in the control panel, although you should seek advice if you have not done this before.)

Three-dimensional graphics: projections and transformations

4.1 Displaying three dimensions on a flat surface

Much of what we have learned about two-dimensional graphics can be applied directly to the representation of three-dimensional objects on a monitor or printer. However, the introduction of a third spatial dimension poses a major problem that we did not have to face in the two-dimensional world: how do we transform a three-dimensional scene so that it may be rendered on a two-dimensional drawing surface?

The fact that this *is* a problem may not be immediately obvious. After all, we are so accustomed to seeing three-dimensional images portrayed on flat surfaces in photographs, television, cinema and so on that we may think it is a quite straightforward process to do this. However, a little thought will show that things may not be quite as simple as we expect.

Let us consider a simple example. Suppose we wish to draw a cube on a monitor screen, but the only information provided to the program is the set of eight three-dimensional points specifying the cube's corners. How do we derive the set of eight corresponding *two*-dimensional points specifying the cube's corners on the monitor?

Solving this problem actually leads us into many of the fundamental areas of three-dimensional graphics. To keep things simple at first, suppose that the cube is a wire-frame model—only its edges are to be drawn (that is, we will not fill in the faces of the cube). What factors will affect the positioning of the edges as drawn to the screen?

It is common, when discussing three-dimensional graphics, to make use of analogies with a camera taking a picture of a scene, or an observer standing at some point and viewing the scene. We will use some of these analogies as well, but it is important to realize that the accuracy of any analogy has its limits. There are many features that can be implemented in a computer-generated three-dimensional image that are not possible with a camera or a human observer.

With these caveats in mind, let us try the analogy of a human observer viewing the wire-frame cube. What influences how the observer perceives the cube?

First, the observer must be a certain *distance* from the cube. Changing the viewing distance has the obvious effect of making the cube look larger or smaller, but it also has another more subtle effect: the relative positions of the front and back of the cube vary as the viewing distance is altered. (It is easiest if you can try some simple viewing experiments yourself as you read this section. If you can build a wire-frame or matchstick-frame cube, so much the better, but even a cardboard box will help in the visualizations.)

Second, the observer must choose a viewing *direction* relative to the cube. If the cube is a large box sitting on the floor, for example, the observer can change the viewing direction by walking around the box, or by moving up or down. Changing the viewing direction changes the relative positions of the edges of the cube as perceived by the observer.

These simple experiments should convince you that there is a fair bit of work to be done in converting the eight three-dimensional points specifying the corners of the cube into two-dimensionsal points that allow the edges to be drawn on a flat surface. There are several methods known as *projections* by which this conversion can be done.

Before we consider projections in some detail, we will give a brief overview of the process for constructing a three-dimensional image.

4.1.1 The viewing pipeline

In the two-dimensional case, the steps required to produce a finished image on a monitor screen or a printer, known as the *viewing pipeline*, could be summarized as follows:

- build the scene in world coordinates by drawing lines and geometric figures, filling areas and so on;
- optionally transform the scene by applying translation, rotation, and so on;
- convert the world coordinates to device coordinates;
- clip the image to the viewport on the display device;
- render the image on the display device.

In three-dimensional graphics, these steps are still present, but some extra steps are often required. In particular, after the transformation step, a *projection* step is necessary to convert the scene from three dimensions to two dimensions.

4.2 Projections

Projection is the process by which a three-dimensional image is converted into a two-dimensional representation. Fortunately, projection is one process where an analogy is not only helpful, but accurate, so we need feel no guilt about using one.

Projections are often divided into two main types: *perspective* projections and *parallel* projections. Since the perspective projection is the most familiar and realistic projection, we will consider it first.

4.2.1 Perspective projections

To construct a perspective projection of the wire-frame cube we considered earlier, you will need, in addition to the cube, a flat projection screen (a piece of white card will do), and a strong, concentrated light source (such as a small, unfrosted light bulb). Position the screen behind the cube, and the light in front of the cube. You should see a sharply-defined shadow of the wire frame on the screen. Keeping the cube and screen fixed, move the light back and forth, and up and down relative to the cube. Note how the shadow outline changes as you do this. The shadow is the *perspective projection* of the cube onto a two-dimensional surface, and represents what we wish to display on the monitor or printer.

Before we get into the mathematics required to calculate this projection, it is helpful to describe the concepts involved in plain English. The light used to create the shadow is located at the *centre of projection* (sometimes called the *viewpoint*). If you removed the light and placed a camera at that position, pointed the camera towards the cube and took a picture, the two-dimensional image of the cube you obtain should be the same shape as the shadow cast by the light.

The projection screen onto which the shadows were projected is known as the *viewing plane* (or just *view plane*). If the view plane is kept perpendicular to the line of sight from the centre of projection to the screen, the only effect that moving the screen relative to the cube can have is to make the projection larger or smaller. (If you rotate the screen so that it is no longer perpendicular to the line of sight, the image of the cube will become distorted, but we will not consider that case just yet.)

The projection of a three-dimensional point (such as one of the corners of the cube) onto the view plane is accomplished by drawing a straight line from the centre of projection (the light) through the point (the cube's corner) and extending the line until it intersects the view plane (the screen). When we have done this for all points in the three-dimensional object, the resulting image on the view plane will be the perspective projection of the three-dimensional object. See Figure 4.1.

Figure 4.1: A perspective projection from centre of projection P (directly in front of the face of the cube) onto the view plane. The two lines show the projections of two corners of the cube.

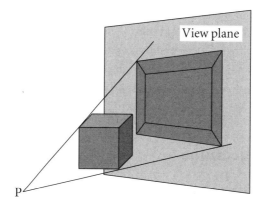

4.2.2 Parallel projections

Returning to our experiment with the light and screen in the previous section, try moving the light further away from the cube and screen. Now consider the angle between two of the projection lines—for example, lines passing through two of the cube's corners. As the light gets further from the screen, this angle becomes smaller and smaller, since the lines are getting closer and closer to being parallel.

If we remove the light to infinity, then the lines will actually be parallel, and the resulting shadow on the screen is known as a *parallel projection* of the cube. (Readers may complain that we can't move a light infinitely far away, and, even if we could, we would then need an infinitely bright light in order for it to cast a shadow. The point of the argument, of course, is that to obtain a parallel projection, we use projection lines that are parallel to each other. Once we have realized that, we don't need the light any more.)

It is possible to simulate a parallel projection with our wire-frame cube model by using the sun as the light source, since its distance is large enough relative to the distance between the cube and the screen that it can be considered infinite for our purposes. The experiment is worth trying, since you should find a qualitative (as well as quantitative) difference between a parallel projection and a perspective projection. See Figure 4.2.

Figure 4.2:
A parallel projection of a cube onto a view plane. The two lines show two of the projection vectors. The cube is directly in front of the plane with one of its faces parallel to the plane, so the projection results in a single square.

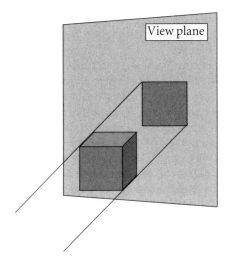

Try both projections with the cube oriented so that one of its faces is perpendicular to the line of sight of the observer. In a perspective projection, you will see that the outline of the front face of the cube (the face closest to the observer) is larger than that of the back face. In a parallel projection, both front and back faces have projections that are the same size.

The experiment illustrates a general feature of these two types of projection. A perspective projection gives a more realistic view of a scene, since to a human observer looking at a scene containing two objects of equal size and shape, the object that is further away appears smaller.

The parallel projection, however, preserves relative sizes and shapes, so that two identical objects at different distances will still appear the same size on the view plane. Thus a parallel projection will not give a realistic view of a three-dimensional scene. However, in cases where it is important to preserve the relative sizes and orientations of the objects in a scene, the parallel projection is the correct one to use. This is the case, for example, in architectural and engineering drawings of buildings or machinery, in which it is important that relative size be preserved. For this reason, blueprints are often drawn using parallel projections.

4.2.3   Three-dimensional coordinates

Before we can analyze projections mathematically, we need to specify the three-dimensional coordinate system. Since we will be using the Java 3D package for most of our graphical display work, we will use Java 3D's coordinate system, but it should be pointed out that other graphics packages (and therefore, textbooks based on these packages) sometimes use other coordinate systems. Caution should therefore be used when applying the methods in this book to other systems.

Java 3D uses a *right-handed* coordinate system, with the *x* axis increasing horizontally to the right, the *y* axis increasing vertically upwards, and the *z* axis increasing towards the observer (that is, coming out of the monitor screen). The default viewing direction is parallel to the *z* axis, looking down from above the *xy* plane. The viewing direction can, of course, be altered in the code, but the starting point is always a bird's-eye view of the *xy* plane.

Note that the orientation of the *y* axis in the Java 3D coordinate system is opposite to that in Java 2D—the *y* axis increases *upwards* in 3D, rather than downwards as in 2D.

In discussing the mathematics of the various types of projections in the next section, we will be dealing with two main coordinate systems. The first is the *world coordinate system*, which is the three-dimensional system used to represent the scene we wish to portray. The unit of length in the world system can be tailored to the system being modelled, and can range from nanometres to light years. We will express coordinates in the world system using variable names without any suffixes, so that a general point would be written as (*x*, *y*, *z*).

The second system is the *view coordinate system*, which is a two-dimensional system used to define locations on the view plane. The unit of length in the view system is the same as that in the corresponding world system. We will write view coordinates with a suffix *v*, so that a point in the view plane would be written (x_v, y_v).

If the unit of length in the world and view systems is not the pixel, a final transformation from the view system to a *device coordinate system* is needed in order that the image projected onto the view plane may be drawn on an output device. This final transformation will involve only a scaling factor, however, so we will simplify the discussions that follow by assuming that the world and view systems both use the pixel as their length unit.

There is one final matter we need to consider before discussing specific projections. Clearly the world system needs three mutually perpendicular axes and the view system needs two axes, but we have not yet specified how these axes are oriented relative to each other.

In the simplest case, the view plane will be parallel to one of the coordinate planes in the world system, and the axes in the view system will coincide with two of the axes in the world system. For example, we might specify the plane *z* = 0 (the *xy* plane) as the view plane, and define the two view axes as identical to the *x* and *y* axes in the world system. This means that whatever projection we are using, the image will be projected onto the *xy* plane in the world system.

Remember also that on a monitor or printer, the device coordinate system is *left-handed*, with the *y* axis increasing downwards. Thus in order to display the final two-dimensional projection on the screen, we must convert from a right-handed to a left-handed coordinate system.

4.2.4   Mathematics of projections

Parallel projections

We will consider the parallel projection first, as it is the simpler of the two projections to analyze. There are actually two types of parallel projection, depending on the orientation of the view plane relative to the projection direction. The simplest case, known as an *orthographic projection*, requires the view plane to be perpendicular to the projection direction. The more general case, where the view plane is not perpendicular to the projection direction, is called an *oblique projection*.

The simplest parallel projection is an orthographic projection where the view plane is the *xy* plane (and the viewing direction is therefore parallel to the *z* axis). In that case, a point with coordinates (*x*, *y*, *z*) projects onto the view plane with coordinates (*x*, *y*), since we can simply ignore the *z* coordinate.

From this simple case, there are several generalizations we can make. We can keep the *xy* plane as the view plane and consider an oblique projection onto it. In this case, the viewing direction is no longer parallel to the *z* axis. Alternatively, we can continue to consider only orthographic projections, but move the view plane so it is no longer parallel to any of the coordinate axes in the world system. Finally, we can consider the most general parallel projection where the view plane can be positioned anywhere in the three-dimensional space, and the projection itself can be orthographic or oblique.

It turns out that the case where the view plane is not the *xy* plane can be handled by transforming the scene so that the view plane *becomes* the *xy* plane. We therefore need only consider the case of an oblique projection onto the *xy* plane.

Figure 4.3: Oblique parallel projection. All points are projected parallel to the projection vector **d** onto the *xy* plane. Point *P* is projected onto point (x_v, y_v).

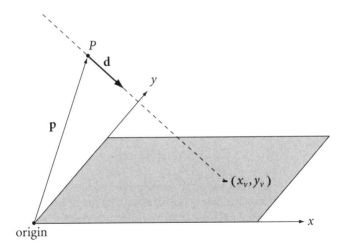

We will derive the equations giving the projection onto the *xy* plane of a point *P* along the direction given by the vector $\mathbf{d} = (d_x, d_y, d_z)$. The equation is fairly easy to derive if we use the vector equation of a line that passes through the point *P* and is parallel to the vector **d**. Let the vector extending from the origin to *P* be $\mathbf{p} = (p_x, p_y, p_z)$ (see Figure 4.3). Then the vector equation of the line is

$$\mathbf{r} = \mathbf{p} + t\mathbf{d} \qquad (4.1)$$

where $\mathbf{r} = (x, y, z)$ is a vector pointing to a point on the line and *t* is a scalar parameter in the range $(-\infty, \infty)$. We need to find the intersection of this line with the *xy* plane. The equation of this plane is simply $z = 0$. Using the *z* component from equation 4.1, we can obtain the value of *t* where the line intersects the *xy* plane, and find that

$$t = -\frac{p_z}{d_z} \qquad (4.2)$$

provided that d_z is non-zero. (If $d_z = 0$, then the projection direction is parallel to the xy plane, so no intersection will occur.)

We can now substitute this value of t back into equation 4.1, and obtain the coordinates in the view plane corresponding to the projection of **p**:

$$(x_v, y_v) = \left(p_x - \frac{p_z d_x}{d_z}, \quad p_y - \frac{p_z d_y}{d_z} \right) \qquad (4.3)$$

As an example, we can reclaim the orthographic projection by setting **d** parallel to the z axis, and pointing in the negative z direction: $\mathbf{d} = (0, 0, -1)$. Then the projection reduces to $(x_v, y_v) = (p_x, p_y)$ as expected.

There are two oblique projections that are used often enough for them to have names of their own: the *cavalier* and *cabinet* projections. Both of these projections are defined by the smallest angle α between the line given by equation 4.1 and the xy plane. If the angle is chosen so that $\tan \alpha = 1$ (so that the angle is $\pi/4$ radians, or 45°), the resulting projection is called a *cavalier projection*, while if $\tan \alpha = 2$, we have a *cabinet* projection.

Specifying $\tan \alpha$ does not specify the projection uniquely, however. We can determine the set of possible projection vectors for a given value of $\tan \alpha$ by using a little more linear algebra and trigonometry.

We begin with the trigonometric identity

$$1 + \tan^2\alpha = \sec^2\alpha$$

Since $\sec \alpha = 1/\cos \alpha$, and $\cos \alpha = \sin(\pi/2 - \alpha)$, we have

$$\sin^2(\pi/2 - \alpha) = \frac{1}{1 + \tan^2\alpha}$$

Using the identity $\cos^2(\pi/2 - \alpha) + \sin^2(\pi/2 - \alpha) = 1$, we have

$$\cos^2(\pi/2 - \alpha) = 1 - \frac{1}{1 + \tan^2\alpha} \qquad (4.4)$$

Usually, the point being projected onto the plane is situated above the xy plane (its z coordinate is positive), so that the projection vector **d** has a negative z component (since it must project the point downwards onto the plane $z = 0$). The angle α is therefore the angle between $-\mathbf{d}$ and the projection plane. The angle between $-\mathbf{d}$ and the *normal* to the plane is therefore $\pi/2 - \alpha$. If **d** is a unit vector, then the scalar product of $-\mathbf{d}$ and the unit vector $\mathbf{z} = (0, 0, 1)$ (along the positive z axis) is $\cos(\pi/2 - \alpha)$:

$$\cos(\pi/2 - \alpha) = -\mathbf{d} \cdot \mathbf{z} = -d_z \qquad (4.5)$$

Having specified the desired angle α for the projection, we can obtain the z component of **d** from equation 4.5. The x and y components of **d** are constrained only by the fact that we specified **d** as a unit vector, so any values of d_x and d_y satisfying the following equation will produce a projection with the desired angle.

$$d_x^2 + d_y^2 = 1 - d_z^2 \qquad (4.6)$$

For example, to produce a cabinet projection, we have $\tan \alpha = 2$, so from equation 4.4, we have $\cos(\pi/2 - \alpha) = 2/\sqrt{5}$ (we consider only the positive square root, since we are dealing only with angles less than $\pi/2$). From equation 4.5 we have $d_z = -2/\sqrt{5}$ and from equation 4.6, we may choose any values for d_x and d_y such that

$$d_x^2 + d_y^2 = \frac{1}{5}$$

An acceptable projection vector is therefore

$$\mathbf{d} = \left(\frac{1}{\sqrt{10}}, \quad \frac{1}{\sqrt{10}}, \quad -\frac{2}{\sqrt{5}} \right) \tag{4.7}$$

Using equation 4.3, we obtain the coordinates in the view plane onto which a three-dimensional point P is projected.

$$\left(x_v, y_v \right) = \left(p_x + \frac{p_z}{2\sqrt{2}}, \quad p_y + \frac{p_y}{2\sqrt{2}} \right) \tag{4.8}$$

Lines parallel to the z axis retain their full length in a cavalier projection, and are foreshortened to precisely half their original length in a cabinet projection. Because we are used to seeing foreshortening in a three-dimensional view, a cabinet projection looks more realistic than a cavalier projection to a human observer. In fact, a popular optical illusion shows a cavalier projection of a cube (see Figure 4.4), and asks the observer to estimate the relative lengths of the edges in the diagram. The edges along the cube's sides look longer than those around the front face, even though they are actually all the same length.

Figure 4.4:
A cavalier projection (left) and a cabinet projection (right) of a cube. All edges in the cavalier projection are the same length, but the cabinet projection looks more realistic.

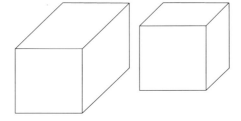

Perspective projections

In a perspective projection, all projection lines emanate from a fixed point C called the *centre of projection*. Thus to find the projection of a point P onto the view plane, we must find the intersection of the line passing through P and C with the view plane.

As with the parallel projection, we will use vector algebra to determine the projection point. We will associate vectors $\mathbf{p}$ and $\mathbf{c}$ with points P and C respectively, and use the xy plane as the view plane (see Figure 4.5). The line passing through points P and C is then

$$\mathbf{r} = \mathbf{c} + t(\mathbf{p} - \mathbf{c}) \tag{4.9}$$

The intersection of this line with the xy plane is found by setting the z component of $\mathbf{r}$ to zero and solving for t. We obtain:

$$t = -\frac{c_z}{(p_z - c_z)}$$

Substituting this into equation 4.9, we obtain the coordinates of the projected point in the view plane.

$$\left(x_v, y_v \right) = \left(c_x - c_z \frac{p_x - c_x}{p_z - c_z}, \quad c_y - c_z \frac{p_y - c_y}{p_z - c_z} \right) \qquad (4.10)$$

We can simplify this equation slightly by putting each component over a common denominator:

$$\left(x_v, y_v \right) = \left(\frac{c_x p_z - c_z p_x}{p_z - c_z}, \quad \frac{c_y p_z - c_z p_y}{p_z - c_z} \right) \qquad (4.11)$$

In this form, we can see the relation between the perspective projection and the orthographic parallel projection, since the latter can be obtained from the former by letting the centre of projection become infinitely far away from the view plane. This is done by taking the limit as $c_z \to \infty$, and in that case we obtain $(x_v, y_v) = (p_x, p_y)$ as expected.

Figure 4.5: A perspective projection. Point C is the centre of projection. Points P and Q are projected onto the xy plane at the points shown. For point P, the projection direction is given by the vector **p** – **c**.

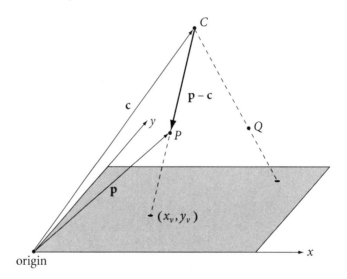

4.3 Three-dimensional transformations

We can apply to three dimensions the same set of affine transformations that we studied in the two-dimensional case: translations, rotations, scaling and shearing. As with two dimensions, it is convenient to express these transformations in homogeneous coordinates, and to derive transformation matrices to represent them. In most cases, these matrices are obvious extensions to the two-dimensional cases, so we need not dwell on their derivations.

4.3.1 Translations

The translation transformation can be written as a simple extension of the two-dimensional case:

$$\begin{bmatrix} x' \\ y' \\ z' \\ 1 \end{bmatrix} = \begin{bmatrix} 1 & 0 & 0 & x_t \\ 0 & 1 & 0 & y_t \\ 0 & 0 & 1 & z_t \\ 0 & 0 & 0 & 1 \end{bmatrix} \begin{bmatrix} x \\ y \\ z \\ 1 \end{bmatrix} \tag{4.12}$$

4.3.2 Scaling

Scaling is also a simple extension from two dimensions. We can scale an image by a different factor in each of the three dimensions, so we obtain:

$$\begin{bmatrix} x' \\ y' \\ z' \\ 1 \end{bmatrix} = \begin{bmatrix} x_s & 0 & 0 & 0 \\ 0 & y_s & 0 & 0 \\ 0 & 0 & z_s & 0 \\ 0 & 0 & 0 & 1 \end{bmatrix} \begin{bmatrix} x \\ y \\ z \\ 1 \end{bmatrix} \tag{4.13}$$

4.3.3 Shearing

Shearing may be done relative to any of the three coordinate axes. Let us consider the case where the x and y coordinates are sheared as we move along the z axis. The shearing factors for x and y can, of course, be different, so the matrix for this particular shearing transformation is as follows.

$$\begin{bmatrix} x' \\ y' \\ z' \\ 1 \end{bmatrix} = \begin{bmatrix} 1 & 0 & x_h & 0 \\ 0 & 1 & y_h & 0 \\ 0 & 0 & 1 & 0 \\ 0 & 0 & 0 & 1 \end{bmatrix} \begin{bmatrix} x \\ y \\ z \\ 1 \end{bmatrix} \tag{4.14}$$

The matrices for shearing relative to the x and y axes are, respectively:

$$\begin{bmatrix} x' \\ y' \\ z' \\ 1 \end{bmatrix} = \begin{bmatrix} 1 & 0 & 0 & 0 \\ y_h & 1 & 0 & 0 \\ z_h & 0 & 1 & 0 \\ 0 & 0 & 0 & 1 \end{bmatrix} \begin{bmatrix} x \\ y \\ z \\ 1 \end{bmatrix} \tag{4.15}$$

and:

$$\begin{bmatrix} x' \\ y' \\ z' \\ 1 \end{bmatrix} = \begin{bmatrix} 1 & x_h & 0 & 0 \\ 0 & 1 & 0 & 0 \\ 0 & z_h & 1 & 0 \\ 0 & 0 & 0 & 1 \end{bmatrix} \begin{bmatrix} x \\ y \\ z \\ 1 \end{bmatrix} \tag{4.16}$$

4.3.4 Rotations

Rotations may occur about any of the three coordinate axes. The matrix for a rotation about a particular axis can be obtained by generalizing the rotation matrix used for two-dimensional graphics.

For example, a rotation counterclockwise (remember we are using a right-handed coordinate system, so counterclockwise rotations are taken as positive) about the z axis may be performed using the following matrix.

$$\begin{bmatrix} x' \\ y' \\ z' \\ 1 \end{bmatrix} = \begin{bmatrix} \cos\theta & -\sin\theta & 0 & 0 \\ \sin\theta & \cos\theta & 0 & 0 \\ 0 & 0 & 1 & 0 \\ 0 & 0 & 0 & 1 \end{bmatrix} \begin{bmatrix} x \\ y \\ z \\ 1 \end{bmatrix} \tag{4.17}$$

Similarly, a rotation about the y axis uses the following matrix.

$$\begin{bmatrix} x' \\ y' \\ z' \\ 1 \end{bmatrix} = \begin{bmatrix} \cos\theta & 0 & \sin\theta & 0 \\ 0 & 1 & 0 & 0 \\ -\sin\theta & 0 & \cos\theta & 0 \\ 0 & 0 & 0 & 1 \end{bmatrix} \begin{bmatrix} x \\ y \\ z \\ 1 \end{bmatrix} \tag{4.18}$$

Finally, a rotation about the x axis uses this matrix:

$$\begin{bmatrix} x' \\ y' \\ z' \\ 1 \end{bmatrix} = \begin{bmatrix} 1 & 0 & 0 & 0 \\ 0 & \cos\theta & -\sin\theta & 0 \\ 0 & \sin\theta & \cos\theta & 0 \\ 0 & 0 & 0 & 1 \end{bmatrix} \begin{bmatrix} x \\ y \\ z \\ 1 \end{bmatrix} \tag{4.19}$$

4.3.5 Composite transformations

As in the two-dimensional case, several transformations can be performed in sequence by multiplying together their respective matrices. Recall that the order in which the transformations are implemented is right-to-left in the matrix product. For example, if we wished to translate a point first, then rotate it about the z axis, we would use the matrix obtained from the product **RT**, where **R** is the matrix in equation 4.17 and **T** is the translation matrix in equation 4.12.

It is important to remember that some combinations of transformations are not commutative—that is, they do not give the same result if the order of the individual transformations within the sequence is changed. Rotations, in particular, are sensitive to the order in which they are performed.

As an example, start with a point at location $(1, 0, 0)$, that is, on the x axis. If we rotate this point by 90 degrees about the z axis and then by 90 degrees about the x axis, it will end up at location $(0, 0, 1)$ on the z axis. However, if we swap the order of rotations, so that we first rotate about the x axis and then about the z axis, the first rotation will have no effect since the point begins on the x axis. The second rotation will then take the point to location $(0, 1, 0)$ on the y axis.

As in the two-dimensional case, we can compose several of the basic transformations given here to obtain a more general transformation. For example, suppose we wish to rotate a point by 30 degrees about the line with equation $y = x$ lying in the plane $z = 0$ (the xy plane). Since we wish to rotate about a line that is not one of the coordinate axes, we cannot use one of the three rotation matrices given above. However, we can first transform the line $y = x$ so that it coincides with one of the coordinate axes (let us choose the y axis). We do this by rotating the system about the z axis through an angle of 45 degrees, by applying the matrix in equation 4.17 with $\theta = \pi/4$ radians. We can now rotate the point about the y axis by 30 degrees, using the matrix in equation 4.18. Finally, we rotate the point about the z axis by $\theta = -\pi/4$ radians to restore the line $y = x$ to its original position. The net effect is to rotate the original point by 30 degrees about the line $y = x$.

Techniques such as this allow us to perform any of the affine transformations relative to any axis in three-dimensional space.

4.3.6 Projections as transformations

As another example of the use of transformations, refer back to equation 4.3 for the oblique parallel projection. We can write this in matrix form as follows (where we simply ignore z_v in the result, since we are only interested in obtaining the projection into the view plane).

$$
\begin{bmatrix} x_v \\ y_v \\ z_v \\ 1 \end{bmatrix} = \begin{bmatrix} 1 & 0 & -d_x/d_z & 0 \\ 0 & 1 & -d_y/d_z & 0 \\ 0 & 0 & 1 & 0 \\ 0 & 0 & 0 & 1 \end{bmatrix} \begin{bmatrix} p_x \\ p_y \\ p_z \\ 1 \end{bmatrix}
\tag{4.20}
$$

By comparing this equation with equation 4.14, we can see that the oblique projection is actually a shearing operation, with the shearing factors in the x and y directions determined by the components of the projection vector **d**.

4.4 View volumes and clipping in three dimensions

Up until now, we have assumed that there is an infinite area available on the view plane for the projection of the three-dimensional scene. In reality, of course, only a portion of the view plane may be displayed within a window on a monitor, or on a printed page. Thus the two-dimensional image that is projected onto the view plane must be clipped so that it fits into the viewport (see Chapter 2 for a discussion of viewports in two dimensions).

Clipping the projected image to fit into a viewport may mean that some of the original three-dimensional objects do not get rendered at all, since their projections lie outside the clipped area. Clearly, a lot of computation can be avoided if these objects are excluded from consideration before the projection calculations are done. We can do this if we can find the volume that is projected onto the viewport, and then exclude any objects that lie outside this volume.

The volume that is projected onto the viewport is called the *view volume*. If the viewport on the view plane is rectangular, the view volume will always be bounded by planes, although its exact shape will depend on the projection being used.

The simplest case is an orthographic parallel projection, since here the projection direction is normal to the view plane, and the view volume is bounded by the four planes that pass through the sides of the viewport. The view volume is infinite in extent in the direction normal to the view plane. (We are assuming that objects lying both in front of and behind the view plane are included in the projection.)

If we are using a perspective projection, the view volume becomes an infinite, four-sided pyramid with its vertex at the viewpoint (see Figure 4.6). Depending on the orientation of the viewpoint relative to the viewport, the pyramid will be skewed at various angles.

Figure 4.6:
The view volume for a perspective projection forms a pyramid with its apex at the centre of projection C.

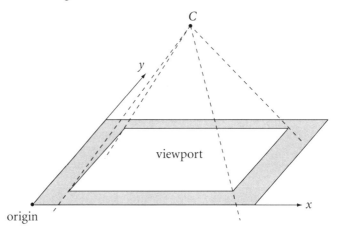

The view volumes we have considered so far are all infinite in extent. View volumes in parallel projections are infinite in both directions along the projection direction, while volumes arising from perspective projections have an apex at the viewpoint, but extend to infinity away from the viewpoint.

In order to restrict the range of objects that are displayed in the final projection, one or two other *clipping planes* are sometimes introduced. These planes are usually parallel to the view plane, and are known as the *front clipping plane* and the *back clipping plane*. For a perspective projection, both planes must be in front of the viewpoint (that is, both planes must intersect the view volume).

Objects closer to the viewpoint than the front clipping plane or further away than the back clipping plane are removed from the projection. The net effect of introducing these two clipping planes is to take a slice out of the original infinite view volume and project to the viewport only objects that are found inside the slice. The resulting truncated view volume is called a *frustum* (from the Latin for 'piece broken off').

Equations for the planes that bound the frustum are fairly easy to derive from the locations of the viewpoint and viewport (see exercises). Once the frustum is known, the only remaining problem is the clipping of the three-dimensional objects relative to the frustum.

For scenes in which all objects are defined in terms of lines or polygons (as many three-dimensional scenes are—see Chapter 6), the Cohen–Sutherland algorithm for clipping lines, and the Sutherland–Hodgman algorithm for clipping polygons (see Chapter 2) can both be extended to three dimensions without too much difficulty, so we will not dwell on the details here. For more general curves and surfaces, more specialized (and computationally expensive) algorithms must be used to perform the clipping.

EXERCISES

1. Verify that the length of any line parallel to the z axis is unchanged in a cavalier projection.

2. Assuming that the projection plane is the xy plane, by what factor are lines parallel to the xy plane scaled in a cavalier projection? In a cabinet projection?

3. Find a projection vector $\mathbf{d}$ that will give a parallel projection in which the projection of a line parallel to the z axis is twice the length of the original.

4. For a unit cube (a cube all of whose edges have unit length) sitting on the xy plane with one corner at the origin, and a centre of projection on the z axis at $z = 2$, use the equations in the text to determine the projection point in the view plane for all eight corners of the cube, and therefore draw the image of the cube projected onto the xy plane. How 'natural' does this projection look when compared with the cavalier and cabinet projections? What effect does moving the centre of projection have?

5. Express a cavalier and a cabinet projection as affine transformations, and derive the transformation matrix associated with each projection.

6. Is it possible to express a perspective projection as an affine transformation?

7. Calculate the equations of the planes bounding the view volume for an orthographic parallel projection. Assume that the viewport is rectangular.

8. Again assuming a rectangular viewport, calculate the equations of the planes bounding the view volume for a general (oblique) parallel projection.

9. Calculate the equations of the planes bounding the view volume for a perspective projection. By considering the intersections of these planes, find the equations of the lines defining the edges of the pyramind making up the view volume.

10. By extending the Cohen–Sutherland algorithm described in Chapter 2, work out an algorithm for clipping lines against each of the viewing volumes calculated in questions 7, 8 and 9.

11. Repeat question 10 for the Sutherland–Hodgman algorithm for polygon clipping.

Java 3D—the basics

C H A P T E R 5

5.1 The Java 3D model

The Java 3D set of packages is a relative newcomer to the Java world and, as such, it is not included with JDK 1.2 or 1.3. However, it is a well-developed collection of classes and may be downloaded and installed in much the same way as the standard JDK.

Beginners to Java 3D are often intimidated by what seems to be a fairly steep learning curve at the outset. While it is true that even the simplest graphics require a basic understanding of how Java 3D works, once these fundamentals are mastered, Java 3D becomes a natural and pleasant environment in which to program.

We will therefore begin this chapter with a discussion of these fundamentals, and illustrate the concepts with a few simple programs.

At the heart of Java 3D is the idea that both the scene to be portrayed *and* the human observer who is viewing the scene should be included in the program. Most earlier (non-Java) graphics packages consider only the objects that are to be drawn to the screen, and treat the observer as a camera that is fixed at a particular point in space and facing in a certain direction.

Java 3D was designed to allow a human observer to move through a 'virtual universe' and view the scenery from various vantage points, all without requiring a major effort on the part of the programmer. It even allows stereoscopic views of the scenery to be produced so that separate images can be projected for each of the observer's eyes. Java 3D can therefore be used not only for the standard, static display that appears on a monitor or printer, but also for producing graphics that can be used with virtual reality helmets and three-dimensional games.

The key to this flexibility is that the graphical entities to be rendered to the screen and the human observer are kept clearly separate in the design and coding stages. The entire universe of graphical objects and observers is brought together in a data structure known as a *scene graph*.

5.2 Scene graphs

The structure of a Java 3D program can seem quite abstract to the beginner, so it is best to keep a specific example of a 3D world in mind when reading over the next few sections.

Suppose we want to create a 3D graphical representation of the house (or block of flats or apartment building) in which we live. If the building itself contains all possible locations that we are going to consider in our program, we can think of the computer's representation of the entire building as a *virtual universe*. The virtual universe determines the maximum boundaries that enclose the world we wish to model. It is important to note that this virtual universe contains not only the objects we wish to portray as graphical images on screen, but also the observer who is to view these images.

The building in which we live will most likely contain several rooms (even if you are a student living in a single room in a residence, the residence itself will have a number of different rooms). If we are building a 'realistic' model of the building—that is, one which a human observer can 'walk through' in much the same way as they could in a real building— then we cannot view more than one room at a time, since the rooms are physically separated from each other by walls and doors.

We can think of each room in the building as a separate *locale*. However, all locales are still part of the overall virtual universe (the model of the building as a whole). When we move from one room to another, we are merely changing locales within the same virtual universe.

Within each room will be a number of items that we wish to appear on screen when the observer is in that room. For example, if we are in a bedroom, we might expect to see a bed, a chest of drawers, a bedside table, and so on. In a kitchen we would expect a fridge, a cooker, a microwave oven, some kitchen cabinets, and so on.

In true object oriented fashion, we can represent each of these items as an *object* at that particular locale. Thus we can create an object to represent each graphical entity that is to appear in a scene, and attach that object to the locale in which it is found.

At this stage, we have an overall virtual universe containing one or more separate locales, and each locale may be populated with several graphical objects which are to be drawn whenever the observer is visiting that locale.

We have not yet mentioned how the observer is to be added to the virtual universe. Java 3D assumes that an observer is connected to a *view platform*, which essentially determines the location and orientation of the observer with respect to the locale in which the observer currently resides. The view platform, together with other attributes that define the observer, make up another object (or collection of objects) which is attached to the currently active locale.

The basic structure of the world to be modelled in a Java 3D program can be drawn as shown in Figure 5.1. The data structure shown in the figure is an example of a mathematical *graph*. This type of graph is not the type with *x* and *y* axes—rather it is a structure consisting of a number of *vertices* or *nodes* connected to each other by *edges*. The fact that the structure is a graph is actually not important in the understanding of Java 3D, apart from the fact that it is known in the Java 3D documentation as the *scene graph*.

The figure shows the virtual universe node at the top, to which is connected a single locale node. (It is possible to have several locales within a virtual universe, but in many applications, this is not necessary.) The locale can have any number of *branch group* nodes attached to it, but if the current locale is active, one of these branch groups must contain the view platform. In Figure 5.1, the branch group on the right leads to the view platform, which we will consider in a minute.

The other branch groups contain the objects to be displayed within that locale. In Figure 5.1 there is only one such branch group (the one on the left), but in a more complex scene there would usually be many more.

Below the branch group node in each branch of the scene graph is a *transform group* node. This node contains information on the transformations (translations, rotations, and so on) that are to be performed on the object within that branch of the graph.

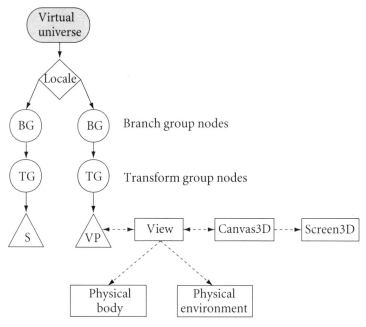

Below the transform group node is the actual object (or view platform) that is to be represented in the scene. In the left branch of the graph in Figure 5.1, there is a triangular node labelled S, which represents a Shape3D node. The Shape3D class in Java 3D represents a geometric shape that can be drawn. A Shape3D object usually has attributes of two types associated with it: *geometry* attributes, which specify the physical shape of the object, and *appearance* attributes which specify such things as the colour.

The right branch in Figure 5.1 contains the view platform node (the triangle labelled VP), to which are attached several other nodes. The essential thing to remember about the view platform is that it contains information on the location and orientation of the human viewing the scene.

A scene graph in Java 3D is designed so that each branch group is independent of the others within the graph. This means that when the scene is rendered onto a two-dimensional display, the branches in the graph can be processed in any order (or even in parallel if you have a multi-processor computer). In the graph shown in Figure 5.1, for example, the object represented in the Shape3D node S on the left may be calculated before or after the properties of the view platform on the right. For this reason, your program cannot use any information from one branch group in any other branch of the graph.

The process of calculating all the branches in a scene graph is called *traversing* the graph. A branch in the graph is traversed by first finding the end node (often called a *leaf node*) of the branch. If this leaf node is a Shape3D object, the object itself is constructred by building its geometry and applying any appearance attributes. Next, the graph node that is immediately above the leaf node (usually called the *parent*) is calculated. In Figure 5.1 this is a transform group node, so any transformations that are specified here are applied to the Shape3D object that was calculated earlier.

The branch group node above the transform group serves more as a place holder than anything else, so there is usually very little work that needs to be done to process this node.

For the view platform branch, the procedure is similar. The view platform itself is built from the various nodes shown in the figure. Once the platform has been defined, it can be transformed in the same way that a Shape3D object can, since the viewer can move about the locale to get a different view of the scene.

After all the branches have been processed, the final scene is constructed by applying a projection (the type of projection is specified in the view platform) to produce the view that would be seen by the observer located on the view platform, and the result is drawn to the display device.

In practice, most simple graphics programs will not need more than one locale vertex in the scene graph, since a locale can in principle cover the entire virtual universe. In our example above, the various rooms in the house *could* be included in a single locale, and the various graphical transformations (mainly translation) could be applied to move the observer from one room to another within that locale.

It is even technically possible to define more than one virtual universe within a single program, but in practice it is hardly ever necessary or convenient to do so.

5.3 A simple Java 3D program

We will deal with the various components of a scene graph in more detail later on. For now, in order that the reader can see how the various parts of the scene graph fit together in an actual program, we will build the Java 3D equivalent of a 'Hello world' program common in textual languages.

We will write a program that makes use of a predefined class called ColorCube, which displays a solid cube with each of the six faces shaded a different colour. Although we are using a predefined shape, we will still build the rest of the program from scratch so you can see how the scene graph is translated into code.

5.3.1 The view platform branch

Since every Java 3D program must have a view platform built in, it makes sense to separate this part of the code into a different class. In fact, Java 3D comes with a utility class called SimpleUniverse which creates a standard view platform and associated view. However, since this class hides most of what is going on in the creation of the view platform, we will not use it here. Instead, we will create a class called BasicUniverse which illustrates how the fundamental pieces of a scene graph are put together. Then we will create another class called Simple3D which creates a BasicUniverse object and adds a ColorCube to it so the observer has something to observe.

The code for the BasicUniverse class is as follows.

```
1   import javax.media.j3d.*;
2   import javax.vecmath.*;
3
4   public class BasicUniverse extends Object
5   {
6       VirtualUniverse universe;
```

```
7      Locale locale;
8      BranchGroup viewPlatformRoot;
9      TransformGroup viewPlatformTransform;
10     ViewPlatform viewPlatform;
11     View view;
12     Canvas3D canvas;
13     float zViewDistance;
14
15     public BasicUniverse(Canvas3D extCanvas,
16         float zViewDist)
17     {
18         canvas = extCanvas;
19         zViewDistance = zViewDist;
20         universe = new VirtualUniverse();
21         locale = new Locale(universe);
22         viewPlatformRoot = new BranchGroup();
23         viewPlatformTransform = new TransformGroup();
24         setupViewPlatform();
25         viewPlatformRoot.addChild(viewPlatformTransform);
26         setupView(extCanvas);
27         view.attachViewPlatform(viewPlatform);
28         locale.addBranchGraph(viewPlatformRoot);
29     }
30
31     private void setupView(Canvas3D extCanvas)
32     {
33         view = new View();
34         view.addCanvas3D(extCanvas);
35         view.setPhysicalBody(new PhysicalBody());
36         view.setPhysicalEnvironment(
37             new PhysicalEnvironment());
38     }
39
40     private void setupViewPlatform()
41     {
42         viewPlatform = new ViewPlatform();
43         setViewingDistance(zViewDistance);
44         viewPlatformTransform.addChild(viewPlatform);
45     }
46
47     public void setViewingDistance(float viewDistance)
48     {
49         zViewDistance = viewDistance;
50         Transform3D transform = new Transform3D();
51         transform.set(new Vector3f(
52             0.0f, 0.0f, zViewDistance));
53         viewPlatformTransform.setTransform(transform);
54     }
55
56     public void addBranchGraph(BranchGroup bg)
57     {
58         locale.addBranchGraph(bg);
```

```
59        }
60
61        public TransformGroup getViewPlatformTransform()
62        {
63            return viewPlatformTransform;
64        }
65
66        public View getView()
67        {
68            return view;
69        }
70    }
```

Since Java 3D contains a number of packages, we must import the correct ones in order for the various calls to methods to be recognized by the compiler. The required import statements can always be determined from the on-line documentation, so we will not dwell on them here. In the BasicUniverse class, we import two packages on lines 1 and 2.

Lines 6 through 12 declare the objects that form the basis of the virtual universe and the observer's branch of the scene graph. The VirtualUniverse and Locale classes correspond directly with their respective nodes in the scene graph.

Once we have the virtual universe and the locale in place, we need to attach the viewer and the objects to be viewed to the locale. Each such object forms a branch in the scene graph, and each branch must begin with a BranchGroup object. The BranchGroup object called viewPlatformRoot, declared on line 8, serves, as its name implies, as the root vertex of the view platform branch in the scene graph. All objects associated with the view platform and the view can be reached only by going through this object.

On line 9 we declare a TransformGroup object. As we saw in Figure 5.1, Java 3D allows the contents of each BranchGroup object to have its own associated transformation, which is defined in a TransformGroup object. If we do not provide one explicitly, Java 3D itself will insert one that contains the identity transformation— that is, it will not transform the object below it.

As we will see a bit later, in order for the observer to see the ColorCube object, we need to move the observer back a bit so that the cube fits into the field of view. For this reason, we need an explicit TransformGroup as part of the view platform branch in the scene graph.

The ViewPlatform and its associated View are declared on lines 10 and 11. As described above, the ViewPlatform determines the location and orientation of the viewer relative to the locale. The View itself takes account of the observer (such as the dimensions and orientation of the user's head) and the physical environment being used (such as the sensors that are being used to interact with the surroundings). For simple graphical rendering, in which we consider only static snapshots of the scene, we will not need to worry about these features.

The View performs one other very important function, however: it does the actual rendering of the scene into a two-dimensional image that can be displayed on screen. The surface onto which the scene is drawn is a Canvas3D object (an extension of the Canvas object from the Java AWT), and so we declare this object on line 12. (A View object can actually render to more than one Canvas3D object, but we will need only one for our simple example.)

The View class is quite large, and contains methods for setting up such things as the type of projection (parallel or perspective) and clipping planes, as well as dealing with the more advanced features such as virtual reality.

The View is technically not part of the scene graph, in the sense that the View object does not constitute a vertex in the graph. Rather, a View is always associated with a ViewPlatform, which *is* part of the scene graph.

The final variable, zViewDistance, declared on line 13, specifies the distance along the z axis from the viewpoint to the origin of the locale. That is, the viewpoint will be positioned at coordinates (0, 0, zViewDistance).

The constructor (lines 15 to 29) sets up the virtual universe, locale, and the view platform branch of the scene graph. The constructor takes two arguments: the Canvas3D object on which the scene is to be drawn, and an initial value for the distance of the view platform from the origin.

The Canvas3D object is the only object which is actually visible in the program's output, and as with the two-dimensional Canvas, it is usually part of some container (such as a JPanel or JFrame) that is displayed within a layout manager. For this reason, the constructor allows the application to specify the Canvas3D outside the virtual universe— in a sense, the Canvas3D is the link between the virtual universe of Java 3D and the outside world, where the person running the program can view the results. We will create the Canvas3D object in a second class below.

The VirtualUniverse and Locale objects are created on lines 20 to 21. The root vertex for the view platform is created on line 22, and the TransformGroup that will be used to move the view platform back from the origin is created on line 23. Then the method setupViewPlatform() is called to initialize the ViewPlatform object.

The setupViewPlatform() method (lines 40 to 45) creates the ViewPlatform object (line 42) and then calls setViewingDistance() (described below) to translate the ViewPlatform along the z axis by the distance zViewDistance.

Like the BranchGroup class, the TransformGroup class is primarily a placeholder class that provides an attachment point for objects that actually perform some function. In this case, a TransformGroup must hold the transformation that is to be applied to the ViewPlatform. A transformation is defined by a Transform3D object.

The method setViewingDistance() (lines 47 to 54) creates a Transform3D object on line 50. We will be seeing much more of the Transfrom3D class in the sections to come, but for now, you can think of it as the main method by which three-dimensional transformations are implemented in Java 3D. The set() method in the Transform3D class is overloaded to the extent that there are 25 different ways of specifying a transformation. The version used on line 51 takes a Vector3f object as its argument.

Vectors and matrices are specified in Java 3D in various sizes and precisions. If the class name for a vector or matrix ends with a number and a letter (as in Vector3f), the number indicates the dimensionality of the class and the letter indicates the precision of its components. Thus a Vector3f has 3 dimensions and its components are specified as floats. There is a Vector3d class which also has 3 dimensions but takes doubles as components.

When the set() method of the Transform3D class is given a vector as its only argument, the vector is taken as a translation vector. Thus the transformation specified on line 51 defines a translation of zViewDistance along the z axis.

Finally (line 53), we set the transform field of the TransformGroup object to be the Transform3D object we just defined.

Returning to the constructor, after setting up the ViewPlatform and its associated TransformGroup, we attach the TransformGroup object underneath the BranchGroup (line 25). The addChild() method is a general purpose method which allows a vertex of the appropriate type to be attached as the child of another vertex.

On line 26 we call setupView() to create and initialize the View. This method is shown on lines 31 to 38. We attach the external Canvas3D object on line 34. Lines 35 and 36 create and attach a PhysicalBody and a PhysicalEnvironment to the View. As mentioned earlier, simple graphics do not require any elaboration of these objects beyond the defaults.

With the View created, we can attach the ViewPlatform to the View (line 27). Finally, we add the whole view platform branch to the Locale object (line 28). At this stage, the virtual universe and locale have been created, and the view platform branch has been fully defined and attached to the locale. The BasicUniverse class we have written could serve as the basis of any 3D graphics program which requires only a single locale and canvas.

5.3.2   Adding a geometry branch

All that remains is to create the BranchGroup for the ColorCube and attach it to the Locale. Branches in the scene graph that contain descriptions of the objects to be drawn (as opposed to the view platform) are often called *geometry branches*.

Rather than include the code for the geometry branch containing the ColorCube within the BasicUniverse class, however, it is better design to do this in a separate class. The reason for this is that, as we just mentioned, the BasicUniverse class is a complete module into which can be plugged any graphic image for viewing. To allow for this, we have added one final method to the BasicUniverse class: the addBranchGraph() method on lines 56 to 59.

This method simply calls the addBranchGraph() method in the Locale class to attach another branch to the scene graph. The intention here is that these other branches will each describe a separate graphical object which is to be viewed by the observer located at the ViewPlatform. We will now examine the other class in our simple example to see how this is done.

We will add a branch like the left branch in Figure 5.1. The ColorCube object will correspond to the triangular S node in this figure. The code for the Simple3D class is as follows.

```
1     import java.awt.*;
2     import java.awt.event.*;
3     import com.sun.j3d.utils.geometry.*;
4     import com.sun.j3d.utils.universe.*;
5     import javax.media.j3d.*;
6     import javax.swing.*;
7
8     public class Simple3D extends JFrame
9     {
10        public Simple3D()
11        {
12            initComponents();
```

```
13          setSize(600, 600);
14          GraphicsConfiguration graphicsConfig =
15              SimpleUniverse.getPreferredConfiguration();
16          Canvas3D canvas = new Canvas3D(graphicsConfig);
17          getContentPane().add("Center", canvas);
18          BasicUniverse universe =
19              new BasicUniverse(canvas, 8.0f);
20          BranchGroup scene = createCubeGraph();
21          universe.addBranchGraph(scene);
22      }
23
24      public BranchGroup createCubeGraph()
25      {
26          BranchGroup objRoot = new BranchGroup();
27          objRoot.addChild(new ColorCube());
28          return objRoot;
29      }
30
31      private void initComponents() {
32          addWindowListener(new WindowAdapter () {
33              public void windowClosing(WindowEvent event) {
34                  exitForm(event);
35              }
36          }
37          );
38      }
39
40      private void exitForm(WindowEvent event)
41      {
42          System.exit(0);
43      }
44
45      public static void main(String args[]) {
46          new Simple3D().show();
47      }
48  }
```

We have presented the complete code for this class so you can see how Java 3D integrates with the GUI (graphical user interface) in which the display is embedded. We will explain the various import statements when we consider the code that requires them.

The class includes an event handler (lines 31 to 43) that allows the program to be halted by clicking in the 'close window' button in the window's title bar, so we need to import the java.awt.event package (line 2). The javax.swing package imported on line 6 is needed for the JFrame object from which Simple3D is derived. This provides the main window for the program.

The ColorCube class is contained in the com.sun.j3d.utils.geometry package (line 3), and most of the other Java 3D methods we use are contained in javax.media.j3d (line 5).

The constructor (lines 10 to 22) first calls initComponents() (line 12) to set up the event handler to close the program. The initial size of the main window is set to 600 by 600 pixels on line 13.

The Canvas3D object that is to be used to display the cube is created on lines 14 to 16, and added to the layout on line 17. The Canvas3D constructor's argument is a GraphicsConfiguration object (part of the java.awt package, so we import this package on line 1), which provides information on the display device used to render the image. The easiest way to obtain this object is to call the static method getPreferredConfiguration() from the SimpleUniverse class. Using the SimpleUniverse class requires importing the com.sun.j3d.utils.universe package (line 4).

With the release of Java 3D version 1.2 (June 2000), the Canvas3D constructor is required to have a non-null argument for the GraphicsConfiguration object (a runtime warning is issued if a null argument is given, although the program will still run). Earlier versions of Java 3D accepted a null argument to the constructor, and if you examine programs written using these earlier versions, you will probably find the Canvas3D constructor called with a null argument.

We then create a BasicUniverse on lines 18 and 19. This provides the VirtualUniverse and constructs the ViewPlatform as described above. Note that we pass it the Canvas3D object that was created in Simple3D, and we also specify that the ViewPlatform should be moved back a distance of 8 metres from the origin of the locale. (Java 3D uses the metre as the default length unit in all calculations.)

On line 20 we call createCubeGraph() to create a BranchGroup containing the ColorCube. The createCubeGraph() method (lines 24 to 29) creates the BranchGroup and adds a default ColorCube object to it. The default cube measures 2 metres on each edge and is centred at the origin.

Note that we have not included a TransformGroup vertex as a child of the BranchGroup, as we did when setting up the ViewPlatform branch. This is because we handled the required transformation in the ViewPlatform. We could, alternatively, put a transform here and remove the one in the BasicUniverse class, or even have transformations in both places. We will see some examples of this later.

Finally, on line 21, we attach the BranchGroup to the BasicUniverse, using the addBranchGraph() method we mentioned above.

The program is now complete, so if we run it, what will we see after all this effort? The result might look a little disappointing, as all we will see is a solid red square on a black background. The reason for this is that our ViewPlatform is aligned so that it is looking at the cube end-on, so all we see is one face of the cube.

5.4 Scene graph traversal

Before we attempt to change the default view by introducing some more transformations, there is one other question that may have occurred to you. Where in the code is the command to actually display the image? In a standard AWT-based graphics program, there is a paint() method which is called implicitly by the virtual machine to display the graphics, but no such method is to be found in either of the classes we have seen.

Java 3D handles rendering by the rule that whenever a BranchGroup is attached to a Locale it becomes *live*, and will be displayed. To prevent any particular BranchGroup from being displayed, all we need to do is disconnect it from its parent in the scene graph, and the Java 3D renderer will ignore it. (You can try this in the Simple3D class by commenting out line 21. The result is that the red square no longer appears.)

This leads us to a more general consideration of how Java 3D calculates and displays the various objects in the scene graph. We mentioned above that Java 3D treats all branches in the scene graph as independent of each other. That is, anything below a particular BranchGroup vertex in the graph must be independent of anything connected to any other BranchGroup vertex. We can therefore consider what calculations are made within a single branch in the scene graph, since the process is repeated for all other branches.

For a branch in the scene graph where a geometric object is stored (such as the ColorCube in the example above), Java 3D will locate the leaf nodes (those nodes that have no children). In a geometry branch, the leaves will contain the instructions for creating the actual shape of the objects to be rendered. All calculations required to create the leaf nodes are performed first within each branch.

As we work up from the leaves we may encounter a TransformGroup node, which contains instructions for applying an affine transform to the objects below it. Each TransformGroup has a Transform3D object associated with it, which consists of a 4×4 matrix specifying the transformation. These transformations are calculated and applied to all geometric objects attached to the TransformGroup.

Since the various branches in the scene graph are independent, Java 3D may process them in any order. This means that, for example, a transformation applied to one branch has no effect on objects in any other branch. This is especially convenient if you are running Java 3D applications on a computer that supports parallel processing, since each branch in the graph can be handled on a separate processor.

More complex scene graphs may have nested BranchGroups, where one BranchGroup has one or more different BranchGroups as its children. In such a graph, the processing rules above are applied recursively.

Processing of the branch containing the view platform occurs in a similar fashion. The view platform branch begins with a BranchGroup vertex, just like any other branch. This is followed by a TransformGroup vertex, which may be used to transform the ViewPlatform object by translating or rotating it, for example.

Once all branches have been processed, so that all geometric objects have been calculated and transformed, and the view platform has been positioned and oriented properly, the View can begin the actual rendering process to produce the image.

The View determines the projection to be used (the default is a perspective projection, but parallel projections can be calculated as well), and applies this projection using the coordinates of the view platform and geometric objects that were calculated before. The result is the two-dimensional image that is drawn to the screen.

It is very important to feel at ease with the way BranchGroups, TransformGroups and leaf nodes are processed in Java 3D, since these techniques are used in every aspect of a Java 3D program.

5.5 Java 3D transformations

In the Simple3D example in the previous section, we had to use a translation in order to move the view platform back a bit so that the cube would fit into the field of view. In the process, we were introduced to the TransformGroup and Transform3D classes.

We will illustrate some simple transformations by showing a different view of the cube (and see that it is, in fact, a cube and not just a red square!). We will begin by performing a rotation of 45 degrees about the *x* axis, which should allow us to see two sides of the cube.

There are several ways we can transform the graphics to get a different view of the cube. First, we can rotate the view platform and leave the cube itself fixed. Alternatively, we can rotate the cube and leave the view platform fixed, or we could rotate both the cube and the view platform.

5.5.1 Transforming the view platform

In the first example, we will rotate the view platform and leave the cube fixed. However, even in this case, we have two choices. We can set up the rotation of the view platform before the BranchGroup in which it resides is added to the scene graph (that is, before it is made live), or we can add the view platform to the scene graph and allow transformations to the view platform *after* it is made live.

To add the transformation to the view platform before it is made live, we replace the setupViewPlatform() method in the BasicUniverse class given above with the following code:

```
private void setupViewPlatform()
{
    viewPlatform = new ViewPlatform();
    setViewingDistance(zViewDistance);

    Transform3D transform = new Transform3D();
    transform.rotX(Math.PI / 4.0);
    Transform3D currentTransform = new Transform3D();
    viewPlatformTransform.getTransform(currentTransform);
    transform.mul(currentTransform);
    viewPlatformTransform.setTransform(transform);

    viewPlatformTransform.addChild(viewPlatform);
}
```

The central six lines of code have been added to transform the view platform by rotating it by $\pi/4$ radians (45 degrees) about the *x* axis. We create a new Transform3D object and call the rotX() method to define the rotation about the *x* axis. Note that the unit used in all methods requiring angles as arguments is the radian, not the degree. Since many common angles are expressed as multiples of π, we use the static definition of π in the Math class to obtain a double-precision value.

The rotX() method defines a 4×4 matrix that contains the correct parameters for a rotation about the *x* axis, although this is hidden from the programmer.

We wish to apply the rotation *after* the initial translation that moves the view platform a certain distance away from the origin. We therefore must obtain the matrix for the initial translation and multiply this matrix by the rotation matrix, with the rotation matrix on the left (since it is to be done after the translation). Recall that the translation was defined in the setViewingDistance() method, and the transform for the TransformGroup was set to this translation at that point. We therefore need to retrieve the translation matrix by calling the getTransform() method for the TransformGroup. Note that this method does not *return* the existing Transform3D object—rather, it requires that a Transform3D object be passed as the argument. It then makes a copy of the existing Transform3D object into the object that was passed as the argument. In other words, a TransformGroup does not allow an external object to change the properties of its Transform3D object directly. We must make a copy of the existing transform, modify the copy, and then use the setTransform() method of the TransformGroup method to reset the transform to the new Transform3D object.

After copying the existing translation transform into the currentTransform object, we use the mul() method to multiply the rotation transform (stored in the transform variable) by the translation (stored in currentTransform). The matrix product is stored in transform.

Finally, we use setTransform() to set the transform to the combined translation and rotation.

If we run the program with these modifications, we obtain the view of the cube shown in Figure 5.2.

Figure 5.2:
The view of the cube after rotating the view platform about the *x* axis.

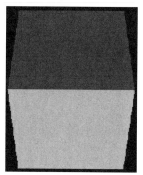

We can see that there are two faces visible. The original red face is at the top, and a new cyan (light blue—dark grey in the figure) face is at the bottom. The perspective view is also clearly evident.

Although we have obtained the desired effect of rotating the cube about the *x* axis, we should be concerned about the poor design of the method we have used. When we created the BasicUniverse class, we did so because we wanted a class that contained a simple template for a virtual universe containing a single locale, and a simple view platform and associated view. The idea was that we could use this class as a starting point for any simple 3D graphics program.

We have somewhat ruined this goal by introducing an extra transformation into the construction of the view platform. It is highly unlikely that we will want an initial rotation of the scene in every application we write.

A much better design would be to add a method to the BasicUniverse class which allows the transformation of the view platform to be set from an external class. We can do this by adding an interface method to BasicUniverse which allows the TransformGroup object associated with the view platform to be read:

```
public TransformGroup getViewPlatformTransform()
{
    return viewPlatformTransform;
}
```

Using this method, an external class can access the TransformGroup, extract its Transform3D object, modify it, and then reset the transform using the setTransform() method, just as we did in the example above.

If we try this, however, we run into a problem. When running the program, a CapabilityNotSetException is thrown. What does this mean?

5.5.2 Capabilities

The crucial difference between the first and second methods of rotating the view platform is that the second method attempts to change the Transform3D object *after* the view platform has been attached to the scene graph.

Because the calculation of transformations and projections and the rendering process itself are computationally intensive activities, Java 3D has a number of optimizations built in. These optimizations become effective whenever a branch in the scene graph is made live (by attaching it to a Locale). In order for these optimizations to be possible, access to many of the internal objects in the branch must be restricted. One of the restrictions is that the Transform3D object in a TransformGroup may not be accessed (read or written) after the branch containing that object is made live.

Clearly, if no modification to any vertex in a branch were possible after that branch is made live, this would severely restrict the abilities of Java 3D. For example, animation of objects within a branch would not be possible, since the initial position and orientation of the objects could not be changed. For this reason, it is possible to define certain features of a vertex that *can* be accessed or changed after the branch containing them is made live. To do this, it is necessary to set a *capability bit* for that vertex.

There are numerous capabilities that can be set for a given type of vertex in the scene graph, but the procedure is the same for all of them, so we will show how to set capabilities that allow the Transform3D in a TransformGroup to be read and written.

Referring back to the code listing for the BasicUniverse class above (page 132), we can insert the following two lines immediately after viewPlatformTransform is created (that is, after line 23):

```
viewPlatformTransform.setCapability
    (TransformGroup.ALLOW_TRANSFORM_WRITE);
viewPlatformTransform.setCapability
    (TransformGroup.ALLOW_TRANSFORM_READ);
```

The quantities ALLOW_TRANSFORM_WRITE and ALLOW_TRANSFORM_READ are static fields in the TransformGroup class, and define the bits in the capability field of a TransformGroup object that must be set in order for the Transform3D to be written or read, respectively, after that TransformGroup becomes part of a live branch in a scene graph.

The various capabilities that can be set may be found either in the class corresponding to the type of vertex (e.g. BranchGroup or TransformGroup) or in one of its ancestor classes such as Group or Node. Consult the Java 3D API documentation for a complete list for each class.

With these modifications to the BasicUniverse class, we can now add code to the Simple3D class to rotate the view platform *after* the BasicUniverse object has been created, rather than during its construction as we did in the first example.

Referring back to the code for the Simple3D class, we can insert the following code after the creation of the BasicUniverse (after line 19, page 136):

```
TransformGroup cubeTransform =
    universe.getViewPlatformTransform();
Transform3D transform = new Transform3D();
transform.rotX(Math.PI / 4.0);
Transform3D currentTransform = new Transform3D();
cubeTransform.getTransform(currentTransform);
transform.mul(currentTransform);
cubeTransform.setTransform(transform);
```

This code is very similar to the code we inserted in the BasicUniverse class earlier. The main difference is that we must first obtain the TransformGroup for the view platform, which we do using the interface method getViewPlatformTransform() we added earlier to the BasicUniverse class. The calculation of the transform to rotate the cube after its initial translation is the same as before, and we finish by using the setTransform() method to set the new transform for the view platform. The result is the same as before (Figure 5.2).

5.5.3 Transforming the cube

The final alternative we may choose to obtain a different view of the cube is to leave the view platform in its initial state (as produced by BasicUniverse) and transform the cube itself. To do this, change the original Simple3D class to implement the rotation in the branch of the scene graph containing the ColorCube.

We can do this by replacing the createCubeGraph() method in the Simple3D class above with the following:

```
public BranchGroup createCubeGraph() {
    BranchGroup objRoot = new BranchGroup();
    Transform3D transform = new Transform3D();
    transform.rotX(-Math.PI / 4.0);
    TransformGroup cubeTransform = new TransformGroup();
    cubeTransform.setTransform(transform);
    objRoot.addChild(cubeTransform);
    cubeTransform.addChild(new ColorCube());
    return objRoot;
}
```

We create the BranchGroup as before, but we then create a Transform3D to rotate the cube about the *x* axis. Note that the argument to the rotX() method is the negative of the angle we used in rotating the view platform. This is because rotating the view platform by an angle *a* about the *x* axis produces the same view as leaving the view platform fixed and rotating all objects being viewed by −*a*.

After setting up the Transform3D, we create a TransformGroup and set its transform to the rotation we just defined. We then add the TransformGroup as the child of the BranchGroup, and then attach the ColorCube as the child of the TransformGroup. This produces the same view as the previous example (Figure 5.2).

Note that in this example, we set the transform *before* making the cube's branch live (by adding it to the Locale). If we wished to transform the cube further after it was part of the scene graph, we would need to set the capability bits on the TransformGroup, just as we did when we rotated the view platform in the earlier example.

5.5.4 Parallel projections in Java 3D

As another example, we will produce the cavalier and cabinet projections of the cube shown in Figure 4.4 (page 121), using the ColorCube to draw the basic cube.

The default projection used in a View is perspective, so we must first see how to instruct the View to draw a parallel projection. This is easily done by inserting the single line of code

```
view.setProjectionPolicy(View.PARALLEL_PROJECTION);
```

during the creation of the View object. Apart from this, we set up the view branch and geometry branch as usual.

The process is similar to the earlier example in which we generated a single perspective view of a ColorCube. In this example, in addition to generating a parallel projection, we will include two cubes in the display (using two BranchGroups), and specify the transformation by means of a full 4×4 matrix, rather than using a convenience method for generating simple rotations, as we did earlier.

We will first write a ParallelUniverse class (with no science fiction-related pun intended) which sets up the view branch for a parallel projection. The code for this is:

```
1    import javax.media.j3d.*;
2    import javax.vecmath.*;
3
4    public class ParallelUniverse
5    {
6        VirtualUniverse universe;
7        Locale locale;
8        BranchGroup viewPlatformRoot;
9        TransformGroup viewPlatformTransform;
10       ViewPlatform viewPlatform;
11       View view;
12       Canvas3D canvas;
13       float scaleFactor;
14
15       public ParallelUniverse(Canvas3D extCanvas,
16           float initScale)
17       {
18           canvas = extCanvas;
19           scaleFactor = initScale;
20           universe = new VirtualUniverse();
21           locale = new Locale(universe);
```

```
22          viewPlatformRoot = new BranchGroup();
23          viewPlatformTransform = new TransformGroup();
24          setupViewPlatform();
25          viewPlatformRoot.addChild(viewPlatformTransform);
26          setupView(extCanvas);
27          view.attachViewPlatform(viewPlatform);
28          locale.addBranchGraph(viewPlatformRoot);
29      }
30
31      private void setupView(Canvas3D extCanvas)
32      {
33          view = new View();
34          view.addCanvas3D(extCanvas);
35          view.setPhysicalBody(new PhysicalBody());
36          view.setPhysicalEnvironment(
37              new PhysicalEnvironment());
38          view.setProjectionPolicy(View.PARALLEL_PROJECTION);
39      }
40
41      private void setupViewPlatform()
42      {
43          viewPlatform = new ViewPlatform();
44          setViewingDistance();
45          viewPlatformTransform.addChild(viewPlatform);
46      }
47
48      public void setViewingDistance()
49      {
50          Transform3D transform = new Transform3D();
51          transform.set(scaleFactor,
52              new Vector3f(0.0f, 0.0f, 5.0f));
53          viewPlatformTransform.setTransform(transform);
54      }
55
56      public TransformGroup getViewPlatformTransform()
57      {
58          return viewPlatformTransform;
59      }
60
61      public void addBranchGraph(BranchGroup bg) {
62          locale.addBranchGraph(bg);
63      }
64  }
```

Much of this class should be familiar from the BasicUniverse class, so we will only describe those features that are new.

The constructor (lines 15 to 29) is identical to that for BasicUniverse. The setupView() method is also the same as that in BasicUniverse, except for the addition of line 38 which tells the View to produce a parallel projection.

The other methods are all the same as in BasicUniverse, with the exception of setViewingDistance() (lines 48 to 54). The default view for a parallel projection often produces an image that is too large to fit into the window on screen. Unlike a perspective projection, moving the view platform has no effect on the size of the image that is projected onto the viewport. We can change the size of the displayed image, however, by scaling the view platform.

To this end, we define a `Transform3D` on line 50 and set its transform on lines 51 and 52. Ideally, we should be able to specify a scale factor only, but it appears that unless we translate the viewing platform, the projection is not visible. The `Vector3f` argument to the `set()` method on line 52 translates the view platform by 5 metres in the z direction. This would appear to be a bug in Java 3D.

The effect of scaling the view platform when the `View` is using a parallel projection is essentially to change the distance of the view platform from the viewing plane. For this reason, the scaling factor seems to produce the opposite effect from what you might expect. In other words, the larger the scaling factor, the smaller the image, because a larger scaling factor means that you are moving further from the viewing plane.

We now examine the class `ParallelProj`, which creates the two `BranchGroups` that draw the two projections of the `ColorCube`. Referring back to equations 4.8 (page 121) and 4.20 (page 125), we see that a cabinet projection is equivalent to a shearing operation with the transformation matrix

$$\begin{bmatrix} x_v \\ y_v \\ z_v \\ 1 \end{bmatrix} = \begin{bmatrix} 1 & 0 & -1/2\sqrt{2} & 0 \\ 0 & 1 & -1/2\sqrt{2} & 0 \\ 0 & 0 & 1 & 0 \\ 0 & 0 & 0 & 1 \end{bmatrix} \begin{bmatrix} p_x \\ p_y \\ p_z \\ 1 \end{bmatrix} \tag{5.1}$$

Using a similar argument to that which resulted in equation 4.8 for the cabinet projection, we can derive the transformation matrix for the cavalier projection, which is defined by the condition that the tangent of the angle between the projection direction and the view plane is 1 (meaning that the angle is $\pi/4$ radians). The result is:

$$\begin{bmatrix} x_v \\ y_v \\ z_v \\ 1 \end{bmatrix} = \begin{bmatrix} 1 & 0 & -\sqrt{2}/2 & 0 \\ 0 & 1 & -\sqrt{2}/2 & 0 \\ 0 & 0 & 1 & 0 \\ 0 & 0 & 0 & 1 \end{bmatrix} \begin{bmatrix} p_x \\ p_y \\ p_z \\ 1 \end{bmatrix} \tag{5.2}$$

Using these transformation matrices, we can create the two `BranchGroups` for the projections of `ColorCube`. The `ParallelProj` class implements the graphics:

```
1    import com.sun.j3d.utils.geometry.*;
2    import com.sun.j3d.utils.universe.*;
3    import javax.media.j3d.*;
4    import javax.swing.*;
5    import javax.vecmath.*;
6    import java.awt.*;
7
8    public class ParallelProj extends JFrame {
9        ParallelUniverse universe;
10
11       public ParallelProj()
12       {
13           initComponents();
```

```
14        setSize(600, 600);
15        GraphicsConfiguration graphicsConfig =
16        SimpleUniverse.getPreferredConfiguration();
17        Canvas3D canvas = new Canvas3D(graphicsConfig);
18        getContentPane().add("Center", canvas);
19        universe = new ParallelUniverse(canvas, 6.0f);
20        addCubes();
21    }
22
23    private void addCubes()
24    {
25        BranchGroup scene = new BranchGroup();
26        Matrix4d cubeMatrix = new Matrix4d(
27        1.0, 0.0, -1.0/(2.0 * Math.sqrt(2.0)), 0.0,
28        0.0, 1.0, -1.0/(2.0 * Math.sqrt(2.0)), 0.0,
29        0.0, 0.0, 1.0,                         0.0,
30        0.0, 0.0, 0.0,                         1.0);
31        Transform3D cubeTrans = new Transform3D();
32        cubeTrans.set(cubeMatrix);
33        TransformGroup objTrans =
34            new TransformGroup(cubeTrans);
35        objTrans.addChild(new ColorCube());
36        scene.addChild(objTrans);
37        universe.addBranchGraph(scene);
38
39        scene = new BranchGroup();
40        cubeMatrix.m02 = -1.0 * Math.sqrt(2.0)/2.0;
41        cubeMatrix.m12 = -1.0 * Math.sqrt(2.0)/2.0;
42        cubeTrans.set(cubeMatrix);
43        Transform3D translateCube = new Transform3D();
44        translateCube.set(new Vector3d(-3.0, 0.0, 0.0));
45        cubeTrans.mul(translateCube, cubeTrans);
46        objTrans = new TransformGroup(cubeTrans);
47        objTrans.addChild(new ColorCube());
48        scene.addChild(objTrans);
49        universe.addBranchGraph(scene);
50    }
51
52    // Other methods are the same as in
53    // Simple3D:
54    // initComponents, exitApplication, and main
55 }
```

The constructor (lines 11 through 21) is very similar to that for Simple3D, except that we create a ParallelUniverse on line 19. The addCubes() method on line 20 creates the BranchGroups and adds them to the virtual universe.

In the addCubes() method, we see how to use a transformation matrix directly to define a Transform3D. We create a Matrix4d by giving its elements as the arguments to the constructor. (Recall that the '4d' in the class name indicates that the matrix is 4 × 4 and takes doubles as its elements.)

Having defined the transformation matrix, lines 31 to 37 create the Transform3D, set its transform to the matrix, create a TransformGroup and add a

ColorCube to it, add the TransformGroup to the BranchGroup and add the BranchGroup to the universe. This completes the branch for the cabinet projection.

The remainder of the addCubes() method alters the two matrix elements (lines 40 and 41) to convert the transformation into a cavalier projection, and then creates and adds the new branch to the universe. The individual matrix elements in a Matrix4d are public data fields so we have direct access to them. Note that the numbering for matrix elements begins with row 0 at the top and column 0 at the left, so that the upper-left element is m00, and the upper-right element is m03.

Note that we add a translation of 3 metres to the left on lines 44 and 45, since we want to display the two cubes side by side.

The result of this program is shown in Figure 5.3.

Figure 5.3:
A cavalier (left) and cabinet projection of the ColorCube.

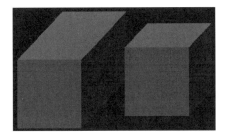

5.6   Clipping planes and the view frustum

As described in Chapter 4, it is often convenient to define front and back clipping planes to restrict the view volume. In this way, objects too near the viewpoint (in a perspective projection) or in the background can be eliminated from the rendered image.

In Java 3D, the View contains the front and back clipping planes, and these can be set easily by means of interface methods in the View class. However, using these methods directly will usually not produce the expected results. To see why, we shall show an example.

We will show a perspective projection of the ColorCube rotated slightly about first the y axis and then the x axis, so that we may see three faces of the cube. The resulting image is shown in Figure 5.4. For this program, we use the BasicUniverse class defined above to create the virtual universe and the view platform branch of the scene graph. The geometry branch, containing the rotated ColorCube, is generated in a class called ClippingDemo, which is similar to the Simple3D class we used in the first example in this chapter.

The constructor for this class is as follows.

```
public ClippingDemo()
{
    initComponents();
    setSize(600, 600);
    Canvas3D canvas = new Canvas3D(null);
    getContentPane().add("Center", canvas);
    universe = new BasicUniverse(canvas, 6.0f);
    addCube();
}
```

Comparing this with the constructor for the Simple3D class will reveal that it is essentially identical. We create the BasicUniverse and its associated view platform, and translate the view platform 6 metres in the positive *z* direction in order to obtain a good view of the cube.

Figure 5.4:
A perspective projection of a rotated ColorCube.

The main difference between ClippingDemo and Simple3D is that the geometry branch is generated by a method called addCube(), the code for which is as follows:

```
private void addCube()
{
    BranchGroup scene = new BranchGroup();
    Transform3D rotateY = new Transform3D();
    rotateY.rotY(Math.PI/6.0);
    Transform3D rotateX = new Transform3D();
    rotateX.rotX(Math.PI/8.0);
    rotateX.mul(rotateY);
    TransformGroup objTrans = new TransformGroup(rotateX);
    objTrans.addChild(new ColorCube());
    scene.addChild(objTrans);
    universe.addBranchGraph(scene);
}
```

We generate a rotation by $\pi/6$ about the *y* axis followed by a rotation of $\pi/8$ about the *x* axis, create the ColorCube and add the branch to the scene graph.

Reading the documentation for the View class reveals that a default View actually comes with both the front and back clipping planes enabled. The front plane is placed at a distance of 0.1 metres from the viewpoint, and the back plane at a distance of 10 metres. Since the ColorCube is created by default with its centre at the origin, and the cube measures 2 metres on each edge, it fits between the planes $z = -1$ and $z = 1$ (rotating the cube will cause it to extend slightly beyond both of these planes, but we know roughly where the cube will be placed in the image). Since we have placed the viewpoint a distance of 6 metres from the origin, the default clipping planes should allow us to see objects between the planes $z = 5.9$ and $z = -4$, so the entire cube should be visible, as it turns out to be.

To see the effect of moving the clipping planes so that they intersect the cube, we might try moving the front clipping plane to a distance of 5 metres from the viewpoint, which, with our current viewpoint position, should place the clipping plane at $z = 1$. We can do this by inserting the lines

```
View view = universe.getView();
view.setFrontClipDistance(5.0);
```

immediately before the call to addCube() in the ClippingDemo constructor above.

If we try this, however, we discover that the cube completely disappears. What has gone wrong?

The problem is that Java 3D uses several different coordinate systems to refer to the geometric objects in the scene, and to the view platform. In fact, in the most general case, 9 different coordinate systems may coexist in a single application.

The coordinate system we have been using up to now for all calculations is known as the *virtual eye* coordinate system, because it treats the viewpoint defined by the position of the view platform as a 'virtual eye' that is used to determine the viewing direction and orientation. By default, however, clipping distances are measured in the *physical eye* coordinate system. For a graphics display consisting of a desktop monitor, the physical eye system attempts to calculate the actual distances perceived by the user sitting in front of the monitor. With the default parameters used in setting up the physical eye system, the net effect is that virtual eye coordinates are scaled by a factor of 0.175 to produce physical eye coordinates. Since the argument to setFrontClipDistance() is interpreted as a distance in the *physical eye* system, it is equivalent to a distance of 5/0.175, or more than 28 metres from the viewpoint. Since this is on the far side of the cube, we don't see anything in the output window.

Rather than attempt to cope with the complexities of the various Java 3D coordinate systems, we will simply use the virtual eye coordinate system for most calculations in this book. To do this, we need a way of telling the View to use virtual eye coordinates for clipping rather than the default physical eye system. The easiest way to ensure that we always use the virtual eye system for clipping is to insert the following two lines in the setupView() method in BasicUniverse:

```
view.setFrontClipPolicy(View.VIRTUAL_EYE);
view.setBackClipPolicy(View.VIRTUAL_EYE);
```

With this alteration, we can now run the ClippingDemo again, and we obtain the image shown in Figure 5.5.

Figure 5.5:
The rotated cube intersected by the front clipping plane.

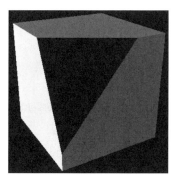

We see portions of the three faces that were fully visible before the clipping plane was moved. We do not see any of the back faces of the cube, since by default, geometric solids are drawn with their back or hidden faces removed. We will see how to change this when we consider the generation of three-dimensional solids in Chapter 6.

5.7 Locales and HiResCoords

As mentioned earlier, it is possible to attach more than one Locale to a VirtualUniverse. Usually, the reason for doing so is that the universe contains several locations that are physically separated by large distances. At each location, some objects are to be rendered, but there is nothing of interest in the intervening space between these locations.

An obvious example of such a situation is an astronomical model of, say, several solar systems, where the space between the solar systems is completely empty. We can define a separate Locale for each solar system, and move the view platform between Locales according to which solar system we wish to view.

The single, default, Locale that we have been attaching to the universe in all examples so far has its origin at (0.0, 0.0, 0.0). In principle, it is a simple matter to add a second Locale to the virtual universe by specifying its location relative to the first Locale.

Java 3D uses a special coordinate system for positioning Locales, however. A Locale's position must be given by a HiResCoord object which, as its name implies, specifies a location using high-resolution coordinates. A HiResCoord consists of three arrays of 8 ints each, one array for each of the three coordinates x, y and z. Let us consider the array X for the x coordinate.

An int in Java consists of 32 bits, so an array of 8 ints contains 256 bits. The array elements of X, from element 0 to element 7, are concatenated to form a block of 256 bits which represent a high-precision floating point number. The first 128 bits, contained in array elements 0 through 3, represent the integer portion of the number, and the remaining 128 bits, contained in array elements 4 through 7, represent the fractional part.

If the number 1.0 is defined to represent a distance of 1 metre, the total range of distances which can be represented by a HiResCoord extends from a smallest distance that is less than the radius of a proton to a largest distance of several hundred billion light years. In other words, a HiResCoord allows a range of distances that covers all sizes with any scientific use.

To produce a HiResCoord, we must convert the desired number into two's complement binary, then split this binary number into the 8 components that are represented by each element in the array. This book is not the place to give a detailed algorithm for producing binary numbers, but a simple example will illustrate the process.

Suppose we wish to represent the number 15.25 as a HiResCoord. We first split the number into the integer and fractional parts. In binary, 15 is 1111 and 0.25 is 0.01. In the 8-element array of ints, only elements 3 and 4 will have non-zero bits: element 3 will contain the 1111 and element 4 the 0.01. We can assign the correct value to X[3] with the assignment X[3] = 15. The assignment to X[4] is a bit trickier, however. Since X[4] is a 32-bit value and we want the first two bits to be 0 and 1, the bit pattern we actually want to store in X[4] is 01000000000000000000000000000000. We could work this out in decimal, but an easier way is to use the bit-shift operator <<. The expression 1 << 30 shifts a single 1-bit 30 places to the left, which is exactly what we want.

The following code snippet creates three int arrays and initializes the X array to store the high-resolution value 15.25. The Y and Z arrays are left in their default states, containing all zeroes.

This set of three int arrays is then used to create a HiResCoord with the coordinates (15.25, 0.0, 0.0). Finally, we use the distance() method in the HiResCoord class to calculate the distance between this HiResCoord and another HiResCoord with coordinates (0.0, 0.0, 0.0). The result is a double, which we can print to verify that the value 15.25 has been stored in the first HiResCoord.

```
int[] X, Y, Z;
X = new int[8]; Y = new int[8]; Z = new int[8];
X[3] = 15;
X[4] = 1 << 30;
HiResCoord hiRes = new HiResCoord(X, Y, Z);
HiResCoord hiResZero = new HiResCoord();
System.out.println("Distance = " +
    hiResZero.distance(hiRes));
```

To create a new Locale in our VirtualUniverse, we need to specify its position with a HiResCoord. This can be done in the Locale constructor. In our previous examples, we have always created a Locale and attached it to a VirtualUniverse by the single statement:

```
Locale locale = new Locale(universe);
```

where universe is a previously created VirtualUniverse. This creates a Locale with its origin at the point (0.0, 0.0, 0.0).

If we have created a HiResCoord named hiRes specfying the origin of a second Locale, we can add this to the VirtualUniverse with the statement:

```
Locale locale2 = new Locale(universe, hiRes);
```

Using the second Locale simply requires that we attach the view platform to locale2. The two Locales can each have their own geometry branches, and the geometry attached to one Locale is visible from a view platform attached to the other, provided that the Locales are close enough to each other and, of course, that the observer is looking in the right direction. The coordinates of any objects in a geometry branch of a Locale are measured relative to the origin of that Locale. This allows us to have several Locales separated by enormous (inter-galactic) distances, and yet have extremely detailed graphics present at each Locale—we use HiResCoords to specify the origins of the Locales, and ordinary doubles to specify the positions and dimensions of the geometric objects at each Locale.

Note that the *only* use (at the time of writing) of HiResCoords in Java 3D is in the specification of Locale origins—we cannot use HiResCoords to define geometric objects. However, it is possible to use some of the methods in the HiResCoord class to do simple arithmetic with HiResCoords.

5.8   Compiling a BranchGroup

Three-dimensional graphics is, at the best of times, demanding of both memory and processor time. As a result, there have been many attempts to optimize the resources used in producing images and animations. The BranchGroup class contains a method called `compile()` which attempts to apply some optimizations to the geometry branches within a Java 3D program.

The `compile()` method might be better named 'optimize', since it doesn't really compile your code in the traditional sense of the word (that is, it doesn't translate your code into machine language). As we mentioned earlier when introducing the geometry branch of a scene graph, geometry consists primarily of `Appearance` and `Shape3D` objects, where the `Appearance` describes aspects of the object such as its colour, and `Shape3D` specifies the physical shape of the object. The `compile()` method attempts to optimize both these attributes by removing duplicate references, merging shapes and so on.

However, calling `compile()` often does not produce any noticeable improvement in a program's speed. One reason for this is that any use of capability bits (such as the two that allowed transform reads and writes that we saw earlier in this chapter) negates most of the benefits of using `compile()`, and as we will see, most Java 3D programs that do anything interesting require some interaction with the geometry branches.

Using `compile()` would not make any significant difference to any of the programs in this book because most of them use capability bits to some extent, and none of them is really big enough for compilation to make much difference in their efficiency.

In practice, however, it can't hurt to call `compile()` for your `BranchGroups` so if you want to maximize the efficiency of your Java 3D programs, you may want to adopt the habit of calling `compile()` for all `BranchGroups` after you have added all the geometry to that branch.

EXERCISES

1. Change the viewing distance of the view platform in the `Simple3D` program in the text by changing the second argument to the `BasicUniverse` constructor on line 19 in the `Simple3D` class code in the text. Verify that the size of the red square changes as you move the viewing platform relative to the cube. At what distance does the cube disappear when you get too close?

2. Change the original `Simple3D` program by rotating the view platform by $\pi/4$ radians about the y axis instead of the z axis. Try to predict what you will see before running the program.

3. Repeat question 2 except rotate the view platform about the z axis.

4. Using the `mul()` method in the `Transform3D` class and starting from the original `Simple3D` program, rotate the view platform by $\pi/4$ about the x axis followed by $\pi/4$ about the y axis.

5. Produce the same effects as those obtained in questions 2, 3 and 4 by rotating the cube instead of the view platform.

6. Produce the same effect as that obtained in question 2, but do it by applying an appropriate rotation of $\pi/8$ to the view platform and another rotation of $\pi/8$ to the cube.

7. Repeat question 5 using a `Matrix4d` to produce the rotations rather than one of the convenience methods in the `Transform3D` class.

8. Modify the parallel projection example in the text to produce a range of projections of the cube. Refer back to Chapter 4 and the discussion following equation 4.3, and produce projections for values of tan α of 0.0, 0.5, 1.0, 1.5, 2.0, 2.5 and 3.0. Draw all the projections on the same canvas by using translations. Is the cabinet projection the most 'normal' looking view of the cube?

9. Adjust the back clipping plane in the program showing the rotated cube so that part of the back portion of the cube is clipped.

10. Find values for the front and back clipping distances in the physical eye coordinate system that give the same results as Figure 5.5 and question 9 (that is, don't change the clipping policy from the default).

11. Express the 3D point (1.125, −178.75, 0.0625) as a HiResCoord. Read the documentation on the HiResCoord class to find an easy way to obtain the negative value for the *y* coordinate. Verify that your answer is correct by using the distance() method (and possibly other methods) in the HiResCoord class.

12. What is the smallest number that would require a non-zero entry in element 2 of an int array in a HiResCoord?

13. Add a second Locale to one of the example programs displaying the ColorCube in this chapter (it doesn't matter which one). Use a HiResCoord to set the origin of the second Locale at (2, 0, 0). Leave the ColorCube attached to the first Locale, but attach the view platform to the second Locale and verify that you get a different view of the cube.

14. Add a panel containing a button to the layout of the program in queston 13. Pressing the button should switch the view platform back and forth between the two Locales, allowing a more dynamic view of the difference between them. To do this, you will need to detach the BranchGroup containing the view platform from its parent and switch it to another parent. Read the documentation on the BranchGroup class to see how this is done. Remember to set the appropriate capability bits.

CHAPTER 6

Creating geometry in Java 3D

6.1 Representing surfaces in three dimensions

In the previous two chapters, we have seen how three-dimensional objects may be transformed and projected onto a two-dimensional surface, and how such objects may be displayed using Java 3D. We have not yet considered how three-dimensional objects may be constructed in the first place.

There are several ways, varying in complexity, of building a representation of a three-dimensional object. In this chapter, we will consider the simplest (and one of the most common) ways—the use of a *polygon mesh*. This is currently the only method supported by Java 3D.

6.2 Approximating a surface with polygons

In the previous chapter, we used Java 3D's ColorCube class to display a cube where each face is a different colour. Clearly, it is easy to construct a cube out of polygonal faces: each of the six sides of a cube is just a square. More general three-dimensional objects may be composed of polygonal faces as well. Objects such as buildings, furniture, and so on can often be portrayed accurately using only simple polygons.

More general scenes, however, usually contain objects with more complex geometry, including curved surfaces which cannot be represented precisely using polygons. In these cases, however, it is still possible to use polygons to provide an approximation of curved surfaces.

Ultimately, of course, all objects that are displayed on a digital display device such as a computer monitor must be represented by polygons, since the display consists of an array of discrete pixels. Thus, even the more general methods for displaying curved surfaces must be reduced to a polygonal representation before they can be rendered.

A polygonal representation of a surface is usually given as an array or list of vertex coordinates. In most cases, the polygons are triangles, since any more complex polygon can always be decomposed into a set of triangles. A first rendering of an object represented in this way would then give a *wire-mesh* image, where only the polygon edges are drawn (see Figure 6.1 on page 159).

To give an object a solid appearance, the surfaces of the polygons must be coloured in some way. The simplest method is just to fill in each polygon with a solid colour, using the filling algorithms in Chapter 1. Provided that the polygon edges are drawn in a colour contrasting with that used for the filling, a solid object with a three-dimensional appearance will be obtained, although no variation in shading over the surface will occur.

The next step could be to add a directional light source, so that parts of the object appear highlighted, and other parts appear in shadow. There are various methods for adding illumination to a model, some of which we will consider in Chapter 8. The simplest method involves calculating how much light is reflected from each polygon and shading that polygon accordingly. More complex illumination models produce a gradient of colour across the surface of each individual polygon, so that even if a surface is composed of a relatively coarse polygon mesh, a more realistic appearance can be obtained.

A final enhancement may be to add a *texture* to the surface. A texture is a pattern which is applied to each polygon, and which is transformed so that if the polygon is viewed in perspective, the texture is transformed so that it is viewed at the same angle.

In addition to building a representation of an object, we must consider the methods by which the object will be drawn. Methods such as *hidden surface removal* (where those portions of the object that are hidden by other portions are identified so that they need not be drawn) must be applied before the final scene is rendered.

As you might expect, drawing 3D graphics can be a costly process with regards both to processing time and memory requirements. It is for this reason that the realism of computer graphics that is being achieved at the moment has had to wait until now—the processing power and memory required were simply not available in most computers until the last few years.

There is very little theory involved in the construction of a polygon mesh for a 3D object. The process of building a mesh is, except for some solids with mathematical descriptions, more an art than a science, and is best left to books on computer art and the use of 3D drawing packages. The handling of a polygon mesh, once it is constructed, is largely dependent on the graphics programming environment, so in the remainder of this chapter we will consider how Java 3D builds and processes representations of 3D objects.

6.3   Polygonal surfaces in Java 3D

In Chapter 5 we mentioned that a geometric object is represented in Java 3D's scene graph by means of a Shape3D node. A Shape3D node must be a *leaf* node, which means that it is not allowed to have any children—we cannot append any further nodes to a Shape3D node within a scene graph.

A given Shape3D node contains a list of Geometry objects (or, to be more precise, since Geometry is an abstract class, a list of objects derived from the Geometry class). The Geometry class is a base class for a number of other classes which allow 3D objects to be built in various ways. If the list of Geometry objects contains more than one element, all objects in the list are drawn when the Shape3D node is processed.

In addition to the Geometry objects, a Shape3D node can contain one (and only one) Appearance object. The Appearance class controls most aspects of an object's appearance except for its geometric shape. Thus, all Geometry objects connected to a single Shape3D node must share the same appearance attributes. This is not really a restriction, since it is always possible to add more Shape3D nodes to a scene graph, and each such node can have a different Appearance object attached to it.

To get a feel for how an object may be created in Java 3D, we will present an example in which we create the simplest solid object with polygonal faces: the tetrahedron. We will use the BasicUniverse class from Chapter 5, and add a second class in which the tetrahedron is constructed. Initially, we will add only the geometry for the tetrahedron, and then add some appearance attributes later.

The first form of the Tetrahedron class is as follows.

```
1    import com.sun.j3d.utils.geometry.*;
2    import com.sun.j3d.utils.universe.*;
3    import javax.media.j3d.*;
4    import javax.swing.*;
5    import javax.vecmath.*;
6    import java.awt.*;
7    import java.awt.event.*;
8
9    public class Tetrahedron extends JFrame
10   {
11       public Tetrahedron()
12       {
13           super("Tetrahedron demo");
14           initComponents ();
15           setSize(600, 600);
16           GraphicsConfiguration graphicsConfig =
17           SimpleUniverse.getPreferredConfiguration();
18           Canvas3D canvas = new Canvas3D(graphicsConfig);
19           getContentPane().add("Center", canvas);
20           BasicUniverse universe =
21           new BasicUniverse(canvas, 4.0f);
22           BranchGroup scene = createTetrahedronGraph();
23           universe.addBranchGraph(scene);
24       }
25
26       public BranchGroup createTetrahedronGraph()
27       {
28           BranchGroup objRoot = new BranchGroup();
29           TriangleArray tetrahedronArray =
30           new TriangleArray(12, GeometryArray.COORDINATES);
31           Point3d coords[] = new Point3d[12];
32           // Base
33           coords[0] = new Point3d(-0.5, -0.5, 0.0);
34           coords[1] = new Point3d(0.5, -0.5, 0.0);
35           coords[2] = new Point3d(0.0, 0.5, 0.0);
36
37           // Side 1
38           coords[3] = new Point3d(-0.5, -0.5, 0.0);
39           coords[4] = new Point3d(0.5, -0.5, 0.0);
40           coords[5] = new Point3d(0.0, 0.0, 1.0);
41
42           // Side 2
43           coords[6] = new Point3d(-0.5, -0.5, 0.0);
```

```
44      coords[7] = new Point3d(0.0, 0.5, 0.0);
45      coords[8] = new Point3d(0.0, 0.0, 1.0);
46
47      // Side 3
48      coords[9] = new Point3d(0.5, -0.5, 0.0);
49      coords[10] = new Point3d(0.0, 0.5, 0.0);
50      coords[11] = new Point3d(0.0, 0.0, 1.0);
51
52      tetrahedronArray.setCoordinates(0, coords);
53      Shape3D tetrahedron = new Shape3D(tetrahedronArray);
54      objRoot.addChild(tetrahedron);
55
56      return objRoot;
57   }
58
59   private void initComponents()
60   {
61      addWindowListener (new WindowAdapter () {
62         public void windowClosing (WindowEvent evt) {
63            exitForm (evt);
64         }
65      }
66      );
67   }
68
69   private void exitForm(WindowEvent evt)
70   {
71      System.exit(0);
72   }
73
74   public static void main(String[] args)
75   {
76      new Tetrahedron().show ();
77   }
78 }
```

The constructor should be familiar from the ColorCube example in Chapter 5. The tetrahedron itself is created in the createTetrahedronGraph() method starting on line 26. This method creates a BranchGroup in which the Scene3D object containing the tetrahedron is to be stored.

To add the geometry of the tetrahedron to the branch, we must recall that the Geometry class is abstract, so we need an instance of one of the classes derived from Geometry. Java 3D provides quite a variety of classes from which to choose. We will consider the various classes in more detail later in this chapter, but for now we need to choose a representation for the tetrahedron.

The GeometryArray class is another abstract class that serves as a base class for a selection of classes that allow geometric objects to be specified by listing the coordinates of their vertices. A figure's geometry can be given as an array of individual points (drawn without lines connecting them), line segments (drawn as points connected in pairs), triangles or quadrilaterals. Although we will see later that there are other, sometimes more efficient, ways of representing some figures, we will begin by using a `TriangleArray` to build the tetrahedron, since its four sides are all triangles.

On lines 29 and 30, we construct a `TriangleArray` object. The first argument of the constructor is the total number of coordinates that will be needed to specify all the triangles in the array. Since we need four triangles, each of which will be specified separately, we need a total of twelve vertices, even though only four of them are distinct. (This is one of the inefficiencies of using the `TriangleArray` to represent an object where many of the triangles share common vertices. We will address this point later.)

The second argument in the constructor on line 30 specifies the type of data this is stored in the array. In addition to storing coordinates, we may also store appearance data such as colour or texture to be associated with each vertex. In this first program, however, we will store only the coordinates of each vertex. The type of data is specified by using one of the static `int` fields in the `GeometryArray` class as an identifier.

The coordinates of the triangles must be stored in one of the three-dimensional `Point` classes. Here, we use `Point3d`, which uses `doubles`. In order to keep the numbers simple, we have placed the base of the tetrahedron in the xy plane, and its vertex directly over the origin at $z = 1$. Since the default orientation of the coordinate system is to allow the user to look down the positive z-axis, we will be looking down onto the tetrahedron from a point directly above its apex.

On line 52 we attach the array of coordinates to the `TriangleArray` object, and then, on line 53, we create a `Shape3D` object and attach the `TriangleArray` to it. This step associates the geometry with the `Shape3D` leaf node. Finally, on line 54, we attach the tetrahedron itself to the scene graph.

Running this program produces a solid white triangle on a black background, which may be a bit of a disappointment. There is no real evidence that we are looking at a tetrahedron, or even at a three-dimensional object.

The reason for this is that by default, Java 3D fills all polygons with the default colour (white) and does not draw the edges of the polygons in a contrasting colour, so there are no visual cues such as edges or shading to give us any hint that we are looking at something solid. Doing this requires adding some appearance attributes.

6.4 The Appearance class

As mentioned earlier, a `Shape3D` node contains two main components: a `Geometry` object and an `Appearance` object. The `Appearance` class allows such things as the colour, line and point attributes (including size, line type, and antialiasing), and several other attributes related to rendering and texture mapping to be specified. As a general rule, once we have the shape of the object defined using a `Geometry`-derived class, the best place to look for all other attributes is in the `Appearance` class.

We will illustrate a typical procedure for using the `Appearance` class by converting the tetrahedron into a wire-frame image, so that only the edges are drawn—the faces are not filled in. Glancing through the documentation for the `Appearance` class, we find a method called `setPolygonAttributes()`, which takes an argument of class `PolygonAttributes`. In the documentation for `PolygonAttributes`, we find a method called `setPolygonMode()`, the argument of which can be a static field in the `PolygonAttributes` class called POLYGON_LINE. This results in the polygon being drawn as lines only, which is what we want.

We can put all this together by adding the following code after line 53 in the `Tetrahedron` class above.

```
PolygonAttributes polyAttr = new PolygonAttributes();
polyAttr.setPolygonMode(PolygonAttributes.POLYGON_LINE);
Appearance appear = new Appearance();
appear.setPolygonAttributes(polyAttr);
tetrahedron.setAppearance(appear);
```

We create a `PolygonAttributes` object and set its polygon mode so that a wire-frame polygon is drawn. We then create an `Appearance` object and attach the `PolygonAttributes` object to it. Finally, we add the `Appearance` object to the `Shape3D` object (`tetrahedron`).

The result is shown in Figure 6.1, where a white wire-frame tetrahedron is drawn on a black background.

Figure 6.1:
A tetrahedron drawn as a wire-frame object.

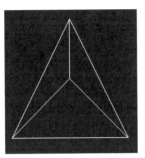

Remember that the view in the figure is from directly above the apex of the tetrahedron. Depending on how we perceive the figure, we might view it so that the centre point is seen as sticking out of the page, or we might see it with the centre point projecting into the page. With a wire-frame model projected into two dimensions, there is no way to be sure what was intended in the original program.

One feature of the `Tetrahedron` class with its added `Appearance` object deserves some emphasis. In our example, we added the `Apperance` object after the geometry had been constructed and added to the `Shape3D` node, but we could also have added it before the geometry was constructed. The important point is that the `Appearance` and `Geometry` objects are only linked once they have both been connected to the `Shape3D` node, and the order in which they are connected does not matter.

The `Appearance` class has many other uses, and we shall meet it frequently in future chapters. To get a feel for the capabilities of the `Appearance` class, you should experiment by applying various attributes to the tetrahedron.

6.5 Strip arrays

One of the problems with the version of the `Tetrahedron` class given above is that each vertex needs to be defined three times. Clearly this is a waste of space, and for larger solids with many polygon faces with shared edges, this redundancy can become a serious problem. Java 3D provides several ways of representing data for shared vertices more efficiently. We will examine how the tetrahedron can be drawn using some of these methods.

One of the subclasses of `GeometryArray` is yet another abstract class called `GeometryStripArray`, which in turn has three subclasses called `LineStripArray`, `TriangleStripArray` and `TriangleFanArray`. Each of these classes allows a series of lines or triangles to be specified in such a way that each line or triangle after the first shares some of its vertices with the previous line or triangle in the array, thus allowing some reuse of common vertices.

As an example, we can replace lines 29 to 53 in the `Tetrahedron` class above with the following code:

```
int[] vertexCounts = {6};
TriangleStripArray tetrahedronStripArray =
    new TriangleStripArray(6, GeometryArray.COORDINATES,
        vertexCounts);
Point3d stripCoords[] = new Point3d[6];
stripCoords[0] = new Point3d(-0.5, -0.5, 0.0);
stripCoords[1] = new Point3d(0.5, -0.5, 0.0);
stripCoords[2] = new Point3d(0.0, 0.5, 0.0);
stripCoords[3] = new Point3d(0.0, 0.0, 1.0);
stripCoords[4] = new Point3d(-0.5, -0.5, 0.0);
stripCoords[5] = new Point3d(0.5, -0.5, 0.0);
tetrahedronStripArray.setCoordinates(0, stripCoords);
Shape3D tetrahedron =
    new Shape3D(tetrahedronStripArray);
```

In a `TriangleStripArray`, the first three vertices form the first triangle. Thereafter, each additional vertex in the array is combined with the last two vertices from the previous triangle to make the next triangle. In the code above, for example, elements 0 through 2 of the `stripCoords` array form the base of the tetrahedron. The next triangle is formed from elements 1, 2 and 3 of the array, then the next from elements 2, 3 and 4, and so on. In this way, we can specify the entire tetrahedron using 6 array elements, rather than the 12 needed in the earlier version. You should convince yourself that this technique will indeed produce the same set of 4 triangles as in our earlier version.

The `TriangleStripArray` constructor used here takes three arguments. The first argument is the number of vertices in the array, the second argument specifies the data type to be stored in each array element (as with the `TriangleArray` class used earlier), and the final argument is an `int` array called `vertexCounts`.

The `TriangleStripArray` allows several separate strip arrays to be stored in a single object, with the `vertexCounts` array specifying the number of vertices to be used in each strip. In the simple example here, we are only using a single strip of triangles to build the tetrahedron, so the `vertexCounts` array contains only a single entry. If we wanted, for example, to display a tetrahedron and an octahedron (an eight-sided solid), we could list all the vertices in a single `TriangleStripArray` object and provide a `vertexCounts` array with two elements, specifying the number of vertices to be used in each of the two solids. The constructor can work out the number of separate strips to be drawn by calculating the size of the `vertexCounts` array.

If we run the program (again with the POLYGON_LINE attribute set so that we get a wire-frame image) we would expect to see the same result as shown in

Figure 6.1. However, all that is visible is a single triangle corresponding to the base of the tetrahedron—the three faces leading up to the apex are missing. What has gone wrong?

6.6 Polygon orientation

In a solid object such as a tetrahedron, it is natural to think of each polygonal facet as having an *inside* and an *outside* face. Java 3D does, in fact, assign each polygon a direction in this way, although up to now the effect has gone unnoticed. The direction of a polygon is determined from the order in which its vertices are specified.

Figure 6.2:
The orientation of polygon faces.
(a) The outward face of an isolated polygon is being viewed if its vertices occur in counter-clockwise order.
(b) In a strip array, the rule for determining the outward face alternates between adjacent triangles.

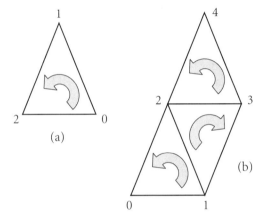

For an isolated triangle (Figure 6.2), if we view the triangle from the side where the vertices appear in counterclockwise order, we are viewing the outside face. Another way of thinking of the rule for finding the outside face of a triangle is to apply a right-hand rule. In Figure 6.2 (a), place your right hand over the triangle and curl your fingers in the direction of the arrow. If you now extend your thumb, it points towards the 'outside' relative to the triangle.

If we applied this rule to the triangles in a strip array, however, the result is not what would be required in most applications. Referring to Figure 6.2 (b), a strip array has been defined using 5 vertices, in the order shown in the figure. The first triangle is drawn using vertices 0, 1 and 2, and has its outward face visible (facing the viewer). The next triangle is drawn using vertices 1, 2 and 3 so if we applied the right-hand rule, its outward face would not be visible—the triangle would be 'upside down'. The next triangle, being composed of vertices 2, 3 and 4, would be facing upwards again.

In most applications, we would probably want all three triangles to be facing the same way, so the convention in a strip array is to alternate the rule for determining the outward face of each polygon. Use the right-hand rule for the first triangle, then a *left-hand rule* for the next triangle, then the right-hand rule again, and so on.

Note that this alternation of the outward-facing rule applies only to subclasses of GeometryStripArray, and *not* to any other subclass of GeometryArray. In particular, the right-hand rule is used to determine the outward faces of *all* triangles in a `TriangleArray`, such as the one we used in the original `Tetrahedron` class.

We can now understand why we see only a single triangle when we draw the tetrahedron with the strip array coordinates above. The first triangle is drawn with its vertices in the order shown in Figure 6.2, so even though it is the base of the tetrahedron, its outward face is directed upwards. If we apply the correct rule to determine the outward face of the other three triangles, we discover that their outward faces are all directed away from the viewer, so they are not visible.

The practice of not rendering the back faces of polygons is known as *back face culling*. There are two reasons why this option may be enforced. First, it is often desirable to omit the back faces in a figure in order to improve the appearance by avoiding cluttering and needless detail. Second, rendering the back face of a polygon uses processor time and slows down the overall graphical display, so if there is no need to do it, it is best avoided.

Assuming we wish to view the full tetrahedron, however, there are two ways of fixing this problem. The first (and probably the best, from a design point of view) is to rearrange the order in which we specify the vertices, so that the base of the tetrahedron faces away from the viewer and the other three sides face towards the viewer. You may wish to give this a try and then view the results to make sure you have it right.

The second way is to turn off back face culling. As you may have guessed, the presence or absence of back face culling is a polygon attribute, and can be altered by setting another flag in the `PolygonAttributes` object that we used earlier to obtain a wire-frame model. Looking up the available options in the documentation, we find that we can turn off back face culling by inserting the following line at some point after the `PolygonAttributes` object `polyAttr` has been created:

```
polyAttr.setCullFace(PolygonAttributes.CULL_NONE);
```

Although this is the easiest method from a programming point of view, you should give some thought as to whether it is the best solution, since it may result in unwanted polygon faces being rendered, and it will also slow down the rendering of the image.

Another exercise you may wish to try is to return to the original `Tetrahedron` class and check the orientation of each of the triangles in the `TriangleArray` object. Are they all facing the correct directions, or were we just lucky in getting a complete image of a tetrahedron in this case? If the latter, you should alter the order of the coordinates to make each triangle face in the proper direction.

6.7   Indexed arrays

The second version of our tetrahedron class, where we used strip arrays, allowed us to reuse some of the vertices, but there was still some redundancy in that we had to specify 6 vertices, while the tetrahedron itself has only 4. Java 3D provides the `IndexedGeometryArray` (which is abstract, so we actually deal with its subclasses) which allow redundancy in the use of vertices to be eliminated completely.

An indexed array uses two subsidiary arrays to store the information required to render an object. In the first array, we store the coordinates of the vertices, but we need to store each distinct vertex only once (no redundancy). In the second array, we store a list of indices into the first array. These indices define how the various polygons are to be constructed with reference to the list of vertices stored in the first array.

It is easiest to see how this works by rewriting the tetrahedron example using an indexed array. There is an indexed array class corresponding to each of the original geometry array classes, so we may use the IndexedTriangleArray to describe the tetrahedron.

We can replace lines 29 to 53 in our original Tetrahedron class above (on page 156) with the following code:

```
IndexedTriangleArray tetrahedronIndexedArray =
    new IndexedTriangleArray(4,
    GeometryArray.COORDINATES, 12);
Point3d indexedCoords[] = new Point3d[4];
indexedCoords[0] = new Point3d(-0.5, -0.5, 0.0);
indexedCoords[1] = new Point3d(0.5, -0.5, 0.0);
indexedCoords[2] = new Point3d(0.0, 0.5, 0.0);
indexedCoords[3] = new Point3d(0.0, 0.0, 1.0);
tetrahedronIndexedArray.setCoordinates(0,
    indexedCoords);
int coordIndex[] = {
// Base
    0, 2, 1,
// Side 1
    0, 1, 3,
// Side 2
    2, 0, 3,
// Side 3
    1, 2, 3
};
tetrahedronIndexedArray.setCoordinateIndices(0,
    coordIndex);
Shape3D tetrahedron =
    new Shape3D(tetrahedronIndexedArray);
```

The IndexedTriangleArray constructor takes 3 arguments. The first is the number of distinct vertices that are to be rendered in the final object; for the tetrahedron, there are 4 vertices. The first argument therefore specifies the length of the first array, which is to contain the data.

The second argument, as usual, specifies the type of data that is stored in the first array (coordinates, in our example). The final argument specifies the size of the second array, which is to contain the indices into the first array. Each index is an int which refers to one of the array elements in the first array. (Note that the JDK documentation states that this third argument is the number of vertices to be rendered, which is incorrect.) In the case of an IndexedTriangleArray, the indices are taken in groups of 3, with each group defining one of the four triangles to be drawn, so we have a total of 12 indices.

After creating the master indexed array in the code sample above, we create the array of coordinate data, called indexedCoords. We specify the four vertices of the tetrahedron only once each. The order in which we list the coordinates does not matter, since the order in which they are drawn is determined by the array of indices.

After attaching the coordinate array to the master indexed array using the setCoordinates() method, we construct the array of indices, called coordIndex. This is an array of 12 ints, with each group of 3 ints within the array corresponding to one of the faces of the tetrahedron. In this case, the order in which we list the indices *does* matter, since this will determine which side of each face is the outside and which is the inside, by means of the right-hand rule described above.

We first define the base of the tetrahedron as being composed of vertices 0, 2, and 1. These indices refer back to the coordinate array, so that the base triangle therefore has vertices at (-0.5, -0.5, 0.0), (0.5, -0.5, 0.0) and (0.0, 0.5, 0.0). The remaining three sides of the tetrahedron are defined in a similar way.

In this example, we have taken care to place the outside face of each triangle correctly, so that the base's outside face is away from the viewer, and the outside faces of all the other edges are towards the viewer. We therefore do not need to turn off back face culling.

Running this program produces the same image as that shown in Figure 6.1.

In this simple example, the use of an indexed array is probably less efficient than the other methods, since we end up using almost as much memory to store the array of 4 vertex coordinates *and* the array of 12 indices as we did in storing the original set of 12 coordinates. However, if we had stored more information (such as colour and other information) at each vertex, and had a large number of triangles sharing vertices, a significant amount of memory could be saved by the use of indexed arrays. The resulting programs are usually easier to understand as well.

However, the use of indexed arrays always results in a performance hit, since the renderer must look up each vertex through the array of indices before drawing it. As such, the use of indexed arrays is not recommended if rendering speed is important. The strip arrays offer a more efficient way of storing the information, without the use of indices.

6.8   Triangulation and the GeometryInfo class

As we can see from the previous sections, specifying the geometry for even a fairly simple scene can be quite tedious, requiring the determination of a large number of coordinates. Since any scene that is rendered in Java 3D must be split into triangles (or at least quadrilaterals), any more complex polygons must be broken up into triangular pieces.

Doing this triangulation by hand would be an insurmountable task for any object with more than a few faces. Fortunately, Java 3D includes some utility classes that automate much of the process.

The GeometryInfo class is similar to the other geometry classes in that it takes an array of coordinates as its input. However, rather than requiring the programmer to specify the geometry as arrays of triangles or quadrilaterals, the GeometryInfo class will divide up an arbitrary polygon into triangles. Other utility classes will generate normal vectors for the vertices of all the triangles (needed if we apply lighting to the object—see Chapter 7), and arrange the triangles into strip arrays for greater efficiency.

Another useful feature of GeometryInfo is that it will allow us to define 'holes' in polygons. We could, for example, draw a polygon representing the side of a house and then draw a few holes representing windows.

Using a GeometryInfo is, if anything, easier than using the other geometry classes we have described earlier. We first create a GeometryInfo object. The constructor requires a single argument, which must be chosen from one of the static parameters defined in the GeometryInfo class:

- POLYGON_ARRAY: allows the array of coordinates to represent one or more polygons. Each polygon can be planar or non-planar, and may contain holes. (We will give examples of all these possibilities later.)

- QUAD_ARRAY: each set of four vertices in the coordinate array represents a quadrilateral.

- TRIANGLE_ARRAY: each set of three vertices in the coordinate array represents a triangle.

- TRIANGLE_FAN_ARRAY: the vertices are used to form a triangle fan.

- TRIANGLE_STRIP_ARRAY: the vertices are used to form a triangle strip, in the fashion of the strip arrays described above.

The most useful option is POLYGON_ARRAY, since the other options can all be duplicated by other classes that we considered earlier.

Once we have created the GeometryInfo, we must assign a list of coordinates to it using setCoordinates(). The coordinates can be specified as arrays of floats or doubles, where the elements must come in groups of three, representing the x, y and z coordinates of each point. Alternatively, the vertices of the polygons can be specified as an array of Point3ds or Point3fs.

Finally, we must tell GeometryInfo what to do with the coordinates. The options here depend on what type of GeometryInfo we created. For all the examples here, we will assume that we specified POLYGON_ARRAY.

First, since the list of coordinates may specify more than one polygon, we must tell GeometryInfo which groups of coordinates to use for which polygons. This is done using an array of ints called the strip count array. Each entry in this array states how many vertices should be used for each polygon. For example, if we have specified 10 vertices where the first 6 vertices specify a hexagon and the last 4 a rectangle, then the strip count array should contain the elements 6 and 4.

There are two important things to note about the strip count array. First, the sum of all the elements in the array must equal the total number of vertices specified in the call to setCoordinates(). Second, if we have specified the coordinates as arrays of doubles or floats, the number of individual coordinates is three times the number of vertices, since each vertex requires three coordinates to specify it. The numbers in the strip count array refer to the number of vertices, not the number of individual coordinates. Thus, in the previous example, if we specified 10 vertices as individual coordinates, the coordinate array would contain 30 elements, but the entries in the strip count array will still sum to 10, not 30.

Finally, if some of the polygons in the coordinate list are to be holes in a surrounding polygon, we must set a contour list. The easiest way to see how a contour list works is to consider an example. Suppose that we have defined two walls of a house, where the first wall consists of a single polygonal outline with two holes for windows and the second wall also consists of a polygonal outline, but with three holes for windows. In total, we need 7 polygons to specify the two main outlines and five windows. We will assume that the outlines of walls are each pentagons (so they require 5 vertices each to specify) and the windows are all rectangular (so they each require 4 vertices). We specify the coordinates in the order: wall, window, window, wall, window, window, window.

The strip count array will therefore contain the entries {5, 4, 4, 5, 4, 4, 4}. To tell GeometryInfo that the first polygon defines a wall and the next two polygons are holes in this wall, we must use a contour list. The contour list is also an array of ints. Each entry in the contour list represents the number of entries from the strip count list that should be combined into a polygon with some holes in it. In our case, the contour list would be {3, 4}. The first entry (3) means that we take the first three entries from the strip count list (5, 4, 4), use the first polygon in this list as the container, and use the remaining polygons in the list as holes in the first polygon. Similarly, the second entry in the contour list (4) means that we take the next 4 entries from the strip count list, use the first polygon as the container, and the rest as holes in that container.

Specifying a contour list is optional, but if we do, it must satisfy a few conditions. First, the sum of the entries in the contour list must equal the length of the strip count array. In our example here, the sum of the entries in the contour list is 3 + 4 = 7, which is the size of the strip count array.

Second, we must ensure that the polygons that are specified as holes lie entirely within the polygon that is used as the container. Failing to do this can cause unpredictable results.

Let us see how all this fits together in a sample program. The class below creates several polygons that define a house. The front and back of the house are each defined by a polygon which is pentagonal in shape but has a notch cut out of the bottom to represent a door. There are also two windows above the door.

The left and right sides of the house are rectangular, but each side contains three windows. Finally, we have covered the house with a peaked roof to give an example of a non-planar polygon.

The output of the program is shown in Figure 6.3. Some lighting (see Chapter 7) has been added to the program to display the sides of the house more clearly.

Figure 6.3:
A house produced using GeometryInfo.

The program uses a BasicUniverse to provide the display as usual. The main class is called GeometryInfoDemo, and is set up in much the same way as previous examples. The complete code may be downloaded from the Web site (see Preface).

We first consider a method that creates the coordinates for the various polygons that make up the house and windows. As the complete list of coordinates is quite long, we will only show those required to display the front side of the house.

```
private double[] createHouseData()
{
    double[] house = {
        // Front of house with a notch for the doorway
        0.0, 0.0, 0.0,
        2.5, 0.0, 0.0,
        2.5, 2.0, 0.0,
        3.5, 2.0, 0.0,
        3.5, 0.0, 0.0,
        6.0, 0.0, 0.0,
        6.0, 5.0, 0.0,
        3.0, 7.0, 0.0,
        0.0, 5.0, 0.0,

        // Left window
        1.0, 3.5, 0.0,
        2.0, 3.5, 0.0,
        2.0, 4.5, 0.0,
        1.0, 4.5, 0.0,

        // Right window
        4.0, 3.5, 0.0,
        5.0, 3.5, 0.0,
        5.0, 4.5, 0.0,
        4.0, 4.5, 0.0,
        // Remaining coords for rest of house
    };
    return house;
}
```

The first block of coordinates defines the outline of the front panel, including the rectangular notch at the bottom for the door. The last two blocks of coordinates define the two windows that will be used as holes in the original polygon.

The addHouse() method uses GeometryInfo to build the house and connect it to the scene graph.

```
1    private void addHouse()
2    {
3        double[] house = createHouseData();
4
5        int[] stripCount = {
6            9,4,4,          // Front + 2 windows
7            4,4,4,4,        // Right side + 3 windows
8            9,4,4,          // Back + 2 windows
9            4,4,4,4,        // Left side + 3 windows
10           6               // Roof
11       };
12       int[] contourCount = {3,4,3,4,1};
13       GeometryInfo gi =
14           new GeometryInfo(GeometryInfo.POLYGON_ARRAY);
```

```
15        gi.setCoordinates(house);
16        gi.setStripCounts(stripCount);
17        gi.setContourCounts(contourCount);
18        Shape3D houseShape = new Shape3D();
19        houseShape.setGeometry(gi.getGeometryArray());
20
21        BranchGroup scene = new BranchGroup();
22            scene.addChild(houseShape);
23    }
```

Line 3 retrieves the array of coordinates from createHouseData(). Lines 5 to 11 create the strip count array. The first three entries define the front of the house—the overall polygon that is serving as the container has 9 vertices, and each of the windows has 4 vertices. The remaining sets of strip counts deal with the other sides and roof of the house. The roof is the only part of the house that does not have any holes in it, so its entry in the strip count array consists of only a single value.

The roof is an example of a non-planar polygon. Its coordinates are given as the last 6 vertices in createHouseData() as:

```
// Roof (non-planar polygon)
0.0, 5.0, 0.0,
3.0, 7.0, 0.0,
6.0, 5.0, 0.0,
6.0, 5.0, -12.0,
3.0, 7.0, -12.0,
0.0, 5.0, -12.0
```

This is a fairly simple non-planar polygon, consisting of two rectangles in an inverted V. The documentation warns that in some more complex non-planar cases, the results of triangulation might not be quite what you expect, so you should use non-planar polygons with some care. If possible, try to separate complex non-planar polygons into either less complex non-planar ones, or even better, into planar polygons.

On line 12, we define the contour count. The entries in this array correspond to the numbers of polygons that are needed to define each of the sides of the house in the strip count array.

Although the results of using contours to define holes in a polygon work well in this example, there have been reports (on the java3d-interest mailing list) of some cases where the insertion of holes does not work properly due to bugs in the triangulation routines.

The remainder of the addHouse() method constructs the GeometryInfo, assigns the coordinates, strip counts and contour counts, and then extracts the geometry from the GeometryInfo so it can be assigned to a Shape3D. Once this has been done, the shape can be attached to the branch group and displayed in the usual way. In the actual program that was used to produce Figure 6.2, some additional components such as appearance, lighting and transformations were applied, but the basic shape as obtained from the GeometryInfo was not changed.

There are three other utility classes that are related to GeometryInfo: Triangulator, Stripifier and NormalGenerator.

The Triangulator class performs the triangulation calculation that divides an arbitrarily-shaped polygon into triangular regions. Although many examples of the use of GeometryInfo on the Web include a separate call to Triangulator, this is not necessary—the GeometryInfo class calls the triangulation routines automatically. There can, however, be some advantage in making a separate call to Triangulator since this class does give us some extra control over the algorithm that is used to produce the triangles.

For example, the default triangulation of the front of the house produced by using GeometryInfo on its own is shown in Figure 6.4. The Triangulator class allows us to produce a random triangulation of a polygon. When this is applied to the front of the house, one possible outcome is shown in Figure 6.5.

To apply Triangulator by hand, we can use the following code:

```
Triangulator tr = new Triangulator(1);
tr.triangulate(gi);
```

The Triangulator constructor takes either zero or one argument. Using the zero argument constructor produces the same results as using GeometryInfo on its own. Passing 1 as the argument results in the random triangulation shown here. (Oddly enough, there are static parameters defined in the Triangulator class that provide readable names for the constructor arguments, but they are private fields and therefore not accessible to programmers.) Random triangulation often results in fewer 'skinny' triangles than the default algorithm.

Having created the Triangulator, we call its triangulate() method to apply it to the GeometryInfo.

Figure 6.4:
The default triangulation produced by GeometryInfo.

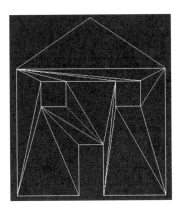

Figure 6.5:
A random triangulation produced using Triangulator.

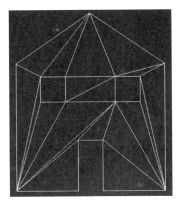

The `NormalGenerator` class generates normal vectors for each vertex in a triangulated `GeometryInfo`. As we shall see when we consider lighting, normals are required if lighting is to be applied to an object. To generate normals, we use the code:

```
NormalGenerator ng = new NormalGenerator();
ng.generateNormals(gi);
```

In those cases where each vertex is used by only one polygon, the normal at that vertex is just the normal to the polygon. If a vertex is shared by two non-planar polygons, `NormalGenerator` will attempt to generate an 'average' normal for the polygons sharing the vertex. The effect of this is to produce more realistic-looking lighting effects.

The `Stripifier` class converts the triangles produced by `GeometryInfo` or `Triangulator` to strip arrays, which usually increases the efficiency of the code. It will not affect the appearance of the graphics, but is often worth doing in more complex geometries. To stripify a `GeometryInfo`, use the code:

```
Stripifier st = new Stripifier();
st.stripify(gi);
```

Normal generation should be done before stripification.

6.8.1 Transformations using the mouse

Although we will study interaction and animation more thoroughly in Chapter 8, it is quite easy to allow scenes to be dynamically rotated, zoomed (scaled) and translated using the mouse, without having to understand the intricacies of the more complex interaction classes. Most of the sample programs in the remainder of the book make use of the three utility classes that allow these transformations, so we will introduce them now.

The three classes are `MouseRotate`, `MouseZoom` and `MouseTranslate`. As all three classes work in much the same way, we will illustrate how to add a `MouseRotate` to a portion of an existing scene. The code is:

```
TransformGroup transGroup = new TransformGroup();
transGroup.
    setCapability(TransformGroup.ALLOW_TRANSFORM_READ);
transGroup.
    setCapability(TransformGroup.ALLOW_TRANSFORM_WRITE);
// Add scene components to transGroup here

MouseRotate mouseRotate = new MouseRotate(transGroup);
mouseRotate.setSchedulingBounds(new BoundingSphere());
scene.addChild(mouseRotate);
```

The mouse utility classes each operate on a `TransformGroup` from the scene graph. `MouseRotate`, for example, will apply rotations to this `TransformGroup` as the user drags the mouse using the left mouse button. Since the transform within the `TransformGroup` is to be modified while it is live, it must have its capabilities set, as shown in the code. All objects that the programmer wishes to be rotated as the mouse is dragged should be children of the `TransformGroup` on which `MouseRotate` is acting.

To add the MouseRotate, we pass the TransformGroup on which it will act as an argument to its constructor. MouseRotate also requires a bounding region within which it will act. The sample code here uses the setSchedulingBounds() method to add a default BoundingSphere (centred at the origin with radius 1.0) as the bounding region, although any class derived from Bounds (which includes BoundingBox, BoundingPolytope (a convex polyhedron), and BoundingSphere) may be used.

Finally, we add the MouseRotate to the scene graph. When this program is run, clicking and dragging the left mouse button will cause the objects connected to transGroup to rotate interactively as the mouse is dragged.

A MouseTranslate can be added in the same way, and is used by clicking and dragging the right mouse button. Finally, MouseZoom zooms the scene in or out, and is activated by clicking and dragging the middle mouse button or mouse wheel. On mice that do not have a middle button or wheel, MouseZoom can be used by holding down the ALT key and then dragging with the left button.

6.9   Visible surface determination—the z-buffer

When more than one object is visible in a scene, it is possible for two or more objects to overlap. In order to display overlapping objects properly, we must be able to determine which object lies nearest the viewpoint and which surfaces it obscures. Surfaces that are obscured should not be rendered.

A number of algorithms exist for *visible surface determination*, but the most common at the moment is the *z-buffer* algorithm. The algorithm is extremely simple in concept, but does require a large amount of memory to implement efficiently. One of the main selling points of a modern graphics card is the amount of RAM it carries, and one of the main consumers of this memory is the z-buffer. (A rival of the z-buffer for memory usage is texture mapping, which is considered in Chapter 8.)

When a scene is to be displayed on screen, it is usually first rendered into an off-screen buffer within the computer's memory, and then transferred to the screen or printer. In animations, where multiple frames must be constructed and displayed in rapid succession, it turns out that this method of building each frame in the off-screen buffer (sometimes called the *frame buffer*) is more efficient than drawing the graphics directly to the screen.

If we are displaying a scene within a viewport, we therefore must reserve for the frame buffer a block of memory proportional to the number of pixels within the viewport. A scene is constructed by determining the colour and intensity values that each pixel must have, and writing these values into the frame buffer at the memory location corresponding to that pixel.

If we have only non-overlapping objects to display, we can get by with only a frame buffer, since we build the scene by traversing the scene graph, applying all the transformations that are specified, adding in any lighting effects (see Chapter 7 for a discussion of lighting) and so on, and then scan the final image (using algorithms similar to the scan-line algorithms for filling polygons discussed in Chapter 1) to calculate the data for each pixel. Portions of objects that face away from the viewpoint (as determined by the rules given earlier for determining the 'direction' of a polygon) can be ignored in these calculations if desired (that is, *back-face culling* can be applied).

Now suppose that some of the objects in a scene overlap. After all the transformations and projections that result in the three-dimensional scene being converted to a two-dimensional image have been carried out, some pixels within the viewport will be occupied by two or more surfaces from the original three-dimensional scene. How do we decide which surface should be used to obtain the value for a given pixel?

The z-buffer algorithm solves this problem in the simplest way possible. We assume that the viewpoint is on the positive z axis and we are looking directly down the z axis towards the scene. For a given pixel, the z coordinates of all surfaces covering that pixel are recorded, and the surface with the largest z coordinate (that is, the surface that is closest to the viewpoint) is the one that is used to draw the pixel.

The determination of the correct surface to draw for each pixel is done as part of the scan-line algorithm that is used to fill in the various polygons that make up each surface. Recall from Chapter 1 that the basic scan-line algorithm (which was described there for two dimensions, but the principle is the same in three dimensions) scans each polygon with a series of horizontal scan lines, and fills in all the pixels on each scan line lying on the 'inside' of the polygon.

Figure 6.6:
Two overlapping polygons. The solid polygon lies in front of the dashed polygon. The horizontal line is a scan line used in the z-buffer algorithm.

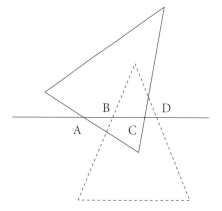

While this scanning is going on, we can also record the z coordinate of each pixel on the polygon, storing it in a separate buffer known, not surprisingly, as the *z-buffer*. At the same time, we write the corresponding colour and intensity for that pixel into the frame buffer.

Later on, when we are scanning another polygon that may overlap the first one, we calculate each z coordinate within the overlap region and compare this coordinate with the value stored in the z-buffer from a previous polygon. If the new z value is less than the stored value, we know that the second polygon must lie further away from the viewpoint than the first one, so we do not render it. If the new z value is larger than the stored one, the new polygon lies in front of the old one, so we save the new z value in the z-buffer and overwrite the corresponding values in the frame buffer with those from the new polygon.

Continuing in this fashion until all the polygons have been scanned will result in a frame buffer where each pixel contains the correct colour and intensity for the surface that is closest to the viewer at that point. (The final values stored in the z-buffer are not used for anything.)

As an example, consider Figure 6.6, where two overlapping polygons are shown. The solid triangle is assumed to be closer to the viewpoint than the dashed triangle. Let us assume that that dashed triangle is scanned first. When the scan line shown in the figure is considered, it intersects the dashed triangle in the line segment BD. Let us suppose that the z coordinate of the dashed triangle varies linearly from 0 to 6 along this line segment, and that there are 7 pixels between points B and D when this triangle is displayed in the viewport. Then the z values written into the z-buffer for the scan line shown in the figure will be:

```
* * * * * * * * * * * * * * * 0 1 2 3 4 5 6 * * * * * * *
```

Here, those pixels represented by * are to be coloured-in using the background colour, since no object yet covers them.

At the same time as we are storing values in the z-buffer, we are also writing pixel values into the frame buffer. We will denote the colour of the dashed triangle as D, so the frame buffer now looks like this:

```
* * * * * * * * * * * * * * * D D D D D D D * * * * * * *
```

Now we scan the solid triangle with the same scan line, which intersects the triangle along line segment AC. Let us assume that the z coordinate of this triangle varies linearly from 1 to 9 along this line segment, and that 9 pixels are required to cover segment AC. The z-buffer values here are

```
* * * * * * * * * * * * 1 2 3 4 5 6 7 8 9 * * * * * * * *
```

We now compare these values with those that were stored earlier for the dashed triangle, which is most easily done if we place the two rows of values next to each other:

```
* * * * * * * * * * * * * * * 0 1 2 3 4 5 6 * * * * * * *
* * * * * * * * * * * * 1 2 3 4 5 6 7 8 9 * * * * * * * *
```

We can see that, in the region where the two triangles overlap, the z values for the second triangle are always greater than those for the first, so the final entries into the z-buffer are:

```
* * * * * * * * * * * * 1 2 3 4 5 6 7 8 9 5 6 * * * * * * *
```

At the same time as the z-buffer is updated, the frame buffer is also updated by overwriting the values originally stored when the dashed triangle was scanned with those from the solid triangle. Denoting the colour of the solid triangle as S, the frame buffer now looks like this:

```
* * * * * * * * * * * * S S S S S S S S S D D * * * * * * *
```

We can see that the correct combination of pixels has been produced for this particular scan line: that portion of the scan line where the dashed triangle is obscured by the solid one has been overwritten by the pixel colour corresponding to the solid triangle. If there were more polygons in the scene, they would all be treated in the same way, so that a complete frame buffer would result at the end of the scanning process. At that point, the frame buffer would be drawn to the screen, making the finished picture visible.

Although, in the current edition of Java 3D, all surfaces are rendered using polygons, the z-buffer algorithm is quite general in that it can correctly identify the pixel values for objects composed of any shape. If a future version of Java 3D should provide spline surfaces (see Chapter 7), for example, the z-buffer algorithm could be used for visible surface determination just as easily.

The z-buffer algorithm obviously requires a lot of memory, especially for high resolution monitors, and it also requires a lot of computing power if the scene is animated so that the objects within a scene are constantly changing their relative positions. The fact that modern graphics cards are capable of running full-screen animations of 3D scenes with a high number of frames per second is due to a combination of the increased memory on these cards and improved hardware techniques for speeding up the processing of graphical data. Many of the animation examples in this book (see Chapter 9) will flicker quite badly if run on machines with less powerful graphics cards, since these cards are unable to keep up with the calculations required to refresh (among other things) the z-buffer for each frame in the animation.

One enhancement of the z-buffer algorithm should be mentioned. The version of the algorithm given above assumes that all objects are totally opaque, so that if one object lies in front of another, the object in the background will be totally obscured. In Java and many other graphics packages, colours may be specified with a *transparency* factor. Objects coloured with a semi-transparent colour allow objects behind them to show through to a certain extent.

In this case, the version of the z-buffer algorithm above obviously would not work, since the *z* components and pixel values of any object lying behind another object are completely overwritten at each stage in the algorithm. One solution to this problem is to maintain a *list* of *z* values for each pixel, and to sort the surfaces in order of increasing distance from the viewpoint. When the scene is ultimately rendered, the most distant object is drawn first, with each successively closer object drawn on top of the more distant objects, with the transparency factor for each surface taken into account at each stage.

It should be obvious, therefore, that dealing with transparent objects dramatically increases the amount of memory and processing that must be done to calculate and render a scene.

6.10   Text in Java 3D

Java 3D provides two ways of adding text to a scene: the Text2D class which creates two-dimensional text on a transparent background that can essentially be used as a 'label', and the Text3D class which creates text strings where the individual characters have a depth or thickness. As these two classes are treated in somewhat different ways, we will consider them separately.

6.10.1   Text2D

A Text2D object is created by defining a rectangle to which the required text is applied as a texture. We will consider texture mapping in Chapter 7 so we will not go into the theory here. The important point is that the text is a pattern that is painted onto a transparent rectangle. The Text2D class inherits Shape3D, so a Text2D object may be attached directly as a child to a TransformGroup or BranchGroup.

The procedure for producing a Text2D is therefore quite simple. Create the object using the constructor and attach it to the scene graph. The Text2D constructor requires the following arguments:

- **text**: the String to be rendered;
- **color**: a Color3f giving the colour of the text;
- **fontName**: a String specifying the name of the font to be used. The standard fonts 'Helvetica', 'Courier' and 'TimesRoman' (no space between 'Times' and 'Roman') are virtually guaranteed to be installed on any system;
- **fontSize**: an int giving the size of the font. Remember that the text will appear larger or smaller depending on how far from the viewpoint it is, so you may need quite a large font size for text on distant objects to be readable;
- **fontStyle**: an int chosen from the various styles in the Font class from java.awt. Typical values are PLAIN, BOLD, and ITALIC.

For example, we could add some text to a scene by saying:

```
Text2D houseText = new Text2D("Some text",
    new Color3f(1.0f, 1.0f, 0.0f),
    "Courier", 200, Font.BOLD);
branchGroup.addChild(houseText);
```

This code creates a Text2D with the string 'Some text', and draws it in yellow, 200-point, bold Courier font. The branchGroup object is assumed to have been created earlier. The default position at which text is rendered is at the origin of the Locale, with the origin at the lower-left corner of the text.

Usually, of course, we would like the text to appear somewhere else in the scene, and often we would like to 'attach' the text as a label on a surface. Doing this requires that we insert a TransformGroup node between the Text2D and the BranchGroup that attaches it to the scene graph. As an example, we will add some labels to the sides and roof of the house scene in the earlier example in this chapter.

First, we will add a label to the front of the house in the lower-left corner. Since the front panel of the house is located with its lower-left corner at the origin, we might think that we need not transform the Text2D at all to have it appear in the correct location. However, we find that if we place the Text2D in exactly the same plane as the polygon on which it is to appear, it may not appear at all, since the two objects are competing for the same layer in the scene. We therefore translate the Text2D so it lies slightly above the front panel of the house. In the code that follows, transRoot is a TransformGroup node that also transforms the house. Thus anything that is attached to this node will transform along with the house. This means that if we add a Text2D to transRoot, it will appear as a label attached to the house.

```
Text2D houseText = new Text2D("Front",
    new Color3f(1.0f, 1.0f, 0.0f),
    "Courier", 200, Font.BOLD);
Transform3D textTrans = new Transform3D();
textTrans.set(new Vector3f(0.0f, 0.0f, 0.01f));
TransformGroup textGroup = new
    TransformGroup(textTrans);
textGroup.addChild(houseText);
transRoot.addChild(textGroup);
```

Since the front panel of the house lies in the plane $z = 0$, we move the Text2D slightly (by 0.01 in the +z direction) above this plane to ensure that it shows up in the rendering.

Next, we can place a label on the left side of the house, as follows:

```
houseText = new Text2D("Left side",
    new Color3f(0.0f, 1.0f, 0.0f),
    "Helvetica", 200, Font.BOLD);
textTrans = new Transform3D();
textTrans.set(new Vector3f(-0.01f, 0.0f, -6.0f));
Transform3D rotTrans = new Transform3D();
rotTrans.rotY(-Math.PI/2.0);
textTrans.mul(rotTrans);
textGroup = new TransformGroup(textTrans);
textGroup.addChild(houseText);
transRoot.addChild(textGroup);
```

This time, we use Helvetica font and draw the text in green. The transformation required here is a bit more complex than for the front panel, as we must rotate the text by $-\pi/2$ radians (that is, 90 degrees clockwise) about the y axis to align the text with the left side of the house. Then we must move the text back (by –6.0 in the z direction) so it appears on the wall, and then move it fractionally out from the wall (by –0.01 in the x direction) so it appears above the surface. We accomplish the rotation with one Transform3D and the translation with another.

Finally, we will put a label on the left side of the roof:

```
houseText = new Text2D("Roof",
    new Color3f(0.0f, 0.0f, 1.0f),
    "TimesRoman", 200, Font.BOLD);
textTrans = new Transform3D();
textTrans.set(new Vector3f(1.0f, 6.0f, -6.0f));
rotTrans.rotY(-Math.PI/2.0);
Transform3D rot2Trans = new Transform3D();
rot2Trans.rotZ(-Math.atan(1.5));
rot2Trans.mul(rotTrans);
textTrans.mul(rot2Trans);
textGroup = new TransformGroup(textTrans);
textGroup.addChild(houseText);
transRoot.addChild(textGroup);
```

This time we use TimesRoman font and draw the text in blue. To position the text properly requires two rotations and a translation. We must first rotate the text by $-\pi/2$ radians about the y axis. Then we must rotate it about the z axis so that the text appears to be lying at the same angle as the roof. The slope of the roof is $2/3$ (as can be seen from the coordinates used to define it in the earlier example) so the angle between the roof and the vertical is $\arctan(3/2)$. We must rotate the Text2D through a clockwise angle of this amount so we use the atan() method in the Math class to calculate the arctangent, and the rotZ() method in Transform3D to do the rotation.

The translation requires moving the text up to the level of the roof (+6.0 in the y direction), back and to the right so it sits in the middle of the roof area (–6.0 in the z direction and +1.0 in the x direction).

The result of adding these three labels to the house is shown in Figure 6.7.

The Text2D class has a setString() method which takes a String argument and allows the text to be changed after the Text2D has been created. There is also a setRectangleScaleFactor() method, taking a float argument, which can be used to change the size of text in an existing Text2D. The method has two bugs, however, that can make its use problematic. The first bug is that to change the size of the text by a factor S, say, the argument that must be passed to setRectangleScaleFactor() is not S as you might expect, it is S/256.0f. That is, the 'base value' for the scaling factor is 1/256, not 1.0.

The second bug is that calling the method on its own has no effect on the display—you must call setString() immediately after a call to setRectangleScaleFactor(), even if you do not wish to change the text that is displayed.

A sample bit of code illustrating how to use the method is therefore:

```
houseText = new Text2D("Roof",
    new Color3f(0.0f, 0.0f, 1.0f),
    "TimesRoman", 200, Font.BOLD);
houseText.setRectangleScaleFactor(0.5f / 256.0f);
houseText.setString("Roof");
```

This code creates a Text2D that displays the string 'Roof', then scales it to reduce its size by half, then calls setString() with the same text as in the original constructor.

6.10.2 Raster images in Java 3D

Although Text2D is useful for creating text labels that transform with the scene, in some applications we would like text labels that always face the viewer and do not change size when the scene to which they are attached is zoomed in or out. The method presented in this section provides a way of creating such labels, and gives a nice illustration of how Java 2D and Java 3D can work together. We will present the code and then describe how it works.

The import statements on lines 1 and 2 are needed in addition to those required for Java 3D.

The idea behind this method is to create a raster image (essentially a bitmap) containing the text label and then attach this image as part of the 3D scene. Raster images, when included in a Java 3D scene graph, are always displayed as rectangular regions of pixels that do not rotate or change size, so any image displayed within a raster will always face the viewer and remain constant in size.

```java
1   import java.awt.font.*;
2   import java.awt.image.*;
3
4   public static Shape3D getTextLabel(String text,
5       Font labelFont, Color background, Color foreground,
6       Point3f attach)
7   {
8       FontRenderContext frc =
9           new FontRenderContext(null, false, false);
10      int width = (int) labelFont.getStringBounds(
11          text, frc).getWidth();
12      int height = (int) labelFont.getStringBounds(
13          text, frc).getHeight();
14
15      BufferedImage image = new BufferedImage(
16          width, height, BufferedImage.TYPE_INT_ARGB);
17      Graphics g = image.createGraphics();
18
19      g.setFont(labelFont);
20      g.setColor(background);
21      FontMetrics metrics = g.getFontMetrics();
22      g.fillRect(0, 0, width, height);
23      g.setColor(foreground);
24      g.drawString(text, 0,
25          height - metrics.getLeading() -
26          metrics.getDescent());
27      g.dispose();
28
29      ImageComponent2D imageComp =
30          new ImageComponent2D(
31              ImageComponent.FORMAT_RGBA8, image);
32
33      javax.media.j3d.Raster raster =
34          new javax.media.j3d.Raster(
35              attach, javax.media.j3d.Raster.RASTER_COLOR,
36              0, 0, width, height, imageComp, null);
37
38      Shape3D s3d = new Shape3D(raster);
39      return s3d;
40  }
```

The getTextLabel() method takes several arguments that allow the programmer to specify the properties of the text label. The text argument contains the actual text to be displayed, and labelFont is a Font object specifying the font to use for the text. The background and foreground colours can then be specified. Finally, attach is a Point3f object which specifies the 3D coordinate where the upper-left corner of the raster's rectangle should be attached in the Java 3D scene.

Lines 8 through 13 find the width and height of the raster by extracting the information from the Font. The FontRenderContext class was discussed when we covered text in Chapter 3.

To create a Raster, we must first construct a BufferedImage (used for creating off-screen graphics, as discussed in Chapter 3) on lines 15 and 16, and then obtain a graphics context to allow us to draw on the image (line 17). Lines 19 through 27 use this graphics context to draw the text label by using simple graphics commands to fill the rectangle with the background colour and draw the text in the foreground colour.

Creating the Raster from the BufferedImage requires first creating an ImageComponent2D (line 29). This class is part of Java 3D, and is used for creating two-dimensional images that are to be included as part of 3D scene.

From the ImageComponent2D, we can create a Raster (line 33). We need to specify the package containing Raster (javax.media.j3d) since there is another Raster class in the 2D graphics package.

The first two arguments in the Raster constructor used here are the point (attach) in the 3D scene at which the Raster is to be attached, and the type of raster being created (here we are creating a raster that contains only colour data, hence the RASTER_COLOR parameter, but rasters can also store depth (z-buffer) data).

Building a raster involves copying, pixel by pixel, the image from a source (in this case, the ImageComponent2D) to the destination (the Raster itself). The source is a rectangular array of pixels originally created in the BufferedImage. The next two arguments in the Raster constructor (both 0 here) specify the x and y coordinates in the Raster where the copy should begin. The next two arguments (width and height) specify the rectangular area in the source that should be copied into the Raster. The next argument imageComp states the source for the pixel data, and the last argument, null here, gives the source for any z-buffer data that is to be copied.

Finally, on line 38, we create a Shape3D from the Raster (one of the constructors for Shape3D accepts a Geometry argument, and Raster inherits the Geometry class).

We can add one of these raster text labels to our house with the code:

```
Font labelFont = new Font("Helvetica", Font.PLAIN, 20);
Shape3D rasterText = getTextLabel("Roof top", labelFont,
    Color.blue, Color.orange, new Point3f(3f, 7f, 0f));
transRoot.addChild(rasterText);
```

Here we are adding a label at the apex of the roof at the front of the house. The result is shown in Figure 6.8.

Note that although the raster label will not rotate or scale with the rest of the image, it will move with its attachment point if that point gets moved as a result of a transformation of the scene.

The raster's position within the scene is determined entirely by the location of its attachment point (the upper-left corner of the raster). This has two effects. First, if part of the scene moves closer to the viewer than the raster, it will obscure the raster (see Figure 6.9). Second, if the attachment point is moved out of the display area (or is clipped by a clipping plane), the entire raster image disappears, even if part of the image would ordinarily be visible in the display area. As far as the Java 3D scene graph is concerned, the raster is represented only by the single 3D point that defines its upper-left corner.

Figure 6.8:
A raster text label.

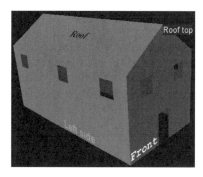

Figure 6.9:
Partly obscuring a raster with other objects in the scene.

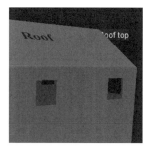

Obviously, this technique of drawing to an off-screen buffer which is then converted to a `Raster` is not restricted to producing text labels—any of the Java 2D graphics classes and methods can be used to produce the image. The sample method given above can therefore be used as a model for including 2D raster images anywhere within a Java 3D scene.

An interesting variant on the text label raster is a raster image constructed from a JPEG image file. In Chapter 3, we saw how to build an off-screen image and save it as a JPEG file. It is just as easy to reverse the process and read an image from a JPEG disk file, convert it to a raster, and display it as part of a Java 3D scene. We leave the details to the exercises, but an example is shown in Figure 6.10, where the Java logo stored in a JPEG file is displayed as a raster object connected to the apex of the roof.

Figure 6.10:
A JPEG image displayed as a raster object in a Java 3D scene.

6.10.3 Billboards

The raster techniques described above allow any Java 2D graphics to be drawn into a rectangle and displayed as a fixed object within a Java 3D scene. Java 3D itself, however, comes with two classes that allow 3D objects to be displayed within a scene so that they are always oriented in the same direction relative to the viewpoint. These classes are `Billboard` and `OrientedShape3D`, the latter being added with version 1.2 of Java 3D.

The `Billboard` class is derived from `Behavior`, which we shall study in Chapter 8. We have included `Billboard` in this chapter, however, since it is most often used to save time and resources in creating the geometry of roughly symmetric objects. A common example used to introduce `Billboard` is that of drawing a tree. Most trees look roughly the same when viewed from any point in a horizontal plane. Constructing a full three-dimensional geometry for a tree can involve a lot of work (and a lot of triangles), so in many applications a suitable shortcut is to draw a two-dimensional projection of a tree and insert it into the scene as a `Billboard`. The `Billboard` ensures that the two-dimensional image of the tree always faces directly towards the viewpoint as the remainder of the scene is rotated or otherwise transformed.

As an example, we will add a few trees around the house in the previous example. We first write a class called `FlatTree`, which extends `BranchGroup` and contains the geometry and appearance of a two-dimensional projection of a tree. This class is left as an exercise since it uses only techniques we have already covered.

We will insert four `FlatTree`s into the house scene, and attach a `Billboard` to each `FlatTree`. A `Billboard` works by being given its own `TransformGroup` on which to operate, since it must apply transforms to keep the tree oriented in the correct direction no matter what other transformations are applied to the scene as a whole. For each tree, therefore, we must create a `TransformGroup` which allows its transform to be written (meaning that we must set the capability ALLOW_TRANSFORM_WRITE). We can insert additional `TransformGroup`s above the `Billboard`'s `TransformGroup` if we wish. In this example, we add a translation to each tree so they are all displayed in different locations around the house.

In addition, a `Billboard` must have a region of influence defined, within which its effects can be felt. This is a typical requirement of several classes in Java 3D, and we shall see further examples when we consider lighting in the next chapter.

The following code adds four `FlatTree`s to the house scene, attaching each tree to a `Billboard`.

```
1   BoundingSphere billSphere =
2       new BoundingSphere(new Point3d(), 100.0);
3   TransformGroup[] treeRotate = new TransformGroup[4];
4   Billboard[] treeBoard = new Billboard[4];
5
6   FlatTree[] trees = new FlatTree[4];
7   TransformGroup[] treeGroup = new TransformGroup[4];
8   Transform3D[] treeTrans = new Transform3D[4];
9   for (int i = 0; i < 4; i++) {
10      trees[i] = new FlatTree();
11      treeTrans[i] = new Transform3D();
12  }
13
14  treeTrans[0].set(new Vector3f(-0.5f, 0.0f, 0.5f));
15  treeTrans[1].set(new Vector3f(0.5f, 0.0f, 0.75f));
16  treeTrans[2].set(new Vector3f(-2.0f, 0.0f, -3.5f));
```

```
17    treeTrans[3].set(new Vector3f(-3.0f, -0.0f, -6.5f));
18
19    for (int i = 0; i < 4; i++) {
20        treeRotate[i] = new TransformGroup();
21        treeRotate[i].addChild(trees[i]);
22        treeRotate[i].setCapability(
23            TransformGroup.ALLOW_TRANSFORM_WRITE);
24        treeBoard[i] = new Billboard(treeRotate[i]);
25        treeBoard[i].setSchedulingBounds(billSphere);
26        treeGroup[i] = new TransformGroup(treeTrans[i]);
27        treeGroup[i].addChild(treeRotate[i]);
28        treeGroup[i].addChild(treeBoard[i]);
29        transGroup.addChild(treeGroup[i]);
30    }
```

On line 1 we specify the region of influence for each Billboard by using the BoundingSphere class. The constructor called here defines a sphere centred at the origin with a radius of 100.

Line 3 defines an array of TransformGroups which will be allocated to the Billboards defined on line 4. As these TransformGroups will have their transforms determined by the Billboards, we do not assign any Transform3Ds to them in the code.

On line 6 we create the array of FlatTrees, and on line 7 we define the array of TransformGroups that will be used to translate the trees to different positions around the house. Note that we must use a different TransformGroup for transformations that are separate from those calculated by the Billboard, so in this example, each tree has two TransformGroups allocated to it. Line 8 creates the array of Transform3Ds that are used to define the translations of the trees on lines 14 to 17.

The loop beginning on line 19 attaches the trees to the scene through the Billboards. The treeRotate array contains the TransformGroups that will be acted on by the Billboards, so we attach the FlatTrees directly to them (lines 20 and 21). On line 22 we set the capability that allows the Billboards to modify the transforms while the program is running.

Line 24 creates the Billboard and passes the TransformGroup on which it will act as the argument to the constructor, and line 25 sets the region of influence for the Billboard.

Lines 26 through 29 create the TransformGroups that will translate the trees to their various positions, and attach the treeRotate transform groups to them. We also attach the Billboard for each tree as a child of the top TransformGroup. Finally, line 29 attaches all the trees to the main TransformGroup (transGroup), which governs the translation of the entire scene (including the house and all four trees). This TransformGroup is the link back to the house program covered earlier in this chapter.

The result of adding the above code to the GeometryInfoDemo class above (it can be added anywhere after the point where transGroup is created since the creation of the trees is independent of the creation of the house) is shown in Figure 6.11.

Figure 6.11:
Adding four
FlatTrees to the
house using
Billboards.

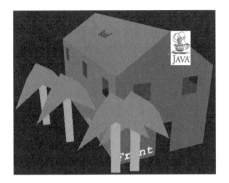

Rotating the scene by applying a rotation transformation to transGroup produces Figure 6.12. We can see that although the viewpoint has changed, the trees all show the same face towards the viewpoint because the Billboard for each tree has calculated the transformation necessary to counter the rotation applied to transGroup. This inverse transformation has been applied to each tree's treeRotate TransformGroup.

Figure 6.12:
Rotating the scene in
Figure 6.11 shows that
the two-dimensional
FlatTrees always present
the same face towards
the view point.

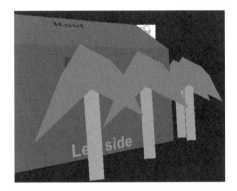

Figure 6.13:
Viewing FlatTrees
from above.

If we rotate the scene so that we view it from above, however, we obtain the result shown in Figure 6.13. The default behaviour of Billboard is that it applies a rotation about the *y* axis only to the TransformGroup which it controls, and it will attempt to move the geometry attached to this TransformGroup in such a way that as much of the original orientation can be maintained as possible. If the overall scene is rotated about an axis that is perpendicular to the y axis, of course, the Billboard cannot compensate for this transformation if it is restricted to rotations about the y axis.

It is possible to change the axis about which a Billboard rotates, or even to change the alignment mode of a Billboard so that it is free to rotate in any direction about a fixed point. For example, we can replace line 24 in the above code with the line:

```
treeBoard[i] = new Billboard(treeRotate[i],
    Billboard.ROTATE_ABOUT_POINT,
    new Point3f(0f, 0f, 1f));
```

The Billboard will now rotate the tree about the point (0, 0, 1) rather than the y axis, so that the tree will now always face the viewpoint for any rotation of the scene. This isn't a very realistic effect for trees, but can be useful for spherically symmetric objects such as the sun or moon.

A new addition to version 1.2 of Java 3D is the OrientedShape3D class. It performs a similar purpose to Billboard, but there are a few differences which should be mentioned.

First, OrientedShape3D extends Shape3D rather than Behavior, so an OrientedShape3D can be added directly as a leaf node to a TransformGroup or BranchGroup. This means that the geometry (or list of geometries) is specified for an OrientedShape3D in the same way as for an ordinary Shape3D. The billboard behaviour of OrientedShape3D is provided by methods which allow the alignment mode (ROTATE_ABOUT_AXIS or ROTATE_ABOUT_POINT), alignment axis and rotation point to be specified. The default values are the same as for a default Billboard: rotation about the y axis.

The fact that OrientedShape3D extends Shape3D means that a single object can only reference a single Appearance. Because a Billboard is attached to a TransformGroup rather than a Shape3D it can affect an entire branch of the scene graph, including different Shape3Ds, each with its own Appearance. The FlatTrees drawn above contain two Shape3Ds, for example: a brown QuadArray for the trunk and a green TriangleFanArray for the leaves. Creating the same tree with an OrientedShape3D would require two separate instances of the class.

Some practice with OrientedShape3D is provided in the exercises.

6.10.4   Text3D

The Text3D class allows three-dimensional text to be added to a scene. A Text3D is created by specifying a two-dimensional font which determines the appearance of the text when viewed face-on, and also specifying an extrusion of that text to give it some depth.

The process of extrusion is similar to squeezing toothpaste out of a tube. With a toothpaste tube, the aperture through which the toothpaste is squeezed is circular—in the case of a Text3D, the aperture is the two-dimensional shape of the text. In the simplest case, the text is squeezed out in a straight line at constant size, so that the resulting text resembles the large magnetic letters and numbers that people (for some reason) often attach to refrigerator doors. The Text3D class, however, allows the extrusion 'aperture' to be varied as the text is squeezed through, so that the depth component can be curved or varied in size.

The main difference between Text3D and Text2D is that Text3D inherits the Geometry class, and can therefore be attached to a Shape3D via the setGeometry() method. A Text2D inherits Shape3D directly so may be added to a BranchGroup as a node in its own right.

To create a Text3D, we must first create a Font3D, which involves specifying the two-dimensional font using the Font class from java.awt, and the extrusion shape using a FontExtrusion. We will begin by examining a Text3D created using default values as much as possible.

The following code produces the text shown (after some transformations have been applied) in Figure 6.14.

```
Font3D font3D = new Font3D(
    new Font("Helvetica", Font.BOLD, 10),
    new FontExtrusion());
Text3D textGeom =
    new Text3D(font3D, new String("Java 3D"));
textGeom.setAlignment(Text3D.ALIGN_CENTER);
Shape3D textShape = new Shape3D();
textShape.setGeometry(textGeom);
```

Figure 6.14:
A Text3D created with default parameters (rotated to show 3D effects).

We create a new Font3D, whose constructor takes two arguments. The first is a standard Font, where we specify a Helvetica, bold, 10-point font. The second argument is a FontExtrusion, and here we create a default one, which produces an extrusion 0.2 metres thick, with a straight edge.

The Text3D itself is created with the Font3D and a String giving the text to render. The call to setAlignment() sets the origin of the Text3D at the centre of the baseline of the text—the default is ALIGN_FIRST, which sets the origin at the bottom-left corner of the text. We have added this alignment to allow the text to be fully visible in the display window.

The last two lines create a Shape3D and set its geometry to be the Text3D. The Shape3D can then be added to a TransformGroup or BranchGroup in the usual way.

Although the default Text3D can produce effective graphics, the real power of the Text3D class is its ability to vary the contour of the text as a function of its depth, and to vary the depth as well.

As a simple example, we will increase the thickness of the text without changing the straight-line contour. To do this, we create a Shape object in a similar way to the examples in Chapter 3. This Shape is then used as an argument to the FontExtrusion. The Shape can be any two-dimensional curve, but there is one restriction: the *x* coordinate in this curve must be monotonically increasing. Put more simply, this means that the curve cannot loop back on itself—it is allowed to vary 'up or down' but must keep heading to the right.

The default Shape used in a FontExtrusion is a horizontal line of length 0.2. We can therefore increase the thickness of a Text3D by just increasing the length of this line. The following code achieves this and produces the result shown in Figure 6.15.

```
Shape lineShape =
    new Line2D.Double(0.0, 0.0, 1.0, 0.0);
FontExtrusion fontExt =
    new FontExtrusion(lineShape);
Font3D font3D = new Font3D(
    new Font("Helvetica", Font.BOLD, 10),
    fontExt);
Text3D textGeom =
    new Text3D(font3D, new String("Java3D"));
```

We use a Line2D.Double to generate the horizontal line of length 1.0, and pass this line as the argument to the FontExtrusion constructor. The Font3D is created using this FontExtrusion as an argument in its constructor, and the Text3D is created in the usual way.

Figure 6.15:
A Text3D with a thickness of 1.0.

A further example shows that the contour followed by the edge need not be a straight line. The text shown in Figure 6.16 is produced by using the following Shape, which describes a parabola:

```
Shape lineShape =
    new QuadCurve2D.Double(0.0, 0.0, 2.5, -1, 5, 0.0);
```

Finally, both Font3D and FontExtrusion allow a tessellation tolerance to be set in their constuctors. This parameter determines how 'smooth' the outlines of the characters and the depth contours are. The smaller the tolerance, the more triangles are used to tessellate (tile) the characters' outlines and the better the result. Of course, the usual tradeoff between quality and efficiency applies—the smaller the tolerance, the more computationally expensive the rendering process.

Figure 6.16:
Text3D with a parabolic outline.

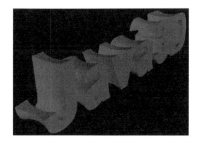

The Font3D class uses a default tessellation tolerance which is calculated from the point size of the Font. The larger the point size, the more triangles are used in the tessellation. This can be changed by adding a third argument to the Font3D constructor which explicitly specifies the tessellation tolerance. For example, if we make the tolerance 1.0 in the previous example, we obtain the result shown in Figure 6.17. A similar effect can be obtained in the depth direction by specifying the tessellation tolerance in the FontExtrusion.

Figure 6.17:
Same Text3D as in
Figure 6.16 but with a
tessellation tolerance of
1.0 specified in the
Font3D.

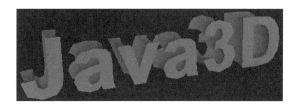

6.11 Level of detail—varying quality with distance

Producing a high-quality image of a three-dimensional object is expensive, both in terms of programming effort and computer resources. However, when an object is placed far away from the viewpoint, not as much detail can be seen as when the object is relatively close. It is therefore a waste of the computer's resources if we use the same geometry to render an object in the distance as we do to obtain a high-quality close-up view of the same object.

Java 3D provides a method whereby the detail stored in an object's geometry can be varied with distance, so that distant objects can be rendered more quickly and use fewer resources. The DistanceLOD (where LOD stands for 'level of detail') class manages the display of an object as its distance from the viewpoint varies.

The idea behind DistanceLOD is that the programmer provides several different versions of the object whose distance is to be varied—the most detailed version for close-up views, and successively less detailed versions to be used as the object moves away from the viewer. DistanceLOD is supplied with a list of distances at which versions should be switched, and with a connection to a Switch object which stores the geometries of the different versions themselves.

The procedure for implementing LOD is fairly straightforward. First, create the Switch and set its capability to Switch.ALLOW_SWITCH_WRITE. (Note that the Switch class—with an upper-case 'S'—is not the same as the ordinary switch statement in Java.) Next, create the set of different versions of the object that are to be displayed at different distances and add these (using addChild()) to the Switch.

Next, create the DistanceLOD and assign a bounding region (as with the Billboard) and a list of distances to it. The distances must be specified in ascending order. Whenever the object is closer to the viewer than the first distance in the list, the first version of the object stored in the Switch is displayed. When the viewer moves past the first distance in the list, the second version of the object is displayed, and so on. Whenever the distance from the viewer to the object is greater than the last value in the distance list, the last version of the object is displayed. Note that since the list of distances specify cross-over points between versions, there must be one more version of the object in the Switch than there are crossover points.

With the Switch and DistanceLOD created and linked, we must connect both these objects into the scene graph. Typically, the Switch and DistanceLOD will both be children of the same group node (usually a TransformGroup), so use the addChild() method from TransformGroup to add the Switch and DistanceLOD.

As an example, we present a program which displays a pawn from a chess game. We will consider the construction of the pawn itself in more detail when we consider lighting in Chapter 7. For now, all we need to know is that the pawn is made from a flat cylinder as the base, a thin cylinder for the main shaft, another flat cylinder on top of the shaft and finally a sphere that sits on top. These four components can all be built using Java 3D's Cylinder and Sphere utility classes. Both these classes construct the geometry by dividing the cylinder or sphere into a triangular mesh surface in the usual way. The quality of the shape can be controlled by specifying how many sections should be used in dividing up the figure. For example, in the Sphere we can specify the number of divisions to be, say, 50, which means that there will be 50 node points used to define one line of latitude on the sphere. A Cylinder has a similar parameter that is used to specify the number of divisions used in one circumference.

We will create three versions of the pawn using different qualities for the Cylinders and Sphere that make up each pawn, and then use a DistanceLOD to switch between these pawn images as the pawn is moved along the line of sight of the viewer. In the code that follows, we will not list the code for the pawn itself, since this is described in the next chapter, and is available in the code on the Web (see Preface). The sample code also changes the colour of the pawn between versions so that we can see the exact point at which the changeover occurs. In practice, of course, we would leave the pawn the same colour, since the main idea of using DistanceLOD is to provide a seamless view of the pawn as it moves into the distance.

```
1    private void addPawn()
2    {
3       BranchGroup scene = new BranchGroup();
4       TransformGroup transGroup = new TransformGroup();
5       transGroup.setCapability(
6       TransformGroup.ALLOW_TRANSFORM_READ);
7       transGroup.setCapability(
8          TransformGroup.ALLOW_TRANSFORM_WRITE);
9       scene.addChild(transGroup);
10
11      Switch pawnSwitch = new Switch();
12      pawnSwitch.setCapability(Switch.ALLOW_SWITCH_WRITE);
13      pawnSwitch.addChild(
14      new Pawn(50, new Color3f(1.0f, 0.0f, 0.0f)));
15         pawnSwitch.addChild(
16         new Pawn(25, new Color3f(0.0f, 1.0f, 0.0f)));
17      pawnSwitch.addChild(
18         new Pawn(10, new Color3f(0.0f, 0.0f, 1.0f)));
19
20      float[] distances = {5f, 10f};
21      DistanceLOD distLOD =
22         new DistanceLOD(distances, new Point3f());
23      distLOD.addSwitch(pawnSwitch);
24      distLOD.setSchedulingBounds(new BoundingSphere());
25      transGroup.addChild(distLOD);
```

```
26          transGroup.addChild(pawnSwitch);
27
28          // Lights added
29
30          // Mouse interaction added
31      }
```

The addPawn() method is part of a class which constructs the scene graph in the usual way, and provides the branch in the scene graph containing the Switch (which in turn contains the set of three pawn versions) and the DistanceLOD. The BranchGroup node and its immediate child transGroup are created, and capabilities set, on lines 3 to 9. Lines 11 to 18 create the Switch, set its capability, and add three Pawns to it. The Pawn constructor's first argument is the resolution of the Cylinders and Sphere that make it up. We have therefore specified a resolution of 50 for the most detailed pawn (line 14) which will be displayed closest to the viewpoint, and resolutions of 25 and 10 for the versions that are displayed further away. The constructor also accepts a Color3f which we have used to set the three versions to red, green and blue respectively.

On line 20 we define the list of crossover distances. The pawn with resolution of 50 will be displayed if the viewing distance is less than 5, the pawn with resolution 25 is shown for distances between 5 and 10, and the resolution-10 pawn is shown if the distance is greater than 10.

Line 21 creates the DistanceLOD. The constructor takes 2 arguments: the first is the distance list, and the second is the point from which the distances are to be measured. Here we have specified a point of (0, 0, 0). On line 23 we connect the DistanceLOD with the Switch containing the versions of the pawn. Lines 24 to 26 attach the bounding region and connect the DistanceLOD and the Switch to the scene graph.

The remainder of addPawn() adds some lighting and the mouse interaction described earlier in the chapter. When running the program the middle mouse button may be used to zoom the pawn in or out, and whenever the distance crosses one of the thresholds in the distances list, the version of the pawn used for the display will change (as will the colour in this demonstration program).

6.12 Drawing general curves and surfaces—splines

Up to now, we have considered algorithms for drawing straight lines, circles, and a few other regular geometric figures in two dimensions, and for approximating surfaces by means of triangular meshes in three dimensions. However, you will no doubt have seen many examples of computer graphics where more general curves and surfaces appear to have been rendered. We will consider some of the simpler techniques for doing this here.

Although algorithms such as Bresenham's algorithms for drawing lines and circles work well to produce regular curves, we have seen that attempting to define a more general curve mathematically and then implement it by scan-converting it to a raster drawing algorithm is far from easy. What is needed is a more general (and computationally less expensive) way of producing arbitrary curves and surfaces. The most commonly used of these general curves are known as *splines*.

The word 'spline' is derived from the term used by draftsmen for the flexible metal strip used to draw a smooth curve connecting several points on a technical drawing. The term evolved from describing the metal strip itself to the mathematical representation of the curves they were used to draw, and ultimately to the curves now seen in computer graphics.

Although splines occur in a wide variety of forms, they are all based on the same general idea. If we have a sequence of discrete points that we wish to connect by a smooth curve, we find polynomial terms that fit successive sections of the overall curve, and impose some mathematical conditions on the points where these polynomial segments join up. The differences between the various types of spline curves can usually be traced to differences in how the curve is made to fit the points, or differences in the conditions imposed at the joining points, or both.

The reason splines have become so popular in computer graphics is that, since they are described exclusively by polynomials, they are relatively simple and quick to calculate, at least compared to more complex terms such as trigonometric functions or square roots. It also turns out that it is usually possible to get a good approximation to almost any geometric shape using polynomials that are no more complex than a cubic (that is, they contain no power higher than the cube).

This remarkable feature of splines has led to them being used to represent regular geometric curves such as circles and ellipses (in preference to more specific algorithms such as those of Bresenham described in Chapter 1), and even to providing mathematical definitions of the fonts used in representing text. In fact, circles and ellipses produced by Java 2D's methods use splines.

By constructing surfaces where the meshes are composed of intersecting spline curves, it is possible to produce three-dimensional models of almost any desired shape.

Despite their power and popularity (and the fact that Java 2D uses them to produce many geometric figures) Java's current support (as of JDK version 1.3 and Java 3D version 1.2) for splines is, sadly, very rudimentary. In Java 2D, support is only provided for quadratic and cubic Bézier curves (which we will consider later in this chapter). In Java 3D, one particular type of spline is used to produce paths along which animations can move, but there is no support for actually drawing more general splines (either as curves or surfaces) in three dimensions.

The authors of Java 3D do not rule out the inclusion of splines in future versions of Java 3D, however, and they are used extensively in other areas of computer graphics, so it is well worth understanding some of the theory behind them. We will also provide a method whereby we can write our own routines for drawing spline curves in three dimensions. Since Java 3D's only support for drawing surfaces relies on the triangular mesh, however, it is a much more difficult job to attempt to write our own spline surface-drawing methods. To do this, we would need a method of producing the spline mesh surface initially, and then an algorithm for converting such a general curved mesh into a triangular mesh, which can then be represented using a Java 3D geometry object such as a `TriangleStripArray`. Although many such algorithms (often called *faceting algorithms* because they produce facets on an irregularly-shaped object, as is done in gem cutting) exist, they are quite complex and are well beyond the scope of this book.

6.12.1   A simple spline

Although the original idea behind the draftsman's metal spline was to draw a smooth curve that actually passed through a set of points, not all mathematical splines do this. At the simplest level, splines can be divided into two main groups: splines that pass through (or *interpolate*) *all* of the points used to define them, and splines that only pass through some (or in some cases, none) of these points.

For splines in the second group (of which the Bézier curves are probably the most commonly used), those points that are not intersected by the spline are said to be *control points* and are used to influence the shape of the curve rather than provide absolute positions through which it must pass.

To begin our study of splines, we will examine the simplest case, in which we specify two points, p_0 and p_1, which serve as the two endpoints of the spline. The methods we develop in this section may seem a bit extreme for dealing with such a simple case, but it is best to understand the ideas in a simple case before progressing to the more general cases.

The simplest curve that can be drawn between two points is, of course, a straight line. We have seen in Chapter 1 several ways of writing the equation of a straight line, but so far, all these equations are of the form $y = f(x)$ or $x = f(y)$, where one coordinate is expressed as a function of the other. This form is fine provided we make allowances for certain special cases, such as vertical and horizontal lines, where one or the other of the two functional forms cannot be used. For example, if we write the equation of the line in slope–intercept form as $y = mx + b$, where m is the slope and b is the intercept, we must add the condition that the line cannot be vertical, since this would require m to be infinite.

Although it is relatively easy to identify and isolate these special cases when we are dealing with straight lines, it is considerably more difficult to do so when we deal with higher order curves such as quadratics and cubics. For this reason, a different method of writing the equations of curves is used when dealing with splines. Curves are written using *parametric equations*, where the coordinates x, y and z are all written in terms of an additional parameter which we shall call u.

To see how a parametric equation works, let us represent a straight line segment between the two points p_0 and p_1 parametrically. In general, a straight line will have parametric equations of the form:

$$x(u) = a_x u + b_x$$
$$y(u) = a_y u + b_y \tag{6.1}$$
$$z(u) = a_z u + b_z$$

What values can the parameter u take on? If the line segment is of finite length, as is usually the case, it is customary to allow u to take on values in the interval $[0, 1]$. For a straight line segment between points p_0 and p_1, this means that when $u = 0$, the values of x, y, and z obtained from equation 6.1 are those corresponding to p_0, and when $u = 1$, they correspond to the coordinates of p_1.

This gives us two independent conditions on each coordinate, from which we can determine the values of the six constants a_i and b_i in equation 6.1. For example, if $p_0 = (1, 1, 2)$ and $p_1 = (2, -1, 4)$, the parametric equations for the line segment are:

$$x(u) = u + 1$$
$$y(u) = -2u + 1 \qquad (0 \leq u \leq 1)$$
$$z(u) = 2u + 2$$

(6.2)

The clever feature of using a parametric form for the equations is that we can use this form no matter what the slope of the line is. A simple exercise for the reader is to derive the values of the six constants a_i and b_i in equation 6.1 for the two cases where the line is vertical and horizontal. The parametric form works equally well in both cases. No special cases need to be identified.

Since splines are always specified in terms of their control points, it would be more convenient if we could eliminate the constants a and b from the equations in favour of these control points. The equations are easier to deal with if we rewrite equation 6.1 as a vector equation:

$$\mathbf{p}(u) = u\mathbf{a} + \mathbf{b}$$

(6.3)

Here, the vector $\mathbf{p}(u)$ traces out the line segment $(x(u), y(u), z(u))$ as u varies between 0 and 1. The constant vectors $\mathbf{a}$ and $\mathbf{b}$ contain the components (a_x, a_y, a_z) and (b_x, b_y, b_z) respectively.

We can make a further refinement to equation 6.3 by finding $\mathbf{a}$ and $\mathbf{b}$ in terms of the two endpoints $\mathbf{p}_0$ and $\mathbf{p}_1$. Although we could do this using some simple algebra, we will use a more general method which will be useful in dealing with more complex splines later in this chapter.

Letting $u = 0$ in equation 6.3, and using the fact that $\mathbf{p}(0) = \mathbf{p}_0$, we have:

$$\mathbf{p}_0 = \mathbf{b}$$

Now, letting $u = 1$, and using $\mathbf{p}(1) = \mathbf{p}_1$:

$$\mathbf{p}_1 = \mathbf{a} + \mathbf{b}$$

We can combine these two equations into a single matrix equation as follows:

$$\begin{bmatrix} \mathbf{p}_0 \\ \mathbf{p}_1 \end{bmatrix} = \begin{bmatrix} 0 & 1 \\ 1 & 1 \end{bmatrix} \begin{bmatrix} \mathbf{a} \\ \mathbf{b} \end{bmatrix}$$

We obtain $\mathbf{a}$ and $\mathbf{b}$ in terms of $\mathbf{p}_0$ and $\mathbf{p}_1$ by inverting the matrix in this equation, to obtain:

$$\begin{bmatrix} \mathbf{a} \\ \mathbf{b} \end{bmatrix} = \begin{bmatrix} 0 & 1 \\ 1 & 1 \end{bmatrix}^{-1} \begin{bmatrix} \mathbf{p}_0 \\ \mathbf{p}_1 \end{bmatrix} = \begin{bmatrix} -1 & 1 \\ 1 & 0 \end{bmatrix} \begin{bmatrix} \mathbf{p}_0 \\ \mathbf{p}_1 \end{bmatrix}$$

(6.4)

We can now rewrite equation 6.3 as a matrix equation:

$$\mathbf{p}(u) = \begin{bmatrix} u & 1 \end{bmatrix} \begin{bmatrix} \mathbf{a} \\ \mathbf{b} \end{bmatrix} = \begin{bmatrix} u & 1 \end{bmatrix} \begin{bmatrix} -1 & 1 \\ 1 & 0 \end{bmatrix} \begin{bmatrix} \mathbf{p}_0 \\ \mathbf{p}_1 \end{bmatrix} = \begin{bmatrix} 1-u & u \end{bmatrix} \begin{bmatrix} \mathbf{p}_0 \\ \mathbf{p}_1 \end{bmatrix}$$

Multiplying out the matrix expression at the end we obtain:

$$\mathbf{p}(u) = (1-u)\mathbf{p}_0 + u\mathbf{p}_1$$

(6.5)

We have now expressed the line segment $\mathbf{p}(u)$ entirely in terms of its two endpoints. The two polynomials, $(1 - u)$ and u, that are used to combine these two endpoints to obtain the line segment are often called *blending functions*, since they blend the control points to create the spline curve.

6.12.2   Joining splines

We now know how to specify a line segment between two fixed points, but usually we need to draw many such segments within a graphical scene. In many cases, we would like to join up several segments to produce a more complex drawing. For example, we might wish to draw a picture of a house by joining up several straight line segments. What conditions might we need to impose on the points where the line segments meet?

The first requirement is, of course, that the two line segments share an endpoint. Mathematically, we must require that the two segments form a *continuous* curve. When talking about joining up spline segments, the join point is usually referred to as a *knot*.

In general, the requirement of continuity on its own does not guarantee a *smooth* join—we will usually have a sharp bend or corner at the knot. In many cases, this may be what we want. If we are drawing a rectangle, for example, the corners of the rectangle must be continuous, but also consist of a right-angle bend.

However, in some cases we will need to ensure that there is no sharp corner where the segments join. If we are dealing with straight line segments, the only way we can eliminate a corner at a knot is to require that the line segments be parallel. (We will see later that, for more general curves, there are varying degrees of 'smoothness' at knots.)

The direction vector $\mathbf{d}$ of a line segment can be determined by taking the vector difference of the two endpoints $\mathbf{p}_0$ and $\mathbf{p}_1$: $\mathbf{d} = \mathbf{p}_1 - \mathbf{p}_0$. Two line segments are therefore parallel if the direction vector of one line is a scalar multiple of the direction vector of the other.

Although it is easy enough to find $\mathbf{d}$ for a line segment whose endpoints have been specified, we will examine a more general method for determining the smoothness of a knot that will prove useful for more general splines. Referring to equation 6.5 in which the line segment is expressed parametrically in terms of its endpoints, we can take the derivative of $\mathbf{p}(u)$ with respect to the parameter u:

$$\frac{d\mathbf{p}(u)}{du} = -\mathbf{p}_0 + \mathbf{p}_1 = \mathbf{p}_1 - \mathbf{p}_0 = \mathbf{d}$$

That is, the parametric derivative of the line segment turns out to be just the direction vector we need. This should not be surprising, since you will recall that the derivative of a curve at a particular point gives the slope of the tangent line at that point. For a curve in three-dimensional space, the derivative provides the tangent vector.

The derivative in the case of a straight line turns out to be a constant because the line segment has a constant direction (that is, a constant tangent vector) at all points along its length. When we consider more general splines, the tangent vector to the spline will vary over its length, so we will need to evaluate the derivative at the endpoints to specify the smoothness of the joining condition, but the principle is the same.

We can therefore specify the condition for a 'smooth' join of two linear spline segments as (1) the line segments must be continuous at the knot and (2) the tangent vectors at the knot must be scalar multiples of each other.

6.13 Cubic splines

With an understanding of the ways in which splines are handled in simple cases, we can now proceed to a study of some 'real' splines—those that are actually used in the construction of curves and surfaces in three-dimensional graphics. The most commonly used splines in graphics are based on cubic polynomials. This is mainly due to trial and error over the years—designers found that lower order polynomials (quadratic and linear polynomials) did not provide enough flexibility in designing curves, while polynomials with higher degrees than cubic tend to be too difficult to control, often producing extraneous 'wiggles' in curves where a smoother look is desired. This is not to say that cubic curves are the only ones used—Java 2D, for example, provides a quadratic spline in one of its packages—it is just that they are by far the most common.

Within the cubic spline family, there are still many different splines from which to choose. In this book, we will examine Hermite splines, cardinal splines, and Bézier splines.

The analogue of equation 6.1 for a cubic spline is:

$$x(u) = a_x u^3 + b_x u^2 + c_x u + d_x$$
$$y(u) = a_y u^3 + b_y u^2 + c_y u + d_y \qquad (6.6)$$
$$z(u) = a_z u^3 + b_z u^2 + c_z u + d_z$$

As before, the parameter u covers the range $[0, 1]$.

Since the equation for each coordinate contains four constants, rather than the two we encountered in the straight line case above, we need four conditions to be able to determine all four constants uniquely. The differences between the various types of cubic splines are largely related to the specification of these conditions.

6.13.1 Hermite splines

The Hermite spline (named after the French mathematician Charles Hermite (1822–1901)) is a cubic spline that is determined by specifying the two endpoints of the curve, and the tangent vector at each endpoint. Together, these conditions provide the four constraints required to determine the constants in equation 6.6. The technique for doing so follows the example in the linear case above fairly closely.

In analogy with equation 6.3, we can write equation 6.6 as a vector equation:

$$\mathbf{p}(u) = u^3 \mathbf{a} + u^2 \mathbf{b} + u\mathbf{c} + \mathbf{d} \qquad (6.7)$$

Evaluating this equation when $u = 0$ and $u = 1$ provides the two conditions at the endpoints:

$$\mathbf{p}_0 = \mathbf{d}$$
$$\mathbf{p}_1 = \mathbf{a} + \mathbf{b} + \mathbf{c} + \mathbf{d} \qquad (6.8)$$

Taking the derivative of equation 6.7 with respect to u, we obtain:

$$\frac{d\mathbf{p}(u)}{du} \equiv \mathbf{p}'(u) = 3u^2 \mathbf{a} + 2u\mathbf{b} + \mathbf{c} \qquad (6.9)$$

and evaluating this derivative at the two endpoints gives us the remaining two conditions:

$$\mathbf{p}'_0 = \mathbf{c}$$
$$\mathbf{p}'_1 = 3\mathbf{a} + 2\mathbf{b} + \mathbf{c} \tag{6.10}$$

Combining all four conditions into a single matrix equation, we obtain:

$$\begin{bmatrix} \mathbf{p}_0 \\ \mathbf{p}_1 \\ \mathbf{p}'_0 \\ \mathbf{p}'_1 \end{bmatrix} = \begin{bmatrix} 0 & 0 & 0 & 1 \\ 1 & 1 & 1 & 1 \\ 0 & 0 & 1 & 0 \\ 3 & 2 & 1 & 0 \end{bmatrix} \begin{bmatrix} \mathbf{a} \\ \mathbf{b} \\ \mathbf{c} \\ \mathbf{d} \end{bmatrix} \tag{6.11}$$

Finally, we can solve for the constants in terms of the endpoints and the derivatives at the endpoints by inverting the 4×4 matrix in the previous equation, to obtain:

$$\begin{bmatrix} \mathbf{a} \\ \mathbf{b} \\ \mathbf{c} \\ \mathbf{d} \end{bmatrix} = \begin{bmatrix} 2 & -2 & 1 & 1 \\ -3 & 3 & -2 & -1 \\ 0 & 0 & 1 & 0 \\ 1 & 0 & 0 & 0 \end{bmatrix} \begin{bmatrix} \mathbf{p}_0 \\ \mathbf{p}_1 \\ \mathbf{p}'_0 \\ \mathbf{p}'_1 \end{bmatrix} \tag{6.12}$$

Combining this result with equation 6.7 allows us to obtain the equation of the Hermite spline in terms of its endpoints and derivatives:

$$\mathbf{p}(u) = \left(2u^3 - 3u^2 + 1\right)\mathbf{p}_0 + \left(-2u^3 + 3u^2\right)\mathbf{p}_1 +$$
$$\left(u^3 - 2u^2 + u\right)\mathbf{p}'_0 + \left(u^3 - u^2\right)\mathbf{p}'_1 \tag{6.13}$$

Here, the four controls (the two points and the two tangent vectors) are blended using the four Hermite blending polynomials:

$$H_0 = 2u^3 - 3u^2 + 1$$
$$H_1 = -2u^3 + 3u^2$$
$$H_2 = u^3 - 2u^2 + u \tag{6.14}$$
$$H_3 = u^3 - u^2$$

The reader should check that equation 6.13 does satisfy the four conditions $\mathbf{p}(0) = \mathbf{p}_0$, $\mathbf{p}(1) = \mathbf{p}_1$, $\mathbf{p}'_0(0) = \mathbf{p}'_0$, and $\mathbf{p}'_1(1) = \mathbf{p}'_1$.

A two-dimensional Hermite spline segment is shown in Figure 6.18. Here, $\mathbf{p}_0 = (-0.5, -0.5, 0)$ and is the point on the left, $\mathbf{p}_1 = (0.5, 0.5, 0)$, $\mathbf{p}'_0 = (1, -2, 0)$ and $\mathbf{p}'_1 = (0, 4, 0)$.

Figure 6.18:
A Hermite spline
in two dimensions.

Note how the tangent vectors at the endpoints govern the overall shape of the curve. The vector $\mathbf{p}'_0$ starts the curve off downwards and towards the right, and the vector $\mathbf{p}'_1$ forces the curve to end with a tangent that is vertically upwards.

Keeping the endpoints the same, but swapping the tangent vectors (so that $\mathbf{p}_0' = (0, 4, 0)$ and $\mathbf{p}_1' = (1, -2, 0)$) results in the spline shown in Figure 6.19.

The fact that the tangent vectors at the endpoints are explicitly specified in a Hermite spline makes it particularly easy to arrange for smooth joins between spline segments. All we need to do to create a smooth join is to set an endpoint in one spline equal to an endpoint in the other, and make the derivatives at the knot equal.

Figure 6.19:
A Hermite polynomial with the same endpoints as in Figure 6.18 but different tangent vectors at the endpoints.

For example, in Figure 6.20 we have joined a second spline onto the one shown in Figure 6.19. The tangent vectors at the common endpoint were both set to $(1, -2, 0)$, ensuring a smooth join.

Figure 6.20:
Two Hermite splines with equal tangent vectors at the knot.

We can characterize the nature of a knot further by comparing successively higher derivatives at the point. From equation 6.13 we can calculate the following derivatives:

$$
\begin{aligned}
\mathbf{p}'(u) &= \left(3u^2 - 4u + 1\right)\mathbf{p}_0' + \left(3u^2 - 2u\right)\mathbf{p}_1' \\
\mathbf{p}''(u) &= \left(6u - 4\right)\mathbf{p}_0' + \left(6u - 2\right)\mathbf{p}_1' \\
\mathbf{p}'''(u) &= 6\mathbf{p}_0' + 6\mathbf{p}' \\
\mathbf{p}^{(4)}(u) &= 0
\end{aligned}
\tag{6.15}
$$

In general, the more derivatives that are equal at a knot, the smoother the join will be. For example, if the splines meet at a knot, but none of their derivatives are equal (or scalar multiples of each other), the join will probably show a sharp bend or corner. If only the first derivatives are equal, there will be a smooth join, but the curvature of the two splines on either side of the join may differ markedly. If the first *and* second derivatives are equal at the knot, the curvatures of the two splines will be similar on either side of the join, and the join itself should look very smooth.

The maximum order of derivative for which the curves match at a knot is referred to as the *order* of continuity at that point. If the curves are continuous but not even the first derivatives match, the knot is said to have *zero-order* continuity, which may be written as C^0 continuity. Similarly, if the first derivatives are equal, we have first-order, or C^1, continuity, and so on.

For Hermite splines, it is interesting to note from equations 6.15 that derivatives of all orders at the endpoints depend only on the values of the first derivatives at the endpoints. In particular, the actual locations of the endpoints have no effect on any of the derivatives at any point on the curve. Therefore, to obtain second order C^2 continuity at an endpoint, it is usually necessary to adjust the *first* derivatives at *both* endpoints in the spline segment.

In the case of a straight line spline, all that was required to ensure a smooth join was that the tangent vectors were parallel—their relative magnitudes did not matter. In the case of a cubic (or any non-linear) spline, however, the magnitude of the tangent vector (as well as its direction) *does* affect the shape of the curve. To illustrate this, Figure 6.21 shows the same splines as Figure 6.20, except that the tangent vector at the knot of the second (lower) spline now has three times the magnitude of the corresponding tangent vector in the first (upper) spline.

Figure 6.21:
Similar to Figure 6.20, except that the tangent vector at the knot of the lower spline is three times the magnitude of the corresponding tangent vector of the top spline.

Although the shape of the upper spline remains unchanged (since none of its control points was altered), the lower spline has a much broader arc on the right. The join between the two splines still looks smooth, but the two figures are noticeably different.

We can see, therefore, that even if the derivative vectors at a knot are not equal, a smooth join can still result if the vectors are at least parallel.

6.13.2 Cardinal splines

Although the ability to specify the tangent vectors at the endpoints of the spline can be useful, in many cases it is desirable to specify all the conditions on the spline as distinct points that can be drawn on the same canvas as that used to draw the spline itself. The *cardinal spline* was designed with this idea in mind.

A cardinal spline is defined by four control points (two of which it passes through) and an extra parameter called the *tension*, which we shall discuss later. The two control points, which are usually not intersected by the spline, are used to define the tangent vectors at the endpoints.

To see how a cardinal spline is constructed, refer to Figure 6.22. The four control points are labelled as $\mathbf{p}_{-1}$, $\mathbf{p}_0$, $\mathbf{p}_1$ and $\mathbf{p}_2$. Points $\mathbf{p}_0$ and $\mathbf{p}_1$ are the endpoints of the curve, as with a Hermite spline. The other two points are used in combination with $\mathbf{p}_0$ and $\mathbf{p}_1$ to determine the tangent vectors at the two endpoints.

The tangent at point $\mathbf{p}_0$ is defined to be proportional to the vector $\mathbf{p}_1 - \mathbf{p}_{-1}$, and the tangent at $\mathbf{p}_1$ is proportional to $\mathbf{p}_2 - \mathbf{p}_0$. These two tangents are shown as dashed lines in Figure 6.22, and an examination of the figure will show that the curve does indeed orient itself so that the tangents at the endpoints match these two dashed lines. Remember when looking at the figure that the dashed line connected to one endpoint determines the tangent vector at the *other* endpoint.

The main advantage of a cardinal spline over a Hermite spline is that the endpoint tangents can be changed interactively by dragging the two control points in an intuitive manner. In the Hermite case, the tangent vectors must be specified directly, which makes an interactive tool for creating them more difficult to build.

Figure 6.22:
The construction
of a cardinal spline.

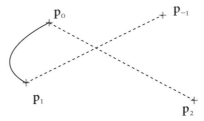

The relations between the control points and the endpoint tangents are given by:

$$\mathbf{p}_0' = \tfrac{1}{2}(1 - t)(\mathbf{p}_1 - \mathbf{p}_{-1})$$

$$\mathbf{p}_1' = \tfrac{1}{2}(1 - t)(\mathbf{p}_2 - \mathbf{p}_0) \tag{6.16}$$

The quantity t in these equations is the *tension* parameter referred to earlier.

We can generate a parametric equation giving the cardinal spline in terms of its four control points by following a similar derivation to that for the Hermite spline. We begin by expressing the four control points in terms of $\mathbf{a}$, $\mathbf{b}$, $\mathbf{c}$ and $\mathbf{d}$. Equation 6.8 is still valid for cardinal splines, so we can use it directly. To express the other two points in terms of $\mathbf{a}$, $\mathbf{b}$, $\mathbf{c}$ and $\mathbf{d}$, we substitute equation 6.16 into the left-hand side of equation 6.10, and using equation 6.8, we arrive at:

$$\mathbf{p}_{-1} = \mathbf{a} + \mathbf{b} + \frac{s - 1}{s}\mathbf{c} + \mathbf{d}$$

$$\mathbf{p}_2 = \frac{1}{s}(3\mathbf{a} + 2\mathbf{b} + \mathbf{c}) + \mathbf{d}$$

where $s = (1 - t)/2$.

Combining these two equations with equations 6.8, we obtain the matrix equation:

$$\begin{bmatrix} \mathbf{p}_{-1} \\ \mathbf{p}_0 \\ \mathbf{p}_1 \\ \mathbf{p}_2 \end{bmatrix} = \frac{1}{s}\begin{bmatrix} s & s & s-1 & s \\ 0 & 0 & 0 & s \\ s & s & s & s \\ 3 & 2 & 1 & s \end{bmatrix}\begin{bmatrix} \mathbf{a} \\ \mathbf{b} \\ \mathbf{c} \\ \mathbf{d} \end{bmatrix}$$

As before, we invert the matrix to solve for $\mathbf{a}$, $\mathbf{b}$, $\mathbf{c}$ and $\mathbf{d}$ in terms of the control points:

$$\begin{bmatrix} \mathbf{a} \\ \mathbf{b} \\ \mathbf{c} \\ \mathbf{d} \end{bmatrix} = \begin{bmatrix} -s & 2-s & s-2 & s \\ 2s & s-3 & 3-2s & -s \\ -s & 0 & s & 0 \\ 0 & 1 & 0 & 0 \end{bmatrix} \begin{bmatrix} \mathbf{p}_{-1} \\ \mathbf{p}_0 \\ \mathbf{p}_1 \\ \mathbf{p}_2 \end{bmatrix}$$

Substituting this into equation 6.7, we obtain the final form for a cardinal spline:

$$\mathbf{p}(u) = \left(-su^3 + 2su^2 - su\right)\mathbf{p}_{-1} + \left((2-s)u^3 + (s-3)u^2 + 1\right)\mathbf{p}_0 + \left((s-2)u^3 + (3-2s)u^2 + su\right)\mathbf{p}_1 + \left(su^3 - su^2\right)\mathbf{p}_2 \tag{6.17}$$

The tension parameter t may be used to vary the amount of 'slack' in the curve. As can be seen from equation 6.16, when $t = 1$ (and therefore $s = (1-t)/2 = 0$), the tangent vectors become zero. From equation 6.17 with $s = 0$, we have

$$\mathbf{p}(u) = \left(2u^3 - 3u^2 + 1\right)\mathbf{p}_0 + \left(-2u^3 + 3u^2\right)\mathbf{p}_1$$

If we define a new parameter $v = -2u^3 + 3u^2$, we can rewrite this equation as:

$$\mathbf{p}(v) = (1-v)\mathbf{p}_0 + v\mathbf{p}_1$$

which is just the parametric equation for a straight line segment between $\mathbf{p}_0$ and $\mathbf{p}_1$, provided that v covers the interval $[0, 1]$, which is easily verified from its definition and the fact that u covers the interval $[0, 1]$.

A tension of 1 therefore defines the 'tightest' curve (a straight line) between $\mathbf{p}_0$ and $\mathbf{p}_1$. All other values of t introduce some slack into the spline, and the further t is from 1, the slacker the curve becomes. If the tension is reduced enough, the spline can even start to 'tangle' by having loops appear along its length. Some examples of cardinal splines with different tensions are shown in Figure 6.23.

Figure 6.23:
The effect of tension on cardinal splines. All four splines have the same control points. The tension is shown in each case.

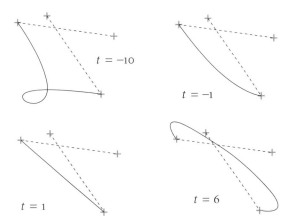

6.13.3 Kochanek–Bartels splines

The Kochanek–Bartels spline is an extension of the cardinal spline that introduces two more tension-like parameters to allow more flexibility (if you'll pardon the pun) in specifying the shape of a curve for a given set of control points. The two extra parameters are the *bias b* and the *continuity c*. For this reason, the Kochanek–Bartels spline is also known as the TCB (for tension–continuity–bias) spline.

To define a Kochanek–Bartels spline, we replace equations 6.16 in the cardinal spline with:

$$\mathbf{p}'_0 = \tfrac{1}{2}(1-t)\left((1+b)(1-c)(\mathbf{p}_0 - \mathbf{p}_{-1}) + (1-b)(1-c)(\mathbf{p}_1 - \mathbf{p}_0)\right)$$

$$\mathbf{p}'_1 = \tfrac{1}{2}(1-t)\left((1+b)(1+c)(\mathbf{p}_1 - \mathbf{p}_0) + (1-b)(1-c)(\mathbf{p}_2 - \mathbf{p}_1)\right)$$

$$(6.18)$$

It can be seen that the relation between the control points and the tangent vectors is no longer as simple as in the ordinary cardinal spline.

A similar procedure to that for the cardinal spline may be followed to obtain the equation for $\mathbf{p}(u)$ in terms of the blending functions.

The Kochanek–Bartels spline is, as of Java 3D version 1.2, the only spline that is implemented in Java 3D. Several classes supporting it can be found in the package com.sun.j3d.utils.behaviors.interpolators, but it is included primarily to provide support for paths followed by objects in animation sequences (see Chapter 8).

6.13.4   Bézier splines

The Bézier spline was invented by Pierre Bézier, an engineer working for the Renault car company in the 1970s. He originally used the curve in the computer-aided design of car bodies, but due to its relative simplicity and flexibility, it has become one of the most popular splines for designing two- and three-dimensional graphics ever since.

Superficially, the Bézier spline is similar to the cardinal spline, in that it is specified by four control points, two of which define the endpoints of the spline and two of which are used to specify the tangent vectors at the endpoints. The main differences (which turn out to be advantages) between the Bézier and cardinal splines are, first, that the endpoint itself is one of the points used in calculating the tangent vector at that endpoint, and second, the Bézier blending functions are of a much simpler form than those used in the cardinal spline.

Although Bézier splines can easily be specified for any degree of polynomial, the cubic form is the most widely used (although the quadratic form is also provided in the Java 2D package), so we will concentrate on that here. The labelling of the control points is, by convention, slightly different to that which we have used for the other splines in this chapter, so the reader is cautioned not to make direct comparisons between the equations for Bézier splines and those presented earlier.

For a cubic Bézier spline, the four control points are specified as $\mathbf{p}_0$, $\mathbf{p}_1$, $\mathbf{p}_2$ and $\mathbf{p}_3$, with $\mathbf{p}_0$ and $\mathbf{p}_3$ being the endpoints of the curve, and $\mathbf{p}_1$ and $\mathbf{p}_2$ being used to specify the tangent vectors at these endpoints. The two tangent vectors are defined by:

$$\mathbf{p}'_0 = 3(\mathbf{p}_1 - \mathbf{p}_0)$$

$$\mathbf{p}'_3 = 3(\mathbf{p}_3 - \mathbf{p}_2)$$

$$(6.19)$$

Given these definitions, we can follow through a similar set of calculations to those done for the Hermite and cardinal splines to arrive at the parametric equation giving the Bézier spline:

$$\mathbf{p}(u) = (1-u)^3\mathbf{p}_0 + 3u(1-u)^2\mathbf{p}_1 + 3u^2(1-u)\mathbf{p}_2 + u^3\mathbf{p}_3 \qquad (6.20)$$

The blending functions in this equation may look familiar, as they are just the terms in the expansion of the binomial expression $((1-u)+u)^3$. This fact illustrates an important property of the Bézier blending functions. Since $(1-u)+u=1$, the sum of the four blending functions for any specific value of u is always exactly 1. This means that $\mathbf{p}(u)$ is always a weighted average of the four control points, with the weighting beginning with 100 per cent $\mathbf{p}_0$ at the first endpoint, then, as we move along the curve, the control point $\mathbf{p}_1$ begins to exert its influence, followed by $\mathbf{p}_2$, and then $\mathbf{p}_3$. As we move past the midpoint of the curve, $\mathbf{p}_0$ begins to lose its influence, followed by $\mathbf{p}_1$ and $\mathbf{p}_2$ until we eventually end up at the other endpoint, which is $\mathbf{p}_3$.

In fact, it is possible to define a Bézier spline to fit any number of control points by simply using the appropriate expansion of the binomial $((1-u)+u)^n$, where n is one less than the number of control points. That is, if we have $n+1$ control points, the Bézier spline that fits these points will have its two endpoints at $\mathbf{p}_0$ and $\mathbf{p}_n$, and will have the form:

$$\mathbf{p}(u) = \sum_{k=0}^{n} \frac{n!}{k!(n-k)!} u^k (1-u)^{n-k} \mathbf{p}_k \qquad (6.21)$$

The individual blending functions thus have the form:

$$B_{k,n}(u) = \frac{n!}{k!(n-k)!} u^k (1-u)^{n-k} \qquad (6.22)$$

and are known as *Bernstein polynomials*.

Figure 6.24:
Two cubic Bézier splines.

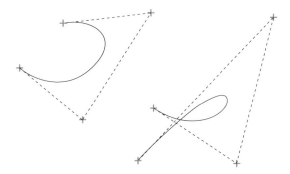

Figure 6.24 shows a couple of Bézier splines. The control points are connected by dashed lines drawn in the order $\mathbf{p}_0$, $\mathbf{p}_1$, $\mathbf{p}_2$, $\mathbf{p}_3$ (it does not matter which endpoint is labelled $\mathbf{p}_0$ as the equations will give the same spline no matter which way the points are labelled). Notice that the dashed lines are tangential to the endpoints they intersect, as opposed to the cardinal spline.

This property provides one way of ensuring that we have first-order continuity at a knot between two Bézier splines. Recall that first-order continuity requires that the first derivatives are equal at the knot. If two Bézier splines are defined by the sets of control points $\mathbf{p}_0$, $\mathbf{p}_1$, $\mathbf{p}_2$, $\mathbf{p}_3$ and $\mathbf{q}_0$, $\mathbf{q}_1$, $\mathbf{q}_2$, $\mathbf{q}_3$ respectively, with $\mathbf{p}_3 = \mathbf{q}_0$ so that they join up at one endpoint, then we can ensure first-order continuity at this point by requiring that $\mathbf{p}_3 - \mathbf{p}_2 = \mathbf{q}_1 - \mathbf{q}_0$.

Figure 6.25:
Two Bézier curves
joined with first-
order continuity.

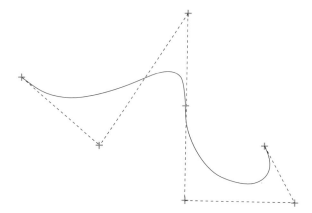

Figure 6.25:
Two Bézier curves
joined with first-
order continuity.

Figure 6.25 shows two Bézier splines joined with first-order continuity. The three control points in a vertical line in the centre of the figure (with the middle point being the join) satisfy the conditions just stated.

6.14   The computation of splines

To draw a spline on a computer display, we must evaluate the blending functions at a large number of values of its parameter u. For all the splines we have considered, these blending functions consist of fixed polynomials, usually cubics. In a complex scene, these calculations can be expensive in terms of processing time.

Most graphics packages, Java 3D included, do not provide any special methods for calculating polynomials, so if we wish to draw a spline, we must calculate the curve at a number of discrete points and join up these points with line segments. This is, in fact, how the drawings of splines in this chapter were produced.

Let us consider the general cubic polynomial of the form

$$f(u) = au^3 + bu^2 + cu + d$$

To evaluate this polynomial for a single value of u, we need to do six multiplications and three additions. However, we can rewrite the polynomial in the form:

$$f(u) = d + u(c + u(b + au)) \tag{6.23}$$

In this form, we need to do only three multiplications and three additions. Since floating-point multiplication is more costly than addition, this represents a significant saving in time over the original brute-force method.

This method still relies on evaluating the polynomial from scratch for each value of u along the spline. If the number of splines in the scene is not too great, and if we are using a fast processor (especially one with optimized floating point calculation), this method is probably adequate for the production of most static scenes.

For the production of complex scenes containing many hundreds or thousands of splines, or the production of animation, there are other more efficient methods of calculating polynomials that involve using earlier values in the calculation to predict later values, or recursive subdivision of the curve to obtain an approximation of line segments.

6.15 Java code for drawing splines

Although Java 2D does provide quadratic and cubic Bézier splines as components in two-dimensional scenes, Java 3D provides no support for drawing splines of any sort in three dimensions (as of Java 3D version 1.2). Therefore, if we wish to include splines in a Java 3D scene graph, we need to provide our own spline-drawing routines. We will illustrate the procedure by providing the code for drawing a Bézier spline.

One way of attaching a spline curve to a Java 3D scene graph is to define a new class which extends the Shape3D leaf node class. Recall that a Shape3D object can be attached at the end of a branch in a scene graph, and can have an associated geometry and appearance. By deriving a new class from Shape3D, we can define the geometry portion of such an object to contain the spline curve as an array of line segments.

The class that draws the spline may have other methods for setting various appearance attributes and so on, but we will examine the method which actually creates the geometry that defines the spline as it will appear on screen.

For example, we can define a class called BezierSpline as follows:

```
public class BezierSpline extends Shape3D
{
    // declarations and methods
}
```

The following method produces a cubic Bézier spline from a given set of control points.

```
 1    public void drawCubicBezierSpline(Point3d[] controls)
 2    {
 3        double bez[] = new double[4];
 4        Point3d[] currentControls = new Point3d[4];
 5        double increment = 1.0 / m_numPoints;
 6        for (int controlPoint = 0;
 7            controlPoint < m_numControls; controlPoint += 4) {
 8            int[] stripCount = {m_numPoints+1};
 9            lineArray = new LineStripArray(m_numPoints+1,
10                GeometryArray.COORDINATES, stripCount);
11            for (int localPoint = 0; localPoint < 4;
12                localPoint++) {
13                currentControls[localPoint] =
14                    controls[controlPoint + localPoint];
15            }
16            int index = 0;
17            for (double u = 0.0; u < 1.0 + increment;
18                u += increment) {
19                double u1 = 1.0 - u;
20                bez[0] = u1*u1*u1;
21                bez[1] = 3.0*u*u1*u1;
22                bez[2] = 3*u*u*u1;
23                bez[3] = u*u*u;
24                lineArray.setCoordinate(index,
25                    calcSplinePoint(bez, currentControls));
```

```
26              index ++;
27          }
28          addGeometry(lineArray);
29      }
30  }
```

The method assumes that the control points have been specified externally (for example, by the user entering values in a dialog box or using the mouse to specify points interactively), and that these points are passed to the method as an array of Point3d objects (line 1). Recall that a Point3d object specifies a three-dimensional point as a set of three doubles. This method will generate any number of Bézier spline segments joined together as a single Shape3D node. It assumes that the controls array has a length that is a multiple of 4, and that each block of 4 elements in the array corresponds to a set of control points for a spline segment.

The array bez on line 3 will be used to hold the values of the Bernstein polynomials during the calculation, and the currentControls array on line 4 holds the current set of control points, extracted from the controls array.

Line 5 defines the increment to be used between successive values of the parameter u. This is determined by an externally supplied variable m_numPoints, which specifies the number of line segments that are to be used to calculate each spline segment.

The main for loop beginning on line 6 iterates over the controls array, and constructs a separate LineStripArray for each spline segment (lines 8 to 10). The loop on line 11 extracts the current set of control points to be used in the calculation of the next spline segment.

The loop beginning on line 17 uses equation 6.20 to calculate the Bernstein polynomial coefficients, and then the method calcSplinePoints() (considered below) is called to calculate the Point3d that is to be added to the LineStripArray. After all points in the current spline segment have been calculated and added to the line array, the line array is added to the Shape3D on line 28.

The method calcSplinePoints() is a simple utility method that calculates a Point3d for any cubic spline:

```
private Point3d calcSplinePoint(double[] blend,
    Point3d[] controls)
{
    Point3d splinePoint = new Point3d();

    for (int point = 0; point < 4; point++) {
        splinePoint.x += controls[point].x * blend[point];
        splinePoint.y += controls[point].y * blend[point];
        splinePoint.z += controls[point].z * blend[point];
    }
    return splinePoint;
}
```

This technique is easily adapted to calculate any of the splines covered in this chapter, since they all follow the same basic pattern. Once the control points have been specified, it is simply a matter of calculating a number of points along the curve given by the spline's equation and plotting them.

1. Using the Tetrahedron program in the text (page 156) as a guide, write a class called Pyramid which draws a pyramid. The base of the pyramid should be a square with a side length of 1 lying in the *xy* plane, with the centre of the square at the origin, and the height of the pyramid should also be 1, with the apex pointing towards the viewer. If you do not use an Appearance, what do you see when the program is run?

2. Add an Appearance to the pyramid in question 1 so that the pyramid is drawn as a wire frame. Try to predict what you will see before you run the program.

3. By consulting the documentation for PolygonAttributes, change the Appearance in question 2 so that only the points that define the corners of the pyramid are drawn.

4. Read the documentation for Appearance and change the program in question 2 so that the lines in the wire frame are drawn as red, dashed lines.

5. [Programming project] Write an application containing a Canvas3D that displays the pyramid as above, but add a control panel containing several components (combo boxes or radio buttons for example) that allow the user to experiment with the various styles and settings available in the Appearance class. Users should be able to set the colour, line style and thickness, and polygon style (filled, wire-frame or points). Note that this program will require that the properties of Appearance be changed after the geometry branch has been made live by adding it to the Locale. You will need to set the appropriate capability bits in order that this is allowed by the program. Failure to do this will result in 'capability not set' errors at runtime—read the documentation for Appearance and the various 'attributes' classes to find the capability bits that you need.

6. Add a TransformGroup (see Chapter 5) to the various pyramid programs in previous questions to allow the pyramid to be viewed from different angles.

7. Rearrange the order of the vertices in the TriangleStripArray specifying the tetrahedron in the text so that the outside of the tetrahedron coincides with the outside faces of all the triangles.

8. Check the code that constructs a tetrahedron using a TriangleArray in the text (page 156). Are the vertices of the triangles specified in the correct order? If not, why was the full tetrahedron visible?

9. Read the on-line documentation for TriangleFanArray and rewrite the code for drawing the tetrahedron using a TriangleFanArray to draw the tetrahedron. Note that since any one vertex of the tetrahedron is shared by only three of the four sides, you will need two strips to specify the full figure.

10. Use a LineStripArray to draw a wire-frame image of the tetrahedron. Try to avoid drawing any edge more than once.

11. Draw the pyramid in question 1 using indexed arrays.

12. Use GeometryInfo to create a model of a car. You will find it easier to sketch the car on graph paper first to work out the coordinates of the vertices. For the first version, keep the outline simple and don't insert any holes for the

windows (so you won't need to use any contour counts). You may also find it easier to download the complete GeometryInfoDemo class and modify it by inserting the coordinates for the car, since that class provides some lighting which will make the car easier to see.

13. Display the car from question 12 as a wire-frame model so you can see how the outline has been triangulated. Add an explicit call to Triangluator to see if this makes any difference (it should if an argument of 1 is passed to the Triangulator constructor).

14. Add some holes representing windows to the car model from question 12. To do this, you will need to add some contour counts as in the house example in the text (page 167). Repeat the experiment from question 13 by drawing the car as a wire frame to see how the triangulation is done when holes are present in the polygons.

15. Use a Text2D to add a 'welcome mat' in front of the house in the example in the text. The Text2D should contain the text 'Welcome', and should be transformed so that it lies on the ground in front of the doorway. Create the text using a 100-point font initially and then scale the text until the size looks right.

16. Use one of the geometry classes to add a vertical post which should appear stuck in the ground in front of the house. Then modify the getTextLabel() method in the text (page 178) so that it creates a 'For sale' sign. Add some simple vector graphics (for example, a box around the 'For sale' string) to the sign, then display it as a Raster attached to the post.

17. Review the procedure in Chapter 3 for saving a BufferedImage as a JPEG file on disk (page 80), and reverse the procedure so that you can read and decode a JPEG file to create a BufferedImage. The required classes can be found by replacing 'output' by 'input' and 'encode' by 'decode' in most cases—see the documentation. Note that the documentation for the com.sun.image.codec.jpeg package is not bundled with the main documentation for either the JDK or Java 3D. If you have the standard documentation set from Sun, look in the folder guide\2d\api-jpeg, and load the file overview-summary.html into your Web browser.

    Use the technique from the getTextLabel() method to convert the BufferedImage to a Raster, and thus display JPEG images in Java 3D. Use your new method to replace the 'For sale' sign in the previous question with a JPEG image of the flag of your favourite country (flag images may be found by searching the Web).

18. Draw the scene graph for the code in this chapter in which four trees are inserted into the scene graph using Billboards. What would you expect to happen if the four TransformGroups assigned to Billboards were replaced by a single TransformGroup which was the parent of the four TransformGroups in the treeGroup array?

19. Using a Billboard with a ROTATE_ABOUT_POINT alignment mode, use a short, flat Cylinder (read the documentation on the Cylinder class to see how it is used) viewed end-on to add a yellow sun to the house scene. The Billboard should allow the flat disk to be viewed face-on no matter how the scene is transformed.

20. Use `OrientedShape3D`s to add the trees and sun to the house scene. How does this class compare with `Billboard` for ease of use?

21. Find parametric equations describing the line segment with endpoints $p_0 = (0, 0, 0)$ and $p_1 = (0, 0, 5)$.

22. Verify that equation 6.13 does satisfy the conditions $\mathbf{p}(0) = \mathbf{p}_0$, $\mathbf{p}(1) = \mathbf{p}_1$, $\mathbf{p}'(0) = \mathbf{p}'_0$, and $\mathbf{p}'(1) = \mathbf{p}'_1$.

23. Using equation 6.6, write a set of parametric equations for the segment of the straight line $y = x$ in the xy plane between the points $(0, 0)$ and $(1, 1)$. The parameter u should vary between 0 and 1 to cover this segment. From your parametric equations, work out the endpoint conditions $\mathbf{p}(0)$, $\mathbf{p}(1)$, $\mathbf{p}'_0$, and $\mathbf{p}'(1)$ and hence use equation 6.13 to write the equation for a Hermite spline that produces this line segment. Check your calculation by verifying that equation 6.13 does return the correct parametric equations that you originally derived from equation 6.6.

24. Consider the segment of the parabola $y = x^2$ between $x = -1$ and $x = +1$. Using equation 6.6, write parametric equations for this segment, using a parameter u that satisfies $u = 0$ when $x = -1$ and $u = 1$ when $x = 1$. From this set of parametric equations, follow the same procedure as in question 23 and derive a formula for the Hermite spline that reproduces this segment of the parabola.

25. In the previous two questions, the Hermite spline was able to reproduce the line and parabola segments exactly. Now repeat the calculation for the segment of the circle $x^2 + y^2 = 1$ in the quadrant where x and y are both positive. You will find it easier to represent the circle as a set of parametric equations in polar coordinates, where the angle from the positive x axis is the parameter. Write these parametric equations in terms of a parameter u that varies from 0 to 1 over the quadrant, and then follow the preceding questions to obtain the equation for the Hermite spline. Generate several values along the circular arc from this spline and compare them with the 'true' circle. How accurate an approximation does the spline give?

26. Extend the previous question by providing three more splines for the other three quadrants of the circle and thus obtain a complete spline representation for a circle.

27. Repeat questions 23 to 26 using cubic Bézier splines.

28. Modify the code in the text for calculating Bézier splines to produce methods for calculating Hermite and cardinal splines, given a set of control points in each case.

29. Modify one of the methods in the text or question 28 to produce a fan where the edge of the fan is defined by a spline curve. This can be done by using a `TriangleFanArray` to store the spline points instead of a `LineStripArray`.

30. Try combining the spline calculation methods with a `GeometryInfo` to produce filled shapes with smoothly curved edges.

Surface rendering and lighting

7.1   Lighting

Although we can draw a three-dimensional scene as a collection of objects with specified geometries, such a scene lacks realism, since no account is taken of the lighting which allows the scene to be viewed. The description of the light and shadow that are present in a real-life scene is very complex, involving not only a mathematical description of the interplay between the light sources and the objects, but also the physics of the interaction between light and matter.

The complexity of the subject means that only more advanced graphics systems are able to approach a truly realistic rendering of light sources and the shadows arising from them. Although Java 3D's provision for including light sources and their effects is not 'industrial strength', enough features are present to allow all the basics of lighting to be implemented in a given scene. In this chapter, we will examine some of the theory behind lighting and give some examples of its implementation in Java 3D.

Lighting theory can be divided into two main areas: the light *sources* and the *materials* on which they act. This distinction is manifest in Java 3D, as all light sources are represented by classes derived from a Light class, and the properties of the objects on which the light shines are contained in a Material class.

7.1.1   Light sources

Let us first examine the various types of light sources. To get a feel for the nature of these light sources, let us assume that we are sitting in a room during the daytime on a cloudy day, and that there are no artificial lights on in the room. We will (assuming the room has a window) still be able to see the objects in the room, but all these objects will be lit more or less uniformly, without any highlights or sharp shadows.

This uniform, background illumination is called *ambient light*, and exists because light reflects from every object to some extent, thus allowing it to reach parts of the room that are not in a direct line with the window. Ambient light is represented in graphics by providing a uniform illumination that is applied to all surfaces of all objects in a scene.

Now suppose that a break appears in the clouds outside and the sun shines into the room. Any object that is lit by the sunlight will, obviously, be more brightly lit than if it were lit from ambient light alone, while surfaces that are not in line with the sunlight will still be visible from the reflected ambient light. The sunlight represents a *directional* light source—a source that provides uniform illumination in a fixed direction. The light source itself is assumed to be very far (ideally, infinitely far) away, so that there is no attenuation of the light with distance. Objects at the back of the room (furthest from the sun) are lit to the same degree as objects near the window, provided that they are in the line of sight to the sun.

After observing the effects of the directional light from the sun, we draw the curtains to shut out the sunlight, and switch on a lamp inside the room. We remove the lampshade, and insert a light bulb that is small and unfrosted (in an attempt to simulate a point light source). The light from the lamp radiates out uniformly in all directions from the light bulb, with the effect that any surfaces of objects that face the light bulb will be lit. There are two main differences between this *point* light source and the directional light source we observed earlier. First, we can move the lamp around, so that the point light source varies its position. This will allow new surfaces to be lit, hide surfaces that were lit before, and allow surfaces to be lit from different angles.

Second, the light from the point source will *attenuate* (get weaker) as we move further away from the light bulb. This means (obviously) that objects further away from the point source will be dimmer than those nearer the light bulb, but there is another effect which is more subtle. An object with a large surface may have some parts of this surface further from the light source than others, so that a gradient of illumination occurs over the surface. To represent this effect realistically, we need to shade the surface so that the intensity of the light varies gradually from one side to the other.

Finally, we put the lampshade back onto the lamp. This restricts the angles from which the point source is visible, creating a *spotlight*. A spotlight is essentially the same thing as a point light source, except that its light is not allowed to radiate in all directions. In particular, the position of the spotlight can be varied, and its light will still attenuate with distance from the source.

Java 3D provides derivatives of the Light class that implement all of these light sources. After we survey the properties of the materials from which objects can be composed and examine the theory of colour, we will look at each of these light sources in more detail.

7.1.2 Materials

Natural materials vary in how they respond to illumination. Probably the most obvious quality of an object is its colour. Objects illuminated with white light do not *appear* white unless the material of which they are made reflects all the wavelengths in the white light that is shone upon it. Objects appear differently coloured because they selectively absorb some wavelengths of light and reflect others. For example, a blade of grass appears green because it reflects primarily green light, absorbing most of the other colours in the spectrum. However, even green grass does not completely absorb, say, red light. If it did, illuminating a blade of grass with red light would cause it to appear black.

The key point here is that in order to describe accurately a surface's appearance in response to illumination, we need to be able to define what fraction of the light at different wavelengths is reflected by an object. This defines the object's colour under various lighting conditions.

Java 3D's Material class allows an object's response to the various types of light sources to be specified in just this way. An object can have its response to ambient light and directional light specified by stating what fraction of the red, green and blue light that is used to illuminate the object is reflected. There are, however, two other types of lighting that can be specified in the `Material` class: *specular* and *emissive* lighting.

Even objects that are primarily a single colour can show subtleties under different lighting conditions. Think of a red snooker or pool ball, for example. Although its primary colour is a uniform red, under most lighting, some highlights are visible on the ball. These highlights are usually white, despite the fact that the ball itself is red. This highlighting effect is very common on any object with a shiny surface—no matter what colour the object itself may be, the highlights are always the colour of the light that is used to illuminate it.

The reasons why this is so are fairly complex, and require some understanding of the physics of solids, so we will not delve any further into them here. However, we should recognize that if we are to produce a realistic lighting model in a scene, we need some way of calculating and adding highlights to an object. This is provided by the *specular* lighting component of the `Material` class, to which we shall return later.

The final lighting attribute present in the `Material` class is the *emissive* lighting property. Emissive lighting allows an object to emit its own light, in addition to any external lighting sources. In effect, it allows the object to 'glow in the dark' (although the light from such an object does not illuminate any other objects in a Java 3D scene). Objects with emissive light will be visible even if all other light sources (even ambient light) are turned off.

7.2   Representation of colour

The phenomenon of colour may be defined either in terms of physics or physiology. In physics, a pure colour may be defined to be light that consists of only a single wavelength, where that wavelength falls into the range perceptible by the human eye. The visible spectrum spans the interval from around 450 nanometres (violet light) to around 700 nanometres (red light).

Such pure colours are very rare in nature (the only reasonably common example today is the laser). Most colours that we perceive in everyday life are composed of a mixture of many different wavelengths. White light is composed of a roughly equal mixture of all wavelengths in the visible spectrum, but even other colours such as red or blue usually have components of light of others colours mixed in with them. Red light only appears red because the dominant wavelengths in it are from the red portion of the spectrum.

From a physiological point of view, colour is believed to be perceived by the human eye by means of specialized cells in the retina that are responsive to various portions of the visible spectrum. A crude model of the retina proposes that certain cells are specialized for seeing each of the so-called *primary* colours of red, green and blue, and the other colours are perceived by combinations of stimuli from groups of these cells.

Computer monitors and colour televisions are based on the principle that most colours can be constructed by combining red, green and blue light in various proportions. The fact that current graphics cards in desktop PCs are capable of supporting upwards of 16 million different colours (many more colours than can be distinguished by the human eye) has led many people to believe that the images rendered by these graphics cards are ultra-realistic. In fact, they are not, and the reason has nothing to do with the amount of memory (and hence, number of combinations of red, green and blue that can be produced) or other capabilities of the card.

Experiments with human subjects have shown that there is a range of wavelengths around 500 nanometres (in the green to blue region of the spectrum) that cannot be represented accurately by a combination of the standard 'pure' red, green and blue colours used in computer monitors. In other words, the RGB model cannot produce all colours visible to the human eye, no matter how fine the gradations allowed in each of the primary colours. Nevertheless, the RGB model is now so ingrained in the available hardware and software that it is not likely to be replaced in the near future, and many of the images that can be produced using that system are certainly impressive.

7.2.1 The RGB model

Java programmers will no doubt be familiar with Java's `Color` class, which allows colours to be specified using the RGB system. The `Color` class has several constructors which allow a colour to be specified in various ways. The method we shall favour in this book defines a colour as a triplet of numbers, each of which is in the range [0.0, 1.0]. A value of 0.0 for a colour component means that component is totally absent, and a value of 1.0 means the component is turned on at maximum intensity. By convention, the three components are listed in the order red-green-blue. For example, pure red is specified as (1.0, 0.0, 0.0) and yellow (a combination of red and green) as (1.0, 1.0, 0.0).

The colours available in the RGB model can be plotted in a three-dimensional coordinate system as points within a cube where each side of the cube has unit length. The three coordinate axes (corresponding to the x, y and z axes) are the three primary colours, red, green and blue.

The corner of the cube at the origin corresponds to the colour with coordinates (0.0, 0.0, 0.0), which is black. The diagonally opposite corner of the cube, with coordinates (1.0, 1.0, 1.0), is white. The other six corners of the cube correspond to one of the three primary colours (red, green, blue) or one of the *secondary* colours, obtained by mixing two of the primary colours in equal proportions (yellow = red + green, magenta = red + blue, cyan = green + blue).

The line connecting the black and white corners defines all points where the red, green and blue values are equal. All such colours are shades of grey. All other points not on this diagonal line represent non-grey colours.

As we saw in Chapter 3 (in Java 2D), an extension of the RGB model is sometimes seen (and is supported both by the Java AWT's original `Color` class and the Java 3D colour classes) in which a fourth parameter called *alpha* is added to the RGB triplet. The alpha or 'A' parameter specifies the *transparency* of a colour, and is also given a value between 0 and 1. A transparency of 0 means the colour is completely opaque so that it totally obscures anything behind it. A value of 1 means the colour is completely transparent, and is in fact not even visible. Intermediate values specify the proportion of the total colour of a pixel is due to the colour with the given transparency value and how much by the background colour that is 'behind' the new colour. For example, if a pixel is to be drawn with an RGBA vector of (1.0, 0.0, 0.0, 0.2), and already has a background colour of solid blue, the resulting colour would be an RGB value of (0.8, 0.0, 0.2).

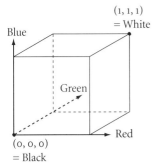

Th RGB colour cube

7.2.2 The HSB model

Although the RGB model is common to all colour monitors, it is not the most intuitive way of describing a colour. For example, even if you know the RGB coordinates of the primary and secondary colours, it is not easy to predict the coordinates of some other common colours, such as orange, pink or brown. Human perception of colour is based more naturally on three different concepts: *hue*, *saturation*, and *brightness*. The HSB model (sometimes known as the HSV—hue, saturation, value—model) was defined with this in mind.

The *hue* of a colour is the property most closely associated with the wavelength of the light, and is the property which most colour words are designed to describe. Thus 'red', 'green', 'blue' and 'orange' describe the hues of various colours.

The *saturation* of a colour describes the intensity or purity of the colour. A pure red appears more intense than a 'washed out' or pale red. If we are painting a picture using oil paints, for example, a paint such as cadmium red fresh out of the tube has maximum saturation. Adding white to the red paint lightens it and reduces its saturation.

The *brightness* of a colour is, roughly speaking, the opposite of saturation. The red paint fresh out of the tube also has maximum brightness, but to reduce the brightness we add black paint rather than white, to produce a darker colour.

Artistically, lightening a colour (reducing its saturation) produces *tints* of that colour, while darkening it (reducing its brightness) produces *shades*. Varying both the saturation and brightness (adding both white and black paint to the original colour) produces *tones* of that colour.

The HSB model is therefore based on the idea that each individual hue is one of the three coordinates in the model, and the other two coordinates vary the pure hue by lightening or darkening it, which is much more in line with the way the human eye perceives colour.

The HSB model is often depicted as a hexagonal cone (Figure 7.1). The apex of the cone corresponds to a brightness *B* of zero (black). At this point, the hue and saturation values are irrelevant.

Figure 7.1:
The HSB colour model.

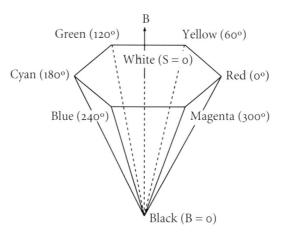

The other end of the cone is a regular hexagon. The vertices of the hexagon correspond to the three primary and three secondary hues. The hue coordinate is given as an angle, with red at 0°, and the other colours arranged at 60° intervals

from this point. The hues are arranged in such a way that two hues that are 180°
apart form *complementary* colours. If two complementary colours are added, the
result is white or grey, depending on the brightness level. Thus red and cyan are
complementary, as are blue and yellow, and green and magenta.

The point at the centre of the hexagon corresponds to a brightness of 1 and a
saturation of 0, and represents white.

The saturation is measured as the *relative* horizontal distance from the central
axis to the colour in question. Any colour on an outside face of the cone has a
saturation of 1, with points in the interior of the cone having proportionately
smaller saturation values. For example, a colour located on the end of the cone, at
a distance halfway between the central axis and the red vertex would have a
saturation of 0.5, a brightness of 1.0 (since it is on the end of the cone) and a hue
of 0° (since it is at the same hue angle as the red vertex). It would appear as a
bright, but washed-out, red colour.

As a second example, imagine a horizontal plane that cuts the cone at a
distance halfway between the black and white points. Any colour in this plane
would have a brightness of 0.5, but a point on the outside edge of this cross-
section would still have a saturation of 1, even though the actual distance from the
central axis to the outside face is smaller here than it is at the top end of the cone.
The saturation is measured as the *fraction* of the horizontal distance from the
central axis to the outside face of the cone.

We can get a better feel for the relation between the RGB and HSB models by
deriving an algorithm to convert between the two systems. First, let us consider
the conversion from RGB to HSB.

We assume that we are given the RGB coordinates of a colour in the form
where each of the three colour coordinates is in the range [0, 1]. For example, we
may have an RGB colour in the form (0.2, 0.5, 0.4). To convert this to HSB, we first
define the brightness B as the maximum of the three RGB coordinates. Thus for
our example, $B = 0.5$. This places the colour halfway up the HSB cone in Figure
7.1. Notice that this definition is consistent with some special cases. Black has an
RGB representation of (0, 0, 0), and thus has a brightness of 0. Similarly, white has
an RGB representation of (1, 1, 1), and thus has a brightness of 1.

To calculate the saturation, we find the maximum and minimum values in the
three RGB coordinates, and take the ratio of the difference (maximum–minimum)
to the maximum value. For our example colour above, the saturation is therefore
$(0.5 - 0.2)/0.5 = 0.6$. Again, notice that this gives the correct saturation value for
some special cases. If the RGB colour is one of the greys, then all three RGB
coordinates are equal, with the result that the saturation is 0. Conversely, a
saturation of 1.0 requires that one of the colours have an RGB coordinate of 1 and
another RGB coordinate of 0, which places the colour on one of the faces of the
HSB cone.

Finally, to calculate the hue angle, we must discover which of the three RGB
coordinates is the maximum. In our example above, the green value is the largest,
so the colour should lie somewhere between 60° and 180° in the HSB cone, since
this is the area where green has the most influence. The hue angles between 60°
and 120° are closer to red than blue, so colours in this region should have red as
the second highest value (after green). Conversely, hue angles between 120° and
180° are closer to blue than red, so here blue should be the second highest value.

The algorithm for the case where green is the maximum value is therefore
defined to be as follows. Let M = maximum RGB coordinate and m = minimum

RGB coordinate. Further, let b = blue coordinate and r = red coordinate. The hue angle in degrees is then $120 + 60 \times (b - r)/(M - m)$.

That is, we express the difference between the blue and red components as a fraction of the spread in all three colour coordinates. If this fraction is positive, then blue is larger than red, and we wish the hue angle to be greater than 120°. We add on a fraction of the 60° segment between green and cyan. Similarly, if red is greater than blue, we subtract a fraction of the 60° between green and yellow.

We can again check this algorithm for some special cases. If the blue and red components are equal, the hue angle is 120°, meaning that the colour is a tone of green. The relative values of the blue and red components compared to the green component will have already been used to determine the brightness and saturation earlier.

If the blue and green components are equal, and red is smaller than both of them, then the difference $b - r$ must be the same as the difference $M - m$, which results in the hue angle being 180°. The colour is then a tone of cyan, which is an equal mixture of green and blue. Again, the brightness and saturation will have been determined earlier.

The algorithm for the other two cases (where red or blue are the maximum coordinates) is very similar.

The converse algorithm for converting from HSB to RGB can be derived from the original RGB to HSB algorithm, and is left as an exercise.

7.2.3 Colours in Java

Java provides two main colour classes: the `Color` class in the `java.awt` package, which has been around since the earliest versions of Java, and several colour-related classes as part of Java 3D, of which we have used `Color3f` in this book.

Both of these classes allow objects to be constructed using only the RGB model, although the `Color` class does have a static method that will return a `Color` object given HSB coordinates.

The best way to understand the effects of the various coordinates in the two models is to experiment with them and view the colours that result. As part of the Swing package, Java provides the `JColorChooser` class which displays a dialog box containing panels that allow the user to select colours based either on the RGB or HSB models and view the results. To use a `JColorChooser`, we can either display it in response to an event such as a button press, or else write a simple stand-alone application in which one is displayed as a child of the master frame. A `JColorChooser` object can be displayed with a single method call:

```
// Need to import the swing package
import javax.swing.*;

// Assumes that 'panel' is a JPanel that has been
//   added to the layout
Color lightColor = JColorChooser.showDialog(panel,
    "Light colour", Color.white);
```

The `showDialog()` method is a static method that creates and displays a `JColorChooser` object. Its three arguments are, respectively, the component that owns the dialog box, a string giving the title of the box, and the initial colour to be displayed in the box. If the user clicks OK in the dialog, the currently selected colour is returned as a `Color` object which can then be used elsewhere in the program. A JColorChooser dialog is shown in Figure 7.2.

Figure 7.2:
A JColorChooser
dialog box.

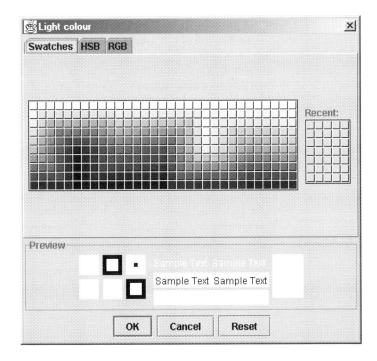

7.3 The theory of lighting

We are now ready to take a more precise look at the theory of light sources and material properties.

7.3.1 Ambient light

The ambient light reflected by an object is determined from two factors: the colour of the ambient light in the scene, and the reflective properties of the object. We can define a vector $\mathbf{c}_a$ to represent the colour of the ambient light:

$$\mathbf{c}_a = (r_a, g_a, b_a) \tag{7.1}$$

The components of this vector are, respectively, the red, green and blue components of the ambient light.

In a similar way, we can define another vector $\mathbf{C}_a$ to represent the material's response to ambient light:

$$\mathbf{C}_a = (R_a, G_a, B_a) \tag{7.2}$$

The components of $\mathbf{C}_a$ give the fraction of the ambient light of that colour that will be reflected by the material. The actual appearance of the material under the ambient illumination can be obtained by defining another vector $\mathbf{A}_a$ whose components are the products of the corresponding components in the vectors given in equations 7.1 and 7.2:

$$\mathbf{A}_a = \left(r_a R_a, g_a G_a, b_a B_a \right) \tag{7.3}$$

For example, if the ambient light in the scene is given by $\mathbf{c}_a = (1.0, 0.5, 0.2)$, and the material's response to ambient light is given by $\mathbf{C}_a = (0.3, 1.0, 0.8)$, then the object will actually be rendered with an ambient colour of $\mathbf{A}_a = (0.3, 0.5, 0.16)$.

This method of calculating ambient reflection can give some surprising effects that are occasionally interpreted as bugs in the program. For example, if the ambient light is defined to be pure red ($\mathbf{c}_a = (1.0, 0.0, 0.0)$), then if the red component of the material's response $\mathbf{C}_a$ to ambient light is zero, the object will appear black. Since the default background colour of a Java 3D canvas is black, the object is invisible on such a canvas, which may lead the programmer to believe that it is not being rendered.

7.3.2 Emissive light

Emissive light is the easiest of the light sources to handle, as it arises from objects, not external light sources. As such, we need add only a single vector describing the colour of emissive light produced by an object:

$$\mathbf{C}_e = \left(R_e, G_e, B_e \right) \tag{7.4}$$

All surfaces of the object for which the emissive light is defined will radiate light with this colour. Remember, however, that although emissive light may be used to make an object glow in the dark, the light from an emissive object does not illuminate any other objects in the scene.

7.3.3 Directional light

Directional light is assumed to have a constant direction and intensity over the entire scene. As mentioned above, a good analogy for directional light in the real world is the illumination of a scene with sunlight.

Unlike ambient light, which illuminates all surfaces of all objects uniformly, the illumination produced by a directed light source depends on the angle between the light's direction and surface which it illuminates. Rather than calculating the angle between a light ray and a surface, it is more conventional in graphics to use the angle between the light ray and the *normal* to the surface. We therefore define the unit vectors $\mathbf{L}$ and $\mathbf{N}$ to be the directions of the light ray and the surface normal, respectively.

To understand why the orientation of the surface makes a difference to the effect of directed light, consider Figure 7.3, where light travelling horizontally left to right illuminates a surface with the normal vector $\mathbf{N}$ shown. The largest possible illumination of a patch of this surface will occur if the normal vector is parallel to the light vector—in that case the light hits the surface face-on. If the surface is at an angle to the light's direction, the same amount of light is now spread over a larger area. In the figure, the light between the bottom two horizontal arrows would cover an area shown by d if the surface were perpendicular to the light's direction (that is, if the normal vector were parallel to the light's direction). If the surface is at an angle to the direction of the light, the same amount of light now covers area h.

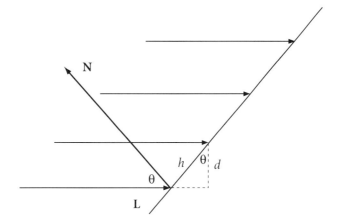

Figure 7.3:
The effect of the angle
between a directed
light ray and the
normal to a surface.

If the angle between $\mathbf{L}$ and $\mathbf{N}$ is θ as shown in the figure, then since h is the hypotenuse of a right-angled triangle, we have $d = h \cos \theta$. The ratio of the amount of light intercepted by a unit area on the surface patch h to that intercepted on the patch d is therefore $\cos \theta$.

In general, the amount of light actually seen by a viewer of such a surface also depends on the angle between the normal vector $\mathbf{N}$ and the direction $\mathbf{E}$ from a point on the surface to the observer's eye. However, for a matte surface such as soft cloth or unpolished wood or stone, a result from physics known as *Lambert's law* states that, for a directed light source, such surfaces appear equally bright from any viewing angle, provided that the relative position of the surface and light source does not change. We can therefore state that for a directional light, the amount of light reflected by a surface is reduced from its maximum value by $\cos \theta$, where θ is the angle between the normal vector and light's direction. With the directions of $\mathbf{L}$ and $\mathbf{N}$ shown in Figure 7.3, we may obtain the value of $\cos \theta$ from the scalar product $-\mathbf{L}{\cdot}\mathbf{N}$ (assuming that both vectors are unit vectors).

In addition to this effect, however, the surface may also have a colour-dependent reflection as in the case of ambient light. As with ambient light, we may define a vector to represent the colour of the light source:

$$\mathbf{c}_d = (r_d, g_d, b_d) \tag{7.5}$$

We may also define a vector to represent the material's response to directional light:

$$\mathbf{C}_d = (R_d, G_d, B_d) \tag{7.6}$$

The colour of a surface with normal $\mathbf{N}$ illuminated by a directional light with direction $\mathbf{L}$ is therefore:

$$\mathbf{A}_d = -\mathbf{L}{\cdot}\mathbf{N}(r_d R_d, g_d G_d, b_d B_d) \tag{7.7}$$

7.3.4 Specular reflection

Any form of directed light source can give rise to highlights in addition to the more general illumination it provides. A highlight is caused by *specular reflection* of the incident light from a shiny surface.

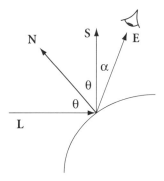

Specular reflection is always observed at a viewing angle such that the angle between the surface normal **N** at a point on the surface and the direction from that point to the observer's eye **E** is equal to (or close to) the angle between **N** and the direction **L** from the point on the surface to the light source. In Figure 7.4, the vector **S** shows the specular direction, where the angle between the normal and the reflected light is equal to the angle between the incident light **L** and **N**.

If the observer's line of sight matched the specular direction **S** (that is, if the vectors **E** and **S** were the same), the maximum highlight would be observed. If the observer moves slightly away from this direction, so that the angle α in Figure 7.4 is non-zero, some highlight may be observed if the distance from the specular angle is not too great. The rate at which the highlight disappears as we move further from the specular direction depends on the shininess of the surface.

There are two common techniques in use for the generation of highlights. The first is derived from the situation shown in Figure 7.4—the intensity of the highlight is set to be proportional to $\cos^n \alpha$, where n is called the *specular reflection exponent*. The higher the value of n, the more concentrated the highlight, and the shinier the surface appears. For a perfect reflector such as a mirror, n is infinite, which means that a highlight is only visible when the observer is exactly aligned with the specular direction. Large, finite values of n correspond to shiny objects such as snooker balls, while very low values of n are used for objects that have some highlights, but are generally matte in apperance.

The method of using a $\cos^n \alpha$ term to calculate highlights was developed in 1975 by Phong Bui-Tuong, and is known as the *Phong illumination model*. Although it provides a realistic highlight on a shiny surface, its main drawback is that it requires the calculation of the specular vector **S**. Although this is a relatively simple exercise in geometry, the calculation can be time-consuming if it must be done repeatedly in the generation of a complex graphical scene. For that reason, a second method known as the *halfway vector* model is often used instead. Java 3D uses this method in preference to the Phong model.

The 'halfway vector' in question is a vector **H** whose direction is halfway between –**L** and **E** (Figure 7.5). If the observer were viewing the object along the specular direction, then **H** would coincide with the normal vector **N**, and the angle β between **H** and **N** would be zero. As **E** deviates from the the specular direction **S**, **H** gets further from **N** and the angle β gets larger. Thus the angle β behaves in the same way as α in the sense that it is zero at maximum highlight and increases as the observer moves away from the specular direction.

The halfway vector model proposes that instead of using a $\cos^n \alpha$ term to determine the intensity of the highlight in a particular viewing direction, we should use $\cos^n \beta$. The advantage of this is that the only vectors we need to know to calculate the angle β are **L** and **E**, which must be known to render the scene anyway. In fact, we can define **H** as the unit vector $(-\mathbf{L} + \mathbf{E})/|-\mathbf{L} + \mathbf{E}|$ so that $\cos \beta = \mathbf{H} \cdot \mathbf{N}$.

Figure 7.5:
The halfway vector model.

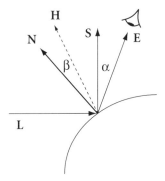

The specular reflection model used by Java 3D uses the halfway vector model, and calls the exponent n the *shininess*. An extra term is added to all light sources (except ambient light) to provide a highlight. Besides the $\cos^n \beta$ factor, the response of the material to the colour of the specular reflection must also be calculated. This is done in a similar way to the method we have already seen for ambient and directional light. Another vector defining the material's response to specular reflections is defined:

$$\mathbf{C}_s = \left(R_s, G_s, B_s \right) \tag{7.8}$$

Since specular reflection can result from any directed light source, this vector is combined with whatever light source is being considered to produce the highlights from that source. For example, if we are using directional light, we combine equation 7.8 with the vector describing the colour of the directional light (equation 7.5) to produce the actual colour of the specular reflection:

$$\mathbf{A}_s = \cos^n \beta \left(r_d R_s, g_d G_s, b_d B_s \right) \tag{7.9}$$

Thus the total illumination provided by directional light is the sum of equations 7.7 and 7.9:

$$
\begin{aligned}
\mathbf{A}_{dir} &= \mathbf{A}_d + \mathbf{A}_s \\
&= -\mathbf{L} \cdot \mathbf{N} \left(r_d R_d, g_d G_d, b_d B_d \right) + \cos^n \beta \left(r_d R_s, g_d G_s, b_d B_s \right)
\end{aligned} \tag{7.10}
$$

Note that although there is only one light source, the material responds in two different ways. The first term contains the material's response to a diffuse illumination, and the second to specular reflection. In most materials, the colour response will be very different in these two cases. Shiny objects of any colour will usually have a specular reflection that matches the colour of the light source, so the most common values for the specular response terms will be $R_s = G_s = B_s = 1$.

7.3.5 Normal vectors

Although we have made much use of the normal vector **N** in the discussion so far, we have not yet indicated how this vector is calculated or evaluated. There are two main approaches to the provision of normal vectors—they can be calculated from the vertex data used to define a surface, or they can be provided as separate data, independently of the vertex data.

In a package such as Java 3D where all surfaces are defined as triangular meshes, it is always possible to calculate the normal vector for any triangular patch. If the three corners of a triangle are given by the vectors **a**, **b** and **c**, then two sides of the triangle are given by **b** – **a** and **c** – **a**. A vector normal to the triangle can then be obtained from the cross product of these two vectors: $\mathbf{N} = (\mathbf{b} - \mathbf{a}) \times (\mathbf{c} - \mathbf{a})$.

Although this method will work for all triangular patches, it can be quite costly in terms of computing time since a fair amount of arithmetic is required in a vector cross product. As a result, many graphics packages, including Java 3D, use the second system, where the programmer is required to supply the normal vectors as additional data.

The method used by Java 3D associates a normal vector with each *vertex* in a Shape3D object, rather than with each polygonal face. For example, the complete specification of a single triangle requires that the coordinates *and* a normal vector be supplied for each of the three vertices of the triangle. Clearly, in most cases, the three normal vectors at the vertices of a triangle will all be the same, so it may seem that such a system could waste a large amount of memory if a scene contains many triangular patches. However, it is possible to generate some interesting effects, especially on curved surfaces that have been approximated by triangular meshes, by making the normals vary over the vertices of each triangle.

The vertex normal method is applied to the calculation of lighting by using equations such as 7.10 to calculate the light colour at each vertex of a triangle. The interior of the triangle is then coloured by interpolating the colour values between the three vertices. Methods for doing this will be considered later in this chapter.

We will see some examples of the use of normal vectors in Java when we consider the coding aspects of lighting below. Before we leave the topic, however, it is worth mentioning one problem that can arise in a system that attaches normals to vertices rather than to surfaces.

The problem can appear in Java 3D when the GeometryArray class and its derivatives are used. In the strip array classes, most vertices are shared between two components (line segments, triangles or quadrilaterals) in the array. If two neighbouring components do not face in the same direction, it is not possible to assign a normal vector to the shared vertex that gives the correct orientation for both faces. If the neighbouring faces are part of an approximation to a curved surface, we might solve the problem by assigning a normal vector that averages the directions of the two normals to the two separate faces—in fact, this might even produce a smoother appearance to the surface under directed lighting.

However, if we are using a strip array to build an object that is intended to have sharp edges and corners, this averaging procedure will not work. The only solution in this case is to avoid the use of strip arrays and define each face as a separate component with its own private set of vertices.

In the case of a cube, for example, we need six separate squares, each with its own set of four vertices (and four associated normal vectors). This, of course, means that each vertex is stored three times in the Shape3D object, which wastes space, but there is no other way to ensure that the normal vectors are defined correctly for each side of the cube.

7.3.6   Point light sources

A point light source is fixed at a particular location in space and radiates equally in all directions from that position. A point light source is distinguished from a directional source in that the light from a point source attenuates with distance from the source.

Strictly speaking, the intensity of light from a point source decreases in inverse proportion to the square of the distance from the source (the inverse-square law). In practice, however, such a strict law often does not give rise to a realistic view in a computer image. For this reason, the formula that is used to calculate attenuation for a point source is more flexible, containing a constant term and a term that depends linearly on the distance, in addition to the standard quadratic term. The attenuation formula used in computer graphics is therefore:

$$a(D) = \frac{1}{a_0 + a_1 D + a_2 D^2} \tag{7.11}$$

where D is the distance from the point light source and a_0, a_1 and a_2 are constants, which may be set independently for each point light source.

With the addition of attenuation, the illumination provided by a point light source can be calculated in much the same way as for a directional light. We define a vector representing the colour of the light source:

$$\mathbf{c}_p = \left(r_p, g_p, b_p \right) \tag{7.12}$$

The material's response to light from a point source is assumed to consist of the same two components as for a directional light: a diffuse reflection and a specular reflection. Therefore, we can write the equation for diffuse reflection from a point source by adapting equation 7.7:

$$\mathbf{A}_p = \left(-\mathbf{L} \cdot \mathbf{N} \right) \cdot a(D) \cdot \left(r_p R_d, g_p G_d, b_p B_d \right) \tag{7.13}$$

Note that the values used for the material's response to the light are the same as those defined in equation 7.6. Also, the vector $\mathbf{L}$ is now the unit vector along the direction from the point light source to the location on the surface where the colour is being evaluated. This vector now varies with the location in the scene, in contrast to the situation with directional light above.

We have also included the attenuation factor $a(D)$ defined in equation 7.11. The variable D is the distance from the point light source to the location on the surface.

We can modify the specular reflection component in a similar way, to arrive at the final illumination at a location on a surface from a point light source (compare with equation 7.10):

$$\mathbf{A}_{point} = a(D) \left(-\mathbf{L} \cdot \mathbf{N} \left(r_p R_d, g_p G_d, b_p B_d \right) + \cos^n \beta \left(r_p R_s, g_p G_s, b_p B_s \right) \right) \tag{7.14}$$

In the specular term, the angle β is still defined as the angle between the halfway vector $\mathbf{H}$ and the normal $\mathbf{N}$. However, $\mathbf{H}$ will now change if we move either the location on the surface or the viewing position, since $\mathbf{H}$ is defined as $(-\mathbf{L} + \mathbf{E})/|-\mathbf{L} + \mathbf{E}|$.

In general, if several light sources of various types are included in a scene, the overall lighting for a particular point is the sum of the contributions from all sources. In some cases, this may give values for the individual components (red, green or blue) that exceed the maximum intensity that can be displayed. Various graphics packages resolve this problem in different ways. Java 3D caps individual colour components at 1.0, so that if the combined light from several sources exceeds 1.0, the colour is just displayed at 1.0. Other packages may work out the components of all three colours and then scale the result so that the component with the highest value is set to 1.0, with the other colour components reduced accordingly.

7.3.7 Polygon shading

Each of the equations given above for computing illumination gives a value for a specific point on an object's surface. If we wish to shade the edges and interior of a polygon, we need some method of setting the illumination at each point within the polygon. We could apply the equations above to each point on each scan line as the polygon is drawn, but this proves to be expensive in computing time, so faster algorithms are often used.

There are three polygon shading algorithms that are in common use. Although Java 3D supports only two of them, we will describe all three in this section.

The simplest method is to use the same colour for all points in the polygon. This method is known as *constant* or *flat* shading. A single colour is chosen, either by choosing the illumination value at one of the vertices or by averaging the values at all vertices, and the scan-line algorithm described in Chapter 1 is then used to fill the polygon with that colour.

The only virtue of the flat shading algorithm is that it is fast. It looks realistic only for objects such as cubes whose sides are intended to be flat facets, and even then, only when these objects are illuminated by a constant directional light. In other cases, some form of shading is needed within each polygon.

Java 3D supports flat shading if rendering speed is a problem, but in general it does not produce a realistic scene.

The simplest shading algorithm that offers a realistic appearance for objects with curved surfaces illuminated under all lighting conditions is called *Gouraud* shading. The main idea of Gouraud shading is to calculate the colour values along the edges of the polygon by interpolating the values at the vertices, and then to calculate the values along each scan line by interpolating the values at either end of the scan line.

The algorithm can be applied at the rendering stage, so it needs to be defined only for two dimensions. After the illumination values at the three vertices of a triangle are calculated, the triangle is projected onto the view plane, and the two-dimensional equivalents of its original three-dimensional coordinates are determined. Let us assume that two of these vertices have coordinates (x_1, y_1) and (x_2, y_2), and that the red components at the two vertices are r_1 and r_2 respectively.

We can work out the red component of a pixel at a point on the edge joining these two vertices by linear interpolation. If the coordinates of a point on the edge are (x_e, y_e), then the red component r_e at that point is

$$r_e = r_1 + (r_2 - r_1)(y_e - y_1)/(y_2 - y_1).$$

Once we have all the colour components calculated for all points on the edges of the triangle, we can work out the colours along each scan line by interpolating between the points at either end of the scan line.

The Gouraud algorithm produces much more realistic shading than flat shading, although considerably more calculation is involved. It is the other shading algorithm supported by Java 3D.

The third commonly used algorithm is known as *Phong shading*. Rather than interpolate the colour values at each point in the polygon directly, Phong shading interpolates the normal vectors at each point, and then uses the equations in the preceding sections to work out the illumination values at each point. This requires considerably more calculation than even the Gouraud model, although methods exist for iteratively calculating the normal vectors from one scan line to the next.

In most cases, Phong shading does produce a better result than Gouraud shading, especially in the calculation of highlights from specular reflection. One striking example of a case where Phong shading provides an improvement over Gouraud is when a highlight occurs entirely within a polygon. This can occur if the polygon in question contains the central area around the specular angle for a point light source. Since the highlight occurs within the polygon, the colour values at the vertices of the polygon will be mostly from diffuse reflection. As Gouraud shading obtains the interior illumination values by interpolating the values found at the vertices, no highlight will appear inside the polygon. Using Phong shading interpolates the normal vectors, so that the area of maximum specular reflection within the polygon will be found by the Phong method, and the highlight will appear.

7.4 Lighting in Java 3D

We will now examine how lighting and material properties are implemented in Java 3D.

Each light source is treated as a separate leaf node in the scene graph, and just like a Shape3D node, a light source can be transformed by a TransformGroup node in the same branch in the graph. For example, we can add a point light source as the child of a TransformGroup node, and move the light source by setting a translational Transform3D object as the transform in the TransformGroup node. We can add other nodes to the scene graph for other light sources, such as ambient light or directional light.

At this point, we will present a simple Java program in which a cylinder is added to the scene graph and lit with various light sources. Certain features in the program will lead us to a consideration of the main points in adding lighting to a Java 3D scene.

First, let us consider the scene graph for the program, as shown in Figure 7.6. The standard view branch is on the right, and is the same as that which we have been using for all our examples.

On the far left is the branch containing the cylinder that is to be rendered. There is a utility class in Java 3D that draws a cylinder without our having to work out the geometry in detail, so we will use that in the program. We can, however, create and attach our own Appearance object to the cylinder and, as shown in the figure, one of the attributes of the Appearance object is a Material object which describes the various material properties discussed above.

The light source is attached as a separate branch, shown in the middle in the figure. Note that the light source has its own TransformGroup so that it can be moved independently of the cylinder which it illuminates. (We could, of course, have combined the cylinder and the light under a single `TransformGroup` object so that they would move as a unit.)

The light node has a `BoundingSphere` object attached to it in the scene graph. We will consider boundaries in more detail after we have examined the example program, but for now all you need to realize is that each light source has a boundary associated with it. Only geometry objects within (or that have some portion within) this boundary are affected by the light source. This provides a way of restricting the influence of a light and also reducing the amount of computation needed by excluding objects outside the boundary.

Figure 7.6:
The scene graph for an illuminated cylinder.

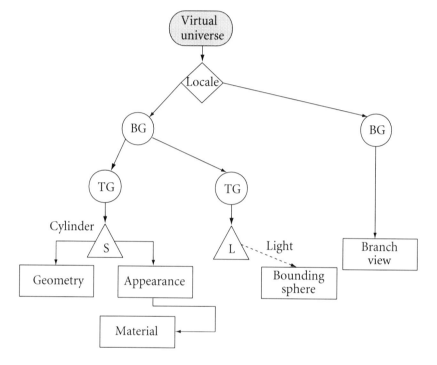

The main class for the cylinder demonstration is `CylinderDemo`, as follows:

```
1    import com.sun.j3d.utils.universe.*;
2    import javax.media.j3d.*;
3    import javax.swing.*;
4    import javax.vecmath.*;
5    import java.awt.*;
6    import java.awt.event.*;
7    import com.sun.j3d.utils.picking.behaviors.*;
8
9    public class CylinderDemo extends JFrame
10   {
11       JPanel m_panel = new JPanel();
12       Canvas3D m_drawingCanvas;
13
14       AmbientLight m_ambientLight;
15       DirectionalLight m_directionalLight;
16       PointLight m_pointLight;
```

```
17
18        CylinderBranch cylinder;
19
20    BasicUniverse universe;
21    BranchGroup scene;
22
23    public static void main(String argv[])
24    {
25        CylinderDemo cylinderDemo = new CylinderDemo();
26        cylinderDemo.setVisible(true);
27    }
28
29    CylinderDemo()
30    {
31        WindowHandler windowHandler = new WindowHandler();
32        addWindowListener(windowHandler);
33
34        setTitle("An illuminated cylinder");
35        getContentPane().setLayout(new BorderLayout());
36        setSize(750,450);
37        getContentPane().add(BorderLayout.CENTER, m_panel);
38        m_panel.setBackground(
39            new java.awt.Color(255,232,221));
40        m_panel.setBounds(0,0,800,450);
41
42        GraphicsConfiguration graphicsConfig =
43            SimpleUniverse.getPreferredConfiguration();
44        m_drawingCanvas = new Canvas3D(graphicsConfig);
45        m_drawingCanvas.setSize(600, 400);
46        m_panel.add(m_drawingCanvas);
47        universe = new BasicUniverse(m_drawingCanvas, 5.0f);
48
49        scene = new BranchGroup();
50        cylinder = new CylinderBranch();
51        scene.addChild(cylinder);
52
53        BoundingSphere behaveBounds =
54        new BoundingSphere(new Point3d(), 5);
55        PickRotateBehavior cylRotate =
56        new PickRotateBehavior(scene,
57            m_drawingCanvas, behaveBounds);
58        scene.addChild(cylRotate);
59
60        setupLightSources();
61        scene.addChild(m_ambientLight);
62        scene.addChild(m_directionalLight);
63        scene.addChild(m_pointLight);
64
65        universe.addBranchGraph(scene);
66    }
67
68    private void setupLightSources()
```

```
69      {
70          m_ambientLight = new AmbientLight();
71          m_ambientLight.setEnable(false);
72          m_ambientLight.setInfluencingBounds
73              (new BoundingSphere(new Point3d(), 2.0));
74
75          m_directionalLight = new DirectionalLight();
76          m_directionalLight.setEnable(true);
77          m_directionalLight.setInfluencingBounds
78              (new BoundingSphere(new Point3d(), 2.0));
79
80          m_pointLight = new PointLight();
81          m_pointLight.setEnable(false);
82          m_pointLight.setInfluencingBounds
83              (new BoundingSphere(new Point3d(), 2.0));
84      }
85
86      // Event handler to exit program omitted
87  }
```

Much of this class should be familiar from earlier examples, so we will concentrate on the code that sets up the cylinder object and the light source. Lines 14 to 16 actually declare three different light sources, one each of AmbientLight, DirectionalLight, and PointLight. The program will show how to set up each of these three types of light, and how to turn them on and off.

Line 18 declares a CylinderBranch object which contains the cylinder object to be drawn. We will consider the CylinderBranch class below.

The code in the constructor (beginning on line 29) should be familiar down to line 47, as this just creates the Canvas3D object and adds it to the layout of the program.

On lines 49 to 51 we create the main BranchGroup and then create and attach the cylinder object to this BranchGroup. This creates the left-most branch in Figure 7.6.

Lines 53 to 58 add the capability to rotate the cylinder by dragging it with the mouse (with the left button pressed). We will consider interaction and animation in more detail in Chapter 8, but we have included this feature here to allow the user to rotate the cylinder in three dimensions so that the effect of viewing it from different angles relative to a fixed light source can be observed. At this point, the reader may simply accept the code as it is given.

On lines 60 to 63 we initialize the three light sources and attach them to the scene graph. We have, in effect, added three more branches to the scene graph here, rather than the single one shown in Figure 7.6, but the idea is the same for all three. We have also omitted the TransformGroup node in each lighting branch, since we will not transform any of the light sources.

Finally, on line 65, we attach the main BranchGroup to the universe to make it live.

The method setupLightSources() beginning on line 68 initializes the three light sources. In each case, we have accepted the defaults for that light source, although each lighting class has its own methods which allow all its attributes to be set. For example, the DirectionalLight class contains a method called setDirection() which allows the direction of the light to be specified. Note that all properties of lighting classes become fixed once the branch containing the light object is made live (by joining it to the Locale object), so if you wish to alter any of these properties after the scene has been rendered, you must set the appropriate capabilities by using the setCapability() method, as described in Chapter 3.

We have switched off the ambient light and point light by calling setEnable() with an argument of false, and switched on the directional light.

The CylinderBranch class is as follows:

```
1    import javax.media.j3d.*;
2    import javax.vecmath.*;
3    import com.sun.j3d.utils.geometry.*;
4
5    public class CylinderBranch extends TransformGroup {
6        public CylinderBranch() {
7            addChild(new Cylinder(1.0f, 1.0f,
8                Cylinder.GENERATE_NORMALS,
9                32, 32, createAppearance()));
10           setCapability(TransformGroup.ALLOW_TRANSFORM_READ);
11           setCapability(TransformGroup.ALLOW_TRANSFORM_WRITE);
12           setCapability(TransformGroup.ENABLE_PICK_REPORTING);
13       }
14
15       private Appearance createAppearance()
16       {
17           Appearance appear = new Appearance();
18           Material material = new Material();
19
20           appear.setMaterial(material);
21
22           return appear;
23       }
24   }
```

Note that we have chosen to define CylinderBranch as an extension of TransformGroup. This allows the methods of the TransformGroup class to be applied directly to a CylinderBranch.

The constructor creates a Cylinder object on line 7 and adds is at a child to the CylinderBranch object. Since CylinderBranch is a derivative of TransformGroup, we are adding a child to the TransformGroup node in the scene graph.

The Cylinder class is one of several convenience classes for common geometric shapes provided by Java 3D. Other classes include Sphere, Box and Cone. All these classes extend the abstract class Primitive (and *not* the Shape3D class!), and objects declared from these classes may be added as leaf nodes to create geometry in a scene graph.

The first two arguments for the Cylinder constructor we have used here specify the base radius and height (1.0 metre each here). The third argument tells the constructor to generate normals for the vertices in the polygons that define the cylinder. As we have seen from the theory of lighting above, normals at the polygon vertices are needed if we wish to illuminate an object. By default, these utility geometry classes do not generate normals unless they are told to, in order to save space and computation time.

The next two arguments specify the resolution of the cylinder in terms of the number of horizontal and vertical divisions used to represent it. Here we have specified that 32 polygons are to be used to represent the circumference and 32 polygons to represent the height. The larger the number of polygons used, the smoother the surface of the cylinder appears, but the more memory and computation time are needed to render it.

The last argument specifies an Appearance object that is to be attached to the cylinder. Here, we create an Apperance object in the createAppearance() method. We create a Material object, accepting all its default values, and attach it to the Appearance.

It is very important to note that if we did *not* attach a Material object to the Appearance, the various light sources would have no effect on the Cylinder. The rule in Java 3D is that lighting only becomes active on an object if that object has a Material object attached to its Appearance. This can be a common source of puzzlement among programmers—even with all light sources set up properly, no lighting occurs if no Material has been set.

The last three lines (lines 10 to 12) in the constructor set some capabilities that are required for the mouse-activated rotation of the cylinder to work. As we will see in Chapter 8, the TransformGroup must allow its Transform3D to be read and written in order for mouse-driven interaction to work. The TransformGroup must also be 'pickable', so that clicking on it with the mouse selects it and starts the interaction.

Running this program as it stands (with only directional light switched on) produces the cylinder shown in Figure 7.7 (after rotating it slightly with the mouse).

Figure 7.7:
A cylinder illuminated with directional light.

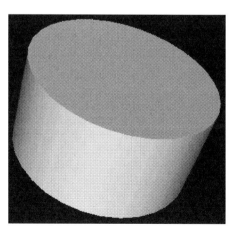

The cylinder's polygons are shaded using Gouraud shading (the default), and the effect appears quite natural, although some vertical lines are visible on the sides of the cylinder, due to the limited resolution used in its construction.

7.4.1 Boundaries and the region of influence

Although a light source can, in principle, illuminate all objects in a scene, Java 3D requires that each light source have an associated boundary of influence. In order for a geometry object to be lit by a light source, all or part of that object must lie with the light's *region of influence*. Geometry objects entirely outside this region are not illuminated by the light source at all, and are excluded from all calculations of the light's intensity.

From a programmer's point of view, boundaries may be used to exclude certain objects from illumination by some or all light sources. From a program-execution point of view, the restriction of a light's effects to objects within a boundary means that any objects outside this boundary need not be considered when calculating the illumination. For complex scenes with many light sources, this can cause a dramatic reduction in the computing time required to render a scene. For this reason, it is a good idea to consider the boundary of each light source carefully when writing the program, and not give in to the temptation to make the boundary very large so that all objects are included within the boundary of every light source.

For example, if a point light source has a negligible effect on objects more than 2 metres away (due to attenuation of the source), it is a good idea to set the boundary of that point source to a sphere of radius 2 metres. This will have no noticeable effect on the resulting scene and will avoid any computation being done on objects that are further than 2 metres away from the light source.

There are two main ways of providing boundaries for light sources. The first method was used in the `CylinderDemo` program above: attach a class derived from the `Bounds` class to the light source using the `setInfluencingBounds()` method.

There are three classes derived from `Bounds` provided in Java 3D: `BoundingSphere` (used above), `BoundingBox` and `BoundingPolytope`. The `BoundingSphere` class provides a sphere of a given radius, initially centred at the origin. `BoundingBox` provides a rectangular box whose axes are parallel to the main coordinate axes, and `BoundingPolytope` provides a general polyhedron, with the condition that it must be convex (loosely, this means there are no dents in the surface).

Any of these `Bounds`-derived classes are affected by `TransformGroups` in the same way as ordinary geometry objects. This may have unexpected effects if two or more light sources access the same boundary object. For example, in Figure 7.8, two light sources both use the same `BoundingSphere`, but one of the lights is the child of a `TransformGroup` while the other has no transform applied to it. Let us assume that the `BoundingSphere` is defined as a sphere of radius 1, initially centred at the origin, and that the `TransformGroup` attached to the first light defines a translation of 5 units in the positive y direction.

If both lights have a position (that is, they are either point lights or spotlights), then the first light will be translated 5 units in the y direction, as expected. However, when the `BoundingSphere` is applied to this translated light, it too will be translated by 5 units in the y direction, so that the region of influence of the translated light will be a sphere of radius 1 centred at the point (0, 5, 0).

For the second, untransformed, light the `BoundingSphere` will not be translated and will apply at its original position, as a sphere of radius 1 centred at the origin.

These effects may or may not be what the programmer wanted. In some cases it is desirable to have the region of influence follow the light around, but in other cases, we may want the region of influence to stay fixed on some particular geometry object while we move the lights around.

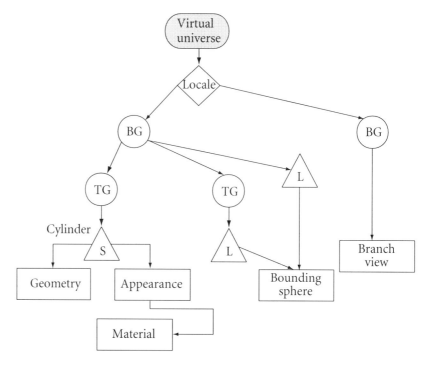

Figure 7.8:
Two light sources
using the same
boundary object.

If the second case is what is desired, the solution is to use a `BoundingLeaf` object instead of a `Bounds` object to specify the region of influence. A `BoundingLeaf` object is a leaf node in the scene graph in its own right, so that it exists independently of any light node. As such, it can be added as a separate branch to the graph, with its own `TransformGroup` parent.

In Figure 7.9 we see two light sources (triangles labelled with 'L') and a `BoundingLeaf` node (triangle labelled with 'BL'). The light on the left is a child of a `TransformGroup` node and can therefore be translated within the scene. However, the `BoundingLeaf` node is a child of its own `TransformGroup`, and can therefore be translated independently of the light source which uses it. In this way, both light sources in the graph can use the same `BoundingLeaf`, but their regions of influence are always the same regardless of how the two lights are moved around.

Using a `BoundingLeaf` is similar to to using a `Bounds` object. A `BoundingLeaf` object can be constructed with a `Bounds` argument in the constructor, as in:

```
BoundingLeaf sphereLeaf =
    new BoundingLeaf(new BoundingSphere());
```

This creates a `BoundingLeaf` with a region of influence given by a sphere of radius 1 centred at the origin. Alternatively, the region of a `BoundingLeaf` can be set by calling the `setRegion()` method, which also takes a `Bounds` object as its argument.

Once a `BoundingLeaf` object has been created, it can be associated with a light source using the `setInfluencingBoundingLeaf()` method which is common to all light classes. If a light source's `BoundingLeaf` is not null, it overrides any `Bounds` object which may have been associated with the light through a `setInfluencingBounds()` call.

Figure 7.9:
Two light sources
using a BoundingLeaf
node.

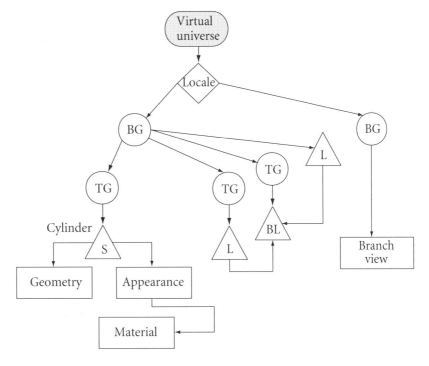

7.4.2 Scopes

The Bounds and BoundingLeaf classes allow general regions of influence to be defined, and lighting that is restricted using either of these classes will affect all objects that lie within the boundaries. In some cases, we would like more precise control over the objects that are to be illuminated by a light source. In this case, it is more appropriate to use the idea of a *scope*.

Rather than specifying an area within the Locale over which the influence of a light is seen, we can specify one or more branches of the scene graph that are affected by a light. Each branch that is to be included in the scope for a light is added to that light's scope list by calling the addScope() method, which takes a single argument of type Group (an ancestor of both BranchGroup and TransformGroup). All objects within a branch that has been added to the scope list of a light will be affected by that light, provided they also lie within the bounds for that light.

Scoping therefore allows us to pick and choose which objects are illuminated by a light without worrying about their physical location. We could, for example, throw a pile of bricks together and add only a few of the bricks within the pile to a light's scope so that these bricks would be lit and all the other bricks in the pile would be left in the dark.

For example, if we have created a DirectionalLight called dLight and a BranchGroup called selectedBricks that contains those bricks we wish to illuminate, all we need to do to restrict dLight so that it affects only the bricks in selectedBricks is make the call:

```
dLight.addScope(selectedBricks);
```

Once a light has some entries in its scope list, it will affect only the items found in that list. If the scope list is empty, the light's scope is assumed to cover the entire virtual universe and any objects within the light's bounds will be lit.

It is quite easy to produce a rather bad design for the scene graph if scoping and transformations are to be combined in the same graph. In the 'pile of bricks' example, if we want only some of the bricks in the pile to be within the scope of a light, but we also want *all* of the bricks in the pile to be within the same transform group (so that if we rotate the pile of bricks all the bricks move together, not just those that are within the scope of the light), we need to make sure that all the bricks are connected to the same TransformGroup node, but that those bricks that are to be within the same scope are within a separate group within the main branch. The situation can get quite complex if there are several collections of shapes, each with its own transformation, and several lights, each containing portions of the various collections of shapes within their respective scopes.

As usual, if we wish to read or write the scope list of a light after that light has been made live, we must set the appropriate capability bits: ALLOW_SCOPE_READ and ALLOW_SCOPE_WRITE.

A group can be removed from the scope list by calling removeScope(), but the required argument here is an int which represents the index number of the group within the scope list, not the actual group itself.

As of Java 3D version 1.2, a class called AlternateAppearance has been added which essentially defines regions of influence for an Appearance. The class works much like a light class, in that a bounds, bounding leaf and scope list can all be defined for it. The effect is that a default Appearance can be defined for a scene, and then a second Appearance can be defined which applies only to those branches within the bounds or scope of the AlternateAppearance. See the exercises for more details.

7.4.3   Backgrounds

Although not strictly an application of lighting, the procedure for setting the background colour in a scene is similar to that for defining a light source. The Background class defines a leaf node which also has a region of influence, which can in turn be specified as either a Bounds object or a BoundingLeaf.

To set the background, create a Background object and add it to the scene graph in the usual way. Several constructors for the Background class exist, and allow a background to be set as a solid colour, a pre-specified geometry, or a two-dimensional image.

The region of influence of a Background is set using either of the methods setApplicationBounds(), which takes a Bounds argument, or setApplicationBoundingLeaf(), which takes a BoundingLeaf argument.

It is also possible to use a textured sphere as the background—we shall see how to do this after we have covered textures later in this chapter.

7.5   Lighting example—a chessboard

We will now present a second example of lighting in Java 3D. In the first example program, we used a predefined shape to provide the geometry object. In this example, we will build a couple of geometry objects using lower-level components to get a feel for how lighting interacts with 'hand-made' objects.

We will build a program which displays a chessboard and single chess piece (a pawn) sitting on the board. Let us consider the class Board which creates the geometry for the chessboard. Its code is as follows.

```
1    import javax.media.j3d.*;
2    import javax.vecmath.*;
3
4    public class Board extends TransformGroup {
5        Shape3D boardShape;
6        Appearance appear = new Appearance();
7        Material material = new Material();
8
9        public Board() {
10           int row, col;
11
12           boardShape = new Shape3D();
13           QuadArray boardArray = new QuadArray(256,
14               QuadArray.COORDINATES |
15               QuadArray.COLOR_3 |
16               QuadArray.NORMALS);
17           Point3d[][] boardVertices = new Point3d[9][9];
18           for (row = 0; row < 9; row ++) {
19               for (col = 0; col < 9; col ++) {
20                   boardVertices[row][col] =
21                       new Point3d((-4.0 + row)/2, (-4.0 + col)/2, 0.0);
22               }
23           }
24
25           Point3d[] squareCorner = new Point3d[256];
26           Vector3f[] normals = new Vector3f[256];
27           Vector3f zNormal = new Vector3f(0.0f, 0.0f, 1.0f);
28           Color3f[] squareColors = {
29               new Color3f(0.2f, 0.2f, 0.2f),
30               new Color3f(0.8f, 0.8f, 0.8f)};
31           Color3f[] colors = new Color3f[256];
32           int colorNum = 0;
33
34           for (row = 0; row < 8; row ++) {
35               for (col = 0; col < 8; col ++) {
36                   int squareNum = 8 * row + col;
37                   colorNum = (row + col) % 2;
38                   squareCorner[4*squareNum] =
39                       boardVertices[row][col];
40                   squareCorner[4*squareNum + 1] =
41                       boardVertices[row][col+1];
42                   squareCorner[4*squareNum + 2] =
43                       boardVertices[row+1][col+1];
44                   squareCorner[4*squareNum + 3] =
45                       boardVertices[row+1][col];
46
47                   normals[4*squareNum] = zNormal;
48                   normals[4*squareNum + 1] = zNormal;
```

```
49          normals[4*squareNum + 2] = zNormal;
50          normals[4*squareNum + 3] = zNormal;
51
52          colors[4*squareNum] = squareColors[colorNum];
53          colors[4*squareNum + 1] = squareColors[colorNum];
54          colors[4*squareNum + 2] = squareColors[colorNum];
55          colors[4*squareNum + 3] = squareColors[colorNum];
56      }
57  }
58  boardArray.setCoordinates(0, squareCorner);
59  boardArray.setNormals(0, normals);
60  boardArray.setColors(0, colors);
61
62  boardShape.setGeometry(boardArray);
63  boardShape.setAppearance(createAppearance());
64  addChild(boardShape);
65  }
66
67  public Material getMaterial()
68  {
69      return material;
70  }
71
72  private Appearance createAppearance()
73  {
74      material.setCapability(Material.ALLOW_COMPONENT_WRITE);
75      material.setCapability(Material.ALLOW_COMPONENT_READ);
76      appear.setCapability(Appearance.ALLOW_MATERIAL_WRITE);
77      appear.setCapability(Appearance.ALLOW_MATERIAL_READ);
78      appear.setMaterial(material);
79
80      ColoringAttributes colorAtt = new ColoringAttributes();
81      colorAtt.setColor(new Color3f(1.0f, 0.5f,0.2f));
82      colorAtt.
83          setShadeModel(ColoringAttributes.SHADE_GOURAUD);
84      appear.setColoringAttributes(colorAtt);
85      PolygonAttributes polyAtt = new PolygonAttributes();
86      polyAtt.setCullFace(PolygonAttributes.CULL_NONE);
87      appear.setPolygonAttributes(polyAtt);
88
89      return appear;
90  }
91  }
```

We construct the board as a QuadArray, which stores a series of quadrilaterals as an array of points, where each group of 4 consecutive points in the array is used as a separate quadrilateral. Since most of the vertices in the chessboard are used by four adjacent squares, we might think that we could save space by using an IndexedQuadArray (there is no QuadStripArray class). However, since the squares sharing a vertex are not all the same colour, we cannot share the vertices. For this reason, we create a QuadArray that stores 256 vertices (64 squares with 4 vertices per square) on line 13.

We need to store three types of information at each vertex: the coordinates of the vertex, the colour at that vertex, and the normal at that vertex, since we will be lighting the chessboard. We therefore must tell the QuadArray constructor that these three types of information will be stored by adding the bit-wise OR of the three parameters on lines 14 to 16.

Although we need to create 64 separate squares, we do *not* actually need to create 256 separate Point3d objects in which to store the vertices. We can create 81 Point3d objects which hold the coordinate information for the 81 different vertices that define the square corners, and then just provide pointers from the main vertex array into this set of 81 vertices.

We will make each square 0.5 metre on each edge, and centre the board at the origin, with the board lying in the *xy* plane. We define the array of Point3d objects on lines 17 to 23. We will refer to this array when we construct the actual array of coordinates that will be attached to the QuadArray a bit later.

The array that will contain the coordinate information that is used by the QuadArray is squareCorner, declared on line 25. Line 26 creates the array of normals, and, since all normal vectors on the chessboard will be the same, we define this normal vector on line 27.

On lines 28 to 30 we define the colours that will be used for the white and black squares on the board. In order to distinguish the squares from the background, and from any white highlights, we define a light and dark grey to use as white and black, respectively, and store these colours in an array called squareColors. (We tend to use the American spelling of 'color' in program code, since all the Java classes that contain 'color' as part of their name use this spelling.) The array of colours that will be attached to the QuadArray is defined on line 31. The parameter colorNum on line 32 is used to determine which colour (white or black) to assign to a given vertex.

The nested for loops beginning on line 34 build the arrays that are to be attached to the QuadArray object. We will use the variable squareNum to step through the 64 squares on the board. For each square, we must store four instances of the coordinates, normals, and colours. The coordinates are assigned on lines 39 to 45 from the boardVertices array created earlier. Note that although the squareCorner array contains 256 components, these are assigned values from the boardVertices array, which contains only 81 different point values. In this way, we save some memory by only creating each distinct vertex on the board once.

Lines 47 to 50 assign all normal vectors to have the same value, and lines 52 to 55 assign the correct colour for each square's four vertices. Lines 58 to 60 attach all three arrays to the QuadArray object.

The last three lines (62 to 64) in the constructor attach the geometry and appearance to the Shape3D object, and then attach the Shape3D object itself to the TransformGroup of which the Board class is a derivative.

The Appearance object created by the createAppearance() method beginning on line 72 is fairly straightforward, but notice that we also include some code that defines a ColoringAttribute for the Appearance object. Although this code will not be used in the current version of the class (as we will see later), we have included it so that we may discuss the various methods by which objects can have colours assigned to them.

The various capabilities that are set on lines 74 to 77 allow various aspects of the Appearance to be altered after it is made live.

Now we consider the class that defines a pawn. Its code is:

```
1    import javax.media.j3d.*;
2    import javax.vecmath.*;
3    import com.sun.j3d.utils.geometry.*;
4
5    public class Pawn extends TransformGroup {
6        Material material = new Material();
7        Appearance appear = new Appearance();
8
9        public Pawn()
10       {
11           Transform3D trans = null;
12           createAppearance();
13
14           // Base
15           TransformGroup baseTransform = new TransformGroup();
16           baseTransform.
17               addChild(new Cylinder(0.2f, 0.05f,
18               Cylinder.GENERATE_NORMALS,
19               50, 2, appear));
20           trans = new Transform3D();
21           trans.setTranslation(
22               new Vector3f(0.0f, 0.025f, 0.0f));
23           baseTransform.setTransform(trans);
24           addChild(baseTransform);
25
26           // Mid-section
27           TransformGroup middleTransform = new TransformGroup();
28           middleTransform.
29               addChild(new Cylinder(0.05f, 0.2f,
30               Cylinder.GENERATE_NORMALS,
31               10, 20, appear));
32           trans = new Transform3D();
33           trans.setTranslation(new Vector3f(0.0f, 0.15f, 0.0f));
34           middleTransform.setTransform(trans);
35           addChild(middleTransform);
36
37           // Top cylinder
38           TransformGroup topCylTransform = new TransformGroup();
39           topCylTransform.
40               addChild(new Cylinder(0.15f, 0.05f,
41               Cylinder.GENERATE_NORMALS,
42               50, 5, appear));
43           trans = new Transform3D();
44           trans.setTranslation(
45               new Vector3f(0.0f, 0.275f, 0.0f));
46           topCylTransform.setTransform(trans);
47           addChild(topCylTransform);
48
49
50           TransformGroup topTransform = new TransformGroup();
51           Sphere topSphere = new Sphere(0.1f,
52               Sphere.GENERATE_NORMALS, 50,
```

```
53              appear);
54          topTransform.addChild(topSphere);
55          trans = new Transform3D();
56          trans.setTranslation(new Vector3f(0.0f, 0.35f, 0.0f));
57          topTransform.setTransform(trans);
58          addChild(topTransform);
59
60          Transform3D rotate = new Transform3D();
61          rotate.rotX(Math.PI / 2.0);
62          trans = new Transform3D();
63          trans.setTranslation(new Vector3d(-0.25, -0.25, 0.0));
64          trans.mul(rotate);
65          setTransform(trans);
66      }
67
68      // createAppearance() and getMaterial() methods
69      // omitted — they are the same as in Board class
70  }
```

The pawn is constructed out of 3 Cylinder objects and a Sphere. We will attach the same Appearance object to all four objects, so we define it as a class variable on line 7, and create it using the createAppearance() method on line 12. This method is the same as that used for the Board class, except that it does not return the Appearance object—it just creates the appear object defined on line 7.

The code for construction of the pawn itself should be fairly straightforward. We create each of the four components and translate it so that it sits in the correct location relative to the other parts of the pawn. When any object such as a Cylinder or Sphere is created, it is centred at the origin, and Cylinders are aligned with their axes along the y axis. We would like the pawn positioned so that its base sits on the xy plane, so we translate the base in the y axis by half its height (line 21). Similarly, the other two Cylinder objects and the Sphere are created and translated along the y axis so they are in the correct position.

Finally, we must orient the pawn so that it sits on the chessboard in the middle of one of the squares. When it is created, the pawn is aligned along the y axis, whereas the board lies in the xy plane, so we need to rotate the pawn by 90 degrees counterclockwise about the x axis (line 61). This will place the pawn on the board, but it will still be centred about the z axis, so we shift it by 0.25 metres in the x and y directions (line 63) to place it in the middle of a square.

The code for the main class (called ChessBoard) is very similar to that in the CylinderDemo class given above. The main difference is that, in ChessBoard, we need to create both a Board and a Pawn and associate them so that any transformations are applied to both objects at once. We can do this by creating a TransformGroup and adding both the Pawn and Board to it. That is, in place of lines 49 and 50 in the CylinderDemo class, we would write:

```
1   TransformGroup pawnBoardTrans = new TransformGroup();
2   board = new Board();
3   pawnBoardTrans.addChild(board);
4   pawn = new Pawn();
5   pawnBoardTrans.addChild(pawn);
6   pawnBoardTrans.setCapability
```

```
7        (TransformGroup.ALLOW_TRANSFORM_READ);
8      pawnBoardTrans.setCapability
9        (TransformGroup.ALLOW_TRANSFORM_WRITE);
10     pawnBoardTrans.setCapability
11       (TransformGroup.ENABLE_PICK_REPORTING);
12
13     scene = new BranchGroup();
14     Transform3D groupTrans = new Transform3D();
15     groupTrans.set(new Vector3f(0.0f, 0.0f, -5.0f));
16     pawnBoardTrans.setTransform(groupTrans);
17     scene.addChild(pawnBoardTrans);
18
19     BoundingSphere behaveBounds =
20         new BoundingSphere(new Point3d(0,0,0),5);
21     PickRotateBehavior boardRotate =
22         new PickRotateBehavior(scene, m_drawingCanvas,
23         behaveBounds);
24     scene.addChild(boardRotate);
25
26     PickZoomBehavior boardZoom =
27         new PickZoomBehavior(scene, m_drawingCanvas,
28             behaveBounds);
29     scene.addChild(boardZoom);
30
31     PickTranslateBehavior boardTranslate =
32         new PickTranslateBehavior(scene, m_drawingCanvas,
33             behaveBounds);
34     scene.addChild(boardTranslate);
```

Lines 1 to 5 in this code create the new TransformGroup and attach the Pawn and Board objects to it. Lines 6 to 11 set some capabilities to allow the scene to be moved around using the mouse.

Before we attach the combined pawn–board branch to the overall scene, we need to move the image back a bit so that it will fit into the viewport. We do this by defining a transformation for the TransformGroup to which we attach the board and pawn (lines 14 to 16). We translate the image back in the z direction by 5 metres, and then add the TransformGroup containing the board and pawn to the scene (line 17).

The remaining code given above sets up the mouse interaction, in a similar way to that given in the CylinderBranch class above. This time, however, we allow rotation, zooming and translation using the mouse. Rotation is done by dragging with the left mouse button, translation with the right mouse button, and zooming with the middle mouse button (or mousewheel on two-button PC mice). The zoom option can also be obtained by holding down the Alt key and dragging with the left mouse button if the mouse has only two buttons and no mouse wheel.

Light sources with various properties can be attached to the ChessBoard class in the same way as we attached them to the CylinderDemo class earlier. With various light sources or combinations of light sources, the rotate, zoom and translate features can be used to view the chessboard under various lighting conditions and from various angles. Programs such as this are useful for experimenting with lighting effects to decide what to put in your own programs.

One view produced by the program is shown in Figure 7.10, which shows the board and pawn after rotation and zooming, under a point light source.

Figure 7.10:
Output of the
ChessBoard program.

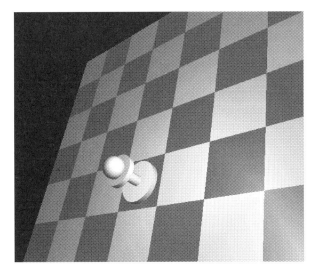

7.5.1 Colour precedence

One thing stands out in the sample programs given above—there are several ways of assigning the colour or colours of an object. The various ways of creating colour do not all work together, so it is important to understand the precedence applied to the various colour-generation methods.

The first thing to understand is that these methods apply to the colour of the *object*, and not of the light source being used to illuminate it. That is, these colour-generation methods are alternative ways of specifying the material colour that is used in the equations earlier in this chapter.

There are three ways of assigning a colour to an object. First, we can assign a colour to each vertex in the geometry, as we did with the QuadArray used to create the chessboard above. Second, we can assign colours to the four material properties (ambient, diffuse, emissive and specular light) as described above. Finally, we can specify a colour for an object by creating a ColoringAttributes object and attaching it to the Appearance of a Shape3D object.

The first thing to remember is that colours defined through a Material object and those defined through ColoringAttributes are mutually exclusive—they are *never* used at the same time. As we mentioned earlier in the chapter, light sources only affect an object if a Material object has been attached to that object's Appearance. If a Material object exists, the colours defined within it are used to determine the object's response to lighting. If no Material object exists for an object, then the colour defined in ColoringAttributes is used. No response to any light source will be shown, so the effect is that all surfaces of the object will be coloured the same colour. Another way of looking at this is that in the absence of a Material, the ColoringAttributes colour is used to provide the ambient light, and no other light sources are used.

However, if the object has been assigned colours by specifying a colour for each vertex in the geometry (as we did with the QuadArray used to create the chessboard above), this method takes precedence over either colours specified in a `Material` object or those in a `ColoringAttributes` object. Note, however, that in the case where a `Material` object exists for an object whose vertex colours have been defined, the vertex colours only replace the ambient and diffuse colours in the `Material`—the emissive and specular colours in the `Material` are still used where appropriate.

In summary, when trying to determine what colour an object will appear, check first to see if there is a `Material` associated with the object. If not, all light sources are ignored, and the colour of the object is determined by first checking to see if individual vertex colours have been specified. If so, these are used. If not, check to see if a `ColoringAttributes` object exists. If so, the colour defined here is used to colour the entire object (no shading is applied). If not, the object is coloured a flat white.

If a `Material` exists for the object, light sources will have an effect on it. Check if individual vertex colours have been defined. If so, these colours replace the ambient and diffuse `Material` values for all lighting calculations. If not, the `Material` colours are used for all lighting calculations. If a `Material` exists, the colours defined in `ColoringAttributes` are ignored.

Referring back to the code for the `Board` class given on page 234, the code on lines 80 to 83 creates an orange colour within a `ColoringAttributes` object. This colour is not used in this class for two reasons. First, a `Material` object exists and is attached to the `Appearance` on line 78. If line 78 were commented out, the `Material` object would no longer be connected to the object, so no light source would have any effect on the object.

However, in this case, the `ColoringAttributes` colour would still not be used, since the chessboard had colours defined for its individual vertices (lines 52 to 55 and 60). If line 60 were commented out as well (and the `COLOR_3` flag on line 15 removed from the constructor), then the `ColoringAttributes` colour would be used to colour the chessboard, with the result that all squares would be the same orange colour.

7.6 Textures

All the shaded surfaces we have seen so far have much the same appearance, in that they are all composed of uniform gradients of colour or shading. Many real-world objects, however, have much more detail or texture in their surface appearance. Common examples of textured surfaces are wood grain, carpet, cloth, stone and concrete. In principle, we could generate the appearance of such surfaces using only the geometry classes we have studied earlier, but the amount of effort, memory and computation time required to produce and process such surfaces would be prohibitive. It would be much easier if we could map an existing image, such as one obtained by scanning in a photograph, onto the triangles making up an existing geometry object. The process of *texture mapping* allows us to do this.

The simplest form of texture mapping uses an image file (such as a JPEG or GIF) as the source of the texture, and defines a *mapping function* which maps pixels from the image onto points within a triangular facet from a three-dimensional object within the scene. The colour from the image may simply replace whatever colour was present on the object, or some form of modulation or blending of the two colours may occur. One example of the latter case is to allow the texture image to be partially transparent, so that the material's colour (and its response to lighting) shows through the applied image.

The texture mapping function used by Java 3D is based on the scan-line algorithm used for filling polygons (described in Chapter 1). Pixels in the texture image (sometimes called *texels*) are identified by assigning a two-dimensional coordinate system to the image (see Figure 7.11). The horizontal coordinate is called *s*, and the vertical coordinate is *t* (some books use *u* and *v*, respectively). Each point in the triangle that is to have the texture applied to it is *mapped* to an (*s*, *t*) coordinate within the texture image. In Figure 7.11, let us map triangle vertex A to texture coordinates (0, 0), B to (0, 1) and C to (1,1).

Figure 7.11:
Mapping a texture onto a triangle. The vertices of the triangle are mapped to (*s*, *t*) coordinates as shown.

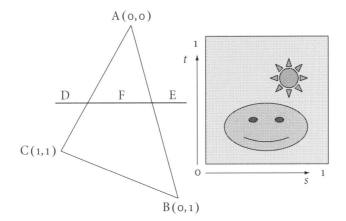

The pixels within the triangle are identified with individual texels one scan line at a time. Consider scan line DE in Figure 7.11. To find which texel maps to point D, we interpolate between points A and C. If D is 40% of the distance along the line from C to A, then its texel coordinates are 0.6C + 0.4A, or (0.6, 0.6). Point D would therefore be mapped to a texel roughly in the location of the sun symbol in the image shown in Figure 7.11.

Similarly, if point E is halfway along the line from A to B, its texel coordinates will be (0, 0.5), and it will be mapped to a texel at the midpoint of the left edge of the image. Finally, point F (halfway between D and E) is mapped to texel coordinates (0.3, 0.55). Other points along the scanline DE are worked out in a similar way.

7.6.1 Textures in Java 3D

At this point, let us see how to apply texture to objects in Java 3D. We will add texture to the squares on the chessboard in the program given earlier in this chapter.

The image files must be prepared externally, and either saved on disk in a standard image format such as JPEG or GIF, or else prepared as a BufferedImage within the program. Any image may be used as a texture, but Java 3D does impose the restriction that the dimensions of the image (in pixels) must be powers of 2. That is, image sizes of 128 × 128, 256 × 16, or even 16 × 1 are all acceptable, but 134 × 256 is not, since 134 is not a power of 2. This restriction is imposed for efficiency reasons.

Images are most commonly obtained by scanning in photographs or by taking original photographs with a digital camera. Image files are also available from the Internet, although you should be careful that the images are not copyrighted if you plan to use them in commercial software.

Once we have obtained the raw image file, we will probably need to adjust its size so that both its dimensions are powers of 2. There are many image editing packages available, many of which are freeware or shareware.

With the image files set up correctly, we can now write the code to add textures to a Java 3D program. Code must be added in two places. First, we need to generate the texture coordinates that map texels from the image file to coordinates in the geometry. Second, we need to add the texture itself to the Appearance object, where we can also set several attributes that modify the texture within the program.

Let us consider first how to add texture map coordinates to a geometry object, by adding these coordinates to the Board class in the chessboard program above. We wish to apply two different textures to the board, one for the white squares and one for the black squares. One way of doing this is to use two separate image files and associate each with a texture. However, doing things this way would require that we separate the white squares and black squares into separate Shape3D objects, since we can only apply a single texture to each Shape3D object. (Actually, as of version 1.2 of Java 3D, multiple textures are allowed, but they are overlaid onto the same object, so that still wouldn't help us.)

An easier way is to combine the textures for the two square colours into a single image file, and then choose the correct texture for each square by means of the texture mapping coordinates. The image file we will use is shown in Figure 7.12.

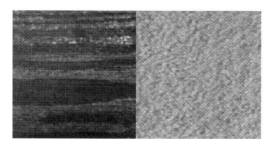

Figure 7.12: The image file used for the chessboard squares.

The images used here are digital photographs of the author's desk and carpet. Each square is 128 pixels on each edge, so the overall image file is 256×128 pixels.

We can now modify the code given in the original Board class above. First, we need to inform the constructor for the QuadArray that defines the chessboard that we will be adding texture coordinates. We modify the declaration of boardArray (on lines 13 to 16 in the original Board class on page 233) to the following:

```
QuadArray boardArray = new QuadArray(256,
    QuadArray.COORDINATES |
    QuadArray.COLOR_3 |
    QuadArray.TEXTURE_COORDINATE_2 |
    QuadArray.NORMALS);
```

The TEXTURE_COORDINATE_2 flag specifies that we will be using a two-dimensional texture.

Next, we need to define the texture map. As we can see from Figure 7.12, the black square is on the left, and its corners have texture coordinates (0, 0), (0.5, 0), (0.5, 1), and (0, 1). Note that extent in the *s* direction from left to right is always taken to run from 0 to 1, no matter how wide the image actually is. Similarly, the vertical *t* direction also has a range from 0 to 1, even if the actual number of pixels is different from those in the *s* direction. Thus the texel coordinates are *relative* coordinates, not absolute ones. The coordinates for the white square are therefore (0.5, 0), (1, 0), (1, 1), (0.5, 1).

As of version 1.2, Java 3D requires that texel coordinates are specified using the TexCoord2f class. This class just contains two data fields for storing the *s* and *t* coordinates as floats. We can therefore define the 8 coordinates of the two squares as:

```
TexCoord2f[] squareTexCoords = {
    // Black square
    new TexCoord2f(0.0f, 0.0f),
    new TexCoord2f(0.5f, 0.0f),
    new TexCoord2f(0.5f, 1.0f),
    new TexCoord2f(0.0f, 1.0f),

    // White square
    new TexCoord2f(0.5f, 0.0f),
    new TexCoord2f(1.0f, 0.0f),
    new TexCoord2f(1.0f, 1.0f),
    new TexCoord2f(0.5f, 1.0f)
};
```

As with the regular coordinates of the square corners, we need an array of 256 TexCoord2f values to associate with the QuadArray. We do this, as before, by referencing the 8 texture coordinates defined in squareTexCoords. We insert the declaration:

```
TexCoord2f[] squareTextures = new TexCoord2f[256];
```

immediately before the for loop on line 34 in the original Board class on page 233. Then we add the following code inside the nested for loop (after line 55 would do) to create the texture coordinates:

```
squareTextures[4*squareNum] =
    squareTexCoords[4*colorNum];
squareTextures[4*squareNum + 1] =
    squareTexCoords[1 + 4*colorNum];
squareTextures[4*squareNum + 2] =
    squareTexCoords[2 + 4*colorNum];
squareTextures[4*squareNum + 3] =
    squareTexCoords[3 + 4*colorNum];
```

Recall that the colorNum parameter alternates between 0 and 1 to identify the colour of the current square.

Finally, we set the squareTextures array as the set of texture coordinates for the QuadArray (after line 60):

```
boardArray.setTextureCoordinates(0, 0, squareTextures);
```

This method call contains three arguments, which requires a bit of explanation. As of Java 3D, version 1.2, all geometry objects can support several *texture coordinate sets*. This is to allow more than one texture to be applied to an object at once, making it possible to overlay textures with different transparency properties. The first argument in setTextureCoordinates() is the index of the coordinate set to which these coordinates are being added. The second argument is the index within that set at which the array squareTextures should be added. If we are only using a single texture coordinate set (as we will in this book), then the first argument will always be 0. (At the time of writing, there are still a number of bugs in the multi-texture code in Java 3D, so the results are unpredictable.)

This completes the assignment of texture coordinates to the QuadArray object.

Now we need to add the texture image itself to the Appearance object. We will not repeat the entire class again, as the number of lines of code that need to be added is not great. First, we need to add an import statement at the start of the Board.java file:

```
import com.sun.j3d.utils.image.*;
```

Then, we add some declarations at the beginning of the class, after line 7:

```
TextureLoader textureLoader;
ImageComponent2D image;
Texture2D squareTexture;
```

We now make some additions to the createAppearance() method by adding the following code after line 87:

```
textureLoader = new TextureLoader("SquareTextures.jpg",
    new java.awt.Panel());
image = textureLoader.getImage();
squareTexture = new Texture2D(Texture.BASE_LEVEL,
    Texture.RGBA, image.getWidth(), image.getHeight());
squareTexture.setImage(0, image);
appear.setTexture(squareTexture);
```

There are several steps which must be followed to load a texture and add it to an Appearance, but if all we wish to do is add a single texture at a fixed resolution, the steps are always the same.

First, we must load the raw image from the disk file. In the example here, the image is stored in the file SquareTextures.jpg. The TextureLoader class simplifies the loading of an image as can be seen from the example code above, but you may wonder what the new java.awt.Panel() argument is doing in the constructor.

All TextureLoader constructors that accept a filename as one of their arguments require an *image observer* as one of their other arguments. A full explanation of image observers would be too much of a digression at this point, but a simple explanation is that Java loads images *asynchronously* (in a separate thread) so that if the image-loading process takes a while, the program can get on with other tasks. This is especially important since texture images can be loaded over the Internet as well as from a disk file, so the time lag while an image loads might be considerable.

The Java AWT is constructed so that any class derived from Component can serve as an image observer, which keeps track of the image-loading process and informs the application when the image is fully loaded. Therefore, we can simply use any object derived from Component (such as a Panel) to fill the role. In many applications, the class in which the texture loading is occurring is itself a descendant of Component (for example, if the class extends the Frame class). In this case, the second argument to the `TextureLoader` constructor may be given as `this`.

Once we have loaded the image file, we extract the image and store it in an `ImageComponent2D` object. Next, we create the texture itself as a `Texture2D` object. The `Texture2D` class contains two constructors, but the one without arguments (which is tempting to use) creates a texture with an image containing no pixels, so is not particularly useful. That explains why we have used the full, four-argument constructor above.

The last two arguments extract the dimensions, in pixels, of the image. Remember that both these values must be powers of 2.

Having created the `Texture2D` object, we assign the image to it, and then attach the texture itself to the `Appearance` object. The final program produces the textured chessboard shown in Figure 7.13.

Figure 7.13:
Textured squares
on a chessboard.

The primitive geometric shapes in the `Sphere`, `Cylinder` and other classes can also have textures applied to them. Recall that in order for lighting to affect a primitive shape, we had to tell the constructor to generate the normal vectors for the shape. In a similar way, we tell the constructor to generate a set of texture coordinates. For example, if we wished to add texture to the `Pawn` class in the chessboard example, we would need to tell each of the four primitive shapes that make up the pawn (three cylinders and a sphere) to generate texture coordinates. Referring back to the code for the `Pawn` class on page 236, we would replace the first constructor call (lines 16 to 19) by:

```
baseTransform.
    addChild(new Cylinder(0.4f, 0.1f,
    Cylinder.GENERATE_NORMALS |
    Cylinder.GENERATE_TEXTURE_COORDS,
        50, 2, appear));
```

with similar modifications for the other three primitive shapes in the `Pawn` class.

The primitive shape uses an internal algorithm to map a single texture image file onto the entire shape, so that parts of the file get mapped to each triangle that makes up the overall surface. The results are not always easy to predict. Perhaps the easiest to interpret is the texture map for a sphere, where the rectangular image file is projected onto the sphere in much the same way as a Mercator projection of the Earth's surface is projected onto a sphere to reclaim an accurate globe of the world.

As an example, we have mapped the image file shown in Figure 7.14 (a photograph of the author's wallpaper) onto each of the four primitives that make up the pawn. The results are shown in Figure 7.15.

Figure 7.14:
The wallpaper image file used as a texture for the pawn.

Figure 7.15:
A textured pawn sitting on a textured chessboard.

7.6.2 Texture coordinate generation

With a more complex scene, the generation of texture coordinates can become quite tedious. Java 3D provides an automatic texture-coordinate-generation class called `TexCoordGeneration` which can replace the process of manually creating an array of `TexCoord2f` objects and attaching it to a geometry.

Automatic coordinate generation is available in two modes: linear projection and spherical projection. We will illustrate the method by applying texture coordinate generation to the chessboard example above.

Before we examine the changes to the code, we need to understand how the coordinate generation is done. As described above, each vertex in a polygon that is to have a texture applied to it must be mapped to a pair of texture coordinates in the image file. The `TexCoordGeneration` class generates each of the two texture coordinates in the pair by calculating the perpendicular distance of the corresponding vertex from a plane that must be specified by the programmer. For example, suppose we wish to generate the s texture coordinate for all vertices on an object by calculating the distance of the vertex from the yz plane. Now consider a triangle within the object with vertices at (0, 0, 0), (1, 0.5, 0) and (0.5, −1.25, 1.75). The s coordinate for the first vertex will be $s = 0$, since the point

(0, 0, 0) lies in the *yz* plane. The second vertex lies at a distance of 1 from the *yz* plane, so its *s* texture coordinate will be $s = 1$. The third vertex will map to $s = 0.5$.

To obtain the *t* texture coordinate for each of these vertices we define a second plane, such as the *xz* plane. In this case, the value of *t* for the first vertex is $t = 0$ and for the second vertex it is $t = 0.5$. What do we do for the third vertex, where the distance to the *xz* plane is 1.25? Since this value is larger than 1.0, which is the maximum possible texture coordinate, we need a rule for interpreting values that lie outside the bounds of [0, 1]. Two options are available: we can *clamp* the value to the maximum or minimum value of the texture coordinate, or we can *wrap* the value so that the texture map repeats itself for values outside the interval [0, 1]. The default in Java 3D is to wrap the coordinates. If we use wrapping, then the *t* coordinate for the third vertex becomes $t = 0.25$.

In order for coordinate generation to work, we clearly need to set up the relation between the scene and the texture image files properly, since we do not have the flexibility provided by being able to generate arbitrary sets of texture coordinates within the program. An example of the type of problem we might encounter is provided by the texturing of the chessboard in the earlier program.

In order to require only a single Appearance object for both white and black squares, we combined the two textures for the two square colours into a single image file, shown in Figure 7.12. It turns out that this file cannot be used to generate texture coordinates, since it is not the same size in the horizontal and vertical directions. That is, we cannot define two planes such that the distances from these planes correctly assign texture coordinates to the vertices of the squares in the chessboard.

The easiest way to fix this problem is to create a new, symmetric image file, as shown in Figure 7.16.

Using this image file, we can now use the *yz* and *xz* planes as the reference planes. Since each square on the board is 0.5 metre on each side, and the squares in the image file have dimensions in texture space of 0.5 on each side, the mapping works perfectly. Note that if we had used a different size for the squares in the chessboard, the mapping would not work without some scaling.

Figure 7.16: The image file used for texture coordinate generation.

We can now examine the changes to the Board class above that are required to use TexCoordGeneration. First, we should comment out the line

```
boardArray.setTextureCoordinates(0, 0, squareTextures);
```

that was added after line 58, since we no longer wish to use the manually-generated coordinates in the geometry class.

Next, since we are using a different image file, we need to change the lines creating the TextureLoader to:

```
        textureLoader = new TextureLoader("Squares4x4.jpg",
            new java.awt.Panel());
```

where Squares4x4.jpg is the name of the image file shown in Figure 7.16.

Finally, we need to add the TexCoordGeneration object to the createAppearance() method:

```
    TexCoordGeneration texCoordGen =
        new TexCoordGeneration(
            TexCoordGeneration.OBJECT_LINEAR,
            TexCoordGeneration.TEXTURE_COORDINATE_2,
            new Vector4f(0.0f, 1.0f, 0.0f, 0.0f),
            new Vector4f(1.0f, 0.0f, 0.0f, 0.0f));

    appear.setTexCoordGeneration(texCoordGen);
```

There are several constructors available for TexCoordGeneration. The one we have used here takes four arguments. The first argument specifies the projection mode—OBJECT_LINEAR uses a linear projection which fixes the texture coordinates to specific vertices on the object, which is what we want.

The second argument specifies that a two-dimensional image file is being used, and the last two arguments specify the two reference planes. The four components of the Vector4f object that defines a plane are the coefficients (A, B, C, D) in the standard equation for a plane:

$$Ax + By + Cz = D$$

Recall that the vector (A, B, C) defines the normal to the plane, and the quantity D defines the minimum distance from the origin to the plane. In the example shown here, the vector $(0, 1, 0, 0)$ defines the xz plane, since this plane passes through the origin $(D = 0)$ and its normal is parallel to the y axis. Similarly, the second vector specifies the yz plane.

With these changes to the code, texture coordinate generation is in effect, and the result is the same as the chessboard shown in Figure 7.13.

7.6.3 Textured backgrounds

As promised earlier in this chapter when we discussed setting the background colour using a Background object, we will now describe how to use a texture as the background image in a 3D scene. The procedure is somewhat more complex than simply defining a uniform colour for the background as we did earlier.

We will present the method addBackground() from the BackgroundDemo class which is available in the source code on the Web. The code is as follows:

```
1   private BranchGroup addBackground()
2   {
3       BranchGroup backgroundRoot = new BranchGroup();
4
5       Background background = new Background();
6       background.setApplicationBounds(bounds);
7       BranchGroup backGeoBranch = new BranchGroup();
8       Sphere backSphere = new Sphere(1.0f,
9           Sphere.GENERATE_NORMALS_INWARD |
10          Sphere.GENERATE_TEXTURE_COORDS, 20);
```

```
11          backGeoBranch.addChild(backSphere);
12          background.setGeometry(backGeoBranch);
13
14          TextureLoader tex =
15              new TextureLoader("carpet.jpg", this);
16          TextureAttributes texAttr = new TextureAttributes();
17          Transform3D textureTrans = new Transform3D();
18          textureTrans.setScale(20);
19          texAttr.setTextureTransform(textureTrans);
20          Appearance backgroundApp = backSphere.getAppearance();
21          backgroundApp.setTextureAttributes(texAttr);
22
23          if (tex != null)
24              backgroundApp.setTexture(tex.getTexture());
25          backgroundRoot.addChild(background);
26          return backgroundRoot;
27      }
```

The addBackground() method creates a BranchGroup which can be added to the overall scene graph. A texture is added to the background by mapping the texture onto the *inside* of a unit sphere (a sphere with radius 1). When this sphere is set as the geometry of the Background object, it is drawn 'at infinity', which means that it surrounds the objects in the scene and appears 'behind' all of them. (Obviously, if the unit sphere were literally drawn infinitely far away, it wouldn't be visible.) We therefore need a way of mapping a texture to the inside surface of a sphere.

The Background is created on line 5 and its bounds set on line 6. Line 7 creates a BranchGroup that will be used to hold the Sphere, which is created on line 8, with the first argument to the constructor specifying a radius of 1.0.

Since we will be viewing the inside of the sphere, we generate inward normals, rather than the default outward-facing normals. We also generate some texture coordinates, and specify that the sphere should be drawn using 20 segments. Lines 11 and 12 attach the Sphere to the Background as its geometry.

On line 14 we load the carpet texture that was used for the chessboad squares earlier in this chapter. If we map this texture directly onto the unit sphere, however, a curious problem arises. As we have no control over how the texture coordinates are set for the Sphere, we cannot use these coordinates to determine the scale at which the pattern is applied to the inside of the sphere. The default behaviour seems to magnify the image in the file by about a factor of 20, which in the case of the carpet texture just produces a blurred beige porridge rather than anything resembling a carpet.

Fortunately, there is another way around this problem. The Appearance class allows a TextureAttributes object to be specified, and one of the abilities of TextureAttributes allows the scale of the texture to be changed. This is what we have done on lines 16 to 21. The code should be fairly obvious—we must define a Transform3D to specify the transformation and apply it to the Appearance.

Finally, we set the texture itself (line 24) and connect the Background to the BranchGroup which is returned.

The full BackgroundDemo program adds a ColorCube in front of the Background, and the initial display is as shown in Figure 7.17.

The program also adds mouse rotate, zoom and translate facilities, except that the TransformGroup on which these transformations act is that of the *view platform*, not any of the objects in the scene. The reason for doing this is that it demonstrates that the background texture really is drawn at infinity. Zooming or translating the view platform changes the location of the ColorCube, but the background remains unchanged. However, rotating the view platform changes the angle at which we view the background, and the carpet texture does indeed rotate when the view platform is rotated.

Figure 7.17:
A ColorCube
displayed on
a textured
Background.

EXERCISES

1. Find the RGB representations of some common non-primary and non-secondary colours, such as orange, brown, purple and so on. Verify your answers by drawing a shape using that colour in Java.

2. For each colour in question 1, use the algorithm in the text to derive the HSB coordinates. Verify your answers using the JColorChooser dialog.

3. Derive an algorithm for converting HSB colours to RGB.

4. If a surface's normal vector makes an angle of 30 degrees with the direction of incoming light, by how much is the brightness of the surface reduced from its maximum value?

5. A cube is to be oriented relative to a directional light source in such a way that three faces appear equally bright (with the other three facing away from the light and thus appearing black). What angle does the normal on each face make with the incident light?

6. A directional light source illuminates a plane. Assuming that neither the light source nor the plane's diffuse reflection colour (as specified in its Material) is orange, find a pair of colours for the light and the plane that will make the plane appear orange.

7. A unit cube (length of each side = 1.0) sitting on the xy plane with the centre of its base at the origin is slowly rotated about the z axis. A directional light source shines down the x axis (with direction $(-1, 0, 0)$) and the observer's eye is on the $+y$ axis. Calculate the specular reflection vector **S** as a function of the rotation angle of the cube. Use the Phong illumination model to determine the range of angles over which the intensity of the specular reflection is greater than 0.5. Try the calculation for several values of the specular reflection exponent n.

8. Repeat question 7, except this time calculate the halfway vector **H** instead of the specular reflection vector **S**.

9. Create a simple polyhedron (tetrahedron or cube) using a `TriangleStripArray`. Specify a normal vector for each vertex and embed the polyhedron in a scene with a single directional light. Add a `PickRotateBehavior` to allow the object to be rotated interactively using the mouse. How does the appearance of the object change as it is rotated relative to the light? Note that since you are using each vertex in more than one face of the object, the results are probably not very realistic.

10. Correct the problem in question 9 by defining each face of the polyhedron as a separate object so that its vertices are not shared with any other face.

11. Construct a cube using the Java 3D utility class `Box`, and have normals generated for the cube (see the documentation for `Box`). Insert it in place of the cube used in questions 9 and 10 and rotate it with the mouse. Can you tell what strategy has been used for attaching normals to vertices?

12. Consider the same setup as in question 7, except replace the directional light source with a point light source at position (2, 0, 0). Derive a formula giving the illumination of each pixel on one face of the cube using the Gouraud shading algorithm. You may assume that each of the four corners of the face has a normal vector that is perpendicular to that face, and that the square face has been subdivided into two triangles. Your formula should give the illumination intensity of a pixel as a function of the location of that pixel within the square, and also as a function of the rotation angle of the cube about the z axis.

13. Repeat question 12 using the Phong shading model. (Since the interpolated normal vector for each point on the square face will be the same everywhere, will Phong shading produce any differences from Gouraud shading?)

14. Consider a unit square panel placed with its centre at the origin, and oriented so that its face is perpendicular to the x axis. The coordinates of its four corners will then be (0, –0.5, +0.5), (0, –0.5, –0.5), (0, +0.5, –0.5) and (0, +0.5, +0.5). Rather than define the normals to be perpendicular to the panel, let us assume that each normal has a component that points radially away from the centre of the panel. This effect might be used, for example, if the square panel was to be included as part of a larger curved surface, and the normals at each vertex were averaged over the perpendicular directions of all polygons using that vertex.

    Thus, the normal at the point (0, –0.5, +0.5) is (1.0, –1.0, +1.0), with normals at the other three points defined in a symmetric fashion so that the normals resemble petals opening in a flower. Assuming a point light source at position (2, 0, 0) and with direction (–1, 0, 0), calculate the specular component of the shading within the square using both the Gouraud and Phong shading models. Is there a significant difference?

15. Experiment with the lit cylinder example in the text (page 224). Try various combinations of ambient, directional, point and spot lights. Read the documentation on these different light classes and try varying as many properties of the various lights as you can. For this question, do not modify

the `Material` from its default value, so that you can observe the effects of the lights on their own.

16. Read the documentation on the `Material` class and experiment with the `Material` attached to the cylinder in the sample program in the text (page 227). In particular, note that you can achieve many of the same effects as in question 15 by using a default, white light source and varying the `Material`'s response to that light source.

17. Experiment with the properties of the `Cylinder` object itself in the lit cylinder program in the text (page 227). What happens if you forget to generate normals for the `Cylinder`? Examine the effect of changing the number of horizontal or vertical divisions used to draw the `Cylinder`, especially with point light sources.

18. Create a scene containing a 5 by 5 square array (in the *xy* plane) of `Spheres`, where each `Sphere` is 0.2 metres in diameter, and the `Spheres` are separated from each other by 1 metre in each direction. (Since a `Sphere` is created at the origin by default, you will need to attach a `TransformGroup` to each `Sphere` to move it to its final location.) Add a point light source at the location (0, 0, 3). Create a `BoundingSphere` for this light so that only the centre `Sphere` is lit. What happens if the light is moved to (2, 2, 3)?

19. Add a second point light source (with a different colour so you can tell them apart) to the scene in question 18. Place it at (−2, −2, 3) with the first light source at its original location of (0, 0, 3). Set the scene up with a `BoundingSphere` so that they both illuminate only the central `Sphere`. What happens if the first light source is now moved to (2, 2, 3)?

20. Change the scene in question 19 by using a `BoundingLeaf` to ensure that only the central `Sphere` is lit no matter where the two lights are moved.

21. Starting with the scene in question 19, change the `BoundingSphere` so that both lights can illuminate all `Spheres` in the scene. Now use scoping so that the first light illuminates rows 1, 3 and 5 in the array and the second light illuminates rows 2 and 4. (The effect will be obvious if the two lights are different colours.) Note that you may want to rearrange the scene graph to achieve the scoping.

22. Read the documentation on the `AlternateAppearance` class. Use this class and scoping to allow a second `Appearance` to be attached to *columns* 1, 3 and 5 in the array of `Spheres` in question 21. In the `Material` of this second `Appearance`, turn off all response to diffuse illumination, so that the `Spheres` show ambient and specular light only. Since this effect is to be combined with the scoping for the light sources in question 21, think carefully about how to arrange the scene graph before writing the code.

23. Read the documentation on the `Background` class, and add a solid yellow (or other colour of your choice) background to the scene in any of the preceding questions.

24. A texture is to be mapped onto a triangle using the setup shown in Figure 7.11. Instead of the image shown on the right of this figure, however, the texture image is a large X drawn on the unit square. That is, a line extends

from $(s, t) = (0, 0)$ to $(1, 1)$ and another line extends from $(1, 0)$ to $(0, 1)$. What image would be drawn inside the triangle on the left of Figure 7.11?

25. Build a scene containing a tetrahedron (formed using one of the GeometryArray classes). Prepare an image file (typically, a JPEG file) containing an image that is 128 pixels square, and map this as a texture onto all four sides of the tetrahedron. (Add a mouse rotator to your scene graph to allow you to view the tetrahedron from any angle to verify that the texture has been applied to all four sides.)

26. Construct a BufferedImage (see Chapter 6) containing an image of your choice drawn using Java 2D commands and create a texture from this image. (Read the documentation on TextureLoader to find the correct constructor to use.) Apply this texture to the tetrahedron from question 25.

27. Use texture coordinate generation to apply the textures in questions 25 and 26 to the tetrahedron.

28. [Research project] Search the Web or other books on computer graphics to discover something about how shadows may be included in a scene. (Creating realistic shadows is quite a complex problem except for the simplest of geometries.)

29. Using one of the methods you discovered in the previous question (or one of your own) write a Java 3D program that displays a single cube (use the utility Box class, not ColorCube) sitting on the *xy* plane. Add a large square sheet to the *xy* plane and a directional light source, and draw the shadow cast by the cube onto the square sheet.

CHAPTER 8

Interaction and animation

8.1 Events

All the graphics programs we have considered so far, both two- and three-dimensional, have been static programs, in that they do not allow the user to interact with them after they have been displayed on screen. They have also been static in the sense that they display a single, fixed image—there is no *animation*.

Readers who have done some programming with the JDK (version 1.1 or later) may have encountered Java's classes for handling user-generated *events*. In the context of a graphical user interface (GUI) program, an event is a signal that is generated when the user interacts with the program by pressing a button, selecting a menu item, or pressing a key on the keyboard. Each event is passed to the running Java program by the operating system, and it is up to the programmer to decide what to do (if anything) with the event when it arrives.

Java handles events in the JDK by means of the various Listener interfaces. For example, to catch the event generated when the user presses a Button, the corresponding Button object must have attached to it an object that implements the ActionListener interface. If this is done, then whenever the Button is pressed, the actionPerformed() method from the ActionListener interface is called, and the code within that method causes the program to respond to the pressing of the button. Other GUI components have their own particular Listener interfaces which allow the various types of events they generate to be caught and processed.

The processing of events generated in GUI programs is not within the scope of this book, as event handling is covered in any good introductory book on Java. In this chapter, we will consider the ways in which the user may interact directly with the graphics that is rendered within the program.

8.2 Interacting with Java 2D

Java 2D does not have any special event handlers beyond those provided in the standard java.awt.event package. However, it is useful to consider how simple interaction with a Java 2D image can be achieved using the mouse or keyboard.

As an example of interaction with a Java 2D program, we will build an application that allows the user to draw an ellipse on a canvas by specifying with the mouse the rectangle enclosing the ellipse. The user clicks the mouse to specify one of the corners of the rectangle and then drags the mouse (moves the mouse while holding the mouse button down) to the opposite corner of the rectangle. When the mouse button is released, the location of the mouse pointer marks the diagonally opposite corner of the rectangle, and an ellipse is drawn to fit within the rectangle.

As an aid to the user, we will also draw an outline of the rectangle as the mouse is being dragged. This outline will move in response to the mouse movement and, because it seems to stretch or shrink to follow the mouse, is often called a *rubber band*.

We begin with the central class that displays the main frame and handles the mouse events.

```
1    import java.awt.*;
2    import java.awt.event.*;
3    import javax.swing.*;
4
5    public class DrawEllipse extends JFrame
6    {
7        JPanel panel = new JPanel();
8        EllipseCanvas m_drawingCanvas = new EllipseCanvas();
9
10       public static void main(String argv[])
11       {
12           DrawEllipse twoDimDemo = new DrawEllipse();
13           twoDimDemo.setVisible(true);
14       }
15
16       DrawEllipse()
17       {
18           setTitle("Mouse events in Java 2D");
19           getContentPane().setLayout(new BorderLayout());
20           setSize(650,450);
21           getContentPane().add(BorderLayout.CENTER, panel);
22           panel.setBackground(Color.red);
23           panel.add(m_drawingCanvas);
24           m_drawingCanvas.setBackground(Color.white);
25           m_drawingCanvas.setSize(600, 400);
26
27           WindowHandler windowHandler = new WindowHandler();
28           addWindowListener(windowHandler);
29
30           m_drawingCanvas.addMouseListener(new MouseHandler());
31           m_drawingCanvas.
32               addMouseMotionListener(new MouseMotionHandler());
33       }
34
35       class MouseMotionHandler extends MouseMotionAdapter
36       {
37           public void mouseDragged(MouseEvent event)
38           {
39               m_drawingCanvas.rubberBand(event.getPoint());
40           }
41       }
42
43       class MouseHandler extends MouseAdapter
```

```
44      {
45          public void mouseReleased(MouseEvent event)
46          {
47              Object object = event.getSource();
48              if (object == m_drawingCanvas) {
49                  m_drawingCanvas.setPoint(
50                      EllipseCanvas.END_POINT, event.getPoint());
51                  m_drawingCanvas.repaint();
52              }
53          }
54
55          public void mousePressed(MouseEvent event)
56          {
57              Object object = event.getSource();
58              if (object == m_drawingCanvas) {
59                  m_drawingCanvas.setPoint(
60                      EllipseCanvas.START_POINT, event.getPoint());
61              }
62          }
63      }
64
65      class WindowHandler extends WindowAdapter
66      {
67          public void windowClosing(WindowEvent event)
68          {
69              System.exit(0);
70          }
71      }
72  }
```

The EllipseCanvas class on line 8 handles the calculation and display of the rubber band and of the ellipse, and will be considered later. The constructor creates the GUI on lines 18 to 25, and adds the usual handler on lines 27 and 28 to allow the window to be closed.

Lines 30 to 32 add the listeners that provide mouse interaction. The Java java.awt.event package provides two types of listeners for mouse events: those that detect mouse button events and those that detect mouse motion events. In drawing an ellipse by clicking and then dragging the mouse, we will need both types of events, so both listeners are attached to the canvas.

Since the various event listener classes are all interfaces, we must implement these interfaces in our own classes in order to use them. A full treatment of event handling is outside the scope of this book (but may be found in any introductory book on Java programming), but we will mention that for any event listener interface containing more than one method, the java.awt.event package provides a corresponding *adapter* class which contains empty implementations of all methods in the interface. If we don't need to implement all the methods, we can simply extend the correct adapter class and override those methods that we do need. This is what we have done in the DrawEllipse class above.

The MouseMotionHandler class (nested inside the DrawEllipse class) on lines 35 to 41 handles the mouse dragging, and the MouseHandler class on lines 43 to 63 handles mouse clicking. To draw an ellipse, the user will first select one of the corners of the rubber-band rectangle and press the mouse button. The mousePressed() method in the MouseHandler class will be called in response to this. This method is passed a MouseEvent by the operating system, from which may be extracted several bits of information about the event, including the object over which the mouse was clicked, and the coordinates of the point selected.

Although there is only a single component in the DrawEllipse application, we have included a test to determine the object clicked by the mouse so the reader can see how it is done. We use the getSource() method on line 57 to extract the object. On line 58 we test the object to make sure it is the canvas. Lines 59 and 60 call a method in the EllipseCanvas class below to store the starting point for the rubber band's first corner. The coordinates of the mouse cursor when the mouse was clicked are obtained from the getPoint() method.

If the user now drags the mouse (moves it with the button still pressed down), the mouseDragged() method on lines 37 to 40 will be called continuously until the user stops moving the mouse or releases the button. In reality, the method is called every few milliseconds, so if we move the mouse quickly, the event is only registered at a few points along the mouse's path. Moving the mouse more slowly causes more events to be registered over the same distance.

In this case, each time a dragging event is registered, the rubberBand() method in the EllipseCanvas class is called. The coordinates of the mouse pointer are provided to this method as well. This method, as we will see, handles the drawing of the rubber-band rectangle.

Finally, when the user releases the mouse button, the mouseReleased() method on lines 45 to 53 is called. Again, we check that the object is the drawing canvas. We then call the setPoint() method in the EllipseCanvas class to store the final corner of the bounding rectangle for the ellipse. The repaint() method is then called to erase the rubber band and draw the ellipse using Bresenham's algorithm, as described in Chapter 1.

We will now examine that part of the EllipseCanvas class that sets up the bounding rectangle and draws the rubber band. The code for drawing the ellipse itself is the same as that given in Chapter 1.

```
1     import java.awt.*;
2
3     public class EllipseCanvas extends Canvas
4     {
5         static int START_POINT = 0;
6         static int END_POINT = 1;
7         Point m_startPoint = null, m_endPoint = null,
8             m_tempEnd = null;
9
10        public void setPoint(int type, Point point)
11        {
12            if (type == START_POINT) {
13                m_startPoint = point;
14                m_tempEnd = point;
15                m_endPoint = point;
16                repaint();
17            } else if (type == END_POINT) {
18                m_endPoint = point;
19            }
20        }
21
```

```
22        public void rubberBand(Point endPoint)
23        {
24            Graphics2D gg = (Graphics2D)getGraphics();
25            float[] dashPattern = {10.0f, 10.0f};
26            gg.setStroke(new BasicStroke(1,
27                BasicStroke.CAP_SQUARE,
28                BasicStroke.JOIN_MITER,
29                10.0f, dashPattern, 0.0f));
30
31            int width = Math.abs(m_tempEnd.x - m_startPoint.x);
32            int height = Math.abs(m_tempEnd.y - m_startPoint.y);
33            int startX = m_startPoint.x < m_tempEnd.x ?
34            m_startPoint.x : m_tempEnd.x;
35            int startY = m_startPoint.y < m_tempEnd.y ?
36                m_startPoint.y : m_tempEnd.y;
37            gg.setColor(getBackground());
38            gg.drawRect(startX, startY, width, height);
39
40            gg.setColor(Color.red);
41            width = Math.abs(endPoint.x - m_startPoint.x);
42            height = Math.abs(endPoint.y - m_startPoint.y);
43            startX = m_startPoint.x < endPoint.x ?
44                m_startPoint.x : endPoint.x;
45            startY = m_startPoint.y < endPoint.y ?
46                m_startPoint.y : endPoint.y;
47            gg.drawRect(startX, startY, width, height);
48            m_tempEnd = endPoint;
49        }
50
51        // Remaining methods draw the ellipse
52    }
```

The setPoint() method serves two functions. If the type parameter is START_POINT, this is a signal that a new ellipse is to be drawn, so the method resets all the Point variables to the single point that was passed in as an argument, and repaints the canvas to clear it.

If the type is END_POINT, the user has dragged the mouse and now wishes to display the final ellipse. In this case, we set the final corner m_endPoint of the bounding rectangle.

The rubber band itself is drawn in the rubberBand() method. The box is to be drawn with one corner at m_startPoint and the other at the point given by the endPoint argument passed to the method.

Since we will be using some Java 2D methods, we need a Graphics2D object, which we obtain on line 24. We will draw the rubber band as a dashed line with a 10-pixel dash followed by a 10-pixel space. We set this up on lines 25 to 29 (see Chapter 3 for details on line styles).

The actual drawing of the rubber band starts on line 31. As we saw above when we considered the mouse dragging event, a series of events will be generated as the mouse is dragged, with each event causing the rubberBand() method to be called with a new value for endPoint. In order to give the impression of a rubber band stretching to follow the mouse pointer, the response to each event should be first to *erase* the box that was drawn on the previous event, and then to draw the new box at the current position of the mouse pointer.

One way of doing this would be to redraw the entire canvas each time, but on most monitors (or rather, with most graphics cards) this will cause a fair amount of flickering in the display. On less powerful systems, some jerkiness in the movement may also appear since if the hardware is unable to keep up with the rate at which mouse dragging events are generated, some updates of the rubber band may simply be skipped.

The technique used in the rubberBand() method here relies on the fact that the rubber band is drawn on top of a uniform background. To erase the earlier box, we set the drawing colour to the background colour and draw over the existing box, then set the colour back to the regular drawing colour and draw in the new box. If this technique is used on top of other objects, rather than on a plain background, the other objects will show 'scratches' in them when the earlier box is 'erased'.

The variable m_tempEnd is used to store the coordinates of the corner of the earlier box. Lines 31 to 36 use m_tempEnd and m_startPoint (which is common to all boxes as the starting corner) to determine the coordinates of the old box. Lines 33 to 36 deal with the possible relative positions of the two corners—one could be to the left or right, or above or below the other corner.

Line 37 sets the drawing colour to the background colour and line 38 draws over the old rectangle to erase it.

Lines 40 to 47 then repeat the procedure to draw in the new box in the foreground colour (red, in this case). Finally, line 48 saves the current endPoint as m_tempEnd so that the current box can be erased if the mouse is dragged further.

Note that all drawing of the rubber band takes place outside the paint() method. Only when the user stops dragging the mouse by releasing the mouse button does the paint() method get called, and this results in only the ellipse itself being drawn—the rubber band disappears at this stage since it is not part of the paint() method.

8.3   Interaction in Java 3D—the Behavior class

Events directed towards objects in a Java 3D scene graph are handled very differently from those produced in response to GUI components in the 2D world. This is due largely to the fact that interactions can result from several different sources in a 3D world. In addition to the standard events such as keyboard presses and mouse events, events in 3D can be generated by the collision of objects in the 3D space and the change of the view platform relative to the objects in the scene. Java 3D provides methods for handling events arising from all these sources.

At the heart of event handling in Java 3D is the abstract Behavior class (note the American spelling!). A Behavior object is similar to a listener in conventional event handling, in that it responds to a particular type of event and contains a method that is processed when an event of that type is received. There are significant differences between a Behavior and a listener, however, so it not wise to read too much into the analogy.

There are several specialized versions of Behavior that may be used in particular situations, but we will begin by describing how to write a simple user-defined Behavior. Although this is not difficult, there are several key features of Behaviors that must be remembered.

First, Behavior is an *abstract* class, which means that it cannot be used directly—we must derive another class from it. The Behavior class is abstract because it contains two abstract methods: initialize() and processStimulus(). Any user-defined class derived from Behavior must provide implementations of these two methods.

As its name implies, initialize() is called when the Behavior object is created, and processStimulus() is called when an event of the type or types to which the object responds occurs. Thus the initialize() method usually defines the type(s) of event that will trigger the Behavior, and processStimulus() contains the code that is executed when one of these events occurs.

The events to which a Behavior should respond are specified by using one of the *wakeup* classes.

Once you have written the Behavior-derived class, you must create an instance of it, provide an area in which it has an effect (the *scheduling bounds*) and connect it to the scene graph (make it live).

Let us illustrate the steps involved in writing and using a Behavior-derived class by adding such a class to our chessboard program from the last chapter. We would like to allow the colour of the directional light to be changed by pressing some of the keys on the keyboard, so that pressing 'R', 'G' or 'B' changes the light to red, green or blue, respectively, and pressing any other key restores the colour to white.

We first write a Behavior class called ColorBehavior which does this.

```
1   public class ColorBehavior extends Behavior
2   {
3       DirectionalLight light;
4       WakeupOnAWTEvent awtWakeup;
5
6       Color3f red3f = new Color3f(Color.red);
7       Color3f green3f = new Color3f(Color.green);
8       Color3f blue3f = new Color3f(Color.blue);
9       Color3f white3f = new Color3f(Color.white);
10
11      public ColorBehavior(DirectionalLight lightSource)
12      {
13          awtWakeup = new
14              WakeupOnAWTEvent(KeyEvent.KEY_PRESSED);
15
16          light = lightSource;
17      }
18
19      public void initialize()
20      {
21          wakeupOn(awtWakeup);
22      }
23
24      public void processStimulus(Enumeration criteria)
25      {
26          WakeupCriterion crit =
27              (WakeupCriterion)criteria.nextElement();
28          AWTEvent[] event =
```

```
29              ((WakeupOnAWTEvent)crit).getAWTEvent();
30          if (event == null) return;
31          KeyEvent key = (KeyEvent)event[0];
32          switch(key.getKeyCode()) {
33          case KeyEvent.VK_R:
34              light.setColor(red3f);
35              break;
36          case KeyEvent.VK_G:
37              light.setColor(green3f);
38              break;
39          case KeyEvent.VK_B:
40              light.setColor(blue3f);
41              break;
42          default:
43              light.setColor(white3f);
44              break;
45          }
46          wakeupOn(awtWakeup);
47      }
48  }
```

In order for a Behavior to have any effect, it must act on one or more of the objects in a scene graph. On line 3, we have specified a DirectionalLight, which is initialized in the constructor on line 16.

On line 4 we specify a wakeup object in the form of the WakeupOnAWTEvent class. This class is one of 20 (as of Java 3D version 1.2) classes which specify event types or combinations of event types that can trigger a Behavior. As its name implies, the WakeupOnAWTEvent class specifies that a trigger should occur if an AWT event is received. AWT events include key presses and mouse actions, so the condition is commonly used to handle user interactions.

Lines 6 through 9 specify some Color3f objects that are used later in the class. As an aside, it is usually a good idea to create variables in which commonly used objects such as colours can be stored, rather than creating a new copy of an object each time it is used. Excessive and unnecessary creation of objects using the new operator is wasteful of CPU time and memory, and in extreme cases can cause a program to crash by running out of memory since Java's garbage collection routines cannot free unused objects fast enough. For this reason, overuse of the new operator is called *memory burn*.

Besides initializing the DirectionalLight object, the constructor also creates the wakeup object on lines 13 and 14. The constructor for the WakeupOnAWTEvent class takes an argument specifying which particular AWT event is to be used as the trigger (an alternative constructor allows several AWT events to be ORed together). In this case, we wish a key press to cause a change in the colour of the directional light, so we specify the KEY_PRESSED event in the KeyEvent class.

Statements in the constructor are executed when the ColorBehavior object is *created*, while statements in the initialize() method are run when the object is *connected* to the scene graph. In this case, we want to tell the ColorBehavior to wake up when a key press is made, so we make a call to the wakeupOn() method on line 21. At this point, the ColorBehavior object is active and awaits a key press before it will do anything else.

When a key press is received, the processStimulus() method is called. The argument to this method is an Enumeration, which allows us to step through the list of events that have yet to be processed.

All the wakeup classes that specify events are derived from the WakeupCriterion class, so we can use this parent class to retrieve events from the Enumeration. In the case where more than one event can trigger the Behavior, we would need to test each criterion to discover its type before deciding on the action to be performed. However, in this simple example, we know the criterion must be a WakeupOnAWTEvent, since that is the only type of criterion that can trigger the Behavior. We therefore just assume that the criterion is of this type, and proceed to extract the actual AWT events (again, more than one event may have triggered the wakeup, so the events are returned as an array) on lines 28 and 29.

Next, we need to discover which key was pressed. We do this by casting event[0] to a KeyEvent object on line 31, and then extracting the *key code* on line 32. By consulting the documentation for the KeyEvent class, we discover the key codes for the various keys, and can therefore add case blocks for each key. For example, if the user pressed the 'R' key, we set the colour of the directional light to red on line 34.

The remainder of the switch statement should be fairly obvious. However, the statement on line 46 is very important (and often forgotten). The original call to the wakeupOn() method in the initialize() method will set the Behavior object to be triggered *once only*. If we want the Behavior to respond to more events, we must remember to reset the trigger at the end of each call to processStimulus(). Omitting line 47 would cause the Behavior to stop responding after the first key press.

At this point, we have written the ColorBehavior class but have not yet added it to a Java 3D scene graph. The procedure for doing this is straightforward, but again there are some points that must be remembered.

First, any objects which are to be altered by the Behavior must have the corresponding capabilities set. Second, the Behavior itself must be connected to the scene graph. Finally, a region of influence (scheduling bounds) must be set for the Behavior so that it includes the objects which are to be modified by the Behavior.

If we wished to add the ColorBehavior to a Java 3D program containing a DirectionalLight and a Pawn, for example, we must first set the capability of the DirectionalLight so that it can be written. We can do this as follows.

```
DirectionalLight m_directionalLight =
    new DirectionalLight();
m_directionalLight.
    setCapability(DirectionalLight.ALLOW_COLOR_WRITE);
```

To create and add a ColorBehavior to the scene graph, we add the following code:

```
ColorBehavior colorBehavior =
    new ColorBehavior(m_directionalLight);
colorBehavior.setSchedulingBounds(new BoundingSphere());
scene.addChild(colorBehavior);
```

We create the ColorBehavior and pass it the DirectionalLight object on which it is to operate. We then set its scheduling bounds by creating a default BoundingSphere object (radius 1, centred at the origin). If the object(s) on which you wish the `ColorBehavior` to operate are outside the default `BoundingSphere`, you will need to define a different set of scheduling bounds to cope with this.

Finally, we attach the `ColorBehavior` object to the scene graph using the `addChild()` method. Here, `scene` is a `BranchGroup` object that was created earlier in the program. Normally, a `Behavior` node can be added anywhere in the scene graph—it is often convenient to attach it to the top `BranchGroup` in the graph.

With these additions, we are now able to change the colour of the light by pressing keys on the keyboard.

8.3.1 Multiple events in a Behavior

The preceding example was fairly simple in that only a single event (a key press) was monitored, and its effect was to change the value of a single object's property (the colour of a light source). In many cases, we need to deal with more than one type of event, and the effects of an event require something more involved than a simple switch of a property.

Another problem which you may have encountered with the example program above is that when the program starts, pressing the keys may have no effect until the mouse is clicked inside the canvas area. We will deal with this problem in this section as well.

We will modify our `ColorBehavior` class by assigning the *focus* to the canvas when the program starts. A component cannot receive events unless it currently has the focus. In almost all GUI applications, a component can be given the focus manually by clicking the mouse within that component's area. However, in the example in the last section, the `Canvas3D` object containing the image of the pawn often does not have the focus when the program starts, so that all key presses are ignored.

As another enhancement to the program, we will add code so that pressing one of the arrow keys causes the pawn to move (translate) in the specified direction. Although this requires only adding some more `case` blocks to the `switch` statement in the `processStimulus()` method, it does involve altering the `Transform3D` object which governs the location of the pawn.

First, let us see how to assign focus to the canvas when the program starts. We would like this to happen automatically, without the need for any user input. Fortunately, there is another wakeup class called `WakeupOnActivation` which causes the `Behavior` object to trigger when it is first made live. But if we wish to add this trigger to our existing `ColorBehavior` class, we are faced with the problem of how to specify *two* different triggers. This is where another family of wakeup classes comes into play.

There are several classes that specify that a `Behavior` should wake up when certain logical combinations of events are received. If we want a `Behavior` to trigger when any one of a number of events happens, we can use the `WakeupOr` class. Let us modify the `ColorBehavior` class to wake up on two different criteria.

```
1   public class ColorBehavior extends Behavior
2   {
3       Color3f red3f = new Color3f(Color.red);
4       Color3f green3f = new Color3f(Color.green);
5       Color3f blue3f = new Color3f(Color.blue);
6       Color3f white3f = new Color3f(Color.white);
7
```

```
8       Transform3D pawnTrans = new Transform3D();
9       Transform3D translate = new Transform3D();
10      static final float MOVEINCREMENT = 0.1f;
11      Vector3f moveLeft =
12          new Vector3f(-MOVEINCREMENT, 0.0f, 0.0f);
13      Vector3f moveRight =
14          new Vector3f(MOVEINCREMENT, 0.0f, 0.0f);
15      Vector3f moveUp =
16          new Vector3f(0.0f, MOVEINCREMENT, 0.0f);
17      Vector3f moveDown =
18          new Vector3f(0.0f, -MOVEINCREMENT, 0.0f);
19
20      Pawn targetShape;
21      DirectionalLight light;
22      WakeupOnAWTEvent awtWakeup =
23          new WakeupOnAWTEvent(KeyEvent.KEY_PRESSED);
24      WakeupOnActivation activationWakeup =
25          new WakeupOnActivation();
26      WakeupCriterion[] wakeups = new WakeupCriterion[2];
27      WakeupOr wakeupList;
28
29      public ColorBehavior(Pawn shape,
30          DirectionalLight lightSource)
31      {
32          wakeups[0] = awtWakeup;
33          wakeups[1] = activationWakeup;
34          wakeupList = new WakeupOr(wakeups);
35          targetShape = shape;
36          light = lightSource;
37      }
38
39      public void initialize()
40      {
41          wakeupOn(wakeupList);
42      }
43
44      public void processStimulus(Enumeration criteria)
45      {
46          WakeupCriterion crit =
47              (WakeupCriterion)criteria.nextElement();
48          if (crit instanceof WakeupOnActivation) {
49              m_drawingCanvas.requestFocus();
50              wakeupOn(awtWakeup);
51              return;
52          }
53          AWTEvent[] event =
54              ((WakeupOnAWTEvent)crit).getAWTEvent();
55          if (event == null) return;
56          KeyEvent key = (KeyEvent)event[0];
57          switch(key.getKeyCode()) {
58          case KeyEvent.VK_R:
59              light.setColor(red3f);
```

```
60              break;
61          case KeyEvent.VK_G:
62              light.setColor(green3f);
63              break;
64          case KeyEvent.VK_B:
65              light.setColor(blue3f);
66              break;
67          case KeyEvent.VK_LEFT:
68              pawn.getTransform(pawnTrans);
69              translate.set(moveLeft);
70              translate.mul(pawnTrans);
71              pawn.setTransform(translate);
72              break;
73
74      // Other directions done similarly
75
76          default:
77              light.setColor(white3f);
78              break;
79          }
80      wakeupOn(awtWakeup);
81  }
```

Lines 3 to 6 define some colours as in the earlier example. Lines 8 through 18 define some quantities that will be used in translating the pawn below.

We have added a Pawn on line 20 since we will be modifying the pawn in response to pressing the arrow keys.

Lines 24 and 25 define the new WakeupOnActivation object. Line 26 creates an array of two WakeupCriterions. The WakeupOr object on line 27 operates on an array of WakeupCriterions, defining a wakeup condition that is the logical OR of all criteria in the array.

In the constructor, we initialize the array on lines 32 and 33, and then define the WakeupOr object by passing it the array on line 34. The wakup condition in the initialize() method is now the wakeupList, so that the Behavior will be triggered whenever *any* of the events in the list occurs.

In the processStimulus() method, we have added some code at lines 48 to 52 to process the WakeupOnActivation criterion. Note that we have used the Java keyword instanceof to discover the class name of the crit object. In this case, we request focus for the drawing canvas on line 49 (we are assuming the ColorBehavior class is embedded within another class in which m_drawingCanvas is defined—if not, the canvas can be passed as an argument to the ColorBehavior constructor).

Once the activation event has been processed, we call wakeupOn() on line 50, but we pass it *only* the awtWakeup object as its argument, since we only want to test for key presses from now on.

Lines 53 to 66 are the same as in the previous example, and handle the colour changes from pressing the 'R', 'G' and 'B' keys. On lines 67 to 72 we have added code to move the pawn left when the left arrow key is pressed.

Before we consider this code, however, remember that the TransformGroup to which the Pawn object belongs must have its capability set to allow reading and writing of its transform. This can be done in the main class where the Pawn is created by adding the lines:

```
pawn.setCapability(TransformGroup.ALLOW_TRANSFORM_READ);
pawn.setCapability(TransformGroup.ALLOW_TRANSFORM_WRITE);
```

On line 68 we read the Transform3D object for pawn and store it in pawnTrans (created on line 8). Next, we set the other Transform3D object (created on line 9) to a translation by assigning it the Vector3f object moveLeft. Referring back to lines 10 to 12, we see that this specifies a translation by 0.1 metres to the left (in the negative *x* direction). We then multiply this translation by the existing transform for the pawn on line 70. Since the translation is on the left, it is done *after* any other transformations that the pawn may already have applied to it. Finally, the pawn has its transform set to translate on line 71 (which now contains the total transformation as calculated by the product on line 70). The result is to take the pawn in whatever orientation or location it may be found and move it 0.1 metres to the left.

Code for the other three arrow keys could be added in a similar way, using the Vector3fs defined on lines 13 to 18.

These examples should make it clear that almost any form of interaction can be specified by writing customized Behavior classes. Although the procedure is straightforward, there are several steps that must be remembered, so we will summarize them here:

- ensure that the appropriate capabilities are set for any objects that are to be modified within the Behavior;

- define a customized class that extends the abstract Behavior class. Provide a constructor, and overridden versions of initialize() and processStimulus();

- specify the wakeup conditions in the initialize() method;

- specify the required actions for each event in the processStimulus() method;

- remember to reset the wakeup conditions (if desired) at the end of processStimulus();

- create a Behavior object in your main class;

- provide some scheduling bounds for the Behavior;

- connect the Behavior to the scene graph.

8.4 Utility interaction classes in Java 3D

Although the Behavior class described in the last section can be used to implement any type of interaction desired, there are some forms of interaction that are common enough for Java 3D to provide some special convenience classes for them. These interactions include using the keyboard or mouse to translate, rotate and zoom one or more objects in the scene graph.

8.4.1 Keyboard utility classes

Simple keyboard interaction can be added by using the KeyNavigationBehavior class, which is derived from the Behavior class. Attaching a KeyNavigationBehavior to an object's transform group has the effect shown in the table.

Key	Effect	Effect with Alt key
Left arrow	Rotate left	Move left
Right arrow	Rotate right	Move right
Up arrow	Zoom in (move forward)	None
Down arrow	Zoom out (move back)	None
PageUp	Rotate Up	Move up
PageDown	Rotate Down	Move down
– (minus key)	Move back clip forward	None
+ (plus key)	Restore back clip	None
= (equals key)	Reset object to centre	None

Using the `KeyNavigationBehavior` class is very simple. For example, we can add keyboard navigation to the program in the previous by replacing the lines where we attach the `ColorBehavior` object with the following code:

```
import com.sun.j3d.utils.behaviors.keyboard.*;

// other code

KeyNavigatorBehavior keyNavBehavior =
    new KeyNavigatorBehavior(pawn);
keyNavBehavior.setSchedulingBounds(
    new BoundingSphere());
scene.addChild(keyNavBehavior);
```

The `import` statement is required since the keyboard utility classes are stored in their own package.

The constructor for the `KeyNavigationBehavior` class requires a `TransformGroup` as its argument. Since we defined the `Pawn` class as inheriting the `TransformGroup` class, we can pass a `Pawn` argument directly to the `KeyNavigationBehavior`. All keyboard events in the table above are now applied to the pawn object.

When we applied the `KeyNavigationBehavior` to the pawn in this example, we first removed the `ColorBehavior` object from the scene graph, by commenting out the line

```
scene.addChild(colorBehavior);
```

that we added in the last section. Although it is possible to attach several different `Behavior` objects to the same object in a scene graph, the results can be unpredictable. For example, if we had left the `ColorBehavior` object attached to the scene graph when we added the `KeyNavigationBehavior`, both `Behaviors` attempt to act upon some of the same keys (the arrow keys). When the author tried this experiment, the left and right arrow keys responded as though they were being handled by the `ColorBehavior`, while the up and down arrow keys responded from the `KeyNavigationBehavior`. However, because the order in which nodes in a scene graph are visited is not specified by Java 3D, we cannot be certain this result will always be obtained. If you *do* attach multiple `Behaviors` to a single object, it is wise to make sure that the events handled by any one `Behavior` are not handled by any of the others.

There is one final caution that should be given in the use of the `KeyNavigationBehavior` class. In the current version of Java 3D (verson 1.2) there seems to be a bug in this class that causes it to use 100% of the processor time when a program containing a `KeyNavigationBehavior` object is run. On older or less powerful systems, this can cause the image to flicker quite badly, even when no interaction with the scene is taking place. (It will also cause other programs to run very slowly, of course.) Until this bug is fixed, it may be better to write your own `Behavior` class based on the example in the previous section.

8.4.2 Mouse utility classes

There are three mouse navigation classes that are very similar to `KeyNavigationBehavior`: `MouseRotate`, `MouseZoom` and `MouseTranslate`. These three classes are all derived from the abstract base class `MouseBehavior`. Using any of these classes requires similar steps to those required for using `KeyNavigationBehavior`. For example, we can add a `MouseRotate` object to the pawn as follows:

```
import com.sun.j3d.utils.behaviors.mouse.*;

// other code

MouseRotate mouseRotate = new MouseRotate(pawn);
mouseRotate.setSchedulingBounds(new BoundingSphere());
scene.addChild(mouseRotate);
```

If this code is added to the program above, the pawn can be rotated by dragging the mouse with the left button pressed. The direction of rotation is determined by the direction in which the mouse is dragged.

The other two mouse navigation classes are used in exactly the same way. The `MouseTranslate` class requires the mouse to be dragged with the right button pressed, and the `MouseZoom` class requires the middle button (or mouse wheel, if one exists) to be pressed. If the mouse has only two buttons (and no wheel), the same effect can be obtained by holding down the Alt key and pressing the left mouse button.

8.4.3 Callbacks

Although the keyboard and mouse navigation classes provide the most commonly-used behaviour, it would also be convenient to allow additional code to be run when a keyboard or mouse event occurs. With the `Behavior` class, this may be done by adding code to the `processStimulus()` method, as described above. Since all the keyboard and mouse navigation classes extend the `Behavior` class, they all have their own versions of `processStimulus()`. For keyboard events, we may write our own class that extends `KeyNavigationBehavior`, and provide our own `processStimulus()` method that overrides that in the base class. If we wish to preserve the responses to the various keys that are provided by `KeyNavigationBehavior`, of course, we must make sure to call the `processStimulus()` method from the base class at some point in our own overridden version. (In practice, it is probably easier to just write our own keyboard event handler by extending the `Behavior` class directly, especially in view of the fact that `KeyNavigationBehavior` saturates the processor, as mentioned above.)

Although the mouse navigation classes could be treated the same way, there is actually a better solution that does not require us to derive our own class that extends one of the mouse navigation classes. We may, instead, use a *callback*.

Callbacks work in much the same way as the listeners that are used to handle events in the Java AWT. A callback may be attached to a mouse navigation object, so that whenever the navigation object traps an event, in addition to handling the event, a method within the callback object is called.

Let us see an example based on the MouseRotate code above. Suppose that, in addition to being able to rotate the pawn by dragging the mouse, we also want the colour of the pawn to change gradually from red to yellow as it is rotated. The rotation of the pawn is handled for us by the MouseRotate, but we can attach a callback to the MouseRotate object that handles the colour changes.

A callback must be an instance of a class that implements the MouseBehaviorCallback interface. Recall that when we implement an interface, we must provide definitions for all the methods declared within the interface. The MouseBehaviorCallback interface declares only a single method called transformChanged().

First, we need to implement the MouseBehaviorCallback interface. We can do this either by creating a new class, or requiring one of the existing classes in the project to implement the interface. If the amount of code we wish to add is fairly small, the latter choice is usually easier, so we will do that here. This requires adding 'implements MouseBehaviorCallback' to the first line of the class, and adding a definition for the transformChanged() method to the body of the class. A method that allows the gradual colour change we want is as follows:

```
public void transformChanged(int type,
    Transform3D transform)
{
    pawnColor.set(1.0f,
        (++changeCount % 256)/256.0f, 0.0f);
    m_directionalLight.setColor(pawnColor);
}
```

Here, we are assuming that the class that implements the MouseBehaviorCallback interface contains an int variable called changeCount (initialized to 0 in the constructor) and a Color3f variable called pawnColor (which can be initialized to any colour we like as it is reset every time transformChanged() is called).

The transformChanged() method is never called explicitly by our own code—it is called automatically by Java whenever a mouse navigation event occurs. (We will see later how to connect a mouse event to this method.) Therefore, the two arguments to the method are also generated externally and passed into the method for us.

The first argument, type, contains a flag that tells the method what type of mouse event has just occurred. The three possible values for type are constants within the MouseBehaviorCallback interface, and are ROTATE, TRANSLATE and ZOOM. (There was a bug in Java 3D version 1.2 resulting in the type value being always set to TRANSLATE, no matter what type of mouse event occurs, but this has been fixed in later releases.)

The code inside the method should be fairly self-explanatory: The red component of pawnColor is set to maximum and the blue component is switched off. The green component is calculated from the current value of changeCount, and will vary from 0 to 1 over the course of 256 mouse events, thus causing the colour to change smoothly from pure red to pure yellow. When the value of changeCount reaches 256, the colour jumps back to red and the cycle starts again.

The only remaining link we must insert is the connection between the MouseRotate object and the MouseBehaviorCallback. This is done by inserting an extra line into the code that creates the MouseRotate object, so that it becomes:

```
MouseRotate mouseRotate = new MouseRotate(pawn);
mouseRotate.setSchedulingBounds(new BoundingSphere());
mouseRotate.setupCallback(this);
scene.addChild(mouseRotate);
```

Note that the setupCallback() method requires an argument of type MouseBehaviorCallback. Since we have required the class containing these four lines of code to implement this interface, we simply pass this as the argument. If we had defined a separate class to implement the callback interface, we would need to create an object from that class and pass that object as the argument to setupCallback().

8.5 Picking

The interaction methods we have described so far in this chapter have all been fairly general, in that they act as event handlers whose only purpose is to trap events of a specific type. After catching an event, the various Behavior classes either rely on the programmer to provide the specific details of what is to happen or, in the case of the utility classes, the effects are applied to an entire branch of the scene graph. These classes do not allow the user to select a specific object or objects directly from the rendered image.

Java 3D provides a package which allows individual objects in a scene to be *picked*. Although the most common method by which an object would be picked is by clicking on its rendered image using the mouse, the basic picking classes do not actually rely on a mouse event to work (although utility mouse-picking classes are provided).

Before we get into the details of some of the picking classes, we should point out that fairly major changes were made to the picking packages with the introduction of Java 3D version 1.2 in June, 2000. These changes mean that some code written using earlier versions will give deprecation warnings if compiled under version 1.2 (or in extreme cases, may not compile at all). The description of picking given here will use code that is compatible with version 1.2.

To see how picking works, suppose that we have an image produced by a perspective projection of some scene. As you will recall from our discussion of projections in Chapter 4, a perspective projection is produced by viewing the scene from a particular *viewpoint*, and projecting all points in the scene from the viewpoint onto the viewing plane (see Figure 4.3, on page 119). If we select a point on the viewing plane by clicking on it with the mouse, we can find what objects, if any, are picked by drawing a line from the viewpoint through the point on the viewing plane that was selected, and extending this line into the scene. Each object in the scene can be tested for an intersection with this line, and if an intersection occurs, the object has been picked. Since the line used for picking an object is identical to the line used for projecting the object onto the viewing plane, any picked objects will appear directly under the mouse pointer when the mouse was clicked.

8.5.1   Utility mouse picking classes

We will begin by looking at the three utility mouse picking classes, since they are very easy to use and contain enough functionality for the most common picking applications. We have seen these three classes used in some of the programs in earlier chapters, but here we shall present a proper introduction.

The three classes are PickRotateBehavior, PickZoomBehavior and PickTranslateBehavior. All three classes extend the Behavior class, but they provide their own implementations of the initialize() and processStimulus() methods, so the programmer does not need to write them. The PickRotateBehavior class picks the object by using the position of a mouse click (but only if the *left* mouse button is clicked) as described above. Dragging the mouse while holding the left button down will then cause the picked object to be rotated about the origin, with the rotation direction determined by the direction of motion of the mouse. Thus the PickRotateBehavior class is very similar to the MouseRotate class, except that it allows a particular object to be picked and then rotated. The PickZoomBehavior and PickTranslateBehavior classes work in a similar way, except that the middle mouse button (or mouse wheel, or Alt + left button if you have neither middle button nor wheel) must be used for zooming, and the right button for translation.

Using one of these classes requires two main steps. First, we must identify which objects in the scene may be picked. Then we must add the picking class to allow selection of these objects.

Since the picking of an object requires determining if a line intersects the geometry of the object, the picking operation can be quite costly in terms of CPU time, especially if the object is composed of a large number of polygons. It is therefore a good idea to restrict the number of objects in a scene that are pickable, if possible. There are two ways this can be done, depending on whether the node in the scene graph that is to be restricted is a leaf or an internal node.

Leaf nodes, such as Shape3D nodes, are pickable by default. To prevent them from being pickable (and thus remove them from the list of objects that are tested for intersection with a picking line), call the setPickable() method with an argument of false.

Internal nodes, such as TransformGroups and BranchGroups, are *not* pickable by default. Since an internal node does not represent any shape that is actually rendered, it may seem odd that they can be made pickable, but allowing an internal node to be pickable merely means that all objects in the branch of the scene graph arising from that internal node are pickable. To make an internal node pickable, its ENABLE_PICK_REPORTING capability must be set. For example, if we have a TransformGroup object called transGroup, we can enable picking for all objects under this node with the statement:

```
transGroup.setCapability
    (TransformGroup.ENABLE_PICK_REPORTING);
```

Setting the ENABLE_PICK_REPORTING capability for a leaf node has no effect—we must rely on the setPickable() method here.

If we are using one of the three mouse picking classes, we *must* enable picking for the TransformGroup above those objects we wish to pick, and not just rely on the objects themselves being pickable. The reason for this is that the mouse picking classes all transform the location or orientation of the objects, and thus must operate on a TransformGroup. Since both read and write access is required for the Transform3D within a TransformGroup, the capabilities for these operations must also be set:

```
transGroup.setCapability
    (TransformGroup.ALLOW_TRANSFORM_READ);
transGroup.setCapability
    (TransformGroup.ALLOW_TRANSFORM_WRITE);
```

A simple example of the use of the PickRotateBehavior class may be found in the CylinderDemo class in Chapter 7 (lines 53–58 on page 225). The relevant portion from that class is reproduced here:

```
import com.sun.j3d.utils.picking.behaviors.*;
// other code

scene = new BranchGroup();
cylinder = new CylinderBranch();
scene.addChild(cylinder);

BoundingSphere behaveBounds =
    new BoundingSphere(new Point3d(), 5);
PickRotateBehavior cylRotate =
    new PickRotateBehavior(scene,
    m_drawingCanvas, behaveBounds);
scene.addChild(cylRotate);
```

Note the import statement that is required for the use of any of the picking classes. This particular picking package is new to version 1.2 of Java 3D, and can be confusing, since the picking package used in earlier versions is the same except that the 'picking' and 'behaviors' words are swapped around at the end of the package path. If you are attempting to compile an older program that you know has picking code in it and you get deprecation warnings from the compiler, try swapping around these two words in the import statement to comply with the newer version.

We create a BranchGroup and then a CylinderBranch object (which draws a cylinder). The cylinder is then added to the BranchGroup. If we examine the code for CylinderBranch (also to be found in full in Chapter 8, page 227), we see that its capabilities are set in its constructor:

```
public class CylinderBranch extends TransformGroup {
    public CylinderBranch() {
        addChild(new Cylinder(1.0f, 1.0f,
            Cylinder.GENERATE_NORMALS,
            32, 32, createAppearance()));
        setCapability(TransformGroup.ALLOW_TRANSFORM_READ);
        setCapability(TransformGroup.ALLOW_TRANSFORM_WRITE);
        setCapability(TransformGroup.ENABLE_PICK_REPORTING);
    }

    // other code
}
```

Note that CylinderBranch extends TransformGroup, so that the class represents a TransformGroup with a Cylinder (one of the primitive geometry classes provided in Java 3D) attached to it. Within the constructor, we set the three capabilities that allow the `CylinderBranch` to be picked, and to have its `Transform3D` read and changed.

With the `CylinderBranch` set up properly, we create a bounding sphere within which the picking will have effect. Picking `Behavior` classes are just like any other `Behavior` class in this respect—a `Bounds` object must be specified in order for them to have any effect. Objects outside the `Bounds` will not be picked, even if they have been enabled for picking.

Next, we create the `PickRotateBehavior` object by calling the constructor. The simpler of the two constructors requires three arguments: a `BranchGroup` (which is usually just the root node from the geometry portion of the scene graph), a `Canvas3D` (which is the canvas on which the rendering of the scene occurs) and the `Bounds`.

Although the `BranchGroup` argument to the constructor may be the root of the scene graph, only those nodes under this root that are enabled for picking will be checked when the mouse is clicked. Thus in order to save cpu time, you should enable only those portions of the scene graph that you really want to be pickable. Objects that are always hidden behind other objects or that are outside the drawing area, for example, can be excluded to save time.

The reader should return to the full definitions of these two classes given in Chapter 7 to verify that no other code is required to allow the cylinder to be rotated by dragging the mouse. All the required code is built in to the `PickRotateBehavior` class.

8.5.2 More general picking

The utility mouse picking classes described in the previous section work by calculating the line from the viewpoint to the point on the viewing plane specified by the mouse when it is clicked, and then checking all pickable objects to see if any of them intersect the line. Although using the mouse to select an object is probably the most common use of picking, there is no reason why the shape used to specify which objects are picked needs to be a line, and no reason why the picking needs to be done with the mouse. We could, for example, specify a `Bounds` as the picking shape, and all pickable objects that are either within the `Bounds` or intersect it should be picked. Rather than use the mouse, we could check for picking when a key is pressed on the keyboard, or even have the picking occur as part of the running of the program, independently of any user-generated event.

There are two main stages in designing a customized picking operation. First, we must specify the picking *shape*, that is, the region within which picking can occur. Next, we need to check the list of pickable objects to see which ones intersect the picking shape. Java 3D's picking classes provide fairly straightforward ways of doing both these things.

There are several classes that may be used to specify the picking shape, but they are all derived from the abstract `PickShape` class. The concrete classes that implement `PickShape` are `PickBounds`, `PickCone`, `PickCylinder`, `PickPoint`, `PickRay` and `PickSegment`. The picking shape defined by most of these classes should be obvious from the name.

The three mouse picking classes described in the previous section all generate a `PickRay` as the picking shape. In geometry, a *ray* is a line with a fixed starting point and extending to infinity in a given direction. In the mouse picking classes, the starting point is the viewpoint and the direction is that specified by clicking the mouse, as described above.

The `PickSegment` class defines a picking shape that is a finite line segment with two fixed endpoints. The `PickBounds` classes defines a picking shape by using a `Bounds` object. We are therefore free to define a picking shape having almost any geometry we wish.

To do the actual picking, we may use the `PickTool` class or its derivative, `PickCanvas`. In addition to setting the `PickShape`, the `PickTool` class allows the level of precision of the picking operation to be specified. The two main *picking modes* are BOUNDS (the default) and GEOMETRY. When in BOUNDS mode, an object will be picked if the picking shape intersects any part of the volume bounded by the object. For example, if a cube is drawn as a wire-frame model, it could be picked by clicking either on one of the edges of the cube or within the area bounded by these edges.

When in GEOMETRY mode, an object will be picked only if the picking shape intersects one of the rendered components of the object. Using the wire-frame cube as an example, the user would need to click the mouse on one of the edges to pick the cube—merely clicking within the space bounded by these edges would not work.

The `PickTool` class also contains several methods that perform the actual picking process. The methods are `pickAll()`, which picks all pickable objects in the scene that intersect with the current `PickShape`; `pickAllSorted()`, which is the same as `pickAll()` except that the objects are sorted in order of the their distance from the viewpoint; `pickAny()`, which selects one of the objects that intersect with the current `PickShape`, and `pickClosest()` which picks the object that is closest to the viewpoint.

The various picking methods in `PickTool` all return their information on which objects were picked in the form of one or more `PickResult` objects. The amount of information about a picked object that is contained in a `PickResult` can be specified by the programmer, depending on how much detail is needed in order to process the picking event. In most cases, we only need a reference to the particular node or nodes in the scene graph that have been selected, but `PickResult` is capable of storing much more information if required. We will not delve too deeply into these levels of detail in this book, but once the basics of using a `PickResult` are understood, the documentation can be consulted for more information.

8.5.3 Example—picking spheres

We will now present a more extended example that uses several picking techniques. The program we will examine generates a small random number of `Sphere` objects, with the radius and location of each sphere also chosen at random. The user may rotate, zoom or translate the entire scene by using the mouse. Clicking on one of the spheres with the mouse will also change the colour of all spheres under the mouse pointer. Finally, by pressing the 'P' key on the keyboard, a random line segment may be generated which is drawn in the scene, but also used as a picking shape, with any spheres that intersect the line segment being coloured red.

The program thus gives another example of the use of the three utility mouse picking classes (used above in the cylinder program). It also illustrates the use of the mouse to pick objects for purposes other than changing their location, and also a use of picking that is independent of the mouse.

We will consider first the class RandSpheres which generates the random collection of spheres.

```
1   import javax.media.j3d.*;
2   import javax.vecmath.*;
3   import com.sun.j3d.utils.geometry.*;
4
5   public class RandSpheres extends TransformGroup {
6       Material[] material;
7       Appearance[] appear;
8       Sphere[] sphere;
9       int m_numSpheres, m_maxSpheres;
10      float m_coordLimit, m_radiusLimit;
11      Vector3f[] sphereCentres;
12
13      public RandSpheres(int maxSpheres, float coordLimit,
14          float radiusLimit)
15      {
16
17          m_maxSpheres = maxSpheres;
18          m_numSpheres =
19              (int)Math.round(Math.random() *
20              (maxSpheres - 2)) + 2;
21          m_coordLimit = coordLimit;
22          m_radiusLimit = radiusLimit;
23          createAppearances();
24
25          TransformGroup[] transGroup =
26              new TransformGroup[m_numSpheres];
27          sphere = new Sphere[m_numSpheres];
28          sphereCentres = new Vector3f[m_numSpheres];
29          Transform3D trans = null;
30
31          for (int sphereNum = 0; sphereNum < m_numSpheres;
32              sphereNum++)
33          {
34              transGroup[sphereNum] = new TransformGroup();
35              float radius = m_radiusLimit * (float)Math.random();
36              sphere[sphereNum] =
37                  new Sphere(radius, Sphere.GENERATE_NORMALS,
38                  32, appear[sphereNum]);
39              sphere[sphereNum].getShape().
40              setCapability(Shape3D.ALLOW_APPEARANCE_READ);
41              sphere[sphereNum].getShape().
42              setCapability(Shape3D.ALLOW_APPEARANCE_WRITE);
43              sphere[sphereNum].getShape().getGeometry().
44              setCapability(Geometry.ALLOW_INTERSECT);
45              trans = new Transform3D();
46              sphereCentres[sphereNum] =
47                  new Vector3f(randCoord(), randCoord(),
```

```
48              randCoord());
49              trans.setTranslation(sphereCentres[sphereNum]);
50              transGroup[sphereNum].setTransform(trans);
51              transGroup[sphereNum].addChild(sphere[sphereNum]);
52              addChild(transGroup[sphereNum]);
53          }
54      }
55
56      public void resetColors()
57      {
58          Material whiteSurface = new Material();
59          for (int sphereNum = 0; sphereNum < m_numSpheres;
60              sphereNum++)
61          {
62              sphere[sphereNum].getAppearance().
63              setMaterial(whiteSurface);
64          }
65      }
66
67      public float randCoord()
68      {
69          return (float)(Math.random() * 2.0 * m_coordLimit -
70          m_coordLimit);
71      }
72
73      private void createAppearances()
74      {
75          appear = new Appearance[m_numSpheres];
76          material = new Material[m_numSpheres];
77          for (int num = 0; num < m_numSpheres; num++) {
78              appear[num] = new Appearance();
79              material[num] = new Material();
80              appear[num].
81              setCapability(Appearance.ALLOW_MATERIAL_WRITE);
82              appear[num].setMaterial(material[num]);
83          }
84      }
85  }
```

This class generates an array of Spheres, each of which must have its own Appearance and Material objects, since we wish to change the colour of each sphere independently of the others. We therefore declare the arrays on lines 6 to 8.

The parameters m_numSpheres and m_maxSpheres represent the actual number of spheres and the maximum allowed number of spheres respectively. On line 10, the parameter m_coordLimit is the upper-bound on a value that may be used as one of the coordinates of the centre of a sphere. In other words, all coordinate values are chosen from the range [–m_coordLimit, +m_coordLimit]. The radius is chosen randomly from the range [0, m_radiusLimit]. The array of Vector3f objects on line 11 is used to store the sphere centres.

The constructor starting on line 13 initializes the various parameters. The number of spheres is randomly chosen on line 18, where we ensure we have at least 2 spheres.

On line 23 we call createAppearances() to set up the arrays of Material and Appearance objects. Since we will be changing the colour of a sphere by replacing its Material object, we set the appropriate capability on line 81.

Since the Sphere class always generates a sphere centred at the origin, we need to translate it to the required location. We therefore need a separate TransformGroup for each sphere, so we create an array on lines 25 and 26. We then create the arrays of Sphere and Vector3f objects on lines 27 and 28.

The for loop beginning on line 31 sets up the properties for each Sphere. The radius is generated on line 35, and the Sphere itself is created on lines 36 to 38. The arguments to the Sphere constructor are the radius, a flag indicating that normal vectors should be generated (since we will be using an external light source), a value (32) indicating how many segments should be used to create the Sphere, and the Appearance for that Sphere.

Lines 39 to 42 allow read/write access to the Appearance for a given Sphere. Note that since the Sphere class does not extend the Shape3D class, we cannot use the setCapability() method directly on a Sphere object. We must use the getShape() method to retrieve the Shape3D that defines the geometry of the sphere, and apply setCapability() to that instead.

Lines 43 and 44 set another type of capability that we have not yet encountered. We will be using GEOMETRY mode (which provides higher precision) when doing the picking later, and this requires that the ALLOW_INTERSECT capability be set for any pickable object.

Lines 45 to 50 create a Transform3D that contains the translation to the randomly-generated centre for the sphere. The coordinates are generated using the randCoord() method on lines 67 to 71, which generates a value in the required range.

Finally, the resetColors() method on lines 56 to 65 refreshes the Material for all spheres so that they return to a white colour. This method is called from the PickDemo class, which we consider now.

```
1       import com.sun.j3d.utils.universe.*;
2       import javax.media.j3d.*;
3       import javax.swing.*;
4       import javax.vecmath.*;
5       import java.awt.*;
6       import java.awt.event.*;
7       import java.util.*;
8       import com.sun.j3d.utils.picking.*;
9       import com.sun.j3d.utils.picking.behaviors.*;
10      import com.sun.j3d.utils.behaviors.keyboard.*;
11      import com.sun.j3d.utils.behaviors.mouse.*;
12
13      public class PickDemo extends JFrame
14      {
15          JPanel m_jpanel = new JPanel();
16          Canvas3D m_drawingCanvas;
17          BasicUniverse universe;
18          BranchGroup scene;
19          RandSpheres randSpheres;
20          Shape3D pickImage;
21          DirectionalLight m_directionalLight;
```

```
22
23      public static void main(String argv[])
24      {
25          PickDemo pickDemo = new PickDemo();
26          pickDemo.setVisible(true);
27      }
28
29      PickDemo()
30      {
31          WindowHandler windowHandler = new WindowHandler();
32          this.addWindowListener(windowHandler);
33          setTitle("Picking in Java 3D");
34          getContentPane().setLayout(new BorderLayout(0,0));
35          setSize(600,600);
36          m_jpanel.setLayout(null);
37          getContentPane().add(BorderLayout.CENTER, m_jpanel);
38          m_jpanel.setBackground(
39              new java.awt.Color(255,232,221));
40          m_jpanel.setBounds(0,0,600,600);
41
42          GraphicsConfiguration graphicsConfig =
43              SimpleUniverse.getPreferredConfiguration();
44          m_drawingCanvas = new Canvas3D(graphicsConfig);
45          m_jpanel.add(m_drawingCanvas);
46          universe = new BasicUniverse(m_drawingCanvas, 25.0f);
47          newRandSpheres();
48          scene = new BranchGroup();
49          scene.setCapability(BranchGroup.ALLOW_DETACH);
50          scene.addChild(randSpheres);
51
52          setupLightSources();
53          scene.addChild(m_directionalLight);
54
55          BoundingSphere behaveBounds =
56              new BoundingSphere(new Point3d(0,0,0), 100);
57          KeyBehavior keyBehavior = new KeyBehavior();
58          keyBehavior.setSchedulingBounds(behaveBounds);
59          scene.addChild(keyBehavior);
60
61          MousePick mouseBehavior =
62              new MousePick(m_drawingCanvas, scene, behaveBounds);
63          scene.addChild(mouseBehavior);
64
65          PickRotateBehavior boardRotate =
66              new PickRotateBehavior(scene, m_drawingCanvas,
67                  behaveBounds);
68          scene.addChild(boardRotate);
69
70          PickZoomBehavior boardZoom =
71              new PickZoomBehavior(scene, m_drawingCanvas,
72                  behaveBounds);
73          scene.addChild(boardZoom);
```

```
74
75        PickTranslateBehavior boardTranslate =
76           new PickTranslateBehavior(scene, m_drawingCanvas,
77              behaveBounds);
78        scene.addChild(boardTranslate);
79
80        universe.addBranchGraph(scene);
81        m_drawingCanvas.setBounds(0,0,600,600);
82     }
83
84     private void setupLightSources()
85     {
86        m_directionalLight = new DirectionalLight();
87        m_directionalLight.setEnable(true);
88        m_directionalLight.setInfluencingBounds
89           (new BoundingSphere(new Point3d(), 100.0));
90     }
91
92     private void newRandSpheres()
93     {
94        randSpheres = new RandSpheres(5, 5.0f, 5.0f);
95        randSpheres.
96           setCapability(TransformGroup.ALLOW_TRANSFORM_READ);
97        randSpheres.setCapability(
98        TransformGroup.ALLOW_TRANSFORM_WRITE);
99        randSpheres.setCapability(
100          TransformGroup.ENABLE_PICK_REPORTING);
101       pickImage = new Shape3D();
102       pickImage.setPickable(false);
103       pickImage.setCapability(Shape3D.ALLOW_GEOMETRY_WRITE);
104       randSpheres.addChild(pickImage);
105    }
106
107    public void newSpheres()
108    {
109       scene.detach();
110       for (int num = 0; num < scene.numChildren(); num++) {
111          if (scene.getChild(num) == randSpheres) {
112             scene.removeChild(num);
113             break;
114          }
115       }
116       newRandSpheres();
117       scene.addChild(randSpheres);
118       universe.addBranchGraph(scene);
119    }
120
121    public void pickSpheres()
122    {
123       LineArray pickLine = new LineArray(2,
124          LineArray.COORDINATES);
125       Point3d[] pickPoint = new Point3d[2];
```

```
126        for (int point = 0; point < 2; point++) {
127            pickPoint[point] = new
128                Point3d(randSpheres.randCoord(),
129                    randSpheres.randCoord(),
130                    randSpheres.randCoord());
131        }
132        pickLine.setCoordinates(0, pickPoint);
133        pickImage.setGeometry(pickLine);
134
135        Transform3D randTrans = new Transform3D();
136        randSpheres.getTransform(randTrans);
137        for (int point = 0; point < 2; point++) {
138            randTrans.transform(pickPoint[point]);
139        }
140        PickSegment pickSeg =
141            new PickSegment(pickPoint[0], pickPoint[1]);
142        PickTool pickTool = new PickTool(scene);
143        pickTool.setMode(PickTool.GEOMETRY);
144        pickTool.setShape(pickSeg, pickPoint[0]);
145        PickResult[] results = pickTool.pickAllSorted();
146
147        randSpheres.resetColors();
148        if (results != null) {
149            for (int p = 0; p < results.length; p++) {
150                Material redSurface = new Material();
151                redSurface.setDiffuseColor(1.0f, 0.0f, 0.0f);
152                Shape3D sphere = (Shape3D)results[p].getObject();
153                sphere.getAppearance().setMaterial(redSurface);
154            }
155        }
156    }
157
158    void exitApplication()
159    {
160        this.setVisible(false);
161        this.dispose();
162        System.exit(0);
163    }
164
165    class WindowHandler extends WindowAdapter
166    {
167        public void windowClosing(WindowEvent event)
168        {
169            Object object = event.getSource();
170            if (object == PickDemo.this)
171                exitApplication();
172        }
173    }
174
175    // Behavior classes inserted here (see below)
176 }
```

The `PickDemo` class is the main class which sets up the usual Java 3D framework. In addition to the usual components, we declare a `RandSpheres` object on line 19, and a `Shape3D` on line 20 that will store the line segment used as a picking shape when the 'P' key is pressed.

We provide a single directional light source (line 21) to light the spheres.

Much of the code in the constructor is the same as in previous examples so we will not dwell on it here. The `RandSpheres` object is created by calling `newRandSpheres()` on line 47. This method (line 92) specifies that we wish a maximum of 5 spheres, and that both the maximum radius and maximum coordinate value for the centre should be 5.0. To prepare for the addition of the three utility mouse picking classes, we allow read/write access to the `TransformGroup` in `randSpheres`, and also enable pick reporting. The method also sets up `pickImage` by specifying that it is not pickable, and that we may alter its geometry.

The main `BranchGroup` is set up on lines 48 to 50. We set the ALLOW_DETACH capability on line 49, since we will be detaching this `BranchGroup` from the live scene graph in order to make some changes to it. More on this later.

The light is created and added to the scene on lines 52 and 53, and a `Bounds` object for use with the various `Behaviors` is created on lines 55 and 56.

Lines 57 to 63 add in the two user-defined `Behaviors` which we will consider a bit later. The `MousePick` class allows all spheres under the mouse pointer to be selected, while the `KeyBehavior` class allows a line segment to be generated and used as a picking shape. Lines 65 to 78 add in the three utility mouse picking classes.

The `newSpheres()` method beginning on line 107 removes the current `randSpheres` from the scene and generates a new one containing a new set of spheres. (The user is able to call this method by pressing the 'N' key on the keyboard, as we will see when we consider the `KeyBehavior` class below.)

Although this operation could be performed with `scene` still a live part of the graph, it is often easier to simply detach the `BranchGroup` from the overall scene graph, make the changes, and reconnect it later. In partciular, this avoids the necessity of setting a large number of capabilities. We do this here on line 109. The `for` loop on line 110 searches `scene` for the `randSpheres` object and removes it. Line 116 calls `newRandSpheres()` to generate a new set of spheres which is added to `scene` on line 117. Line 118 reattaches `scene` to the virtual universe, making it live again.

The `pickSpheres()` method on line 121 is called (as we will see) in response to the user pressing 'P' on the keyboard. It creates a line segment which is both displayed in the scene as `pickImage` and used as a picking shape. Lines 123 to 133 generate random coordinate values for `pickImage`'s endpoints and construct the line segment from them.

Alert readers may suspect a potential problem here. We have allowed the three mouse picking classes to rotate, zoom and translate the set of spheres, so that the locations of the spheres will probably not be the same after a few transformations as they were when they were created. However, we have calculated the coordinates of `pickImage`'s endpoints in the original, untransformed coordinate system used by `randSpheres` when it was first created. Do we need to transform the coordinates of `pickImage` to retain the correct relative position of the line segment relative to the spheres?

The answer is 'no', since `pickImage` was added as a child to `randSpheres` (line 104). Since the mouse picking classes apply their transformations to the randSpheres (which is derived from TransformGroup), any transformation applied to randSpheres will apply to all its children as well, so that pickImage will be transformed right along with the spheres.

However, it is important to remember that pickImage is *not* the object that is used by the program to specify the picking shape—it is merely a graphical object that renders the picking shape as part of the scene. We have not yet created the picking shape in the program. Since this picking shape will not be part of the randSpheres branch in the scene graph, it will not be automatically transformed whenever the user moves the spheres using the mouse. We therefore must transform the coordinates used to define the picking shape before we create the shape itself. This is done on lines 135 to 139.

The creation of the picking shape is done on line 140. We define a PickSegment that uses the transformed endpoints to define its extent. Next (line 142) we create a PickTool and attach it to the scene. We set the PickTool's mode to GEOMETRY to provide the greatest precision in picking (line 143) and then associate the shape we just created with the PickTool (line 144).

The actual picking operation occurs on line 145, where we call the pickAllSorted() method to retrieve an array of PickResults, sorted by their distance from the viewpoint.

To display the results of the picking operation, we first reset the colours of all the spheres to white (line 147). If the picking shape (the line segment) did not intersect any of the spheres, the results array will be null. If there are some intersections, we loop through the array (lines 149 to 154) and change the Material in each picked sphere so that its diffuse colour is red.

Readers may wonder why we used the pickAllSorted() method on line 145 instead of the pickAll() method, since we do not make any use of the fact that the results array is sorted. This is because there appears to be a bug in the pickAll() method which results in some intersections with picked objects being incorrectly calculated. Until this bug is fixed in a future release of Java 3D, it is better to use the pickAllSorted() method if all intersections are required.

We will now have a look at the KeyBehavior class which allows the user to call the pickSpheres() and newSpheres() methods. Its code, which is nested within the PickDemo class above, is:

```
1    public class KeyBehavior extends Behavior
2    {
3        WakeupOnAWTEvent awtWakeup = new
4        WakeupOnAWTEvent(KeyEvent.KEY_PRESSED);
5        WakeupOnActivation activationWakeup = new
6        WakeupOnActivation();
7        WakeupCriterion[] wakeups = new WakeupCriterion[2];
8        WakeupOr wakeupList;
9
10       public KeyBehavior()
11       {
12           wakeups[0] = awtWakeup;
13           wakeups[1] = activationWakeup;
14           wakeupList = new WakeupOr(wakeups);
15       }
16
17       public void initialize()
```

```
18      {
19          wakeupOn(wakeupList);
20      }
21
22      public void processStimulus(Enumeration criteria)
23      {
24          WakeupCriterion crit =
25              (WakeupCriterion)criteria.nextElement();
26          if (crit instanceof WakeupOnActivation) {
27              m_drawingCanvas.requestFocus();
28              wakeupOn(awtWakeup);
29              return;
30          }
31          AWTEvent[] event =
32              ((WakeupOnAWTEvent)crit).getAWTEvent();
33          if (event == null) return;
34
35          KeyEvent key = (KeyEvent)event[0];
36          switch(key.getKeyCode()) {
37          case KeyEvent.VK_N:
38              newSpheres();
39              break;
40          case KeyEvent.VK_P:
41              pickSpheres();
42              break;
43          }
44          wakeupOn(awtWakeup);
45      }
46  }
```

This class should be familiar from the `Behavior` example given earlier in this chapter (page 260). The `KeyBehavior` class listens initially for `WakeupOnActivation` or a key press event. When the application is started, the canvas requests the focus so that subsequent key presses are directed to this `KeyBehavior` object. From that point on, only key presses are handled, and then only the 'N' and 'P' keys result in any action.

Figure 8.1 shows a sample from the program, where 3 spheres have been generated, and a picking segment intersects the two on the right.

Figure 8.1:
A pick segment intersecting two spheres.

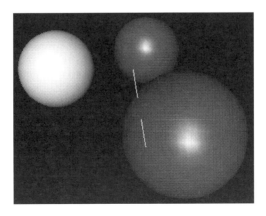

Finally, we examine the `MousePick` class, which extends the `PickMouseBehavior` utility class:

```
1    public class MousePick extends PickMouseBehavior
2    {
3       Material redSurface = new Material();
4
5       public MousePick(Canvas3D canvas, BranchGroup branch,
6          Bounds bounds)
7       {
8          super(canvas, branch, bounds);
9          setSchedulingBounds(bounds);
10         pickCanvas.setMode(PickTool.GEOMETRY);
11         setTolerance(0.0f);
12         redSurface.setDiffuseColor(1.0f, 0.0f, 0.0f);
13      }
14
15      public void updateScene(int xPos, int yPos)
16      {
17         randSpheres.resetColors();
18         pickCanvas.setShapeLocation(xPos, yPos);
19         PickResult[] results = pickCanvas.pickAllSorted();
20         if (results != null) {
21            for (int i = 0; i < results.length; i++) {
22               Shape3D shape = (Shape3D)results[i].
23               getNode(PickResult.SHAPE3D);
24               shape.getAppearance().setMaterial(redSurface);
25            }
26         }
27      }
28   }
```

This class is designed to generate a ray passing through the point selected by the mouse click and pick all spheres intersecting this ray. All picked spheres are coloured red, as in the `pickSpheres()` method.

The `PickMouseBehavior` class is a utility class derived from `Behavior` that provides default implementations of the `initialize()` and `processStimulus()` methods. These methods listen for mouse clicks and generate a `PickRay` for each mouse click. If this is all we want a mouse click to do, we need not override the `initialize()` or `processStimulus()` methods, which is what we have done here.

The constructor for `MousePick` requires three arguments: the canvas on which mouse clicks are to be detected, the `BranchGroup` to be searched for pickable objects, and `Bounds` inside which events are handled. The initialization of the first two of these parameters is done in the `PickMouseBehavior` constructor, so we call that using the `super()` method on line 8. For some reason, the `Bounds` are not set in the base class constructor, so we still must do that ourselves (line 9).

The `PickMouseBehavior` class contains a `PickCanvas` object which may be used to do the actual picking. As mentioned earlier, `PickCanvas` extends the `PickTool` class, and adds a few features useful for mouse picking. In the constructor, we set the picking mode to GEOMETRY (line 10) for more precise determination of intersections.

Line 11 calls the `setTolerance()` method, which specifies how close to an object (in pixels) the mouse pointer must be in order for that object to be picked. Specifying a tolerance of 0, as we have done here, means that the mouse must be clicked directly over part of the object. The default tolerance is 2 pixels, which means that the mouse may be clicked anywhere within 2 pixels of the object to be picked. Setting a non-zero tolerance is useful if we wish to allow picking of very small or thin objects such as points or lines. The tolerance of 0 used in the program makes sense, since the objects being picked are all spheres with a reasonable extent, so they are easy to select with the mouse.

Although we do not need to provide a `processStimulus()` method in `MousePick`, we do need some way of telling the class what should be done when a picking operation has been performed. The `PickMouseBehavior` class provides the `updateScene()` method for this purpose. This method is called from the default version of `processStimulus()`, and is passed as arguments the pixel coordinates of the mouse pointer when the picking request was made.

On line 17 we reset the colours as before. On line 18 we call the `setShapeLocation()` method, which is part of the `PickCanvas` class. This method creates a `PickRay` from the viewpoint that intersects the viewing plane at the point given by the xPos and yPos arguments to the method, and sets the `PickShape` of the `PickCanvas` to this ray.

On line 19 we generate the array of `PickResults` by calling `pickAllSorted()` as before, and the remainder of the method duplicates the code from `pickSpheres()` above.

The examples given here should give a feel for what can be done with picking. The reader is encouraged to explore the documentation to see what other features are available.

8.6 Animation in two dimensions

Although the examples given so far in this chapter have involved moving part or all of the objects in the scene around, we have not yet seen true *animation*. The difference between interaction and animation is usually taken to be that *interaction* requires the intervention of the user to make things happen, while animation is a movement of the objects in a scene without any user intervention. Thus while we were able to make the rubber box grow or shrink in the first example in this chapter, the movement of the box was only possible if the user dragged the mouse to make it happen. An animation of a scene may be started or stopped by user actions, but in between the motion should continue without any input from devices such as the keyboard or mouse.

We will begin our study of animation by looking at a two-dimensional example. Unlike Java 3D, where several features have been built in to make animations easier to construct, there are no special features available in Java 2D to ease the job of the animator.

The basic idea in constructing a two-dimensional animation is to use the same technique as that used in creating animated cartoons seen on television. We create a series of static drawings and then show them in rapid succession to give the appearance of movement. The easiest way of doing this is to call the `paint()` method of the component (such as a `Canvas`) repeatedly to display each frame, with a delay of a fixed time between each pair of frames.

Although such an approach will work, there is a problem that rapidly becomes apparent once the application is run—the animation seems to take total control of the program. The main effect of this is that all attempts to interact with the program (including shutting it down) seem to be ignored, so that the only way of stopping it is to type Ctrl-C in the shell window from which the program was started (if you are running the program on a UNIX system or from a DOS window) or Ctrl-Alt-Delete if you need to kill the program in Windows.

8.6.1 Threads

The reason this happens is that Java is a *threaded* language, meaning that it is capable of running different parts of a program in different *threads*, or subprocesses. Every running Java program has several threads that run automatically, dealing with such things as display of the interface and garbage collection. Unless the programmer creates a separate thread in which the animation is run, it must share the main thread that is used to run the program. Since a continuous animation never has any pauses, it grabs all the CPU time in the main thread, meaning that the program will not pay any attention to attempts to communicate with it.

The solution to this problem, as you have probably guessed, is to create a separate thread in which Java can run the animation, leaving the main thread free to listen for user-generated events such as mouse clicks.

Creating and using threads in Java is actually quite simple, despite the complexity of the thread management that is taking place behind the scenes. Each thread is an instance of the Thread class. When a thread is created, it must be associated with an object that implements the Runnable interface. This interface contains a single method, run(), which is called when a Thread starts running. The code inside the run() method tells the Thread what to do.

Let us look at a simple example of animation. The program that follows initially displays a blank canvas. When the user clicks the mouse over the canvas, a new Thread is created which begins the animation. The animation itself displays an ellipse (drawn using our code from Chapter 1) which starts off in the upper-left corner of the canvas and moves diagonally down and to the right. When the ellipse hits an edge of the canvas, it 'bounces' off and continues its journey until it hits another edge, where it bounces again and so on. Clicking the mouse again will pause the animation. Another click of the mouse will restart the animation from where it left off, and so on.

We will first examine the AnimatedEllipse class, which handles the interaction with the mouse and sets up the thread.

```
1   import java.awt.*;
2   import java.awt.event.*;
3   import javax.swing.*;
4
5   public class AnimatedEllipse extends JFrame
6       implements Runnable
7   {
8       JPanel panel;
9       EllipseCanvas drawingCanvas;
10      Thread animation;
```

```
11    boolean threadRunning = false;
12    int cornerX = 0, cornerY = 0;
13    int diameterX = 55, diameterY = 15;
14    int incrX = 5, incrY = 5;
15    int canvasX = 537, canvasY = 400;
16    int updateInterval = 15;
17
18    public static void main(String argv[])
19    {
20        AnimatedEllipse twoDimDemo = new AnimatedEllipse();
21        twoDimDemo.setVisible(true);
22    }
23
24    AnimatedEllipse()
25    {
26        WindowHandler windowHandler = new WindowHandler();
27        addWindowListener(windowHandler);
28        setTitle("Animation in Java 2D");
29        getContentPane().setLayout(new BorderLayout());
30        setSize(650,450);
31        getContentPane().add(BorderLayout.CENTER, panel);
32        panel = new JPanel();
33        panel.setBackground(Color.red);
34        drawingCanvas =
35            new EllipseCanvas(new Dimension(canvasX, canvasY));
36        panel.add(drawingCanvas);
37        drawingCanvas.setBackground(Color.white);
38        drawingCanvas.addMouseListener(new MouseHandler());
39    }
40
41    public void run()
42    {
43        while (threadRunning) {
44            drawingCanvas.setEllipse(new Rectangle(cornerX,
45                cornerY, diameterX, diameterY));
46            if (cornerX + incrX > canvasX-diameterX ||
47                cornerX + incrX < 0) {
48                incrX = -incrX;
49            }
50            if (cornerY + incrY > canvasY-diameterY ||
51                cornerY + incrY < 0) {
52                incrY = -incrY;
53            }
54            cornerX += incrX;
55            cornerY += incrY;
56            drawingCanvas.repaint();
57            try {
58                Thread.sleep(updateInterval);
59            } catch (Exception e) { }
60        }
61    }
62
```

```
63    class MouseHandler extends MouseAdapter
64    {
65        public void mousePressed(MouseEvent event)
66        {
67            Object object = event.getSource();
68            if (object == drawingCanvas) {
69                if (threadRunning) {
70                    animation = new Thread(AnimatedEllipse.this);
71                    threadRunning = true;
72                    animation.start();
73                } else {
74                    threadRunning = false;
75                    animation = null;
76                }
77            }
78        }
79    }
80
81    class WindowHandler extends WindowAdapter
82    {
83        public void windowClosing(WindowEvent event)
84        {
85            System.exit(0);
86        }
87    }
88 }
```

The class is declared as implementing the Runnable interface on line 6, which is necessary if we wish to use this class to run a Thread. As mentioned above, implementing Runnable requires that we include a run() method, which we will discuss later.

The EllipseCanvas object declared on line 9 (considered below) handles the drawing of the ellipse. Line 10 declares the Thread and line 11 creates a boolean flag that indicates if the Thread is currently running. (Since JDK version 1.1, we must pause or stop threads by examining the state of such a flag, rather than by calling the (now deprecated) suspend() or stop() methods from the Thread class.)

The remaining variables declared on lines 12 to 16 are all parameters used in displaying the ellipse and running the animation. The variables cornerX and cornerY define the upper-left corner of the rectangle that bounds the ellipse, and diameterX and diameterY define the major axes of the ellipse in the x and y directions respectively. The values of incrX and incrY specify how far in the x and y directions the ellipse should move between each pair of frames in the animation. Initially, both these quantities are positive since the ellipse will move to the right and downwards, but after a bounce off one of the edges, one or both of these values could become negative to indicate a change of direction.

The dimensions of the drawing canvas are specified by canvasX and canvasY, and updateInterval gives the time, in milliseconds, between successive frame updates.

The constructor on line 24 is relatively straightforward, as it just sets up the usual event handlers and initializes the frame and drawing canvas.

Before we examine the run() method on line 41, we should have a look at how the Thread is created. We wish the animation to start in response to a mouse click, so we have added a nested class called MouseHandler on line 63. We only need to implement the mousePressed() method since no other mouse events are to be handled.

After testing that the mouse was clicked over the canvas (line 68), we must decide whether the animation should be started or stopped. We test the threadRunning flag (we could also test if animation == null, since we set the Thread to null each time we stop the animation). If the animation is not running, we create a new Thread (line 70). When a Thread is created, we must associate a Runnable object with it so that the Thread has a run() method to call when it starts. In the example given here, we have added Runnable to the AnimatedEllipse class, but we could also have created a separate class that implements Runnable and used an instance of that.

After creating the Thread, we set the threadRunning flag (line 71) and then call the Thread's start() method (line 72). Calling start() causes the Thread to begin execution by calling the run() method in the Runnable object that associated with that Thread when it was created. In this case, the Thread will begin running by calling the run() method in the AnimatedEllipse class, on line 41.

The run() method consists of a single loop which continues as long as threadRunning is true. As mentioned earlier, as of JDK version 1.1 it is not acceptable to use the stop() or suspend() methods in the Thread class (for technical reasons that we will not pursue here) to interrupt a Thread. The preferred method is to cause the run() method to exit when the Thread should stop or pause. The easiest way of doing this is the method we have adopted in this example—use a boolean flag to indicate whether the Thread should be running or not, and exit the run() method when this flag becomes false.

The one disadvantage to using this method is that, depending on the time interval between frames in the animation, the response of the Thread to a mouse click may not appear instantaneous, since the loop goes through a single iteration once for each update of the image, and will only stop after a complete iteration has been performed. In the example given here, the iteration time is only 15 milliseconds (just over one-hundredth of a second) so the response will appear immediately, but with a longer time interval, the delay will be noticeable. If this is unacceptable, further tests of the threadRunning flag can be placed at various points inside the loop.

The code inside the run() method should be fairly obvious—the new position of the ellipse is specified by defining its bounding rectangle (lines 44 and 45). Lines 46 to 53 check if the ellipse will reach one of the boundaries of the canvas on the next iteration and, if so, reverse the corresponding increment value so that the motion in that direction will change. Lines 54 and 55 add the increment to the coordinates, and line 56 redraws the canvas to update the position of the ellipse in the display. Finally, the static sleep() method in the Thread class is called to pause between successive frames in the animation. Note that the sleep() method can throw a non-runtime exception and must therefore always be enclosed in a try–catch block.

Returning to the mousePressed() method, if the thread is running when the mouse is clicked, the threadRunning flag is switched off (line 74) and the Thread itself is set to null. This will cause the loop in the run() method to exit with the next iteration, causing the animation to stop. Clicking the mouse again will create a new Thread, but since we have not reset any of the values defining the position of the ellipse, the animation will pick up from where it left off.

We will now examine the relevant portions of the EllipseCanvas class.

```
1    import java.awt.*;
2    import java.awt.image.*;
3
4    public class EllipseCanvas extends Canvas
5    {
6
7       Point m_startPoint = null, m_endPoint = null,
8       m_tempEnd = null;
9       Dimension preferredSize;
10
11      Point centre = new Point();
12      Rectangle newEllipse;
13
14
15      public EllipseCanvas(Dimension prefSize)
16      {
17         preferredSize = prefSize;
18         newEllipse = new Rectangle();
19      }
20
21      public void setPreferredSize(Dimension prefSize)
22      {
23         preferredSize = prefSize;
24      }
25
26      public Dimension getPreferredSize()
27      {
28         return preferredSize;
29      }
30
31      public void setEllipse(Rectangle ellipse)
32      {
33         newEllipse = ellipse;
34         m_startPoint = new Point(ellipse.x, ellipse.y);
35         m_tempEnd = m_startPoint;
36         m_endPoint = new Point(ellipse.x + ellipse.width,
37            ellipse.y + ellipse.height);
38      }
39
40      public void paint(Graphics g)
41      {
42         Graphics2D gg = (Graphics2D)g;
43         if (m_startPoint == null || m_endPoint == null)
44            return;
45         centre = new Point((m_startPoint.x + m_endPoint.x)/2,
46            (m_startPoint.y + m_endPoint.y)/2);
47
48         gg.setColor(Color.black);
```

```
49        int axisA = Math.abs(m_endPoint.x - m_startPoint.x)/2;
50        int axisB = Math.abs(m_endPoint.y - m_startPoint.y)/2;
51        if (axisA > 0 && axisB > 0) {
52            drawBresenhamEllipse(gg, centre, axisA, axisB);
53        }
54    }
55
56    // Remaining methods implement Bresenham's algorithm
57 }
```

This class is very similar to the class we used when drawing ellipses at the beginning of this chapter. The main difference is that we have replaced the setPoint() method in the earlier class by a setEllipse() method here (line 31). This is because we are now able to specify all the dimensions of the ellipse at once, rather than in the earlier example where the initial corner was specified when the mouse was pressed and the final corner when the mouse was released.

The paint() method is essentially identical to the earlier class, as it invokes Bresenham's algorithm to draw the ellipse. This code was covered in Chapter 1.

8.6.2   Double buffering

The example we have just considered contains all the basics of writing an animation in Java 2D. We must create a separate thread in which to run the animation and calculate the geometry required to draw each successive frame, then redraw the image using a Graphics2D object.

Depending on the speed of your computer (in particular, the graphics card), you may find that the bouncing ellipse program produces some flickering when the animation is running. The flickering is caused by the fact that a call to the repaint() method first calls the update() method (defined in the Component class) before it calls the paint() method that we have written in the EllipseCanvas class. The first thing the default version of update() does is to clear the canvas by filling it with the current background colour, thus erasing whatever graphics were there. Slower graphics cards will not be able to refresh an entire canvas at once, with the result that part of the canvas will appear to flicker as the background is repainted. As you might expect, the flickering gets worse if the canvas area gets larger, or the image that is to be drawn gets more complex.

Although there is no way to eliminate flickering entirely (apart from buying a more powerful graphics card), there are some techniques that can reduce it. The most common of these is known as *double buffering*.

In the AnimatedEllipse example above, all the graphics were drawn directly onto the monitor, which means that there is a lot of traffic between the running program and the computer's hardware. The idea behind double buffering is that the drawing process can be made more efficient by constructing the graphics for a single frame as an image in the computer's memory, and then transferring the entire image from memory to screen in a single operation, rather than carrying out each individual drawing operation directly onto the screen.

Double buffering is fairly easy to do in Java, as a special Image class is provided for this purpose. The procedure is to create an Image object, obtain its Graphics2D object and use it to construct the *off-screen buffer* by sending all the drawing commands to the Image rather than directly to the screen. When the Image is complete, it can be drawn onto the monitor using the `drawImage()` method in the `Graphics2D` class.

There is one common source of problems in using the `Image` class, however. An `Image` can only be created by calling the `createImage()` method from an existing and fully defined component (such as a `Frame` or `JFrame`). If an attempt is made to create an `Image` from another component before that component has been fully created itself, the `createImage()` method will return `null`. What this means in practice is that the component that is being used to create the `Image` should actually be visible on screen before the call to `createImage()` is made.

We will now illustrate the use of double buffering by showing modified versions of `AnimatedEllipse` and `EllipseCanvas`.

The changes required in the `AnimatedEllipse` class are quite minor so we will refer back to the previous version (on page 286) rather than reproduce the entire class. First, in the `main()` method, we insert the following line after line 21:

```
twoDimDemo.initImage();
```

This creates the `Image` by calling the `initImage()` method, which may be added anywhere within the `AnimatedEllipse` class:

```
public void initImage()
{
    Image ellipseImage = createImage(canvasX, canvasY);
    drawingCanvas.setImage(ellipseImage);
}
```

This creates an `Image` by calling the `createImage()` method (giving the dimensions of the required image). Since `AnimatedEllipse` extends the `JFrame` class, it is the `createImage()` method from the `JFrame` class that is being called (actually, since `JFrame` ultimately extends the `Component` class, it is the `createImage()` method in the `Component` class that is being called). We therefore must ensure that the `JFrame` is fully created *before* the call to `createImage()`. This is done by the original call to `setVisible()` on line 21 in `main()`. When the frame is displayed, we can be sure it is fully specified. Readers should experiment with the placement of the call to `initImage()` to see where it is possible to create the `Image`.

The `Image` is then passed to the drawing canvas with a call to `setImage()`, which is a method we will insert into the `EllipseCanvas` class below.

The final change to `AnimatedEllipse` is to replace the call to `repaint()` on line 56 in the `run()` method with a call to a method which we shall call `redraw()`:

```
drawingCanvas.redraw();
```

This method will draw the frame's image to an off-screen buffer, which will then be transferred to the screen in a single operation.

The changes to `EllipseCanvas` are also not extensive. First, we add an `Image` variable at line 6 in the code listing given above (on page 290):

```
Image ellipseImage;
```

We then add the `setImage()` method called from `AnimatedEllipse`:

```
public void setImage(Image image)
{
    ellipseImage = image;
    ellipseGraphics =
```

```
        (Graphics2D)ellipseImage.getGraphics();
    ellipseGraphics.setPaint(Color.white);
    ellipseGraphics.fill(new
        Rectangle(0, 0, preferredSize.width,
            preferredSize.height));
}
```

After initializing ellipseImage, this method obtains a Graphics2D object for use with the Image, and clears the background to solid white.

Finally, we replace the paint() method in the original EllipseCanvas with a new redraw() method:

```
1    public void redraw()
2    {
3        if (m_startPoint == null || m_endPoint == null)
4            return;
5
6        ellipseGraphics.setPaint(Color.white);
7        ellipseGraphics.fill(new
8            Rectangle(0,0,preferredSize.width,
9                preferredSize.height));
10       centre = new Point((m_startPoint.x + m_endPoint.x)/2,
11           (m_startPoint.y + m_endPoint.y)/2);
12
13       ellipseGraphics.setColor(Color.black);
14       int axisA = Math.abs(m_endPoint.x - m_startPoint.x)/2;
15       int axisB = Math.abs(m_endPoint.y - m_startPoint.y)/2;
16       if (axisA > 0 && axisB > 0) {
17           drawBresenhamEllipse(ellipseGraphics, centre,
18               axisA, axisB);
19       }
20       Graphics2D canvasGraphics = (Graphics2D)getGraphics();
21       canvasGraphics.drawImage(ellipseImage, null, this);
22   }
```

The code in redraw() is mostly the same as the code that was in the paint() method earlier. The main difference is that all the drawing is done to ellipseGraphics rather than to the graphics context of the monitor directly. Since drawing to an off-screen buffer does not call the update() method, we need to provide our own code to erase the canvas before each new drawing, which is done on lines 6 to 9. The ellipse itself is drawn on lines 13 to 19.

Line 20 obtains the main Graphics2D object that relates to the monitor, and line 21 calls the drawImage() method to render the completed image onto the screen.

The last two arguments to drawImage() may require some explanation. The second argument is an optional AffineTransform which may be used to transform the Image before it is rendered. In our case, we don't want any transform, so the argument is set to null.

The last argument is an ImageObserver, which may receive reports of the progress of the rendering of the Image. This is useful in cases where the rendering is expected to take some time, but in our case we will not make use of it. Any object derived from Component can serve as an ImageObserver, so we have just used the `EllipseCanvas` class itself (which is derived from `Canvas` which is in turn derived from `Component`).

If you did not notice any flickering running the original version of `AnimatedEllipse`, running the double-buffered version will probably not make any noticeable difference. The main advantage to double buffering is with computer systems that have less powerful graphics cards or a small amount of memory. However, if the scene being rendered for each frame in the animation is more complex, there may be some advantage from using double buffering even on more more powerful systems.

One final improvement is still possible with this program. Since the only difference between successive frames in the animation is that a single ellipse moves slightly across the canvas, it is a bit of a waste of time to redraw the entire canvas. All that really needs to be redrawn are the old and new locations of the ellipse in each case. We can restrict the area drawn by a `Graphics2D` object by setting a clipping region, as we saw in Chapter 3 when drawing textured text. We could therefore work out what regions actually need to be redrawn for each new frame and restrict the update to that region using the `setClip()` method in the `Graphics2D` class. The implementation of this technique is left to the exercises.

8.7 Animation in Java 3D

Simple animation in Java 3D is a considerably easier task than in Java 2D, since there are several classes provided expressly for that purpose in the Java 3D libraries. The two main classes (and their derivatives) that are used for animation in 3D are `Alpha` and `Interpolator`. To get an idea of how these classes are used, let us consider a specific case—displaying a simulation of the Earth revolving in its orbit about the Sun. The geometry involved is quite simple—we will use a yellow sphere to represent the Sun and a blue sphere to represent the Earth. Drawing a snapshot of the Sun–Earth system is therefore easy, but we need to consider what is involved to create an animation.

There are two main aspects to any animation: the properties of the object that are to change and the timescale over which the change takes place. The most obvious property that can change during an animation is the position or orientation of an object, but other properties such as the colour or transparency of an object can also be varied dynamically.

8.7.1 The Alpha class

The `Alpha` class generates a periodic waveform (similar to a sine wave) where the period and shape of the waveform can be specified by the programmer. A single cycle in an `Alpha` waveform is divided up into four sections or phases. The first phase, known as the 'increasing alpha' phase, begins with a value of 0.0 and increases to a value of 1.0. In the default version of the `Alpha` class, the increase is linear, but it is possible to modify the shape of the curve slightly by setting additional parameters.

The second phase, known as 'alpha at one' is a length of time during which the value of an `Alpha` object is constant at 1.0. The third phase is 'decreasing alpha', where the value drops linearly from 1.0 to 0.0, and the fourth phase is 'alpha at zero' where the value is constant at 0.0. (Figure 8.2). The length of time spent in each of these four phases, along with the total number of cycles, may be specified by the programmer. An optional *phase delay* may be specified which causes the first cycle to be delayed a specified amount of time after the Alpha object is triggered.

Figure 8.2:
The Alpha waveform. The Alpha object is triggered at time t_0. An optional *phase delay* may be specified before the first waveform starts at time t_1. The four phases of a waveform are the 'increasing alpha' phase (t_1 to t_2), the 'alpha at one' phase (t_2 to t_3), the 'decreasing alpha' phase (t_3 to t_4) and the 'alpha at zero' phase (t_4 to t_5). The complete first cycle lasts from t_1 to t_5. The second cycle begins at t_5.

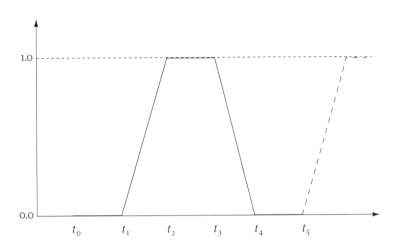

An Alpha object need not use all four of its phases. For example, the default version of Alpha uses only the 'increasing alpha' phase.

To see how an Alpha is used to govern an animation, let us consider the Earth–Sun simulation. We would like the Earth to revolve about the Sun at a constant rate. We can do this by requiring that the rotation angle of the Earth (relative to some fixed starting point) vary from 0 to 2π radians in some fixed time (say 5 seconds), and that this pattern should repeat indefinitely. We can manage this by creating an Alpha with only an increasing alpha phase, and specify that the time spent in this phase is 5 seconds on each cycle. We can also tell the Alpha that it should continue to generate cycles indefinitely. Such an Alpha would then begin with a value of 0.0 and increase linearly from 0.0 to 1.0 over a time interval of 5 seconds. After completing one cycle, the value will jump from 1.0 back to 0.0 immediately (since we have omitted phases two to four) and begin to rise back to 1.0 over the second period of 5 seconds, and so on.

The values generated by the Alpha can be mapped onto the angles occupied by the Earth in its orbit by multiplying the Alpha value by 2π. Since an angle of 2π is the same (geometrically speaking) as 0, the rotation will appear to be continuous.

If we change the Alpha so that it contains both its increasing and decreasing phases (but neither of the constant phases), each with time intervals of 5 seconds, then the Earth would make one revolution around the Sun in one direction, then immediately reverse direction and make another revolution in the opposite direction, and then switch back to the original direction for the third revolution, and so on. Introducing the two constant phases into the Alpha waveform would cause the Earth to pause after each revolution.

We can see, therefore, that the Alpha class provides a flexible method by which any periodic motion can be modelled.

8.7.2 The Interpolator classes

The abstract `Interpolator` class and its various implementations are responsible for determining which of an object's properties are altered during an animation. Several utility classes allow an object to be moved dynamically, either by rotating it or by moving it along some specified path. Other classes allow the colour or transparency of the object to vary.

The `Interpolator` class is derived directly from the `Behavior` class, so the principles behind its operation are similar to those we studied above. An `Interpolator` is awakened by certain events occurring, and processes these events to produce the animation. However, the default `initialize()` and `processStimulus()` methods usually do not need to be overridden by the programmer, since they are set up to respond to events produced by an accompanying `Alpha` object.

We will see a few examples of the use of `Interpolator` and its derivative classes, but we will begin with a summary of what is required to animate an object in Java 3D.

First, of course, we must create the object itself. In anticipation of the animation that is to be performed on it, we must also set the capabilities for the object. For example, if we wish to rotate or move an object, we must ensure that a `TransformGroup` has been created exclusively for the object that is to be moved, and that this `TransformGroup` has the ALLOW_TRANSFORM_WRITE capability set so that the `Interpolator` can change the object's position.

Next, we must create an `Alpha` object to define the time course of the animation. Then, the appropriate `Interpolator` is created and connected (usually by means of parameters passed through the constructor) with the `Alpha` object and the object to be animated.

Since the `Interpolator` class is derived from the `Behavior` class, we must also set some scheduling bounds for it. Any target objects lying outside these bounds will not be animated by the `Interpolator` even if they have been included in the target list.

Finally, the `Interpolator` must be connected to the scene graph, like any other `Behavior`. Note that the `Alpha` object is not connected directly to the scene graph—it is connected only to the `Interpolator`.

8.7.3 Example—an orbiting sphere

As a first example, we will present the code for the simple simulation mentioned above, in which one sphere representing the Earth orbits about a larger sphere representing the Sun. Apart from the `BasicUniverse` class, the entire program is contained in a single class called `SolarSystem`.

```
1    import com.sun.j3d.utils.geometry.*;
2    import com.sun.j3d.utils.universe.*;
3    import javax.media.j3d.*;
4    import javax.swing.*;
5    import javax.vecmath.*;
6    import java.awt.*;
7    import java.awt.event.*;
8
```

```
9      public class SolarSystem extends JFrame
10     {
11         JPanel jpanel = new JPanel();
12         Canvas3D drawingCanvas;
13
14         BasicUniverse universe;
15         BranchGroup scene;
16         DirectionalLight directionalLight;
17
18         Color3f blue3f = new Color3f(Color.blue);
19         Color3f yellow3f = new Color3f(Color.yellow);
20         Sphere sun, earth;
21
22         public static void main(String argv[])
23         {
24             SolarSystem solar = new SolarSystem();
25             solar.setVisible(true);
26         }
27
28         SolarSystem()
29         {
30             WindowHandler windowHandler = new WindowHandler();
31             this.addWindowListener(windowHandler);
32             setTitle("Interpolators in Java 3D");
33             getContentPane().setLayout(new BorderLayout(0,0));
34             setSize(800,600);
35             jpanel.setLayout(null);
36             getContentPane().add(BorderLayout.CENTER, jpanel);
37             jpanel.setBounds(0,0,800,600);
38
39             GraphicsConfiguration graphicsConfig =
40             SimpleUniverse.getPreferredConfiguration();
41             drawingCanvas = new Canvas3D(graphicsConfig);
42             jpanel.add(drawingCanvas);
43             universe = new BasicUniverse(drawingCanvas, 5.0f);
44
45             scene = new BranchGroup();
46             setupLightSources();
47             scene.addChild(directionalLight);
48
49             sun = new Sphere(0.5f, createAppearance(yellow3f));
50             earth = new Sphere(0.15f, createAppearance(blue3f));
51
52             Transform3D groupTrans = new Transform3D();
53             TransformGroup earthTransform = new TransformGroup();
54             groupTrans.
55                 setTranslation(new Vector3f(0.0f, 0.0f, 1.5f));
56             earthTransform.setTransform(groupTrans);
57             earthTransform.addChild(earth);
58
59             TransformGroup earthRotTrans = new TransformGroup();
60             earthRotTrans.setCapability(
```

```
61              TransformGroup.ALLOW_TRANSFORM_WRITE);
62          Alpha alpha = new Alpha(-1, 5000);
63
64          BoundingSphere behaveBounds =
65              new BoundingSphere(new Point3d(0,0,0), 10);
66          RotationInterpolator rotInt =
67              new RotationInterpolator(alpha, earthRotTrans);
68          rotInt.setSchedulingBounds(behaveBounds);
69          scene.addChild(rotInt);
70          earthRotTrans.addChild(earthTransform);
71          scene.addChild(earthRotTrans);
72          scene.addChild(sun);
73
74          universe.addBranchGraph(scene);
75          drawingCanvas.setBounds(0, 0, 800, 600);
76      }
77
78      private Appearance createAppearance(Color3f color)
79      {
80          Appearance appear = new Appearance();
81          Material material = new Material();
82          material.setDiffuseColor(color);
83          appear.setMaterial(material);
84          return appear;
85      }
86
87      private void setupLightSources()
88      {
89          directionalLight = new DirectionalLight();
90          directionalLight.setEnable(true);
91          directionalLight.setInfluencingBounds
92              (new BoundingSphere(new Point3d(), 500.0));
93      }
94
95      void exitApplication()
96      {
97          this.setVisible(false);
98          this.dispose();
99          System.exit(0);
100     }
101
102     class WindowHandler extends WindowAdapter
103     {
104         public void windowClosing(WindowEvent event)
105         {
106             Object object = event.getSource();
107             if (object == SolarSystem.this)
108                 exitApplication();
109         }
110     }
111 }
```

The program creates two Spheres (lines 49 and 50), each with its own Appearance. The sun sphere is yellow and 0.5 metres in radius, while the earth sphere is blue and 0.15 metres in radius. A directional light source has also been added.

The key to running an animation involving rotation or motion is to arrange the TransformGroups properly. In this example, the sun object is created at the origin and is not moved, so we do not need a TransformGroup for it.

In the case of the earth object, however, we need to consider things a bit more carefully. When we create the Sphere for the earth on line 50, it is created at the origin, so clearly the first thing we need to do is move it away from the origin to its correct location in the orbit. We therefore create a TransformGroup called earthTransform and its associated Transform3D on lines 52 and 53, and initialize the transformation to a translation of 1.5 metres in the +z direction. The initial display of the program will therefore be a larger yellow sphere at the origin with a smaller blue sphere directly in front of it.

To introduce the animation, we need to rotate the blue sphere about a vertical axis passing through the origin (that is, the y axis). We can use a RotationInterpolator (an implementation of the Interpolator class) to do this, but we must specify on which TransformGroup the RotationInterpolator should act. On first thought, it might seem reasonable to apply the interpolator to earthTransform, since that is the TransformGroup that controls the location of the blue sphere. However, the problem is that an interpolator overwrites the Transform3D object within the TransformGroup, rather than just multiplying the existing Transform3D by a new matrix. Since a RotationInterpolator deals exclusively with rotations, the initial translation that we applied on lines 54 and 55 will be lost, and the blue sphere will return to the origin.

To solve this problem, we introduce a second TransformGroup above the existing one in the scene graph. The new TransformGroup called earthRotTrans, is created on lines 59 to 61, and its capability is set to allow writing. Note that we add this new TransformGroup *above* earthTransform in the scene graph, since transformations are applied to an object from the leaves of the scene graph upwards towards the root. We need the translation away from the origin to be applied first, followed by the rotation, so the translation must be lower down in the graph.

On line 62 we create the Alpha object which controls the speed of the orbit. The Alpha class has several constructors, but one of the simplest is the one used here. The first argument indicates the number of cycles that should be provided—the value of –1 indicates that the waveform should be supplied indefinitely. The second argument is the length of a full, single cycle in milliseconds. The value of 5000 thus indicates that each cycle should last 5 seconds.

If no other parameters are specified for an Alpha object, the default is to enable only the increasing alpha phase, so this Alpha will generate a linearly increasing sequence of values from 0.0 to 1.0, followed by a jump back to 0.0 for the beginning of the next cycle.

Lines 64 and 65 prepare the scheduling bounds for the interpolator, which is created on lines 66 and 67. The RotationInterpolator class also has several constructors, but the simple one we use here specifies the Alpha object and the TransformGroup which are to be associated with it. The default axis of rotation is the y axis through the origin, and the default range of rotation angles is from 0 to 2π, giving a complete revolution.

The remainder of the code connects the interpolator and the the spheres (together with their TransformGroups) into the scene graph. A frame from the animation is shown in Figure 8.3.

Figure 8.3:
A frame from the
solar system
animation.

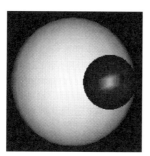

One aspect of the solar system program may have struck the reader as odd—there was no mention of threads, even though we produced an animation that runs forever. In fact, the animation is run in a separate thread, but the code for constructing and managing the thread is concealed within the Alpha and Interpolator classes. It is therefore possible to add extra Behavior objects which listen for events such as key presses or mouse events.

8.7.4   Using the Alpha class

The solar system example above used only the simplest form of Alpha object to produce its animation. In this section, we will explore some other ways that Alpha can be used.

An Alpha object may exist in two modes: INCREASING_ENABLE or DECREASING_ENABLE (the two modes can both be enabled in the same object). The INCREASING_ENABLE mode activates the 'increasing alpha' phase. Similarly, the DECREASING_ENABLE mode activates the 'decreasing alpha' phase. By ORing together the two modes, an entire cycle can be activated. The default Alpha is in the mode INCREASING_ENABLE.

The duration of each phase can be specified either by using one of the constructors which allows this, or by using interface methods on an existing Alpha.

For example, if we replaced the creation of the Alpha object on line 62 (on page 298) of the SolarSystem class above with the three lines

```
Alpha alpha = new Alpha();
alpha.setMode(Alpha.DECREASING_ENABLE);
alpha.setDecreasingAlphaDuration(5000);
```

the blue sphere would orbit the yellow one in the opposite direction.

Using instead the following four lines causes the blue sphere to make one orbit in one direction followed by another orbit in the opposite direction:

```
Alpha alpha = new Alpha();
alpha.setMode(Alpha.DECREASING_ENABLE |
    Alpha.INCREASING_ENABLE);
alpha.setIncreasingAlphaDuration(5000);
alpha.setDecreasingAlphaDuration(5000);
```

We can now see that the constructor that we used on line 62 of the SolarSystem class is equivalent to:

```
Alpha alpha = new Alpha();
alpha.setMode(Alpha.INCREASING_ENABLE);
alpha.setIncreasingAlphaDuration(5000);
```

Note that the argumentless constructor creates an Alpha that cycles indefinitely.

Although it is possible to duplicate an Alpha in INCREASING_ENABLE mode by creating a general purpose Alpha and just setting the durations of all its modes except the increasing alpha mode to zero, it is actually more efficient to define the Alpha as using INCREASING_ENABLE mode directly. Less CPU time is used in its calculation.

The examples so far have all produced animations that run at a constant rate. In some cases, an animation would look more natural if there were a gradual acceleration at the beginning of the increasing and decreasing alpha phases and a deceleration at the ends of these phases. An animation of a car starting from rest or of a pendulum swinging would benefit from such an effect, for example.

The Alpha class provides two 'sub-phases' called *ramps* that allow this effect. Separate durations for ramps on the increasing and decreasing alpha phases may be specified. For example, we could add ramps to the example above containing both increasing and decreasing alpha phases by adding the following two lines:

```
alpha.setIncreasingAlphaRampDuration(1000);
alpha.setDecreasingAlphaRampDuration(2000);
```

The time specified in these method calls is taken out of each end of the specified time for the corresponding phase. For example, since we specified 5000 milliseconds for the increasing alpha phase in the example above, adding the call to setIncreasingAlphaRampDuration(1000) would result in the first 1000 milliseconds of that time being used to accelerate and the last 1000 milliseconds being used to decelerate. As a result, the actual speed of the motion in the middle 3000 milliseconds is faster than in the case where we omitted the ramps, since the entire cycle must still finish in a total of 5000 milliseconds.

8.7.5   Starting and stopping an animation

Most of the other methods in the Alpha class are easy to use, with the help of the documentation. However, there is one effect that, it would seem, *should* be included in the Alpha class, but is not: the ability to start and stop an Alpha during its lifetime; for example, in response to a mouse click or key press.

It turns out that this is not too difficult to do, but to accomplish it we need to understand a little more about how Alpha generates its values. An Alpha object reads the current time (in milliseconds) from the system clock and compares this time to the time when the Alpha was started. The difference between the two values gives the total time the Alpha has been running. This time can then be mapped to the durations of the various phases in the Alpha's waveform to determine which value should be generated.

Since an Alpha always manifests itself through an Interpolator, we can stop an animation by simply setting the Alpha value in the Interpolator to null. If we wish to restart the animation where we left off, however, we must also record two other times: the system time when the Alpha was first started, and the system time when we stopped it. A static method in the System class called currentTimeMillis() allows us to do this.

To restart the animation in response to a user event such as a key press, we first retrieve the system time when the key was pressed. The time interval between the time when the Alpha was stopped and the time when the key was pressed is a dead time interval during which the value of Alpha should not change if we want to resume the animation where it left off. We can 'fool' the Alpha into restarting at the correct place in its cycle by just adding this dead time interval to the original start time of the Alpha and then reconnect the Alpha to its Interpolator. This has the effect of shifting the Alpha waveform back by the exact number of cycles that would have elapsed during the dead time interval, thus effectively 'rewinding' it to the point where it was when it was stopped.

We will illustrate the procedure by adding a Behavior class to our SolarSystem class that allows the motion of the blue sphere to be stopped and started by pressing any key on the keyboard. The Behavior class is as follows.

```
1    public class AlphaBehavior extends Behavior
2    {
3        WakeupOnAWTEvent awtWakeup =
4            new WakeupOnAWTEvent(KeyEvent.KEY_PRESSED);
5        WakeupOnActivation activationWakeup =
6            new WakeupOnActivation();
7        WakeupCriterion[] wakeups = new WakeupCriterion[2];
8        WakeupOr wakeupList;
9        long startTime, pauseTime;
10       Interpolator interpolator;
11       Alpha alpha;
12
13       public AlphaBehavior(Interpolator extInterpolator)
14       {
15           interpolator = extInterpolator;
16           wakeups[0] = awtWakeup;
17           wakeups[1] = activationWakeup;
18           wakeupList = new WakeupOr(wakeups);
19       }
20
21       public void initialize()
22       {
23           wakeupOn(wakeupList);
24       }
25
26       public void processStimulus(Enumeration criteria)
27       {
28
29           WakeupCriterion crit =
30               (WakeupCriterion)criteria.nextElement();
31           if (crit instanceof WakeupOnActivation) {
32               alpha = interpolator.getAlpha();
33               startTime = alpha.getStartTime();
34               drawingCanvas.requestFocus();
35               wakeupOn(awtWakeup);
36               return;
```

```
37          }
38          AWTEvent[] event =
39              ((WakeupOnAWTEvent)crit).getAWTEvent();
40          if (event == null) return;
41          if (interpolator.getAlpha() != null) {
42              interpolator.setAlpha(null);
43              pauseTime = System.currentTimeMillis();
44          } else {
45              startTime += System.currentTimeMillis() -
46                  pauseTime;
47              alpha.setStartTime(startTime);
48              interpolator.setAlpha(alpha);
49          }
50          wakeupOn(awtWakeup);
51      }
52  }
```

Most of this class should be familiar from our discussion of Behaviors earlier in this chapter. We have added some extra class variables on lines 9 to 11. The system time is expressed as a long (it is actually the number of milliseconds from midnight on January 1, 1970, so is a fairly large number by now!), so we declare three long variables for storing the starting time for the Alpha, and the time when a key was pressed to pause the animation.

The constructor on line 13 requires that the Interpolator object to which the Alpha is attached be passed in as an argument. The remainder of the constructor sets up the wakeup conditions as described earlier in this chapter.

In the processStimulus() method, we extract the Alpha object from the Interpolator when the program is first started, and also record the Alpha's starting time.

After the initial activation of the program, the only event that will trigger this Behavior is a key press. Since we want alternate key presses to stop and start the animation, we must sort out which state the Alpha is in on each key press. We do this by retrieving the Alpha from the Interpolator. If the returned value is not null (line 41), the animation is currently active, so we stop it by setting the Alpha value in the Interpolator to null (line 42) and record the time at which this was done (line 43).

Otherwise (line 44), we need to retrieve the system time when the key was pressed to restart the animation and subtract off the time when the last key was pressed to stop the animation. The start time is offset by this amount (line 45). The Alpha then has its start time reset to this new value (line 47) and is reconnected to the Interpolator (line 48).

8.7.6   Using the Interpolator classes

The only example of an Interpolator class in use that we have seen so far is of the RotationInterpolator which was used to produce the orbit of the Earth about the Sun in the solar system animation. There are several classes in the Interpolator family, most of which work in a similar way to the RotationInterpolator.

The ColorInterpolator operates on a Material object and, given starting and ending Color3f objects and an Alpha, varies the diffuse colour of the Material.

The PositionInterpolator operates on a TransformGroup, just as the RotationInterpolator. It provides animation by translating an object between two specified locations on the *x* axis. Although it may seem restrictive that translation is only allowed on a single axis, the class allows its local coordinate system to be transformed so that its local *x* axis coincides with whatever line of translation is required in the main scene. Thus, the PositionInterpolator provides straight-line animation in any direction. (For an example using the PositionInterpolator see the snooker program later in this chapter.)

There are two other simple Interpolator classes: ScaleInterpolator and TransparencyInterpolator that provide animation by changing the scale and the transparency of an object respectively.

There is one other group of Interpolator classes known as *path interpolators*. Associated with a path interpolator is an array known as a *knot vector*. A knot vector in a path interpolator must consist of a sequence of values, where the first value is 0.0, the last is 1.0, and all intermediate values must form a strictly increasing sequence. For example, a legal knot vector is {0.0, 0.25, 0.5, 0.75, 1.0}.

Associated with each value in a knot vector is a particular value of the parameter that is being varied in the animation. For example, if an object is being rotated, the sucessive angles of rotation that could be associated with the 5-component knot vector given above might be {0, $\pi/2$, π, $3\pi/2$, 2π}.

The link between a knot vector and a sequence of parameter values such as the list of angles in a rotation is provided by the Alpha object. Recall that an Alpha generates a sequence of values ranging from 0 to 1 which determines the time course of an animation. An Interpolator reads each value from the Alpha and changes the parameters of the object being animated accordingly.

In a path interpolator, a value in the knot vector is taken to be a value of Alpha at which the object must be in the state given by the corresponding value in the list of parameter values. In the example above, when the Alpha starts, its value is 0.0, so the object must have the rotation angle that corresponds to the knot vector component of 0.0, which is 0 radians. As Alpha increases from zero, the path interpolator must compare the values generated by the Alpha with the values in the knot vector. When Alpha reaches 0.25, the interpolator must ensure that the rotation angle has reached its corresponding value of $\pi/2$ radians. It is the interpolator's job to provide a sequence of rotation angles between 0 and $\pi/2$ so that a smooth animation is produced over this interval. Similarly, in the next interval as Alpha varies between 0.25 and 0.5, the rotation angle must vary smoothly between $\pi/2$ and π, and so on.

There are several path interpolators that allow various types of animation to be defined with respect to knot vectors. The base class for all these classes is PathInterpolator, but this is an abstract class and cannot be used on its own. The RotationPathInterpolator and PositionPathInterpolator classes provide path interpolators for rotating and translating objects respectively. Two other classes, RotPosPathInterpolator and RotPosScalePathInterpolator, allow rotations, translations and scaling to be combined in a single interpolator.

Finally, there is a small family of interpolators that provides motion along spline curves. These are based on the Kochanek–Bartels spline curve mentioned in Chapter 7. The abstract base class for this family is KBSplinePathInterpolator, and there is a single implementation of this class called KBRotPosScaleSplinePathInterpolator, which allows the spline formula to be used to calculate animations involving rotation, translation and scaling all at once. If nothing else, this class must take the prize for the longest class name in the Java 3D library.

As the uses of all these path interpolators is fairly similar, we will give a single example in which the orbit of the Earth about the Sun is implemented using a `RotationPathInterpolator` instead of the `RotationInterpolator` used originally.

Understanding the code involved will require a slight diversion into the many ways Java 3D has of representing rotations. Precisely why Java 3D uses so many different ways of defining a rotation about an axis (and why there isn't more consistency among the various classes in the ways rotations are represented) is something of a mystery, but until the situation is clarified in a future release, we must spend some time understanding the current situation.

As we recall from Chapter 4, a rotation in three dimensions is ultimately defined in terms of a rotation matrix. The matrix representation is also available in Java 3D, and a rotation in a `Transform3D` may be defined by specifying this matrix. However, Java 3D provides two other methods which may also be used to define rotations: *axis angle classes* and *quaternion classes*.

The axis angle classes (`AxisAngle4f` and `AxisAngle4d`) are slightly simpler, so we will consider them first. An axis angle may be defined by specifying a fixed vector and a fixed angle. The axis angle then represents a rotation by the given angle about the given vector.

An axis angle object on its own is not much use, since a rotation does not become visible until it is applied to some object. Therefore, usually an axis angle is converted to a standard matrix rotation by applying it to a `Transform3D` object. Two of the `set()` methods in the `Transform3D` class accept axis angles as arguments, and produce a standard rotation matrix within the `Transform3D` as a result.

The other method of representing a rotation that is used in the code sample below is the *quaternion*. A quaternion is a mathematical object that has been studied extensively for its own sake, but fortunately we do not need to delve that deeply into its properties to see how it is used in Java 3D. A quaternion, like an axis angle, may also represent a rotation by a fixed angle about a fixed vector. Unfortunately, the relation between the vector, angle and quaternion is not immediately obvious (involving, as it does, cosines and sines of the angle), but fortunately, methods exist in Java 3D for creating a quaternion out of an axis angle. Unless you have some experience in using quaternions in their own right, it is probably easiest to take this route to their creation, as we have done in the example code here.

Having realized that axis angles and quaternions are two different ways of representing a rotation by an angle about a vector, we can now explain the code. Referring back to the `SolarSystem` class above (page 298), we can replace lines 66 to 72 with the following.

```
1    int numKnots = 5;
2    float[] knots = new float[numKnots];
3    Quat4f[] quats = new Quat4f[numKnots];
4    for (int q = 0; q < numKnots; q++) {
5        knots[q] = q / (numKnots - 1.0f);
6        quats[q] = new Quat4f();
7        AxisAngle4f axisAngle =
8        new AxisAngle4f(0.0f, 1.0f, 0.0f,
9        knots[q] * 2*(float)Math.PI);
```

```
10        quats[q].set(axisAngle);
11    }
12    RotationPathInterpolator rotPath =
13        new RotationPathInterpolator(alpha, earthRotTrans,
14            new Transform3D(), knots, quats);
15    rotPath.setSchedulingBounds(behaveBounds);
16    scene.addChild(rotPath);
17    earthRotTrans.addChild(earthTransform);
18    scene.addChild(earthRotTrans);
19    scene.addChild(sun);
```

The `RotationPathInterpolator` requires a knot vector, represented as an array of `float`s, and an array of corresponding angle values, represented by quaternions, as manifested by the `Quat4f` class. In this example, we use arrays of size 5, which are created on lines 2 and 3.

The loop on line 4 initializes both these arrays. We will use an array of equally spaced knots, so that the rotation will occur at a constant rate. Line 5 defines the knot vector to be {0.0, 0.25, 0.50, 0.75, 1.0}.

As mentioned above, the easiest way of creating a quaternion is to create the corresponding axis angle and convert it to a quaternion. We create an `AxisAngle4f` on lines 7 to 9. The constructor for the `AxisAngle4f` requires 4 parameters. The first three specify the vector about which the rotation is to occur. Since we want the rotation to occur in the horizontal plane, we use the y axis (0.0, 1.0, 0.0) as the rotation axis. The fourth argument is the angle of rotation (in radians), which we specify as 2π multiplied by the corresponding knot value. This gives an evenly spaced sequence of angles between 0 and 2π.

Line 10 takes advantage of the fact that the `Quat4f` class contains a `set()` method that converts an `AxisAngle4f` to a `Quat4f`.

Lines 12 to 14 create the `RotationPathInterpolator`, whose constructor takes 5 arguments. The first two are the `Alpha` and `TransformGroup` on which the interpolator acts. The third argument is a `Transform3D` which may transform the coordinate system used by the interpolator. In this case, we do not need to transform it, so we simply create a default `Transform3D` (which contains an identity transformation) to satisfy the constructor. The last two arguments are the arrays of knots and quaternions.

The remainder of the code adds in the scheduling bounds and connects the various objects into the scene graph, as we did in the original `SolarSystem` class.

When this version of the program is run, the result should appear to be the same as in the original version. Although the path interpolator version is more complex, it is also more flexible, since we can, for example, cause the rotation to vary its rate (or even change its direction) at various points around the orbit by using non-uniform knot or parameter values in the two arrays.

As a final example of interpolators (and the use of the axis angle classes) we will see how we can change the axis of rotation to whatever we please.

The default rotation axis for an interpolator is the positive y axis, so that objects appear to rotate counterclockwise when viewed from above. Obviously, we need to be able to move the rotation axis for some applications.

Changing the rotation axis involves producing the `Transform3D` that is passed as the third argument in the `RotationPathInterpolator` constructor. For example, suppose we wished to use the x axis as the rotation axis, resulting in the Earth orbiting the Sun in a vertical plane. We can do this as follows:

```
AxisAngle4f angle =
    new AxisAngle4f(0.0f, 0.0f, 1.0f,
        -(float)Math.PI/2.0f);
Transform3D rotAxis = new Transform3D();
rotAxis.set(angle);
```

The `Transform3D` object `rotAxis` is then passed as the third argument to the `RotationPathInterpolator` constructor.

The `AxisAngle4f` object generates a rotation of $-\pi/2$ about the z axis, and this rotation is converted to a `Transform3D` object by the `set()` method in the last line. However, *what* exactly is being rotated? The key here is to realize that the default axis of rotation in a `RotationPathInterpolator` is the y axis and it is this axis that is being transformed by the `rotAxis` transform. If the y axis is rotated by $-\pi/2$ about the z axis, it is transformed into the x axis, so this becomes the new axis of rotation.

We can shift the axis so that it does not pass through the origin by adding a translation to the `rotAxis` transform. For example, we can add the line:

```
rotAxis.setTranslation(new Vector3f(0, 1, 0));
```

after the other lines above to shift the axis up by 1 unit in the y direction. The resulting rotation axis is still horizontal but lies 1 unit above the origin. The Earth still rotates in a circle, but the Sun is no longer at the centre of the orbit.

8.8   Morphing

Morphing is an effect in which one shape changes gradually into another. It is most commonly seen as a special effect in films (after the werewolf gets killed, his hairy face gradually transforms back into a human face, and so on). In the early days of films, before computers were available to generate special effects, morphing was achieved by showing successive frames in which each frame was a photograph of a slightly modified real object. In computer-generated morphing, the effect is achieved by mathematically interpolating the coordinates of the start and end objects to produce a smooth transition between the two.

Java 3D supports a limited form of morphing which nevertheless can be used to good effect. To produce a morph, begin by generating two or more key frames in the animation. The main restriction placed on morphing in Java 3D is that all of these key frames must be of the same class (any of the classes derived from `GeometryArray` may be used, but for any given morph, all frames must use the same class). Further, the number of vertices must be the same in all frames.

Although these two restrictions may seem to limit morphing to very simple examples, this is not really the case. Although all frames must contain the same number of vertices, several of these vertices can be the same geometric point. The trick, therefore, to produce a morph where the *apparent* number of vertices changes in the course of the animation is to work out which frame contains the greatest number of *distinct* vertices and set that number as the number of vertices present in *all* frames. In those frames where fewer distinct vertices are visible, just make the redundant vertices coincide with one of the visible ones and all will be well.

Java 3D provides a `Morph` class to manage the transition between frames. `Morph` does not itself provide any animation, however—that must be done in the usual way using an interpolator together with an `Alpha`. The job of `Morph` is to store an array of frames (that is, an array of `GeometryArrays`) and an array of *weights*. Given these two arrays, `Morph` will generate a new `GeometryArray` which is built by calculating a weighted average of all the `GeometryArrays` it contains.

For example, suppose we have three `GeometryArrays` representing a tetrahedron, a pyramid (with a square base) and a cube, respectively, and we want to morph one shape into the next. Let us call the three `GeometryArrays` $\mathbf{G}_t$, $\mathbf{G}_p$ and $\mathbf{G}_c$, and the array of weights w_t, w_p and w_c. `Morph` calculates its new `GeometryArray` using the formula

$$\mathbf{G}_{\text{morph}} = w_t\mathbf{G}_t + w_p\mathbf{G}_p + w_c\mathbf{G}_c$$

`Morph` requires that the array of weights always sums to 1.0, so we might begin with $w_t = 1$ and $w_p = w_c = 0$. To morph between the tetrahedron and the pyramid, we gradually decrease w_t from 1 to 0 and at the same time increase w_p from 0 to 1, maintaining the relation $w_t = 1 - w_p$ (and keeping $w_c = 0$). Once the pyramid is fully formed, we can use a similar procedure to morph between the pyramid and the cube.

The animation is provided by defining an interpolator class which varies the weights according to a time scale set by an `Alpha`. The weights are transmitted back to the `Morph` which produces the new `GeometryArray` and renders it, once per frame, to produce the morphing effect.

The morphing effect applies not only to the physical shape of the object, but to all the properties that may be defined in a `GeometryArray`. Referring back to Chapter 5 (or consulting the documentation on `GeometryArray`) we see that effects such as the colour, texture and normal vector may also be attached to a `GeometryArray`, so all of these properties may be morphed along with the actual coordinates of the vertices. We must ensure, however, that the information type(s) stored at each vertex is the same for all `GeometryArrays` in the array assigned to the `Morph`. In the example above, we could not, say, assign coordinates only to the tetrahedron and attempt to add colour information to the pyramid. If one of the `GeometryArrays` has colour information, they all must have it.

Also note that the morphing model used by `Morph` allows any number of the frames to be combined using the weights array. Although the most common application of morphing is a transition between two frames, we could combine any number of frames to produce the morphed `GeometryArray`, provided that the weights still sum to 1.0.

As an example of morphing, we will produce a simple animation of a seed that sprouts to give a plant with two leaves. The plant then produces a stalk with a bud on the end, and finally the bud opens to show a flower with four petals. The entire animation is produced using only four frames, relying on `Morph` to generate the animation between successive frames. The individual frames are shown in Figure 8.4.

Figure 8.4:
The four frames used in the morphing demo: seed, two leaves, leaves with bud, flower.

Clearly, the frame with the largest number of visible vertices is the one showing the flower, and a count will show that 23 vertices are needed here (using a LineStripArray). In this simple example, we are including coordinates only in the geometry—there are no colour, normal or other data.

We can therefore create four LineStripArrays, each with 23 vertices. In the first three frames, we will just make all the redundant vertices equal to one of the visible vertices in that frame. In the first frame (the seed) for example, the bottom vertex is at the origin, and we have therefore made 20 of the 23 vertices equal to the origin.

To build in the morphing, we use the following method to add a Morph and its associated Behavior class (considered below) to the scene graph.

```
1    private void addFlower()
2    {
3        BranchGroup scene = new BranchGroup();
4        GeometryArray[] geomArray = new GeometryArray[4];
5        geomArray[0] = createSeedArray();
6        geomArray[1] = createLeavesArray();
7        geomArray[2] = createBudArray();
8        geomArray[3] = createFlowerArray();
9
10       Morph flowerMorph = new Morph(geomArray);
11       flowerMorph.setCapability(Morph.ALLOW_WEIGHTS_WRITE);
12
13       Alpha alpha = new Alpha(-1, 5000);
14       MorphBehavior flowerBehav =
15           new MorphBehavior(flowerMorph, alpha, 4);
16       flowerBehav.setSchedulingBounds(new BoundingSphere());
17       scene.addChild(flowerMorph);
18       scene.addChild(flowerBehav);
19
20       universe.addBranchGraph(scene);
21    }
```

Line 4 creates the array of GeometryArrays which will hold the four frames in the morphing. These four frames are created by calling four separate methods (lines 5 to 8), each of which just creates a LineStripArray from a list of coordinates. (The full program may be downloaded from the Web—see Preface.)

The Morph is created on line 10 and passed the array of frames as its argument. A capability must be set on line 11 to allow the weights within the Morph to be changed during the animation.

Line 13 creates an Alpha that runs forever (first argument is –1) with a period of 5 seconds, which will be the full period for the animation. A MorphBehavior (see below) is created which will generate the new weights at each stage in the animation and pass them back to the Morph so that it can generate the new image to be displayed.

The remaining lines in the method just add the Morph and its bounds object to the scene graph.

To get the Morph to run, we need to attach a MorphBehavior to it. The complete code for this class is as follows.

```
1    import javax.media.j3d.*;
2    import java.util.Enumeration;
3
4    public class MorphBehavior extends Behavior
5    {
6       Morph targetMorph;
7       Alpha alpha;
8       int numWeights;
9       double[] weights;
10      WakeupCondition trigger = new WakeupOnElapsedFrames(0);
11
12      MorphBehavior(Morph target, Alpha morphAlpha, int numWts)
13      {
14         targetMorph = target;
15         alpha = morphAlpha;
16         numWeights = numWts;
17         weights = new double[numWeights];
18      }
19
20      public void initialize()
21      {
22         wakeupOn(trigger);
23      }
24
25      public void processStimulus(Enumeration criteria)
26      {
27         for (int i = 0; i < numWeights; i ++) {
28            weights[i] = 0.0;
29         }
30         float alphaValue = numWeights * alpha.value();
31         int alphaIndex = (int) alphaValue;
32         weights[alphaIndex] = 1.0 - (alphaValue - alphaIndex);
33         if(alphaIndex < numWeights - 1) {
34            weights[alphaIndex + 1] = 1.0 - weights[alphaIndex];
35         } else {
36         weights[0] = 1.0 - weights[alphaIndex];
37         }
38      }
39      targetMorph.setWeights(weights);
40      wakeupOn(trigger);
41      }
42   }
```

The MorphBehavior's main job is to calculate the weights that are to be applied to the Morph for each frame in the animation. This class works in much the same way as any other Behavior-derived class, in that it requires a wakeup condition to trigger it. In this case, the condition is not a user-generated event such as a mouse click; rather, it is the end of a single frame in the animation as specified by the Alpha. The condition is set on line 10—the WakeupOnElapsedFrames class sets a trigger after the specified number of frames has been generated by the Alpha. Using a value of 0 as we have done here means that the trigger should be generated at the end of the current frame, so that the animation is refreshed continually. (Setting a higher value for the number, such as 10 or 20, of elapsed frames can produce an interesting 'strobe' effect, since the Alpha continues to feed new weights to the Morph, but only every 10th or 20th frame gets displayed.)

The constructor (line 12) and initialize() (line 20) perform standard initialization tasks. The real work is done in processStimulus() (line 25).

Each time this method is called, the weights are initialized to 0.0 (lines 27 to 29). The current value of the Alpha is found (line 30), then multiplied by the number of weights (which is also the number of different elements in the array of geometries) and then truncated to get an int between 0 and 3. This value, and the value just above it, represent the two frames between which the morph is currently occurring. Since the lower frame is decreasing in influence as time progresses, line 32 sets the weight for this frame to be 1.0—(fractional part of alphaValue). Lines 33 to 37 set the next higher weight to be the complement of this value. If the lower frame is currently the last frame (that is, the one showing the flower), the frame is morphed with the first frame (the seed). The net effect is that the animation begins with the seed, shows two leaves sprouting from the seed, then the bud stalk grows and turns into a flower, and finally the flower and leaves collapse back into a seed where the cycle starts over again.

8.9   Detecting collisions

Java 3D allows an object to detect a collision between itself and any other object in the scene graph. In principle, adding collision detection to an object is quite simple, but there are a number of pitfalls which we will examine in due course.

Collisions are monitored by attaching a Behavior to an object and using one of the three collision wakeup classes to define the events to which the Behavior responds. The classes are WakeupOnCollisionEntry, WakeupOnCollisionMovement and WakeupOnCollisionExit. The first class causes the Behavior to trigger when the object in question first collides with another object in the scene graph. The second class triggers when an object that has entered a collision moves relative to the object with which it has collided, but the two objects remain in contact. The final class triggers when an object loses contact with the other object.

As a simple example, the following Behavior could be used to change the colour of an object every time it collided with something else.

```
1    import java.util.Enumeration;
2    import javax.media.j3d.*;
3    import javax.vecmath.*;
4
5    public class ObjectCollide extends Behavior {
6        Color3f collideColor = new Color3f(1.0f, 0.0f, 1.0f);
7        Material collideMaterial =  new Material();
8        boolean inCollision;
9        Shape3D shape;
10       Material objectMaterial;
11       Appearance shapeAppearance;
12
13       WakeupOnCollisionEntry collideStart;
14       WakeupOnCollisionExit collideEnd;
15
```

```
16        public ObjectCollide (Shape3D s) {
17            shape = s;
18            collideMaterial.setDiffuseColor(collideColor);
19            shapeAppearance = shape.getAppearance();
20            objectMaterial = shapeAppearance.getMaterial();
21            inCollision = false;
22        }
23
24        public void initialize() {
25            collideStart = new WakeupOnCollisionEntry(shape);
26            collideEnd = new WakeupOnCollisionExit(shape);
27            wakeupOn(collideStart);
28        }
29
30        public void processStimulus(Enumeration criteria) {
31            inCollision = !inCollision;
32            if (inCollision) {
33                shapeAppearance.setMaterial(collideMaterial);
34                wakeupOn(collideEnd);
35            } else {
36                shapeAppearance.setMaterial(objectMaterial);
37                wakeupOn(collideStart);
38            }
39        }
40    }
```

This class, when attached to a particular Shape3D in the scene graph, will listen for collisions between this object and any other object in the scene. When a collision is detected, the object's colour is changed to magenta (by changing the diffuse colour attached to the object's Material). The colour remains magenta until the collision finishes (the two objects lose contact), at which point the colour returns to the object's original colour.

Line 6 defines the magenta colour, and line 7 defines a Material to be used as the temporary Material assigned to the object while it is in collision with something else. The boolean variable on line 8 is true when the object is in contact with another object. The Shape3D on line 9 stores a reference to the object on which collisions are being detected, and lines 10 and 11 store its original Material and Appearance.

The constructor (line 16) is called to attach a collision detector to a Shape3D, passed in as an argument. Lines 19 and 20 extract the Material and Appearance from the object so they can be restored when the collision finishes.

The initialize() method (line 24) sets up the two wakeup conditions and attaches them to the shape.

When processStimulus() (line 30) is called the first time, inCollision will be false, so line 31 inverts to true, causing line 33 to set the shape's Appearance to the Material containing the magenta diffuse light. Line 34 then sets the wakeup condition so that it will next be triggered when the two object lose contact. When this happens, processStimulus() is called again, this time with inCollision starting off as true. Line 31 again inverts it to false, causing line 36 to restore the object's original Material, and reset the wakeup condition so that it waits for another collision to start.

We could also have included a `WakeupOnCollisionMovement` in this class if wanted to, say, gradually change the colour of the object as it moved relative to the object which collided with it.

To use `ObjectCollide`, we attach an instance of it to the desired `Shape3D` in the usual way, and also attach the `ObjectCollide` to the scene graph:

```
Shape3D newShape;

// Initialize newShape to desired geometry

ObjectCollide collide = new ObjectCollide(newShape);
BoundingSphere behaveBounds = new BoundingSphere();
collide.setSchedulingBounds(behaveBounds);
addChild(collide);
```

All this may look relatively straightforward, but there are several points that will come up before the programmer has used the collision behaviour for very long.

First, the default behaviour of the wakeup collision classes is to specify that the 'bounds' of the object be used in detecting collisions. In practice, Java 3D calculates the bounds of an arbitrary geometry by finding the smallest rectangular box that encloses the geometry. The bounds for a sphere, for example, would be a cube that just touches the sphere on all six sides of the cube. For other more general shapes, the bounding box is fairly easily calculated by finding the maximum and minimum values of the x, y and z coordinates over all triangles of which the geometry is composed.

Clearly, using a bounding box will significantly decrease the amount of work that must be done to determine when two shapes first intersect, but it also has the disadvantage of causing 'collisions' to occur when the objects themselves are still some distance apart. Using the sphere as an example again, a collision will be detected when a corner of the enclosing cube touches any other object in the scene, and the corner of the cube is some distance away from the actual surface of the sphere.

The wakeup collision classes do allow the precise geometry of a shape to be used in collision detection, rather than just the bounding box. We could, for example, replace line 25 in the code above by:

```
collideStart = new WakeupOnCollisionEntry(shape,
    WakeupOnCollisionEntry.USE_GEOMETRY);
```

Doing so, however, will result in a massive degradation in performance unless shape contains a fairly simple geometry (that is, contains a small number of triangles or line segments). Since collision detection is most often used in conjunction with animation, remember that the detection calculations must be done for each frame in the animation, which means they must usually be done many times each second. Attempting to use the actual geometry in collision detection in a scene that contains only a few spheres can cause the program to grind to a halt, since each sphere is typically composed of several dozen triangles.

Another problem that will no doubt have occurred to the reader is that of determining which object in the scene collided with the shape in question. All we did in the `ObjectCollide` class above is change the properties of the object to which `ObjectCollide` is registered—we did not attempt to access the *other* object with which it collided. How do we do this?

Fortunately, the various wakeup collision detectors have some methods that help us deal with this problem. We can access the other Shape3D that was involved in the collision by using the following two lines of code:

```
SceneGraphPath path = collideStart.getTriggeringPath();
Shape3D otherShape = (Shape3D)path.getObject();
```

The getTriggeringPath() method retrieves a SceneGraphPath that contains information on the path in the scene graph from the Locale right down to the object that caused the collision. The SceneGraphPath class contains a variety of methods that allow us to get information on the nodes in this path, but the one we are interested in here is getObject(), which returns the 'terminal node object' in the path—in our case the Shape3D leaf. Once we have access to the Shape3D, we can alter its Appearance and other properties, provided the correct capability bits have been set.

8.10   Example—the beginnings of a snooker game

One of the most commonly seen examples of collisions, at least on British television, is the game of snooker. If the reader is not one of the millions who spends all of their idle moments watching or playing snooker, don't worry. All that is required to follow the example in this section is an understanding that the white ball (the cue ball) must be hit by the player and caused to collide with one of the other coloured balls. In the process, the white ball may bounce off one of the edges of the table.

Since a full implementation of snooker is quite a challenging task, involving an understanding of the physics of motion and friction, we will restrict this example to a very early stage in the development of such a project. We will display all the balls in their initial state on the table, but only the cue ball can move. The player should be able to select the cue ball by picking it with the mouse, and be able to select the point to which the cue ball moves by clicking the point on the table. Note that this latter action may involve clicking on an area of the canvas where no objects are present, so we can't rely on the picking examples earlier in this chapter where we always picked one of the objects in the scene graph.

The edges of the table (the cushions, in snooker terminology) are drawn as lines, and if the cue ball hits an edge, it should bounce off at the same angle with which it hit (the 'angle of incidence equals angle of reflection' law familiar from optics). If the cue ball hits one of the other balls on the table, it should just stop.

Although the game is far from a playable version of snooker, it does illustrate (and extend) many of the features introduced in the chapter. We must be able to pick the cue ball with the mouse, and we must also be able to pick an empty point on the canvas and interpret it as a 3D point to which an object can be moved. Once the cue ball and its destination have been picked, we must use an interpolater and an alpha to move the cue ball to its new location. We must also be able to detect collisions between the cue ball and the other objects (both balls and lines) in the scene. Finally, we need to be able to change an interpolator in mid stride to implement the bounce of the ball off a cushion.

The full program is relatively long, so we will not present all the code in the text—the reader may download the full program from the Web site (see Preface).

8.10.1 Setting up the table

To set up the table in its initial configuration, we need to define the snooker balls and the cushions. Let us consider the cushions first. Each cushion is to be represented by a single line segment, but we need to be able to detect collisions between a cushion and a ball. (Although we will only be allowing the cue ball to move in this simple version, in general all the balls will be able to move.) Our first thought might be to use a rectangle or even a single line strip array to represent the four cushions as a single shape. However, since we are using bounds rather than geometry to detect collisions, defining the four cushions as a single shape would include the entire table top within the bounds, so that any object within that region would be in collision with the cushions.

The simplest method, therefore, is to represent each cushion as a separate object consisting of a single line segment. We define a class TableEdge to represent a single edge of the table.

```
1    public class TableEdge extends BranchGroup
2    {
3        float[] endPoints;
4        float[] normals = {0f, 0f, 1f, 0f, 0f, 1f};
5        float xScale = 1.0f;
6        float yScale = 1.0f;
7
8        public TableEdge(float[] coords, int id, Snooker parent)
9        {
10           LineArray tableLine =
11           new LineArray(2,
12               LineArray.COORDINATES | LineArray.NORMALS);
13           endPoints = coords;
14           for (int I = 0; i < 2; i ++) {
15               endPoints[i*3] *= xScale;
16               endPoints[i*3 + 1] *= yScale;
17           }
18           tableLine.setCoordinates(0, endPoints);
19           tableLine.setNormals(0, normals);
20           Shape3D edgeShape = new Shape3D(tableLine);
21           edgeShape.setAppearance(
22               createMaterialAppearance(black));
23           edgeShape.
24               setCapability(Shape3D.ALLOW_APPEARANCE_READ);
25           edgeShape.
26               setCapability(Shape3D.ALLOW_APPEARANCE_WRITE);
27           edgeShape.getGeometry().
28           setCapability(Geometry.ALLOW_INTERSECT);
29
30           BallCollide edgeCollide =
31               new BallCollide(edgeShape, id, parent);
32           edgeCollide.setSchedulingBounds(behaveBounds);
33           addChild(edgeCollide);
34           addChild(edgeShape);
35       }
36   }
```

The class consists only of a constructor which accepts the endpoints of the line (coords), an ID label which identifies which edge of the table it is, and a reference to the parent Snooker object which is passed along to the collision detector later. (The Snooker class is the main class which runs the program.)

After initializing the LineArray, we have inserted a loop (line 14) which allows the line to be scaled. This allows the program to vary the margin size between the cushions and the window frame containing the display. In order to bounce the cue ball off a cushion, the player first selects the cue ball and then clicks on a point in the margin outside the cushions. The cue ball will head towards the clicked point and bounce off the cushion when it reaches it.

The remaining lines up to line 28 set up the appearance of the edge and turn on some capabilities needed later.

Line 30 attaches a collision detector to the edge. The BallCollide class is similar to ObjectCollide given above, so we will examine only the processStimulus() method from that class.

```
1    public void processStimulus(Enumeration criteria) {
2        inCollision = !inCollision;
3        if (inCollision) {
4            SceneGraphPath path =
5                collideStart.getTriggeringPath();
6            Shape3D ballSphere = (Shape3D)path.getObject();
7            Snooker.SnookerBall ball =
8                parent.findBall(ballSphere);
9            if (ball == parent.getCueBall())
10                shapeAppearance.setMaterial(collideMaterial);
11            if (shapeID == parent.BALL) {
12                ball.getMoveBall().setAlpha(null);
13            } else {
14                parent.bounceBall(shapeID, ball);
15            }
16            wakeupOn(collideEnd);
17        }
18        else {
19            shapeAppearance.setMaterial(ballMaterial);
20            wakeupOn(collideStart);
21        }
22    }
```

Up to line 6, we extract the Shape3D object that caused the collision. (In this simple version of the program, this will always be the Shape3D component of the Sphere representing the cue ball, but in a more complete implementation this could be any of the balls on the table.) However, as we will see below, we are using a new class called SnookerBall, nested inside the Snooker class, to represent the balls, so merely having the Shape3D is not enough to allow us to access the SnookerBall object. We have therefore provided a method called findBall() (called on line 7) in the Snooker class which can locate the SnookerBall given the Shape3D of the ball within it. We will consider the method shortly.

If the ball causing the collision is the cue ball, we change the Material of the object with which it collides (which is the object attached to this instance of BallCollide) so that its colour changes to magenta. Later in processStimulus(), we change the colour back again if the cue ball bounces away from the object. For the table edge, therefore, the cushion will briefly flash from black to magenta to black as the cue ball bounces off it. Since we are just causing the cue ball to stop dead if it hits any other ball, the ball that it hits will remain magenta until the cue ball is moved away by the user clicking it with the mouse.

On line 11 we check the shapeID of the object hit by the cue ball and, if it is another ball, we stop the cue ball by stopping its Alpha. As we will see later, each ball has its own PositionInterpolator and Alpha to make it move in a straight line. The getMoveBall() method retrieves the PositionInterpolator.

If the object hit by the cue ball is not another ball, it must be one of the cushions, so we call bounceBall() (line 14) to bounce the cue ball off the cushion.

The code on lines 19 and 20 restores the appearance of the object hit by the cue ball (whether it is another ball or one of the cushions) when the collision is over.

The balls themselves are represented by the SnookerBall class, which is nested inside the main Snooker class. The geometry of each ball is represented by a Sphere, but a number of auxiliary objects need to be attached to each ball to allow it to move and collide with other objects, so it is better to encapsulate all these objects within a separate class.

```
1    public class SnookerBall extends BranchGroup
2    {
3        TransformGroup startPosGroup, interpolatorGroup;
4        PositionInterpolator moveBall;
5        Alpha alpha;
6        Sphere ballSphere;
7        int ballNumber;
8
9        public SnookerBall(int index, Vector3f position,
10           Color3f colour, Snooker parent)
11       {
12           ballNumber = index;
13           ballSphere = new Sphere(BALL_RADIUS,
14               createMaterialAppearance(colour));
15           ballSphere.getShape().getGeometry().
16           setCapability(Geometry.ALLOW_INTERSECT);
17
18           ballPosTransform = new Transform3D();
19           ballPosTransform.set(position);
20           startPosGroup = new TransformGroup(ballPosTransform);
21           startPosGroup.setCapability(
22               TransformGroup.ALLOW_TRANSFORM_READ);
23           startPosGroup.setCapability(
24               TransformGroup.ALLOW_TRANSFORM_WRITE);
25           startPosGroup.addChild(ballSphere);
26
27           interpolatorGroup = new TransformGroup();
28           interpolatorGroup.addChild(startPosGroup);
29           interpolatorGroup.setCapability(
30               TransformGroup.ALLOW_TRANSFORM_READ);
31           interpolatorGroup.setCapability(
32               TransformGroup.ALLOW_TRANSFORM_WRITE);
33           addChild(interpolatorGroup);
```

```
34
35              moveBall = new PositionInterpolator(
36                  null, interpolatorGroup);
37              moveBall.setSchedulingBounds(behaveBounds);
38              addChild(moveBall);
39              alpha = new Alpha();
40
41              if (index != CUE_BALL) {
42                  BallCollide cueCollide = new BallCollide(
43                      ballSphere.getShape(), BALL, parent);
44                  cueCollide.setSchedulingBounds(behaveBounds);
45                  addChild(cueCollide);
46                  ballSphere.getShape().setPickable(false);
47              }
48          }
```

Each ball needs to have two TransformGroups since the ball needs to be translated from the origin (where all Spheres are initialized) to its location on the table, and the PositionInterpolator also needs a TransformGroup on which to act. Recall that interpolators always overwrite any transform in a TransformGroup when they act on it, so we cannot store both transformations in the same TransformGroup. These two groups are declared on line 3, with startPosGroup being the static translation of the ball to its initial position, and interpolatorGroup being the group on which the PositionInterpolator acts.

The constructor does all the work in this class as well, although there are a few 'get' functions not shown here that are needed to retrieve some of the fields from a SnookerBall object. The arguments to the constructor (line 9) are an index number to keep track of which ball we are creating, the initial position of the ball as a Vector3f, the colour of the ball, and a reference to the parent Snooker object.

Lines 13 to 16 set up the Sphere, lines 18 to 25 set up the static translation transform to place the ball in its initial position, and lines 27 to 33 set up the TransformGroup for the PositionInterpolator to act on. This latter TransformGroup contains only the identity transform at the moment, since the ball has not moved from its initial position.

Lines 35 to 39 set up the PositionInterpolator and Alpha for this ball. Note (line 36) that the interpolator is assigned a null Alpha initially, since we do not want any motion until the user selects the ball and tries to move it.

Finally, lines 42 to 45 add a collision detector to any ball that is not the cue ball, and line 46 turns off picking for any ball other than the cue ball since the cue ball is the only ball that the player should be able to move directly.

This class is called 22 times to set up all the balls at the beginning of a frame of snooker. The result is shown in Figure 8.5.

Note that the 15 red balls in the triangle on the left are drawn with spaces between them, contrary to the way they should be set up in a real snooker game. This is one drawback of having to use bounds to specify collisions rather than geometry—placing the red balls any closer together than this would cause them all to 'collide' with each other even though they are not actually touching, since the bounding cubes overlap. However, attempting to use geometry in the collision detector for this program makes it so slow that it barely runs.

Figure 8.5:
The initial display of
the Snooker program.
The rectangle is
composed of four
separate line segments,
each of which
represents a
cushion.

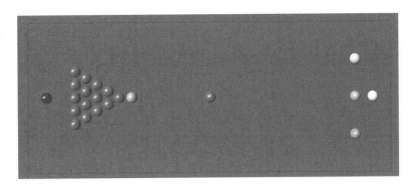

8.10.2 Moving the cue ball

Having set up the cushions and balls, we now need some code to allow us to pick
the cue ball and specify the location on table to which it should be moved. As in
the earlier sphere-picking example in this chapter (see section 8.5), we will use an
extension of the PickMouseBehavior class to allow the picking. We call the class
MousePick and its code (nested inside Snooker) is as follows.

```
1    public class MousePick extends PickMouseBehavior
2    {
3        Point3d origin = new Point3d();
4        Snooker parent;
5        SnookerBall ball;
6        TransformGroup startPosGroup = new TransformGroup();
7        TransformGroup interpolatorGroup = new TransformGroup();
8
9        public MousePick(Canvas3D canvas, BranchGroup branch,
10           Bounds bounds, Snooker owner)
11       {
12           super(canvas, branch, bounds);
13           setSchedulingBounds(bounds);
14           pickCanvas.setMode(PickTool.GEOMETRY);
15           setTolerance(0.0f);
16           parent = owner;
17       }
18
19       private void moveBalls()
20       {
21           endShot.sub(startShot);
22           Vector3d direction = new Vector3d(endShot);
23           Vector3d xAxis = new Vector3d(1, 0, 0);
24           double angle = xAxis.angle(direction);
25           if (endShot.y < 0) angle = -angle;
26               Transform3D directionTrans = new Transform3D();
27               directionTrans.rotZ(angle);
28
29           Alpha alpha = ball.getAlpha();
30           alpha.setStartTime(System.currentTimeMillis());
31           alpha.setIncreasingAlphaDuration(2000);
32           alpha.setLoopCount(1);
```

```
33
34          PositionInterpolator moveBall = ball.getMoveBall();
35          moveBall.setAxisOfTranslation(directionTrans);
36          moveBall.setStartPosition(0.0f);
37          moveBall.setEndPosition((float)direction.length());
38          moveBall.setAlpha(alpha);
39      }
40
41      public void updateScene(int xPos, int yPos)
42      {
43          pickCanvas.setShapeLocation(xPos, yPos);
44          PickResult[] results = pickCanvas.pickAllSorted();
45
46          if (results != null) {
47              Shape3D shape = (Shape3D)results[0].
48              getNode(PickResult.SHAPE3D);
49              ball = parent.findBall(shape);
50              startPosGroup = ball.getStartPosGroup();
51              interpolatorGroup = ball.getInterpolatorGroup();
52              SceneGraphPath path =
53              results[0].getSceneGraphPath();
54              if (path != null) {
55                  Transform3D ballTransform = path.getTransform();
56                  origin.set(0.0, 0.0, 0.0);
57                  ballTransform.transform(origin);
58                  startShot = origin;
59                  shotInProgress = true;
60              }
61          } else if (shotInProgress) {
62              endShot =
63              Snooker.canvasToVworld(xPos, yPos, canvas);
64              shotInProgress = false;
65              interpolatorGroup.setTransform(new Transform3D());
66              ballPosTransform.set(new Vector3d(startShot));
67              startPosGroup.setTransform(ballPosTransform);
68              moveBalls();
69          }
70      }
71  }
```

The constructor (line 9) takes as arguments the canvas on which picking is allowed, the BranchGroup that should be explored to search for picked objects, the scheduling bounds, and a reference to the main Snooker object. We use GEOMETRY mode for the picking tool, since this is much more accurate than just using the bounds and not as computationally expensive as in collision detection. The tolerance is set to 0 (line 15) so that the cue ball can be picked only by clicking directly over it.

We now examine the updateScene() method (line 41) since this is called first when a pick operation is performed. This method must be able to handle two different cases: picking the cue ball and picking over any other part of the table. Let us consider what happens if the player picks the cue ball.

As in the earlier example in this chapter (section 8.5), we retrieve the `results` list using `pickCanvas` (lines 43 and 44). If `results` is not `null`, we have picked the cue ball, since it is the only pickable object in the scene (recall that we explicitly set all other balls to be non-pickable above). Thus the code within the block starting on line 47 is only called if the cue ball has been picked.

We need to retrieve the `SnookerBall` object representing the cue ball, since this contains the two `TransformGroups` which must be acted on to move the ball. We first retrieve the `Shape3D` from the `Sphere` for the cue ball on line 47, using the `getNode()` method. When this method has an `int` argument chosen from the static parameters in `PickResult`, it searches backwards from the end of the `PickResult` until it finds the first node of the type specified. In this case, we are searching for a `Shape3D` node.

On line 49 we use the `findBall()` method mentioned earlier to locate the `SnookerBall` object corresponding to shape. From here, we can get the two `TransformGroups` (lines 50 and 51). We need these two groups since we must determine the path that is to be followed by the `PositionInterpolator`. At this stage, the user has clicked on the cue ball and has not specified the other end of the path yet, so we need to find the current location of the cue ball when it was picked. One way of getting this information is to find the `SceneGraphPath` to the cue ball (line 52). A `SceneGraphPath` allows us to extract the total `Transform3D` that has been performed along its length. In this case, that will be the translation from the origin to the current location of the cue ball, which is what we want. We therefore find `ballTransform` on line 55 and use it to transform the origin (lines 56 and 57) to find the location of the cue ball when it was picked. Note that this will give the coordinates of the *centre* of the cue ball no matter where on the cue ball the mouse was clicked. We save this information in the `startShot` variable (of type `Point3d`), and switch the boolean flag `shotInProgress` on to indicate that the cue ball has been successfully selected.

Next, we assume that the player clicks somewhere else on the table. For now, we will assume that this location is within the cushions, so we don't have to worry about any bounces. In this case, `results` on line 44 will be `null` since we haven't picked any actual object in the scene, so `updateScene()` continues with line 62.

At this stage, we need to convert the location of the mouse click to a coordinate in the 3D virtual world of the snooker table. Although it would seem that this would be a commonly-needed conversion, Java 3D does not provide any methods for doing this, so we will need to build our own. A method called `canvasToVworld()` has been added as a static method in the Snooker class. It takes as arguments the *x* and *y* coordinates (in pixels) of the mouse cursor and the `Canvas3D` on which the mouse was clicked, and returns a `Point3d` corresponding to the location in the *xy* plane in the 3D virtual world. The code from the Snooker class is as follows.

```
1    static public Point3d canvasToVworld(int xPos, int yPos,
2        Canvas3D canvas)
3    {
4        Point3d mouseImagePlate = new Point3d();
5        canvas.getPixelLocationInImagePlate(
6            xPos, yPos, mouseImagePlate);
7        Transform3D imagePlateToVWorld = new Transform3D();
8        canvas.getImagePlateToVworld(imagePlateToVWorld);
9        imagePlateToVWorld.transform(mouseImagePlate);
```

```
10      Point3d eyeImagePlate = new Point3d();
11      canvas.getCenterEyeInImagePlate(eyeImagePlate);
12      imagePlateToVWorld.transform(eyeImagePlate);
13      double t = 0.0;
14      if (mouseImagePlate.z - eyeImagePlate.z != 0.0) {
15          t = eyeImagePlate.z / (mouseImagePlate.z -
16              eyeImagePlate.z);
17      }
18      Point3d mouseVWorld = new Point3d();
19      mouseVWorld.x = eyeImagePlate.x - t *
20          (mouseImagePlate.x - eyeImagePlate.x);
21      mouseVWorld.y = eyeImagePlate.y - t *
22          (mouseImagePlate.y - eyeImagePlate.y);
23      return mouseVWorld;
24  }
```

Although Java 3D provides no direct method for transforming mouse coordinates into canvas coordinates, it *does* provide methods for transforming to and from the *image plate*. The image plate is a plane that represents the display surface (usually the monitor screen) where the projected 3D image is assumed to be rendered. We can therefore use the image plate as an intermediary to get from the mouse to the actual canvas.

On line 5 of this method, we obtain the location of the mouse click in the image plate, which is returned as a Point3d. Next (lines 7 and 8) we find the Transform3D that converts from image plate coordinates to virtual world coordinates, and apply this (line 9) to the mouse coordinates.

We now have the mouse coordinates in virtual world coordinates, but this location is not in the virtual world's *xy* plane since the image plate is assumed to be some distance from the observer. The final transformation that we must make is a projection of mouseImagePlate onto the *xy* plane in the virtual world. For this we are left entirely on our own, but fortunately it is a fairly simple exercise in linear algebra (see exercises). The centre of projection in the virtual world is a location known in Java 3D as the *centre eye* (since Java 3D is designed to allow stereo projections, one from each eye, the single point of projection for a monoscopic view is assumed to be at a point halfway between the two eyes, called the centre eye). Line 11 finds the location of the centre eye in image plate coordinates and line 12 converts this to virtual world coordinates. The remainder of the method finds the intersection of a line through the centre eye and the mouse click point with the *xy* plane.

If we now return to the MousePick class above, line 62 finds the point on the table selected by the player and stores it in endShot. We now have the two endpoints of the line segment over which the cue ball should move.

If the cue ball has been moved before, its current position will result from a combination of translations in the two TransformGroups startPosGroup and interpolatorGroup. The position of the cue ball before its previous move will be stored in startPosGroup and the motion from this point to the endpoint of the previous move will be stored in interpolatorGroup since it was generated by the PositionInterpolator during the move.

In order to set up the TransformGroups correctly for the next move, we clear the transformation in interpolatorGroup (line 65) and set the transform in startPosGroup to correspond to the current location of the cue ball (lines 66 and 67). Finally, we call moveBalls() to start the cue ball in motion.

The moveBalls() method (line 19) must calculate the direction of motion of the cue ball. Recall that a PositionInterpolator always assumes motion along the *x* axis, so we must find the transform to convert the *x* axis into the required direction of motion. Lines 21 and 22 calculate the vector from start-point to end-point, line 23 is a unit vector along the *x* axis, and line 24 finds the angle between these two vectors. The angle() method from Vector3d, however, only returns angles between 0 and 180 degrees, so if the *y* component of the direction of motion is negative, we must also negate the angle (line 25). Finally, we get the required transformation to convert the *x* axis into the direction of motion of the cue ball (line 27).

On lines 29 to 32 we set up the Alpha that governs the motion of the cue ball. We set its start time to the current system time, its duration to 2 seconds, and its loop count to 1 so that the ball just goes from its start-point to its end-point and stops. (Note that trying to set these parameters in the Alpha's constructor for some reason does not work.)

On line 34, we retrieve the PositionInterpolator for the cue ball, set its axis, start and end positions and Alpha. We give the end position as the length of the direction vector calculated earlier so that the ball covers the correct distance and ends up exactly where the mouse was clicked.

8.10.3 Bouncing off an edge

The final feature that we will add to the snooker program is the ability of the cue ball to bounce off the cushions. The code for this is contained in the method bounceBall() in the main Snooker class:

```
1    public void bounceBall(int id, SnookerBall ball)
2    {
3        PositionInterpolator moveBall = ball.getMoveBall();
4        Alpha alpha = ball.getAlpha();
5        TransformGroup startPosGroup = ball.getStartPosGroup();
6        TransformGroup interpolatorGroup =
7            ball.getInterpolatorGroup();
8
9        Transform3D axis = moveBall.getAxisOfTranslation();
10       Matrix3f rotMatrix = new Matrix3f();
11       Vector3f transVector = new Vector3f();
12       float scale = axis.get(rotMatrix, transVector);
13       switch (id) {
14       case TOP_EDGE:
15       case BOTTOM_EDGE:
16           rotMatrix.m01 = -rotMatrix.m01;
17           rotMatrix.m10 = -rotMatrix.m10;
18           break;
19       case LEFT_EDGE:
20       case RIGHT_EDGE:
21           rotMatrix.m00 = -rotMatrix.m00;
22           rotMatrix.m11 = -rotMatrix.m11;
23           break;
```

```
24        }
25        moveBall.setAlpha(null);
26        axis.set(rotMatrix, transVector, scale);
27        Transform3D collideTrans = new Transform3D();
28        interpolatorGroup.getTransform(collideTrans);
29        Transform3D origTrans = new Transform3D();
30        startPosGroup.getTransform(origTrans);
31        collideTrans.mul(origTrans);
32        startPosGroup.setTransform(collideTrans);
33        interpolatorGroup.setTransform(new Transform3D());
34
35        float alphaValue = alpha.value();
36        long duration =
37           (long)(alpha.getIncreasingAlphaDuration() *
38              (1f - alphaValue));
39        alpha.setStartTime(System.currentTimeMillis());
40        alpha.setIncreasingAlphaDuration(duration);
41        alpha.setLoopCount(1);
42
43        moveBall.setAxisOfTranslation(axis);
44        moveBall.setStartPosition(0.0f);
45        moveBall.setEndPosition(moveBall.getEndPosition() *
46           (1f - alphaValue));
47        moveBall.setAlpha(alpha);
48     }
```

In principle, the bounce off an edge is quite simple to implement. If we bounce off the top or bottom edge, we are effectively changing the angle of the direction vector calculated in the moveBalls() method above to its negative, so all we need to do is change the corresponding entries in the Transform3D matrix. Similarly, if we are bouncing off a left or right edge, the angle is changing from its initial value, θ, say, to $\pi - \theta$, which means that the sine of the angle changes sign, so again we change only the corresponding terms in the Transform3D matrix.

This is what we have done in this method. Lines 3 to 7 retrieve the main objects governing the motion of the ball. Line 9 obtains the current Transform3D used to transform the x axis into the axis of translation in the PositionInterpolator. On line 12 we retrieve the rotation matrix (and translation vector, although this will be zero, but there is no method in Transform3D which allows only the rotation matrix to be retrieved).

The id parameter contains the type of edge at which the bounce occurs, so we use this in a switch statement to determine which matrix elements to change. The Matrix3f class provides public access to the individual elements of the matrix, so we can change them directly (lines 14 to 22). (Refer back to Chapter 4 if you have forgotten the form of the rotation matrix.)

However, changing the axis of translation is only part of the story. We need to stop the PositionInterpolator by setting its Alpha to null, reset the two TransformGroups attached to the cue ball, and restart the PositionInterpolator.

We stop the interpolator's Alpha on line 25, and reset the axis of translation on line 26. Next, we need to find the location of the cue ball when it collided with the edge. We can do this by retrieving the two Transform3Ds attached to the two TransformGroups (lines 27 to 30). We combine the transforms on line 31, transfer the net transform to `startPosGroup` and clear `interpolatorGroup` (lines 32 and 33).

To reset `Alpha`, we find its value when it was stopped (line 35) and scale the new `Alpha`'s duration so that it runs from the value when it was stopped until it reaches the final value of 1.0 (line 36).

Finally, we reset the `PositionInterpolator` with its new axis (line 43) and change its end position so that it only runs the distance left to run when it collided with the edge.

One point should be mentioned concerning the detection of collisions during motion governed by an `Alpha`. An `Alpha` produces animation by generating a series of frames, using an interpolator to work out the position of the object being moved at each frame. The collision detector checks for a collision event *only once per frame*. This means that if the cue ball is moving fairly fast so that there is a large distance between frames, a collision between the cue ball and another ball or a cushion will not be detected when the cue ball first contacts the other object (and in fact may be missed entirely).

This effect is easily observed in the snooker program. Start the cue ball off at one end of the table and aim it at another ball at the other end of the table. In most cases, we will find that the cue ball stops only after partially embedding itself in the other ball. If we aim the cue ball at another ball that is quite close, it is more likely that the cue ball will stop when first contact is made.

If we want pixel-perfect collision detection, we cannot obtain it by using the wakeup collision detection classes. In the case of the snooker program, we would need to keep track of the positions of all the balls and provide a method that calculates the exact point of collision between the cue ball and the other ball, once the cue ball's path is known. For the snooker program, this would not be too difficult to do, since all the shapes are spheres and all the paths of motion are straight lines (although in a real game of snooker it is possible to make the cue ball follow a curved path by putting spin on it, but that is getting complicated). In more complex geometries, this sort of calculation would be very difficult.

8.11 Epilogue

This last example should convince you that doing even apparently simple things in Java 3D can sometimes take a lot of work, research and patience. The main problems with the Java 3D package (at least at the time of writing) can be summed up in three main areas.

First, since the package is still evolving and is an area of active work at Sun Microsystems, there are still quite a few bugs sprinkled throughout the package. This can lead to a sense of frustration—if something doesn't work is it your fault or is it a bug in the system? The best way of coping with this situation is to become a member of Sun's `java3d-interest` newsgroup (details are given in the preface) and post your problems there. Although a response is not guaranteed, many of Sun's Java 3D engineers read this group and provide replies.

Second, Java 3D, being written in Java, suffers from Java's overall sluggishness compared to fully compiled languages such as C++. Three-dimensional graphics is renowned for the amount of processor time it eats up, even on optimized systems, so it should come as no surprise that running such graphics under Java is not going to break any speed records. This is most evident in scenes containing a lot of geometry or a lot of animation. In the snooker example above we saw that attempting to use accurate geometry for detecting collisions produces a program that is unrunnable, while using bounds produces a game where collisions are far from accurate.

Finally, Java 3D is still somewhat limited in what it can do compared to more mature packages such as OpenGL. There are no provisions, for example, for spline curves and surfaces, ray tracing, fractal landscapes, and so on in Java 3D. As it continues to evolve and grow, however, we can expect more, and more powerful, features to be added.

These disadvantages, although not negligible, must be weighed against the advantages of the elegant, powerful, and relatively simple scene graph model that is used for constructing Java 3D worlds. In addition, Java 3D was designed with many sophisticated features, such as stereo viewing, head-mounted displays and so on, that we have not covered in this introductory book.

But perhaps the main benefit that Java 3D has going for it is that it allows us to write graphics programs *in Java*. Over the years that Java has been in existence, it has proven itself to be a much cleaner language than C++, its main competitor, and considerably more enjoyable as a coding environment. It is the author's view that Java 3D is worth knowing for that reason alone.

EXERCISES

1. Write a Java 2D program which draws a few simple shapes (lines, rectangles, etc.) on a canvas. The user should then be able to pick one of these shapes with the mouse and drag it to a new location on the canvas. Use techniques similar to those in the 'rubber band' program in this chapter (see section 8.2).

2. Write a `Behavior` class which detects keyboard presses and prints out (using `System.out.print()`) the key that was pressed.

3. Modify the class written in question 2 so that it stores the key presses in a `String` until the user presses 'Enter' and then constructs a `Text3D` (see Chapter 6) from the `String`. The `Text3D` should be displayed in the scene.

4. Modify the program in question 3 so that a `Text3D` with the current system time is displayed when the program starts up. (Read the documentation on the `System` class to see how to obtain the time.) Do this by using a `WakeupOnActivation`, and then accept key presses as in question 3. When the user presses 'Enter', the existing `Text3D` should be modified to display the new text.

5. Attach a `MouseRotate` to the `Text3D` in question 4 so that the text can be rotated using the mouse. By using a callback, change one or more properties of the text (such as its thickness or colour) as it rotates.

6. Using a square array of `Spheres`, such as that created in question 18 in Chapter 7, add a class similar to `MousePick` in this chapter to allow individual `Spheres` to be selected and highlighted in a different colour using the mouse. Experiment with the mode of the `PickCanvas` (try BOUNDS as well as GEOMETRY) to see how accurately a shape needs to be specified in order to be picked.

7. Using a grid of Spheres as in question 6, adapt the three mouse picking classes to allow one of the Spheres to be picked and then rotated, zoomed or translated by dragging the mouse.

8. Use a LineArray to construct a wire-frame model of a cube. Write a class extending PickMouseBehavior that allows single edges of the cube to be picked and highlighted in a different colour. Experiment with setTolerance() to see how difficult it is to select an individual line with various tolerances.

9. Write a Java 2D program which begins with a square displayed at the centre of the canvas. Clicking the mouse within the square should cause the square to move randomly in one of four directions (up, down, left, right) for a fixed distance at a constant speed. If the square hits the boundary of the canvas, it should bounce back in the direction from which it came.

10. Modify the program in question 9 so that the square decelerates as it moves. A simple algorithm that may be used is to decrease the distance moved from one frame to the next by a constant fraction such as 0.75.

11. Modify the programs from questions 9 or 10 by adding several other (non-overlapping) squares to the display. Make these additional squares a different colour to the first one so that it is easy to find the original square. Now, whenever the first square hits another square, the first square should stop and the square it hit should continue the motion in the same direction for the remaining travel time. Try to make the program more efficient by storing the list of positions of the squares in sorted order so you don't need to search the entire list of squares to determine which one may be hit.

12. Further increase the efficiency of the program in question 11 by keeping track of which part of the canvas needs to be redrawn at each frame in the animation. This can be done by working out a rectangle that encloses the combined positions of the square that is currently moving before and after its motion, and using the setClip() method in Graphics2D to clip the rendering area to this rectangle.

13. Add another 'planet' representing Mars to the SolarSystem program in the text (see section 8.7.3). To make the properties of the new planet roughly equivalent to the real Mars, make the Sphere red and about half the size of Earth. It should orbit the Sun about twice as far away as Earth and take twice as long to complete a single orbit.

14. Modify the Alpha in the SolarSystem program in the text so that the Earth pauses for 1 second at the point in its orbit where it appears closest to the observer.

15. Assume that the SolarSystem program has been modified by having the AlphaBehavior class given in the text added to it, so that it is possible to start and stop the orbit by pressing a key on the keyboard. Modify the program so that the Earth turns green whenever it is paused, and returns to blue when the motion resumes.

16. Add a ColorInterpolator to the original SolarSystem program so that the colour of the Earth changes continuously between green and blue as it orbits the sun.

17. Use a `PositionPathInterpolator` to write an animation in which a `Sphere` rolls up one side of a hill and down the other, then repeats the motion in the opposite direction. Represent the hill by an inverted V, so that motion up and down the hill consists of two straight line segments. Make the motion look more realistic by having the `Sphere` slow down as it nears the top and speed up as it reaches the bottom of the hill.

18. Using the program from question 13 in which there are two planets rotating about the sun, change the axis of rotation of Mars so that it makes an angle of 30 degrees to that of Earth's axis.

19. Write a program which morphs a tetrahedron into a cube. Remember that morphing requires that both shapes be represented using the same type of class, and that they both have the same number of vertices.

20. Modify the morphing program in question 19 so that the colour of the tetrahedron starts off as pure red, and gradually morphs into green as the tetrahedron itself morphs into the cube.

21. Write a program containing two `Spheres`, each of which may be picked by the mouse and translated by dragging the mouse. Add a `Behavior` which detects collisions between these two `Spheres`, causing a `Sphere` to change colour during the course of the collision. Experiment with using bounds or geometry in the collision detector to see how close the spheres can get before a collision occurs in each case.

22. Add successively more `Spheres` to the program in question 21 and compare the efficiency of using geometry against that of using bounds in collision detection. How many spheres do you need to add before you would judge the program to be too slow when running in geometry mode?

23. Extend the snooker example by allowing one or more of the coloured balls to move when hit by the cue ball. Initially, handle a collision by stopping the cue ball at the point of impact (as is done in the existing program) but make the coloured ball move off in the same direction as the cue ball was moving. A more sophisticated collision handler would need to consider the conservation of momentum law from Newtonian physics, so that if the cue ball hits the target ball at an angle, both balls move off in different directions with different speeds. If you are familiar with elementary physics, try to extend the program to handle this case.

24. One way of coping with the problem of inaccurate collision detection is not to use Java 3D's collision detection mechanism at all. Instead, use some algebra to determine which object will be hit by the cue ball, and where the cue ball will be when the impact occurs. Use a `PositionInterpolator` to move the cue ball as usual, but replace the collision detection code with code that checks to see when the ball reaches the collision point and stops the animation at that point. Using this method should also allow you to place the cue at exactly the right point after the collision, rather than finding it embedded in the target ball.

Index